Starting Small

Starting Small

Celebrating First Steps When Adopting Curricular Changes K–16

Edited by Lauren Madden

ROWMAN & LITTLEFIELD
Lanham • Boulder • New York • London

Rowman & Littlefield
Bloomsbury Publishing Inc, 1385 Broadway, New York, NY 10018, USA
Bloomsbury Publishing Plc, 50 Bedford Square, London, WC1B 3DP, UK
Bloomsbury Publishing Ireland, 29 Earlsfort Terrace, Dublin 2, D02 AY28, Ireland
www.rowman.com

Copyright © 2025 by Lauren Madden

All rights reserved. No part of this publication may be: i) reproduced or transmitted in any form, electronic or mechanical, including photocopying, recording or by means of any information storage or retrieval system without prior permission in writing from the publishers; or ii) used or reproduced in any way for the training, development or operation of artificial intelligence (AI) technologies, including generative AI technologies. The rights holders expressly reserve this publication from the text and data mining exception as per Article 4(3) of the Digital Single Market Directive (EU) 2019/790.

British Library Cataloguing in Publication Information available

Library of Congress Cataloging-in-Publication Data available

ISBN 9781538191668 cloth | ISBN 9781538191675 paperback | ISBN 9781538191682 epub

For product safety related questions contact productsafety@bloomsbury.com.

∞™ The paper used in this publication meets the minimum requirements of American National Standard for Information Sciences—Permanence of Paper for Printed Library Materials, ANSI/NISO Z39.48-1992.

Contents

Introduction   vii
Lauren Madden

1. Little Kids Making Big Decisions   1
   Tiffany Robles

2. Small Changes, Meaningful Impact: Number Talks in the Elementary Mathematics Classroom   11
   Heather West Jerez, Temple A. Walkowiak, Briana Pelton, Kristin Hord, and Jennifer Tymkin

3. Wonder Walks as a Nature-Based Teaching Practice   23
   Steph N. Dean

4. A Small Step toward a Meaningful School: Collaboration in Experimentality for Curriculum Integration   37
   Ivan Salinas, Natalia Albornoz, and Magnolia Guerrero

5. Taking Small Steps toward Inquiry-Based Science Teaching   49
   Zora M. Wolfe

6. Creating a Discourse-Driven Classroom   57
   Jillian Plum

7. Stepping Stones on Mount Project-Based Learning (PBL)   67
   Maggie Demarse and Anne-Lise Halvorsen

8. Stories That Need to Be Told   79
   Clancy Bishop, Tiffany Coleman, Nikki Collins, and Melissa Ewing

9. The Naughty List—Time for a Change   89
   Carolyn Davidson Abel and Tingting Xu

10. Nurturing the Writer Within   101
    Melissa Ewing, Courtney Kozelski, and Elizabeth Crocker

11	Empowering Middle School English: Small Steps in a Journey of Literacy Transformation *Mona Zignego*	113
12	Beyond Checking Boxes: Enacting Equitable Practices in English Language Arts *Katie F. Whitley, Erin Riley-Lepo, and Ashley Pollitt*	123
13	Conferencing in the High School STEM Classroom *Lauren Bsales and Tanner Huffman*	137
14	Creating Multiple Pathways for Outcomes and Unit Themes through Standards *Samantha Shane*	151
15	Small Steps toward Amplifying More Voices in Your Social Studies Classroom: An Exercise in Critical Literacy *Ashley Wright*	161
16	Think Big, Start Small: A Story with Strategies for Curriculum Change *Emily S. Meixner and Rachel Scupp-Jorge*	173
17	A Simulation Activity: Supporting Preservice Teachers through the Response-to-Intervention Process *Molly D. Keough*	185
18	A "Small but Meaningful" Framework for Improving Postsecondary Courses *Amy L. Clay*	199
19	Exploring Cosmopolitan and Critical Perspectives in a Writing Course *Grace Y. Kang*	211
20	Flip, Switch, Reverse: A New Faculty Member Tackling a New Course and Content Area *Abby C. Emerson*	221
21	Incorporating Lesson Study: An Improvement Process for Elementary Social Studies Teacher Candidates *Alexander S. Butler*	233
22	Collaborate with Librarians: How Adding New and Relevant Materials Matters *Ewa Dziedzic-Elliott*	243
23	Jagged Learning Profiles for Culturally Responsive Classrooms *Serena Morales*	251
24	Creating a Classroom Community That Values Disabled School Citizens *Steve Singer*	261
Index		273
About the Editor		287
About the Contributors		289

Introduction

Starting Small: Celebrating First Steps When Adopting Curricular Change K–16

Lauren Madden, PhD

As a college professor at a small school, I wear a lot of hats. Few days look the same. Some days, the bulk of my time is spent teaching, grading, and planning my next class. Others are spent collecting data for research projects and writing. Still others are full of committee meetings and other administrative appointments. The variety in my workdays minimizes boredom, but also offers other benefits that one might not notice on the surface. One of these is the ability to view situations from multiple perspectives and, perhaps more importantly, to separate parts from wholes.

The bulk of my research and a good deal of my teaching focuses on climate change education. In recent years, my state, New Jersey, adopted learning standards to support climate change education across grade levels and subject areas. I found myself in a new position—my work was propelled into the public eye and started getting noticed by others including the news media. I was often asked about *my* recommendations and opinions regarding the best way to introduce climate change into New Jersey classrooms. And I wasn't quite sure how to respond.

The *right answer* is to integrate climate change across the curriculum. To create student-centered, multidisciplinary, solution-based, arts-integrated learning experiences that take place inside and outside the classroom. To collaborate with community members, government agencies, nonprofit organizations, and local businesses. To bring real-time data, justice-oriented perspectives, and student-led inquiries to the forefront of the discussion on climate. And don't get me wrong. This is the *right answer*.

But I spend a lot of time in K–12 classrooms. And I know that teachers are taxed beyond measure. They are given more tasks and fewer resources every day. So if I were to recommend the kinds of changes described in the *right answer* above, a very small number of teachers might follow that recommendation. Most would feel overwhelmed and, at best, might show an explanatory video to "tick the box" that climate change was included. And this left me thinking about how we might make meaningful changes in a way that was actually feasible.

What if a fifth-grade teacher shared a newspaper article, like Aimee Nezhukumatathil's *New York Times* opinion piece[1] about the effects of climate change on vanilla beans? The flavor and scent is widely considered to be a favorite around the world, and is surely something that all fifth graders are familiar with. But due to our changing climate, the delicate conditions needed to grow the plant that produces the vanilla bean pods are threatened. Instead of simply describing climate change itself, the article would spark interest and discussion among students. And it might generate more questions that could lead a teacher to find some more resources about how plants and foods are affected by our changing climate. It might also spark further curiosity in children who may not have cared much about climate change previously.

That fifth-grade teacher wouldn't have to turn her curriculum inside out to integrate this new reading and discussion—she could swap out another opinion piece for this one, and craft a few discussion questions. This change is small, but purposeful.

There are so many shades of gray between box-ticking and overhauling entire curricula. Making purposeful and meaningful choices can lead to salient learning experiences that spark further changes. In sum, small changes to our teaching can:

1. Shift the kinds of discussions and questions that come up in our classrooms, leading to increased student engagement.
2. Allow students to make connections between classroom experiences and their interests and beliefs.
3. Fit within the existing scope and sequence of the school year without overburdening teachers.

The chapters in this book share many examples of small but meaningful changes that address a range of topics and subject areas. Each can serve as a jumping-off point for additional incremental adjustments to support student learning. The book starts with several chapters focused on the elementary years, then moves up in scope to include middle school, high school, and postsecondary experiences. The book finishes with suggestions that can be useful in classrooms across the board. Some chapters focus on strategies, while others are content-specific. Taken together, these tools can help teachers get started with small changes that lead to big outcomes.

NOTE

1. Aimee Nezhukumatathil, "This Is How the World's Favorite Scent Disappears," *New York Times*, August 4, 2024, https://www.nytimes.com/2024/08/04/opinion/vanilla-cooking-climate-change.html.

Chapter 1

Little Kids Making Big Decisions

Tiffany Robles

Project-based learning (PBL) is an effective teaching method where students actively acquire knowledge through engaging in personally meaningful and authentic real-world projects.[1] Despite its proven effectiveness, PBL curriculum is often tailored toward older students, leaving early childhood educators with limited support and resources for successful integration. This chapter aims to provide guidance and support for implementing PBL in K–2 classrooms by incorporating small but meaningful changes into their practice.

Project-based learning, characterized by hands-on learning, enables students to build skills and knowledge through various activities.[2] It involves students responding to a complex question, problem, or challenge through active participation and learning while working toward a final project or product.[3] Finally, PBL gives students the opportunity to present their final project to an authentic audience in some way. Unfortunately, much of the research on PBL extends beyond the early childhood classroom, raising concerns about its application to younger students who are still developing foundational skills, especially in literacy.

In a typical PBL unit, students are encouraged to think deeply, collaborate with peers, conduct research, make big decisions, and respond to challenges, all while teachers adopt a hands-off approach, facilitating learning rather than providing explicit instruction. However, skepticism often arises regarding the ability of early childhood students to navigate a project-based learning unit effectively, particularly considering their ongoing literacy development. As literacy proficiency is a pivotal component of the early childhood classroom, questions arise about how young students, still in the process of learning to read and write, can create final projects or respond to guiding questions.

Yet, the evidence suggests that early childhood students can participate in PBL and thrive when given the opportunity. Beyond its broader benefits, PBL has proven to be an effective and invigorating approach to teaching reading and writing with young children.[4] By offering young students choice and autonomy, PBL enhances engagement,[5] leading to heightened intrinsic motivation.[6] When early childhood students are actively engaged in their learning, the potential for academic growth is significantly increased.

As the title of this chapter suggests, little kids are more than capable of making big decisions. They can respond to guiding questions, make plans, and exercise choice over their learning. All they need is the opportunity. The rest of this chapter explores four small yet impactful changes that early childhood educators can make to incorporate PBL into their teaching practice in K–2 classrooms: adjusting mindset, crafting a guiding question, incorporating choice, and looking for literacy and language opportunities.

SMALL CHANGE #1: ADJUST YOUR MINDSET

Implementing a new teaching and learning approach in the classroom, such as PBL, can be challenging. The first and most important change required is a shift in mindset. Project-based learning is inherently dynamic and may require educators to step outside their comfort zones. Teachers should view challenges as opportunities, be open to trying new things, and learn from the evolving needs of their students. Deciding to incorporate PBL with young children can be intimidating as it requires teachers to relinquish some control, transforming them into facilitators of learning. In PBL, teachers guide students as they explore, breaking away from the traditional passive learning model. Transitioning one's mindset from doubting the capabilities of young kids in PBL to expecting and supporting their success is crucial. Sometimes, teachers have concerns that the results may not be grandiose or meet expectations, which requires a shift in perception.

Implementing PBL does come with challenges, including time, resources, classroom management, teacher self-control, and integration of a unit.[7] Finding time for both planning and execution proves challenging, while a lack of resources, coupled with the emphasis on student choice, adds complexity. Despite these challenges, evidence supports PBL's potential to enhance literacy growth. Before jumping into the practical aspects of PBL implementation in K–2 classrooms, educators must adjust their mindset. This requires transitioning from the traditional teacher-centered approach to more of a student-centered and inquiry-based philosophy.

Taking the initial leap involves changing one's perspective on what PBL should entail for early childhood students. Instead of adopting the mindset of "But they can't do this," it is essential to reframe to a mindset of, "But they can do this." This approach reflects an asset-based mindset. An asset-based mindset focuses on what a student can do by targeting the student's unique strengths and skills to guide their learning[8] Asset-based teaching encourages educators to challenge their previous assumptions and focus on what a student understands and can do. Table 1.1 provides illustrative examples of how to make this shift in thinking.

Embarking on the journey of implementing PBL in early childhood education requires a fundamental shift in mindset. Educators must overcome doubts about the capabilities of young students in PBL and embrace a perspective that sees challenges as opportunities for growth. The shift involves relinquishing control, becoming facilitators of learning, and fostering an environment where curiosity thrives. By reframing hesitant perceptions into positive affirmations, teachers can begin the process of implementing PBL in their classrooms.

Table 1.1. Examples of Mindset Shifts from the Deficit Model to Asset-Based Teaching

My students CAN'T do this.	My students CAN do this.
How will the students learn to read if I do project-based learning?	In what ways can I incorporate literacy into our lessons to increase student reading proficiency?
The final project won't be that great.	Look at what my students accomplished!
There is no way _____ will stay focused throughout the project.	How can I give _____ choices to keep them engaged in the project?
My students are too young. I will end up having to do it all for them.	In what ways can I scaffold the curriculum to help students be successful!
How will I know that my students learned anything?	What do I want my students to learn, and how will I embed it throughout the unit?
This is going to be a mess!	This may look different than some of the learning that normally goes on in this classroom, and that's okay.
What am I giving up?	What are my students gaining?
Some students don't even know all of their alphabet letters. How can they present on a topic at our final showcase?	The final showcase will look different for each student. How can I help all of my students be successful at the end?

SMALL CHANGE #2: START WITH AN OPEN-ENDED GUIDING QUESTION

Are you ready to dip your feet into the PBL pond but not go all the way in? Begin by taking one of your current units or groups of common standards and determining an age-appropriate guiding question to go with the unit.

Choosing a guiding question for PBL in an early childhood classroom requires careful consideration of young children's developmental needs, interests, and abilities. Guiding questions are open-ended and relevant to your students. Frame the guiding question in an open-ended way that encourages curiosity and investigation. Avoid questions with a simple yes/no answer, as you want to foster exploration and inquiry. Choose a question that is relevant and meaningful to the children's daily lives. This could be related to their interests, their experiences, and, particularly for early childhood students, the community around them.

As mentioned, if you want to tie a guiding question to one of your current units or a set of standards, ensure that the guiding question aligns with educational standards and learning objectives for early childhood education. This helps to maintain a balance between child-led exploration and academic goals. The question can incorporate a multidisciplinary approach and cover standards throughout the different disciplines. Aim for a question that lends itself to hands-on and active learning experiences. Early childhood learners benefit greatly from interactive, sensory-rich activities that involve exploration and play.

Examples of guiding questions that can be adapted for common early childhood learning units include the following:

- How can we help those who are hungry in our community?
- How do community helpers contribute to our community?

- How can we create an escape plan in our homes in case of emergency?
- How can we help new students get to know our community?
- How can we plant and take care of a garden?
- How can we, as designers, design our own toys to make recess more fun?
- How can we keep our bodies happy and healthy?
- How can we teach others in our building how to reduce, reuse, and recycle?
- How can we use art to tell a story?
- How can we bring a story to life using light and sound for an audience?

As teachers incorporate guiding questions into existing units, students embark on a journey of questioning, critical thinking, and decision-making, laying the groundwork for a gradual introduction to the components of project-based learning. This small change empowers students to delve deeper into their learning experiences, setting the stage for meaningful exploration and growth.

SMALL CHANGE #3: INCORPORATE CHOICE

A third small change that can be implemented in the classroom involves planning for and applying opportunities to incorporate student choice in a current lesson or unit.

Choice is a powerful motivator for learners of all ages, and K–2 students are no exception. Incorporation of choice within PBL allows young learners to take ownership of their projects. Providing choices for young students profoundly impacts student engagement, motivation, and confidence, especially for young children who often have adults making most of the decisions for them. Research has shown that providing choices to students of all ages often increases their intrinsic motivation and collaboration skills.[9] Beyond fostering increased engagement and responsibility, offering students a voice and choice in projects also enhances authenticity. This authenticity is showcased when students witness the real-world impact of their projects.

It is important to remember to start small in offering choice, especially for young students. Too much choice could be overwhelming for some students. Offering choice should also fit within the boundaries of your learning goals. Start with incorporating small opportunities for students to choose what they do and how they do it. By incorporating small choices into the classroom, you can empower young students to take ownership of their learning, fostering a sense of autonomy and enthusiasm for the project.

Table 1.2 provides examples of ways to incorporate choice into a PBL unit with the guiding question, "How can we help those who are hungry in our community?"

The incorporation of student choice is an impactful small change that can transform the dynamics of a classroom. This small change prompts a shift in mindset from apprehension to appreciation, asking educators to consider not what they are giving up but what their students are gaining through the empowerment of choice.

Table 1.2. Ways to Incorporate Choice into a Project-Based Learning Unit

Selecting Topic of Interest	Allow students to choose specific aspects related to hunger that interest them. For example, they could focus on food drives, community gardens, or organizing events to raise awareness about hunger.
Choosing Project Format	Provide various project formats for students to choose from. Some may prefer creating posters, while others may enjoy putting together a skit, writing a song, or making a video to present their findings.
Deciding on Outreach Strategies	Give students the opportunity to decide how they want to raise awareness. This might include organizing a food drive, creating informational pamphlets, or planning a community event.
Selecting Research Approaches	Offer a variety of research methods for students to explore. Some may enjoy conducting interviews with community members, while others might prefer reading books or watching age-appropriate videos about hunger issues.

SMALL CHANGE #4: EMBED LITERACY AND LANGUAGE IN PBL

Literacy development is a fundamental aspect of early education, and PBL provides a unique platform to enhance literacy skills in meaningful ways. PBL is an excellent way for educators to intentionally embed literacy opportunities within projects. From storytelling and journaling to creating written or multimedia presentations, the integration of literacy not only supports language development for young learners but also enhances the overall quality of PBL experiences for K–2 students. PBL is conducive to literacy instruction because projects often involve a great deal of reading and writing.[10] Moreover, research has found that when young students read and write for authentic, specific purposes beyond mastery of a standard, they are more likely to experience growth.[11]

A fourth small change involves purposeful planning to embed language and literacy opportunities within your unit. Begin by thinking through the literacy components you can tie to your guiding question. Read-alouds, shared writing, journals, word walls, predictable text, and more can all lead to enhancing student literacy skills. Select the literacy opportunities that align with the content of your unit.

At the beginning of a PBL unit, teachers can introduce key vocabulary, read related books aloud, and engage in discussions to build background knowledge. These components allow students to share their thoughts, ask questions, and express ideas verbally, which helps develop oral language skills. Providing sentence stems gives students the opportunity to explain their thinking and writing. This process can foster language and literacy skills by encouraging students to ask questions, share ideas, and collaboratively brainstorm solutions, laying the groundwork for language development.

During the project implementation, educators can guide students in expressing their ideas through written or drawn plans, fostering literacy skills in a purposeful context. There are many practical ways to embed literacy into project planning, such as creating project journals, labeling materials, and using writing as a tool for communication within collaborative groups.

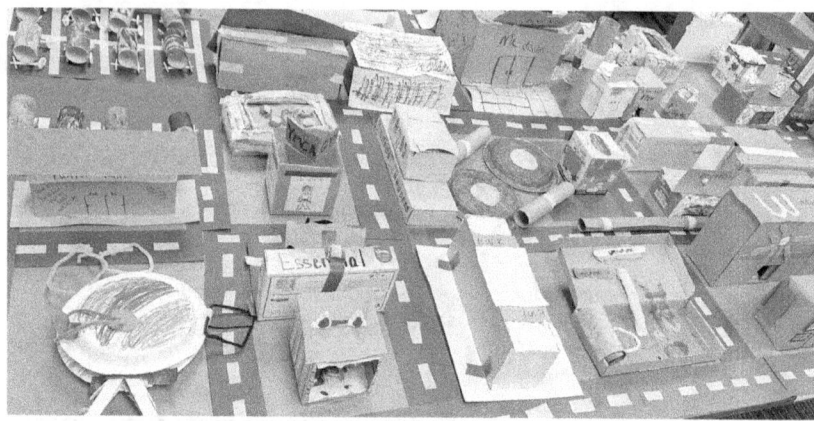

Figure 1.1. Photo of a first-grade group of students' community project. Students used their literacy skills to label the parts of their community. T. Robles.

The final project and reflection stage of a PBL unit provides opportunities for literacy integration through presentations and reflection activities. Teachers can facilitate literacy-rich culminating events, such as creating books, posters, or presentations. Reflective discussions and written reflections contribute to a deeper understanding of the project and reinforce language development.

It is essential to scaffold activities based on individual student needs and adjust as necessary to ensure that literacy skills are being developed in a supportive and engaging manner. Try to tie the literacy opportunities to the needs of your students. Early childhood students may not know how to read and write yet, so focus on what they can do. Can they label a drawing they made? Can they add the beginning letter of their picture? Can they add details to their picture or writing? Can they track print with a familiar text? Meet your students where they are in their literacy development while supporting and growing them as readers throughout the unit. Scaffolding activities based on individual needs ensure that literacy skills are developed in a supportive and engaging manner. This small change enhances literacy skills and enriches the overall learning experience, making PBL a dynamic and language-rich approach for early childhood education.

SMALL CHANGES IN ACTION

Implementing a PBL approach in early childhood education can greatly enhance engagement and learning. The following is an example that guides an early childhood educator through the process of enacting PBL with the four simple but meaningful changes discussed in this chapter. The example incorporates early childhood learning objectives based on the environment and the students' community.

Step 1: Adjusting Your Mindset

Embrace the role of a facilitator who nurtures curiosity and active participation. Acknowledge that environmental stewardship can start at a young age and recognize the capacity of young learners to contribute meaningful ideas and actions toward environmental care. Prepare to support and expand on children's suggestions and initiatives.

Step 2: Choosing an Open-Ended Guiding Question

Utilize the question, "How can we take care of our environment and inspire others to help us?" This question encourages students to think critically about sustainability and their role in the wider community. It invites them to explore concrete actions they can take and how they can communicate these actions to influence others positively.

Step 3: Incorporating Choice

Provide students with choices that allow them to explore their interests and strengths. Options could include:

- Choosing specific environmental issues to focus on (recycling, reducing waste, saving water, etc.).
- Deciding how they will present their findings and suggestions to the school or community (through posters, a video, a classroom presentation, etc.).
- Selecting tasks or roles within the project, such as researching, creating, or speaking.

Step 4: Embedding Language and Literacy

Incorporate activities that enhance literacy skills while deepening environmental understanding:

- Reading: Introduce age-appropriate books about the environment, conservation, and stories of young eco-heroes.
- Writing: Have students write persuasive letters or create informational brochures to spread awareness about their chosen environmental issues.
- Speaking/Listening: Encourage students to conduct interviews with each other, school staff, or family members about everyday actions that help the environment.

Overall, PBL is an engaging teaching method that has shown great success with young students. Evidence suggests that with thoughtful adjustments, even the youngest learners can actively engage in and benefit from PBL experiences. Implementing the four small changes introduced in this chapter will provide insight into the effectiveness of PBL for early childhood students. Empowering young students with the ability to engage in PBL not only fosters their academic growth but also cultivates a mindset where even little kids can make big decisions.

NOTES

1. Buck Institute for Education, "What Is PBL?" PBLWorks, 2017, https://www.pblworks.org/what-is-pbl.
2. Tiffany G. Robles, "The Impact of a Literacy Program on Summer Reading Setback: Providing Access to Books and Project-Based Learning" (EdD diss., University of South Carolina, 2023).
3. Nurul Farhana Jumaat, Zaidatun Tasir, Noor Dayana Abd Halim, and Zakiah Mohamad Ashari, "Project-Based Learning from Constructivism Point of View," *Advanced Science Letters* 23, no. 8 (2017): 7904–6.
4. Nell K. Duke, *Inside Information: Developing Powerful Readers and Writers of Informational Text Through Project-Based Instruction* (New York: Scholastic, 2014).
5. Alpaslan Sahin and N. Top, "STEM Students on the Stage (SOS): Promoting Student Voice and Choice in STEM Education through an Interdisciplinary, Standards-Focused Project Based Learning Approach," *Journal of STEM Education: Innovations and Research* 16, no. 3 (2015), https://www.jstem.org/jstem/index.php/JSTEM/article/view/1911.
6. Fien De Smedt, Amélie Rogiers, Sofie Heirweg, Emmelien Merchie, and Hilde Van Keer, "Assessing and Mapping Reading and Writing Motivation in Third to Eight Graders: A Self-Determination Theory Perspective," *Frontiers in Psychology* 11 (July 2020).
7. Seth A. Parsons, Salem Rainey Metzger, Jeanna Askew, and Ashley R. Carswell, "Teaching Against the Grain: One Title I School's Journey toward Project-Based Literacy Instruction," *Literacy Research and Instruction* 50 (2010): 1–14.
8. Shannon Renkly and Katherine Bertolini, "Shifting the Paradigm from Deficit-Oriented Schools to Asset-Based Models: Why Leaders Need to Promote an Asset Orientation in Our Schools," *Empowering Research for Educators* 2, no. 1 (2018): Article 4, https://openprairie.sdstate.edu/ere/vol2/iss1/4.
9. Dimitra Kokotsaki, Victoria Menzies, and Andy Wiggins, "Project-Based Learning: A Review of the Literature," *Improving Schools* 19, no. 3 (2016): 267–77.
10. Nell K. Duke, "Project-Based Instruction: A Great Match for Informational Texts," *American Educator* 40, no. 3 (2016): 4.
11. Victoria Purcell-Gates, Nell K. Duke, and Joseph A. Martineau, "Learning to Read and Write Genre-Specific Text: Roles of Authentic Experience and Explicit Teaching," *Reading Research Quarterly* 42, no. 1 (2007): 8–45.

BIBLIOGRAPHY

Buck Institute for Education. "What Is PBL?" PBLWorks, 2017. https://www.pblworks.org/what-is-pbl.

De Smedt, Fien, Amélie Rogiers, Sofie Heirweg, Emmelien Merchie, and Hilde Van Keer. "Assessing and Mapping Reading and Writing Motivation in Third to Eight Graders: A Self-Determination Theory Perspective." *Frontiers in Psychology* 11 (July 2020). https://doi.org/10.3389/fpsyg.2020.01678.

Duke, Nell K. *Inside Information: Developing Powerful Readers and Writers of Informational Text through Project-Based Instruction*. New York: Scholastic, 2014.

Duke, Nell K. "Project-Based Instruction: A Great Match for Informational Texts." *American Educator* 40, no. 3 (2016): 4.

Jumaat, Nurul Farhana, Zaidatun Tasir, Noor Dayana Abd Halim, and Zakiah Mohamad Ashari. "Project-Based Learning from Constructivism Point of View." *Advanced Science Letters* 23, no. 8 (2017): 7904–6. https://doi.org/10.1166/asl.2017.9605.

Kokotsaki, Dimitra, Victoria Menzies, and Andy Wiggins. "Project-Based Learning: A Review of the Literature." *Improving Schools* 19, no. 3 (2016): 267–77. https://doi.org/10.1177/1365480216659733.

Parsons, Seth A., Salem Rainey Metzger, Jeanna Askew, and Ashley R. Carswell. "Teaching against the Grain: One Title I School's Journey toward Project-Based Literacy Instruction." *Literacy Research and Instruction* 50, no. 1 (2010): 1–14. https://doi.org/10.1080/19388070903318413.

Purcell-Gates, Victoria, Nell K. Duke, and Joseph A. Martineau. "Learning to Read and Write Genre-Specific Text: Roles of Authentic Experience and Explicit Teaching." *Reading Research Quarterly* 42, no. 1 (2007): 8–45. https://doi.org/10.1598/rrq.42.1.1.

Renkly, Shannon, and Katherine Bertolini. "Shifting the Paradigm from Deficit-Oriented Schools to Asset-Based Models: Why Leaders Need to Promote an Asset Orientation in Our Schools." *Empowering Research for Educators* 2, no.1 (2018): Article 4. https://openprairie.sdstate.edu/ere/vol2/iss1/4.

Robles, Tiffany G. "The Impact of a Literacy Program on Summer Reading Setback: Providing Access to Books and Project-Based Learning." EdD diss., University of South Carolina, 2023.

Sahin, Alpaslan, and N. Top. "STEM Students on the Stage (SOS): Promoting Student Voice and Choice in STEM Education through an Interdisciplinary, Standards-Focused Project Based Learning Approach." *Journal of STEM Education: Innovations and Research* 16, no. 3 (2015). https://www.jstem.org/jstem/index.php/JSTEM/article/view/1911.

Chapter 2

Small Changes, Meaningful Impact

Number Talks in the Elementary Mathematics Classroom

Heather West Jerez,* Temple A. Walkowiak,*
Briana Pelton, Kristin Hord, and Jennifer Tymkin

After implementing Number Talks in my third-grade classroom for just a few months, I noticed more students using mental math and building off one another's ideas when explaining their strategies.

—Kristin, veteran teacher and chapter coauthor

Are you looking to make a small change in your math instruction that will support your students' fluency with number and operations and encourage talking about their math ideas? As evident in the testimonial from Kristin, adding a brief routine in the form of a Number Talk is a small change that we have found supports this goal. Number Talks, typically five to fifteen minutes in length, are designed to further develop students' number sense and mental math skills.[1] In this chapter, we share one school's initiative to incorporate Number Talks into their math instruction. We provide information on the background and benefits of Number Talks, take you inside one of our classrooms, outline steps for implementation, and offer advice for both teachers and school leaders who are interested in implementing this small change. While we write with a first-person point of view as we present our experiences with Number Talks, we will also refer to each author by first name (third-person point of view) to provide clarity to our readers. Our author team includes Briana, school principal; Jen, second-grade teacher; Kristin, third-grade teacher; Temple, university-based mathematics teacher educator; and Heather, mathematics educator and researcher.

NUMBER TALKS: BACKGROUND, BENEFITS, AND OUR CONTEXT

A Number Talk includes either a single expression or a string of expressions that build on each other (see table 2.1 for examples of both). The teacher displays an expression on the board or chart paper, asks students to mentally evaluate the expression, records students' strategies as they share orally, and facilitates discussion about similarities and differences among particular strategies based on the goal of the Number Talk. When using a string of expressions, the teacher presents one expression at a time. This enables students to apply strategies used for each expression to subsequent expressions in the sequence. The chosen expression(s) should support students' mental computation, understanding of a given strategy, and ability to explain their strategies.[2] The learning that unfolds during Number Talks results in numerous benefits for students, the broader classroom community, and the teacher.

Table 2.1

Grade Level	Example	Goal
Kindergarten	(three 10-frames)	This string can be used to focus on how many more is needed to make 10. Note: Each 10 frame is a single expression, presented one at a time, to make the string of three expressions.
First Grade	(two 10-frames)	This expression, consisting of two 10 frames to model 9 + 4, can reinforce the Break-Apart-to-Make-Ten strategy[a] (i.e., move 1 counter from "4" to fill the first 10 frame: 9 + (1 + 3) = (9 + 1) + 3)
Second Grade	43 + 27	This expression can be used to elicit strategies based on place value and making tens.
Third Grade	153 – 100 151 – 98 173 – 160 171 – 158	This string can be used to draw students' attention to keeping a constant difference (i.e., The distance on the number line between the minuend and subtrahend in each pair of expressions is the same).
Fourth Grade	8 × 16 4 × 32 2 × 64	This string can be used to develop a doubling and halving strategy (i.e., doubling one factor and halving the other does not change the value of the expression).
Fifth Grade	$\frac{1}{2}$ of $\frac{1}{4}$	This expression encourages students to visualize part of a part (which is fraction multiplication).
Resources for Number Talks	*Making Number Talks Matter: Developing Mathematical Practices and Deepening Understanding, Grades 3–10* by Cathy Humphreys and Ruth Parker *Digging Deeper: Making Number Talks Matter Even More, Grades 3–10* by Ruth Parker and Cathy Humphreys *Number Talks: Whole Number Computation* by Sherry Parrish *Number Talks: Fractions, Decimals, and Percentages* by Sherry Parrish	

a Douglas Clements and Julie Sarama, *Learning and Teaching Early Math: The Learning Trajectories Approach*, Third Edition (New York: Routledge, 2021).

Number Talks provide a range of benefits for students as individual learners. This routine is an inclusive approach to supporting students' development of accurate, flexible, and efficient use of strategies.[3] Number Talks contribute to students' overall mathematical proficiency as well as foster a positive environment for their learning. During Number Talks, students leverage their understanding of number relationships and reasoning skills to evaluate an expression, rather than rely on memorized procedures.[4] As teachers build on students' responses to help them make meaningful connections to important math concepts, Number Talks serve as a powerful tool for building students' confidence in math. With an emphasis on the process for arriving at a solution, rather than on the correct value, all students are encouraged to contribute. In doing so, they become more comfortable making mistakes and see this as an opportunity to deepen mathematical understanding.[5] This is closely aligned with the work of developing a growth mindset.[6]

Number Talks provide an opportunity to engage all students in meaningful discussions that enrich the classroom community. Teachers elevate math discourse by asking probing questions that elicit student thinking and help them make sense of each other's strategies and reasoning.[7] Students who may otherwise be reluctant to participate can share their thinking in a safe environment, knowing their unique way of thinking is not only accepted but offers valuable contributions to the discussion.[8] Number Talks encourage students to be sense makers and convey the message that all students are capable of understanding and engaging in class.[9]

In addition, Number Talks offer opportunities for teachers to grow in their practice. There are times when teachers face challenges implementing new instructional ideas due to curricular, time, or planning demands. However, Number Talks provide teachers with a practical and incremental approach to strengthening their instruction. These brief and manageable routines offer a small, yet impactful way for teachers to experiment with questioning and talk moves. Moreover, Number Talks are designed to be time-efficient and require no additional materials other than markers to record strategies, making the routine accessible for teachers who are already experiencing constraints with time and resources. In our own context, teachers recognized these benefits for their students, classrooms, and professional growth when they started exploring Number Talks.

In the fall of 2019, Briana reached out to Temple, a university-based teacher educator, about providing professional development in math for teachers at the elementary school where Briana was serving as principal. While the initial primary goal was to evaluate and increase rigor of math tasks, a secondary goal was to focus on supporting students' computational fluency. Temple facilitated professional development in support of both of these goals. In addition to an initial session at the beginning of the school year, Temple met with grade-level teams for more focused work and participated in group walk-through observations and reflections with teams of teachers and school leaders. After the initial session, there was quick evidence that teachers, including Kristin and Jen, were trying out Number Talks in their classrooms to support their students' fluency with the operations. We attribute this quick evidence to the small change teachers had to make to instruction when adding this number routine, but we also emphasize that this small change involves complexity and practice in facilitation. To illustrate how facilitation plays out, we now enter Jen's classroom during a Number Talk.

Vignette: A Number Talk in Action

This Number Talk takes place in Jen's second-grade classroom in January, almost halfway through the school year. Her students were gathered on the rug eagerly waiting as she wrote the expression 47 + 33 + 56 + 84 on chart paper. Jen intentionally chose these numbers to encourage students to use prior knowledge of decomposing numbers by place value (e.g., 47 is 40 plus 7) and making tens (e.g., 4 and 6 make 10).

Jen: If you have a strategy, show me a quiet thumb on your chest. [Jen models a fist with a thumb up close to her chest. She pauses for about 15 seconds.] *If you have a second strategy, show me a quiet second finger.* [She models and pauses again until most students have a thumb up.] *Raise your hand if you have a value for this expression. Remember, all responses are valued and important.* [She calls on students; five different values are shared and recorded: 210, 220, 200, 213, and 225.]

Jen: Raise your hand to share your strategy.

As students share, Jen writes their name on the chart paper to honor their thinking, as well as their strategy, for all students to see (figure 2.1). This acknowledges and validates each student's contribution and empowers them to actively participate in the discussion.

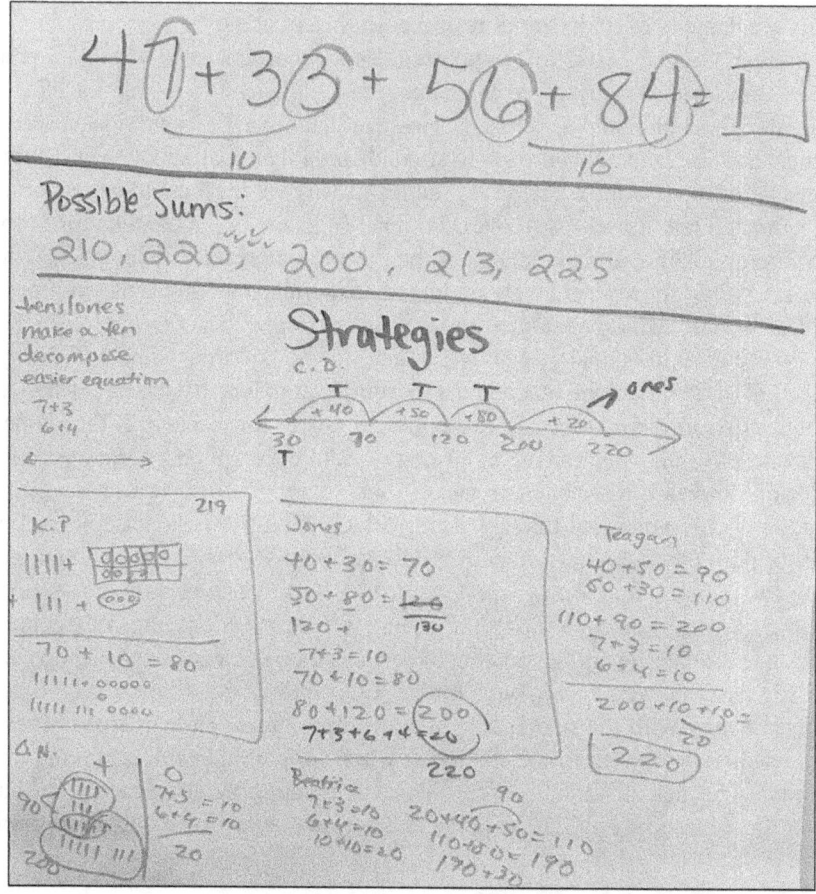

Figure 2.1. Students' recorded strategies for solving 47+33+56+84 during a Number Talk. J. Tymkin.

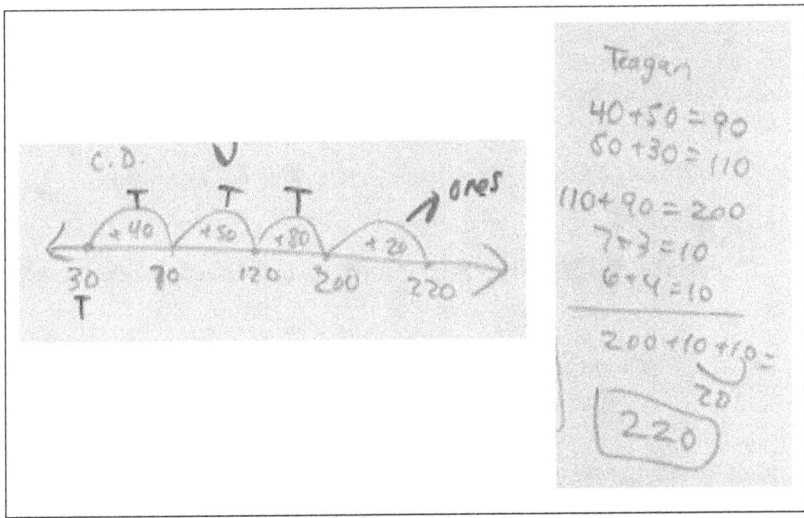

Figure 2.2. Jen purposefully selects two students' strategies for further discussion. J. Tymkin.

After several strategies have been recorded, Jen circles back to the strategies of two students, CD and Teagan (figure 2.2). She selected these strategies because she noticed that together, the two strategies would allow her to highlight decomposing numbers by place value, making tens, and using an open number line.

Jen: How are the strategies of CD and Teagan similar? How are their strategies different? Use these sentence frames. [Jen points to sentence frames on the wall and reads aloud:] *The strategies are similar because _____. The strategies are different because _____. Now, turn and talk to a partner.*

By asking students to turn and talk, Jen encourages all students to actively participate in the Number Talk, even those who may be reluctant to share their thinking with the larger group. After a couple of minutes of sharing, Jen asks for her students' attention.

Jen: Raise your hand if you would like to share how CD's and Teagan's strategies are similar or different.

Thomas: They both combined the ones together, uh, the 7, 3, 6, and 4.

Jen: Where are the ones in CD's strategy?

Thomas: In that last jump on the number line, 20. [Jen points to the +20 jump on the number line to confirm and labels the jump with "ones".]

Jen: I like how many of you noticed that 7 and 3 make 10, and 6 and 4 make 10. And together that makes 20! Is there another way the strategies are similar or different?

Olivia: They also both combined the tens.

Jen: What do you mean by that?

Olivia: They both added the 40, 50, 80, and 30. They just did it in different ways.

Jen: Tell me more.

Olivia: Um, well I see those numbers on Teagan's strategy, but . . .

Jen: So you see the 30, 40, 50, and 80 from the tens place from the original equation in Teagan's strategy. [Jen points to the equation and Teagan's recorded strategy.] *Where are those numbers in CD's strategy?* [Jen waits to give students a chance to think.]

Taylor: The 40, 50, and 80 are jumps on the number line in CD's strategy.

Jen: Where is the 30?

Olivia: I see it now! The 30 is where CD started, then added all the other numbers!

Jen: CD, why did you start at 30?

CD: Um, um . . . I wanted to start with the smallest number so I started with the 30 from 33.

Jen: Even though CD and Teagan used different strategies, we see connections between how they decomposed into tens and ones, and how they made those tens! Great work, everyone! And I want to leave you with one question to ponder: Whose strategy did you find the most efficient?

When Jen asks several students to share their ideas, she is able to clarify and extend their thinking. Note that she concludes the Number Talk with statements about making tens and decomposing by place value. She also revoices students' responses (e.g., *So you see the 30, 40, 50, and 80 . . . in Teagan's strategy. Where are those numbers in CD's strategy?*) and asks probing questions (e.g., *What do you mean by that?*) to support her goal for the Number Talk.

Adding Number Talks as a routine is a small change to instruction; however, we acknowledge that this work requires continued practice. For educators seeking to incorporate Number Talks into their classrooms, the following section offers guidance and practical strategies for successful implementation.

GUIDE FOR IMPLEMENTING NUMBER TALKS

The versatility of Number Talks allows K–12 teachers to easily integrate this activity into existing math routines. Number Talks can be used as part of a daily warm-up activity, in a small group setting to reinforce a particular math concept, or even in a whole-group extended discussion. Here are some specific strategies and teacher actions that can help you implement these in your classroom.

- Plan for intentionality. That is, the intentionality behind your chosen expression(s) is important. Which strategies are you trying to develop or reinforce through your choice in number selection or ordering of the string? In our vignette, Jen was intentional with her selected expression based on strategies she wanted to highlight. Table 2.1 includes examples and a list of resource books.
- Designate a location in the classroom where students gather closely on a rug near a board or chart paper. This allows you to record students' responses for all to see.

- Write the expression horizontally, like Jen did in the vignette, if the expression involves an operation. This discourages the use of procedures.[10]
- Provide wait time so students have ample time to silently and mentally evaluate the expression.
- Ask students to hold their hand in a fist by their chest. Show them how to raise a thumb to signal they have a strategy and to raise a second finger to signal a second strategy. These quiet signals by their chests are less distracting and disruptive to thinking than raised hands.
- Elicit answers (i.e., values for the expression) after most students have indicated they have a solution. All values are accepted and recorded on the board, both correct and incorrect (Note: five different values were shared for the expression in our vignette).
- Elicit strategy sharing by asking students to "Raise your hand if you'd like to share."[11] Record the student's name and their strategy as they describe. This validates the student's thinking and promotes ownership of their learning. Ask probing questions to encourage clear communication of mathematical thinking.
- Remind students to listen to others so they can pose questions or build on their classmates' ideas.[12] Display sentence frames to support students responding in a productive and respectful manner. For instance, "I would like to defend the answer _____ because _____," and "I respectfully disagree with you because _____."
- Make meaningful connections across strategies and to the goal of the Number Talk by asking for similarities and differences among strategies, like when Jen asked her students to compare the strategies of CD and Teagan (Note: Jen provided sentence frames to support her students to compare).
- Be confident that students know the "correct" value for the expression at the conclusion of the Number Talk, either by noticing that students have self-corrected as they hear other students' strategies or by asking students to analyze why various responses are reasonable or unreasonable.

With these strategies and teacher actions in mind, we offer additional advice; we have found that sharing our experiences, as well as successes and challenges, can help others integrate these routines into their math instruction.

ADVICE FOR TEACHERS AND SCHOOL LEADERS

Three of us were deeply embedded in the school's initiative to utilize Number Talks. Kristin and Jen both made incremental changes as they started to implement Number Talks in their classrooms, observing improvement in their own facilitation and encouragement for students to share their strategies over time. Briana had the vantage point of observing implementation and changes across classrooms. We share pieces of advice based primarily on these three teachers' observations; however, we also draw on Temple's observations to a lesser extent, as an external partner who interacted with teachers and leaders at the school. We encourage you to consider all advice because the collective list provides a "big picture" perspective, but we organize the advice into

Are You a Teacher Who Is Interested in Number Talks?

Build on What You Are Already Doing in Your Classroom

When planning for Number Talks, consider these not as a new practice, but rather as a natural extension of what is already happening in your classroom. Reflect on where elements of math talk are already a part of your classroom culture and in place during your math lessons—your students' explanations of various strategies to solve problems, the use of sentence starters or word walls to reinforce math vocabulary, and the questions you pose to students to elicit their thinking. The initial process of introducing Number Talks takes time, but leverage the strengths of your existing instruction. If student talk during math instruction has been less present in your classroom, start by setting clear expectations and model what it looks like by thinking out loud about your own computational strategies. Above all, have fun and infuse your own creativity into the routine, as you know what will engage your students most effectively.

Start Small, Practice Regularly, and Keep Trying

While Number Talks are indeed a small change, they are still a sophisticated and complex component of instruction—so we encourage you to start small. You might start by trying a Number Talk once or twice per week, or you might start with a small group of students, rather than your whole class. No matter what you choose to do, the key is to practice regularly. Recording students' strategies while also asking probing questions is not easy; however, practice helps. We noticed when first trying Number Talks that we and other teachers tended to restate what students shared, rather than probing them about their thinking. We also noticed that sometimes when facilitating a Number Talk, we gave our own strategy too early in the Number Talk, which sometimes shut down student thinking. This all changed over time. Like any skill, such as playing the piano or shooting a basketball, with repeated practice we saw improvement in how we recorded students' strategies, connected across strategies, and probed students' thinking. We recommend video recording yourself periodically and noting your improvements over time.

We also saw improvement in students. Perhaps most important to note, both Kristin and Jen saw students grow exponentially in their abilities to decompose numbers and utilize a variety of strategies. These improvements skills trickled into other components of math instruction. For instance, students applied strategies learned during Number Talks while solving math tasks and playing math games during other parts of lessons. Furthermore, students improved in their overall abilities to communicate their mathematical ideas with others.

Utilize Tools to Support Your Students

When we first started Number Talks, we noticed that students had varied levels of comfort in sharing their strategies orally. To increase comfort, we utilized tools students were familiar with, like "turn and talk" and sentence frames. Asking students to turn and talk to a peer helps them clarify their ideas and increases their confidence to share their strategies with a larger group. Opportunities to turn and talk are often helpful for multilingual speakers for whom English may not be their first language, and for students who experience anxiety when prompted to talk in larger group settings. Similar to the use of turn and talk, sentence frames also provide structure and support for students. We have found that sentence frames (e.g., "I agree with _____'s strategy because _____.") help students more clearly communicate, allowing them to focus on their mathematical processes rather than on how to structure their sentences when explaining. Finally, we noticed that using sentence frames simultaneously with a turn and talk, like Jen did with her class in the vignette, can effectively promote meaningful student-to-student dialogue and build collaboration among students. For instance, to support students as they engage in that conversation, the first student in the pair might say: "The strategy I used is _____ because _____." The second student follows with: "My strategy is _____ and is similar to/different from your strategy because _____." Together, we have found that these two supports helped students learn to share their mental math strategies orally.

Elevate the Impact of Number Talks through Extensions

Once you have practiced and feel more comfortable with Number Talks, we recommend elevating their impact through extensions. We have used writing extensions, strategy evaluation on assessments, analysis of efficiency and accuracy, and attention to mathematical relationships in story problems. First, a writing extension helped deepen our students' understanding of concepts and their ability to make connections over time. For instance, after a Number Talk, Jen often gives her students time to record strategies and explanations in their math notebooks. This serves as a reference when students are prompted to make connections across strategies in future Number Talks. Students enjoy documenting their strategies and revisiting the evolution of their thinking over time. This documentation highlighting student progress can also be shared with parents during conferences. Second, we have noted the utility of including Number Talk strategy evaluation on written assessments. We recommend taking pictures of recorded strategies, like Jen did for the vignette above, to inform your assessments and to actually use pictures of select strategies on assessments for students to explain. Third, we often engage our students in assessing the flexibility and accuracy of shared strategies during Number Talks. This might be reflecting on whose strategy seems most efficient, why a shared value seems unreasonable, or how and why a strategy for solving does not work. Finally, while Number Talks typically involve computational expressions without context (i.e., "naked numbers"), you might also consider targeting mathematical relationships in story problems. For example, after first focusing on developing her students' computational skills, Kristin used numberless story problems during a Number Talk where the purpose was to talk about the mathematical relationships between the missing numbers in the story. All of these extensions further demonstrate the meaningful impact Number Talks can have in your classroom.

Are You a Principal or Instructional Leader Looking for School-Wide Recommendations?

Start Small and Celebrate Along the Way

Initiate the integration of Number Talks within your school gradually. Start small with one classroom, one grade level, or even a grade band. Encourage teachers to try out this practice once per week and share artifacts with one another. This may include chart paper, a picture of the board, or a video recording. This can spark interest and create a supportive space for teachers to learn from and celebrate both successes and challenges together. When visiting classrooms, you may observe variations in implementation among teachers; some may feel comfortable probing students' thinking and making connections across their strategies, while others may need more time to hone these skills. This variation is okay; with regular practice, improvement will happen. This approach of starting small, sharing experiences, and celebrating efforts helps build a collective positivity that encourages other teachers to willingly join in, fostering a culture of collaboration.

Give Teachers Meaningful Opportunities to Learn Together and from Each Other

As with any new initiative, we have found that a set of shared learning opportunities is critical. In our case, teachers participated in a school-wide professional development session with Temple and follow-up opportunities with their grade-level teams. These opportunities included watching videos, planning together, self-analysis after video recording, and visiting other teachers' classrooms to observe. Together, this helped establish a culture of collective professional growth as teachers learned from and with each other. Jen and Kristin emphasize the power of being given the opportunity to visit other teachers' classrooms to observe Number Talks. While watching videos is important and beneficial, watching Number Talks live can be particularly transformative because it allows teachers to gain ideas and insights about the diverse ways a Number Talk can be implemented.

Participate in the Learning Opportunities with Teachers

At this school, the instructional leaders' participation in the learning opportunities with teachers was a critical foundation for teacher buy-in. In our case, Briana as well as the assistant principal and instructional coach participated in the initial professional development session and numerous follow-up learning opportunities. Temple noticed that Briana was engaged and brought an eagerness to learn, offering explicit ideas for teachers to build on what they were already doing. Her participation, along with other leaders, communicated the value and priority of the work, coupled with a message of "we're all in this together" as they embarked on the initiative.

CONCLUSION

As you can see, starting small with Number Talks can act as a catalyst for continuous growth and progressive expansion of opportunities throughout the year. Number Talks serve to deepen students' number sense and computational strategies, but their impacts extend beyond the math curriculum. Number Talks serve to foster a discourse-rich community where students' ideas are positioned as important and valid, both in math and in other disciplines. This routine also builds support for acknowledging, leveraging, and celebrating students' conceptions, including misconceptions that are expected.

In their simplest form, Number Talks allow ALL students the opportunity to mentally, collaboratively, and verbally share and elaborate on a strategy. These are life skills, used across all academic disciplines, that also build a respect for differing opinions, differing mindsets, and differing starting points of understanding . . . all of which are needed to prepare students for our world.

NOTES

* Co-lead authors

1. Sherry Parrish, "Number Talks Build Numerical Reasoning," *Teaching Children Mathematics* 18, no. 3 (2011): 198–206.

2. Cathy Humphreys and Ruth Parker, *Making Number Talks Matter* (Portsmouth, NH: Stenhouse, 2015); Sherry Parrish, *Number Talks: Whole Number Computation* (Sausalito, CA: Math Solutions, 2014); Dawn Woods, "Building a Math-Talk Learning Community Through Number Talks," *Journal of Mathematical Behavior* 67 (2022): 100995.

3. Parrish, "Number Talks Build Numerical Reasoning."

4. Humphreys and Parker, *Making Number Talks Matter.*

5. Cathy Humphreys, "Number Talks in High School," *New England Mathematics Journal* 49, (2016): 28–39.

6. Jo Boaler, *Mathematical Mindsets* (San Francisco: Jossey-Bass, 2015).

7. Laura Bofferding and Melissa Kemmerle, "Elementary Teacher Candidates' Use of Number Strings: Creating a Math-Talk Learning Community," *Mathematics Teacher Educator* 3, no. 2 (2015): 99–115; Magdalene Lampert, Heather Beasley, Hala Ghousseini, Elham Kazemi, and Megan Franke, "Using Designed Instructional Activities to Enable Novices to Manage Ambitious Mathematics Teaching," in *Instructional Explanations in the Disciplines*, eds. Mary Kay Stein and Linda Kucan (New York: Springer, 2010), 129–41.

8. Kathy Sun, Erin Baldinger, and Cathy Humphreys, "Number Talks: Gateway to Sense Making," *Mathematics Teacher* 112, no. 1 (2018): 48–54.

9. Woods, "Building a Math-Talk Learning Community Through Number Talks"; Sun, Baldinger, and Humphreys, "Number Talks: Gateway to Sense Making."

10. Sherry Parrish, *Number Talks: Whole Number Computation.*

11. Humphreys and Parker, *Making Number Talks*; Parrish, *Number Talks: Whole Number Computation.*

12. Ruth Parker and Cathy Humphreys, *Digging Deeper: Making Number Talks Matter Even More, Grades 3–10* (Portsmouth, NH: Stenhouse Publishers, 2018).

BIBLIOGRAPHY

Boaler, Jo. *Mathematical Mindsets.* San Francisco: Jossey-Bass, 2015.

Bofferding, Laura, and Melissa Kemmerle. "Elementary Teacher Candidates' Use of Number Strings: Creating a Math-Talk Learning Community." *Mathematics Teacher Educator* 3, no. 2 (2015): 99–115.

Humphreys, Cathy. "Number Talks in High School." *New England Mathematics Journal* 49, (2016): 28–39.

Humphreys, Cathy, and Ruth Parker. *Making Number Talks Matter*. Portsmouth, NH: Stenhouse, 2015.

Lampert, Magdalene, Heather Beasley, Hala Ghousseini, Elham Kazemi, and Megan Franke. "Using Designed Instructional Activities to Enable Novices to Manage Ambitious Mathematics Teaching." In *Instructional Explanations in the Disciplines*, edited by Mary Kay Stein and Linda Kucan, 129–41. New York: Springer, 2010.

Parker, Ruth, and Cathy Humphreys. *Digging Deeper: Making Number Talks Matter Even More, Grades 3–10*. Portsmouth, NH: Stenhouse Publishers, 2018.

Parrish, Sherry. "Number Talks Build Numerical Reasoning." *Teaching Children Mathematics* 18, no. 3 (2011): 198–206.

Parrish, Sherry. *Number Talks: Whole Number Computation*. Sausalito, CA: Math Solutions, 2014.

Sun, Kathy, Erin Baldinger, and Cathy Humphreys. "Number Talks: Gateway to Sense Making." *Mathematics Teacher* 112, no. 1 (2018): 48–54.

Woods, Dawn. "Building a Math-Talk Learning Community Through Number Talks." *Journal of Mathematical Behavior* 67 (2022): 100995.

Chapter 3

Wonder Walks as a Nature-Based Teaching Practice

Steph N. Dean

A line of fourth graders walks slowly and silently along the school campus boundary, following their teacher as she leads them past a wooded area filled with various trees and ground shrubs. At first glance, this appears to be a typical elementary school line, with students moving purposefully, albeit unhurriedly, toward the building. A closer inspection, however, reveals some anomalies: One student stops to pat a piece of moss, another twirls a large piece of grass in her hand while her eyelids flutter. Some students simply look up at the sky and take deep breaths while others appear to be simply, but deliberately, walking. The teacher picks something up from the grass, examines it, and then passes the object back down the line, each student receiving a chance to handle the mystery item.

As they near the door to the building, the students instinctively form a circle, accustomed to the debrief routine with which they engage on a regular basis.

Once everyone is grouped, the class collectively takes some deep breaths. In and out, in and out. After a comfortable silence stretches over the circle of students, the teacher finally asks, "Who wants to share their wonderings?"

Hands fly up. One student starts to speak but then remembers to wait her turn. Students are eager to share.

A fourth grader cradles the mystery item the teacher picked up just a few moments ago, ready to explain his hypothesis regarding both its origin and identification.

The teacher smiles—this may be routine, but it doesn't get old. This is a wonder walk.

The concept of wonder is not easy to define. Scholars in a variety of fields have wrestled with this rather abstract concept in an attempt to describe and delineate *what* wonder is and whether it can be classified as a state of mind, an emotion, or simply an idea. Within the field of education, particularly science education,[1] there has been a growing awareness of wonder as a starting point for inquiry[2] as well as an important component of mindfulness.[3] Its definition is slippery, yet I am of the opinion that wonder's elusiveness adds to the splendor and mystery of all that it represents.

I have personally adopted the following explanation of wonder from a former fourth-grade student: "Wonder starts with noticing the world around us. It is being in awe of nature and letting curiosity take over. It's like lifting your open mouth to the sky to catch a raindrop."

Wonder is beauty. It is fascination.

Wonder often involves a sense of admiration.

It is novel.

It is ancient.

It is constantly changing, yet still consistent in its resonance.

Yes, wonder looks and feels differently for everyone.

A wonder walk is similar in its open-endedness, and can be difficult to define because individual approaches vary. Regardless of the specifics, a wonder walk involves walking in nature while paying attention to things that fill one's mind with awe, fascination, or wonder. Within an educational context, wonder walks typically include a mindful walk out in the schoolyard wherein students are encouraged to notice and wonder about the world around them.

My own journey with wonder and wonder walks has drastically impacted my role as an educator, encouraging me to both model and cultivate an openness to experience that has enhanced my perception of the world. This small classroom change—of letting wonder take a prominent role through a simple schoolyard walk—has also had positive effects on my students in myriad ways.

But let's start at the beginning, with my growing realization that our current educational approach often does not create enough space for curiosity and authentic, genuine inquiry. Let's start with my brief break from the public education system and then a subsequent road trip around the United States.

WONDER-FILLED JOURNEYS

I was only a couple of years into my teaching career, and I was starting to feel burned out. It wasn't workload or student behavior, although those were challenging. What slowly wore away at my momentum and spirit was the way in which I fought a system that quantified my students based on academic achievement rather than fostering a love and passion for learning. The innovative learning opportunities that I was presenting to my classes each year were deemed a *success* or a *failure,* not based on student holistic well-being or their development of twenty-first-century skills, but on a single end-of-year test score.

I had reached a point as an educator that presented a crossroads: keep teaching or try something else. I opted for the latter option, handed in my letter of resignation, and decided to take a yearlong road trip around the United States visiting all the national parks. Yes, it was slightly drastic and perhaps reactionary to my experiences, but in June 2016 I took off, towing my teardrop trailer armed with the essentials that I would need for a year.

It was an incredible experience, and I could write a book on each of the ideas I discovered, the people I met, and the things that I learned. One of which was wonder.

Wonder found me in the darkened chambers of Mammoth Caves. It stared me straight in the face when I paddled amid mangrove trees in Biscayne National Park.

Wonder startled me with a sunset when I crested the overlook at Black Canyon of the Gunnison (figure 3.1). And it crept up on me as I sat for an hour watching banana slugs in the Redwood Forest (figure 3.2).

Wonder effectively reset my brain and catapulted me back into the love of learning and teaching. Part of this came about by my solo experiences immersed in the

Figure 3.1. Sunset in Black Canyon of the Gunnison National Park.

Figure 3.2. Banana slug in Redwood Forest National Park.

federally protected outdoor environments. The other part involved ranger-led interpretive programs that included place-based knowledge at its finest.

I had rediscovered the joy of learning experiences and the beauty of being fascinated by the natural world.

I knew that I had to share this with students. Back to my fourth-grade classroom.

I tentatively began teaching again, intent on finding moments to get my students outside to learn *in place,* experiencing the natural world in a way that mirrored my own outdoor excursions. I quickly learned that wonder came easier to many of my students than it did for me; it simply required an opportunity for my class to observe, play, and explore outdoors. The unstructured moments in between lessons lent themselves for time spent in wonder-filled encounters.

The problem was that time is such a commodity, especially in public schools.

After a few weeks of gradually letting wonder take its rightful place within my daily rhythms, I realized that I was "falling behind" on my district's pacing guide. I knew I had to continue meeting expectations in this regard while still finding creative possibilities for infusing wonder into my class culture and regular routines.

Our morning circle time became an opportune time for wonder-filled sharing as I, and eventually my students, brought in various objects from nature to pass around for both appreciation and speculation: A nautilus shell found at the beach. A giant heart-shaped leaf from a catalpa tree. A fragile oak gall. A growing avocado seed, balanced on toothpicks in an empty baby food jar.

I also begin to align science instruction with ecological learning objectives as a way to get my students outside while also creating space for wonder. In order to authentically engage my class with science practices, I found wonder to be an incredible starting point for various learning endeavors but was still grappling with how to infuse it into our regular class schedule.

After a few months back in the classroom, two things happened simultaneously: I began to read more about wonder from a scholarly perspective as I pursued my PhD, and I met Nancy (pseudonym), a like-minded teacher from a nearby school.

"I take my second graders on wonder walks," Nancy told me one day, casually, like it wasn't the most genius idea of the year.

I prompted Nancy to tell me more.

She went on to explain how she incorporated it into the school's character education program and then connected it to mindfulness. Nancy would use wonder walks as a transition after recess, in between specials, or whenever her students needed some time outside to ground themselves. She quietly led her students in a single-file line along the edge of their schoolyard or into the forested area adjacent to the school. Nancy encouraged her class to independently notice and wonder, calling on volunteers at the end of the walk to share these with the whole group.

After hearing more about Nancy's experiences, I knew I just had to try wonder walks for myself.

I couldn't wait to see how my students reacted, and I was convinced that this would be a creative approach to infusing wonder into our daily routines.

FAILURE, THEN SUCCESS

At the time, we were well into the school year, and my current group of fourth graders had experiences exploring the natural environments of our school campus. They had become used to a certain type of freedom during these moments of free play in the wooded area adjacent to our soccer field. I erroneously assumed they would take to wonder walks as a natural extension of their already-established connection with nature.

The first time I tried a wonder walk was a heroic failure. Students were talking with their peers, chatting about recess, friends, and other topics that interest nine- and ten-year-olds. I reminded them rather harshly that this was a wonder walk and must be completed in absolute silence. My class then proceeded to walk stoically in a line, eyes on the back of the head of the individual in front of them. It was as if we were inside the school hallway, trying to get from point A to point B as quickly and efficiently as possible.

Wonder was absent.

I rethought my approach and used interactive modeling to show my students what this might look like. After recess, we gathered together, and I demonstrated how to walk quietly but with an eye for the environment around me. I pointed out some curiosities I saw, and then asked for student volunteers to demonstrate as well. I told the class, "At the end of our walk, I'm going to ask you what you noticed and what filled you with wonder."

That day, our walk was only about fifty feet. It was long enough to give them a chance to notice the birds flitting in the boundary line's thicket, and short enough that students didn't become bored. I taught them how to stand in a circle and had a few brave souls share out their wonders.

Little by little we got better, and part of the reason was my own approach toward wonder walks. There needed to be enough structure that students were encouraged to have a wonder-filled experience, yet freedom is an inherent part of the wonder process. My wonder walk goal was to balance student autonomy while ensuring *all* students in the class had an accessible wonder walk experience (figure 3.3).

Most days I would have specific "look fors" that I would offer up for students who preferred some more solid teacher direction, as described in table 3.1. This enabled me to incite more curricular connections based on the particular prompt. I began to notice that our science and wonder walk concepts overlapped considerably as the year progressed, the result of intentionality on my part but also the natural curiosity of my fourth graders.

One day when I was absent, I didn't a write wonder walk into my substitute teaching plans, figuring that the process was too complicated to explain in writing and that whoever filled in for me wouldn't need an additional outdoor activity. The next day, I heard about it from exasperated students.

"Why didn't the sub take us on our wonder walk?"

"We went *right back inside* after recess."

It was then that I realized my small change had made a big difference. After a month of wonder walks, my students relished the opportunity to engage with wonder on a daily basis, and even began to request it on rainy days after our indoor recess

Figure 3.3. A student noticing an arrangement of sticks, leaves, and acorns.

cleanup. It was a slow start, but we grew together in our ability to be open to new experiences and to find fascination in our own backyard (figure 3.4). In fact, it would be a slow start every year I led my students in wonder walks. Building the routine takes time, as does the buy-in.

One year, I had a twice-exceptional student, Jordan (pseudonym), who was vocally opposed to wonder walks. "These are stupid," Jordan would retort on a regular basis.

The other students tried to ignore him, but it was hard for them to find contentment. The class often struggled to find joy or curiosity while Jordan so vocally expressed his frustration with the activity.

"It's only five minutes!" I practically begged Jordan to use the time to zone out and just enjoy being outside.

Table 3.1. Sample Wonder Walk Scaffolds

Name	Description	Example(s)
"Look Fors"	Teacher challenges students to look for a particular phenomenon.	- Different colored leaves - Flying insects - Cloud types
Classroom Connections	Teacher asks students questions to extend in-class concepts that they have recently explored.	- How has water changed the land? - How does the structure of the plant help it survive?
Change over Time (phenology)	Teacher reminds students to notice what has changed since the last time the class did a wonder walk in a specific area.	- Weather - Flora and fauna - Human impact, such as landscaping
Soundscape	Teacher invites students to pay attention to the sounds they hear as they walk, rather than looking around.	- Birds - Insects - Wind and plants - Vehicles
Freeze Walk	Teacher calls out "freeze" or uses another signal during the wonder walk to signal students to stop, observe, and wonder.	N/A

Part of the problem was Jordan's limited engagement; his mind couldn't handle a walk in nature without something to captivate him. I was at a crossroads and spent time reflecting on ways that I could encourage him to engage with wonder rather than simply monitor his behavior.

One day a salamander turned things around.

I was, per usual, keeping an eye on Jordan while we went on a wonder walk one rather dry spring. He was dragging his feet in protest, when suddenly he stopped, dropped to his stomach, and let out a cry of surprise.

The back of the line turned as one and rushed to where Jordan was lying. My own curiosity got the best of me, so I walked quickly over to see what had caused my most reluctant wonder-er to stop in his tracks.

There, in Jordan's hand, was a salamander.

It was highly unusual, as the nearest water source was over a hundred feet away, and we hadn't gotten rain for quite some time. Yet there was the salamander, cupped into Jordan's palm.

And there was Jordan, a big grin on his face.

The other students crowded in to see, with lots of conversations and a little pushing and shoving. My heart soared, and I decided to do our regular debrief right then and there. After students circled up, I cautioned Jordan against holding the salamander in his bare hand, as the oils from our skin aren't good for them. He immediately found a large leaf to create a semi-shelter for his newfound friend. We talked about the surprise of the salamander, and it became a type of show-and-tell, with Jordan looking to me for support as we shared our wonders all around. The salamander was ceremoniously given a name and then released closer to the creek that runs adjacent to our property.

From that point on, there was a marked difference in Jordan during wonder walks. Yes, he was still learning to monitor his volume, but Jordan began to make it his

Figure 3.4. A student finding wonder in the grassy field.

mission to find the "coolest" specimen of that day. Whether it was a speckled rock aptly named "Leopard" or a leaf "the size of [his] face," Jordan became one of the best observers of the group. His excitement was contagious.

At the end of the year, Jordan announced: "The best part of fourth grade were the wonder walks, even though I didn't like them at the beginning." For Jordan, the benefits of wonder walks were an increase in confidence and an overall excitement about the natural world. The rest of the class mirrored this interest, leaning into the sense of mystery that wonder walks offered.

Behavior Improvements

In general, I was amazed at the positive outcomes of this small change. The improvements in behavior that I noticed were initially rather nuanced and then soon became quite evident. There were smoother transitions back into learning after a high-energy recess and an increase in students' overall capacity to focus in the afternoons (figure 3.5). Students demonstrated a greater propensity toward self-regulation when engaged in hands-on learning activities.

Figure 3.5. An exceptionally wonder-filled day during the first snowfall of the season.

Mental Health

I also noticed that the mental well-being of my class seemed to improve on wonder walk days. Students reported that wonder walks made them feel happier or more peaceful. Some explained that it was a time in the day where they didn't have to think too hard if they didn't want to, and that it allowed their brain to rest. As a teacher, I also found wonder walks grounding for me, especially after the class got over that initial hump and I was able to relax throughout the experience. It was peaceful, contemplative, and a great midday boost for my own morale. The joy that I saw during wonder walks had a positive impact on my own mental health, further iterating the benefit of being and learning outdoors while simultaneously creating space for wonder.

Curricular Connections

I became better at intentionally including the curriculum into our wonder walks, a really important benefit that emerged as I got better at explicitly pointing out these connections. For instance, when students became interested in a specific organism, I might ask, "How does the structure of that [plant/animal] help it survive?" Or "What might help that plant spread its seeds this fall?"

I was purposeful about drawing students' attention to the impact of Earth processes on humans and our subsequent effect on the natural environment, some key fourth-grade earth science concepts. I became more excited to teach science standards, and this was reflected in my students' overall interest in the subject that now substantiated their own wonders.

My class began to naturally make these scientific connections, as well. When learning about erosion and weathering, students pointed to evidence of these, confidently stating their current knowledge and then offering curiosity questions regarding cause and effect. At times wonder was a powerful force within the scientific inquiry; other times, wonder had a gentler presence during our walks as students expressed a cognitive desire to know more about a phenomenon. I tried to let the class lead, knowing that the benefits of these wonder walks were multifaceted and often subtle, the outcomes sometimes only noticeable after substantial time spent collectively engaging in wonder.

SUGGESTIONS AND CONSIDERATIONS FOR OTHER EDUCATORS

It is my hope that the above stories are inspirational, that perhaps they might nudge you toward trying wonder walks yourself, whether it's in a preschool setting, a middle school classroom, or with your university students. As educators, we all feel curricular pressures, and wonder is often relegated to a lesser role rather than taking its rightful place in the driver's seat.

Personal Wonder

My first suggestion for those looking to implement this small change within their regular routines is to find wonder yourself. It might not be through a national parks trip, but wonder is accessible regardless of your geographic location, activity, age, or other factors. My earlier story regarding my park pilgrimage reiterates the personal starting point for wonder. It cannot be contrived—it must be an authentic feeling/thought/dream/encounter that *starts with the teacher.* Yes, there are students who are prone to wonder and can inspire their peers but, as an educator, you hold so much influence over the young hearts and minds of your students.

Begin looking for wonder every day, finding at least one thing that fills you with awe, fascination, or curiosity. Be intentional about going outside, sitting, and letting wonder come to you. We cannot authentically instigate wonder walks unless we, as educators, understand the role of wonder in our own lives, including how to share that with students.

Let your students see the childlike wonder as you pass around a rock you found on a nature walk. Talk about an interesting phenomenon you spotted at recess. Share your wonder-filled questions with your students, showcasing your need for future investigations. Get excited about learning new things about the natural world, discovering as a co-learner alongside your class. Laugh at the wonder-filled stories that follow those who are open to new experiences.

Stick with It

My second recommendation is: don't give up. Students, whether young or old, need time to adjust to a wonder walk rhythm. We live hurried lives, rushing from one place to the next. Very rarely do we slow down, walk leisurely, and look for wonder to join us. As my above stories demonstrate, building routines is a process, and there will be some trial and error as you practice them with your class. In order for wonder walks to be authentic, there needs to be a certain degree of freedom, as well. Balancing the structure and freedom is a learning process for educators, and one that often takes some fine-tuning depending on the class. I have found interactive modeling to be very helpful, along with the other scaffolding structures mentioned in table 3.1. The end goal is for students (and teachers) to be intentional about finding wonder and letting wonder settle within their hearts and minds.

Seek Out Other Wonder-Filled Practices

My final suggestion rests on these other scaffolding structures. Wonder walks might not be feasible for your particular group of students, or it might not be the best fit for your given situation. Be open to other ways to infuse wonder.

Wonder journals are a great way to support student literacy, mindfulness, and attentiveness to the natural world. I have used these in the past before I began wonder walks, and later, as a supplement to wonder walks. Students can be free to sketch, write poetry, label diagrams, ask questions, execute plant rubbings, or any other engagement with the natural environment that they wish. These, too, may require some teacher support depending on the age of your students. Laws and Lygrend's *How to Teach Nature Journaling* is a great resource and a fantastic starting point. The authors list both mindfulness and wonder as key reasons behind nature journaling and make many connections to academic standards.[4] Whether it's a science journal, nature journal, or wonder journal, there are lots of access points for students to encounter wonder-filled moments inspired by the natural or human world.

Sit Spot is another wonder walk–adjacent activity. Rather than walking together as a class, students choose (or are assigned) a place to sit in nature. This should be a regular activity, perhaps once or twice a week. Students can observe the world around them, note changes, let questions roll around in their mind, and simply *be* in the outdoors. Wonder might not be the focus of Sit Spot, but the two are closely related and emerge from a place of connecting in/with nature. Jon Young's book, *Coyote's Guide to Connecting with Nature,* describes how to introduce and sustain successful Sit Spots in educational settings.[5]

FINAL WONDER-FILLED THOUGHTS

The tendency might be to view wonder (and wonder walks) as *one more thing* for educators to take on in an already full schedule. Some may argue that there isn't time for wonder with all the curricular pressures that seem to continuously compound. Yet many scholars and educators, myself included, argue that wonder is innate to humans and needs to be fostered and nurtured in children so that it can grow.[6] Wonder is not an optional add-on, but a valuable and necessary component of a child's mind, heart, and spirit. Washington[7] uses the term *birthright* to describe the intrinsic, yet fragile, sense of wonder inside each human being. Our question as educators then becomes: How do we let wonder retake its rightful place within education? How do we cultivate a child's inborn sense of wonder, providing opportunities for them to contemplate and connect to the local, natural world?

I believe that wonder walks are a starting point, a small change, that can empower students to think, feel, and relate to nature in a way that honors their sense of awe and imagination. I believe that the benefits far outweigh any curricular checkboxes. I believe that we can't afford to *not* let wonder play a prominent role within our education system, starting with regular class rhythms. "[Wonder] can be buried—yet it can also be reawakened. Our task is to hold onto our wonder and rejuvenate it so that it continues to burn brightly."[8]

NOTES

1. Andrew Gilbert and Christie Byers, "Wonder as a Tool to Engage Preservice Elementary Teachers in Science Learning and Teaching," *Science Education 101,* no. 6 (2017): 907–28.

2. Steph Dean and Andrew Gilbert, "What Scientists Do: Engaging in Science Practices Through a Wonder-Framed Nature Study," *Interdisciplinary Journal of Environmental and Science Education* 17, no. 4 (2021): e2255.

3. Elizabeth K. Zimmerman, "N.O.W.—Notice with Open Wonder: A Mindfulness-Based Program for Children Ages 4–5 Years," PhD diss., Chicago School of Professional Psychology, 2019. ProQuest (10977681).

4. John Muir Laws and Emilie Lygren, *How to Teach Nature Journaling: Curiosity, Wonder, Attention* (Berkeley: Heyday, 2020).

5. Jon Young, Ellen Haas, and Evan McGown, *Coyote's Guide to Connecting with Nature* (Santa Cruz: OWLLink Media, 2016).

6. Rachel Carson, *The Sense of Wonder* (New York: Harper, 1965).

7. Haydn Washington, *A Sense of Wonder Towards Nature: Healing the Planet Through Belonging* (Abingdon, UK: Routledge, 2019).

8. Washington, *A Sense of Wonder*, 37.

BIBLIOGRAPHY

Carson, Rachel. *The Sense of Wonder*. New York: Harper, 1965.

Dean, Steph, and Andrew Gilbert. "What Scientists Do: Engaging in Science Practices Through a Wonder-Framed Nature Study." *Interdisciplinary Journal of Environmental and Science Education* 17, no. 4 (2021): e2255. https://doi.org/10.21601/ijese/11136.

Gilbert, Andrew and Christie Byers. "Wonder as a Tool to Engage Preservice Elementary Teachers in Science Learning and Teaching." *Science Education* 101, no. 6 (2017): 907–28. https://doi.org/10.1002/sce.21300.

Laws, John Muir, and Lygren, Emilie. *How to Teach Nature Journaling: Curiosity, Wonder, Attention*. Berkeley: Heyday, 2020.

Washington, Haydn. *A Sense of Wonder Towards Nature: Healing the Planet Through Belonging*. Abingdon, UK: Routledge, 2019.

Young, Jon, Ellen Haas, and Evan McGown. *Coyote's Guide to Connecting with Nature*. Santa Cruz: OWLLink Media, 2016.

Zimmermann, Elizabeth K. "N.O.W.—Notice with Open Wonder: A Mindfulness-Based Program for Children Ages 4–5 Years." PhD diss., Chicago School of Professional Psychology, 2019. ProQuest (10977681).

Chapter 4

A Small Step toward a Meaningful School

Collaboration in Experimentality for Curriculum Integration

Ivan Salinas, Natalia Albornoz, and Magnolia Guerrero

This book converges toward the concept of "starting small." We are reminded of the concept of large problems being addressed one step at a time. Weick referred to addressing the scale of social problems by redefining their size as "small wins." In his words,

> A small win is a concrete, complete, implemented outcome of moderate importance. By itself, one small win may seem unimportant. A series of wins at small but significant tasks, however, reveals a pattern that may attract allies, deter opponents, and lower resistance to subsequent proposals. Small wins are controllable opportunities that produce visible results . . . Once a small win has been accomplished, forces are set in motion that favor another small win. When a solution is put in place, the next solvable problem often becomes more visible.[1]

In this chapter we tell a story about a small win or a small step that is geared toward a contested and big problem: school curricula in times of high-stakes standardized testing and specialized disciplines. We highlight a recent story about El Salitre, a Chilean public school where a small step has taken place; we have named this "experimentality with curriculum integration."

Experimentality points to a concept that has a long but interrupted tradition in Chile's education: experimental education.[2] Experimental education was an important innovation during the twentieth century in Chile's public education system. Inspired by US scholars and the Deweyan notion of experiential learning,[3] several experimental schools were formed in Chile during the mid-twentieth century. Experimental education was interrupted by a military coup on September 11, 1973, which changed the landscape of the entire educational system—diminishing the role of public education, incorporating a voucher system to fund privately owned schools, and increasing stakes and accountability measures for school competition. This last idea has pressed for standardization of curriculum, which today means that schools are pressured to "teach to the test." This change in the landscape has been continuously reformed in the last three and a half decades, including curricular reforms, but they have mostly deepened the idea of having a curriculum that is testable for accountability measures and favoring particular school subjects (e.g., math and language arts). The COVID-19 pandemic defied the entire organization of schools' teach-to-the-test curriculum, gearing school communities toward care and inclusion. Somehow, it provided a window of opportunity for trying out new things. Because the historical context is not the same as when experimental schools were created, we presented the idea of experimentality in education. While it does not yet have a formal definition, we understand experimentality in education as a twenty-first-century reinterpretation of the spirit of experiential learning, taking into consideration its democratic character, and singular rather than universal approaches to problems that are real and meaningful to communities. Curriculum integration[4] is a large social and educational problem today, and making it happen in a school is a small win or a small start in a process of change. Curriculum integration shares roots with experiential learning, which has at its core a commitment to making school relevant and meaningful to students and the whole community, and a democratic design of curriculum. It also involves trying new things in a contested context, risking innovations to provide school experiences. Much more like the experimental schools of the past, we feel there is experimentality in today's attempts for curriculum integration at El Salitre school.

CONTEXT

El Salitre is a public school located in Pudahuel, a commune in the northwest corner of Chile's capital city, Santiago. This commune has a total population of over 250,000.[5] A particular feature of this commune, one of fifty in the Metropolitan Region of Santiago, is that it has an extensive rural geographic zone while also having an urbanized zone with high connectivity to the rest of the city of Santiago. The school is located in the urban zone of Pudahuel and is considered at high social risk, according to the Ministry of Education (MINEDUC).[6] All public schools in Pudahuel are managed by the Barranca's Local Service of Education (LSE), an autonomous state institution in charge of managing the public schools in Pudahuel and the two adjacent communities: Cerro Navia and Lo Prado. In total, the Barranca's LSE manages over fifty-four schools in these three communes.

El Salitre school served 262 children in 2023, from kindergarten to whole basic education. Basic education in Chile includes grades 1–8. Children attend school for a total of 38 hours a week. Most public schools in Chile serve low-income populations. El Salitre is no exception: it serves a low-income community, children whose families have low socioeconomic status according to MINEDUC's indicators.[7] In 2020, 79 percent of student enrollment was categorized as priority or preferent students, with a vulnerability index of 89 percent. The vulnerability index can be compared to the index for free or reduced-price lunches in American schools. El Salitre also faces the issue of high rates of low student attendance, which the COVID-19 pandemic exacerbated with a prolonged closure of in-person school. Starting with this emergency scenario, the initiative or small step to curriculum integration began to take shape.

UNDERSTANDING THE PROBLEM

The current principal of the El Salitre, Magnolia, a coauthor of this chapter, became part of the school community in 2018 as the head of the technical-pedagogical unit (UTP), a pedagogical leadership role that each school in Chile should have. In the years 2018–2019, one of the main concerns in the school was the low standardized test scores of students and low attendance at early grade levels. The school leadership and teachers were concerned about what they perceived as persistent low participation and low interest on the part of students and their families. Families, parents, and guardians seemingly perceived the school spaces as irrelevant, not important to their lives, and not pertinent to their children's education. Additionally, the teachers and leadership had the perception that parents and families held very traditional views about learning. This was mostly due to anecdotal evidence that showed parents understood learning as the result of repetitive activities associated mostly with mandated curricular content. In other words, parents might think that children who do not have written notes in their notebooks or those whose notebooks are not filled with copied activities are children who have done nothing in school and have not learned.

Within this scenario, in 2019, Magnolia led an initiative to have parents and families learn about their children's experiences. To this end, "public lessons" were implemented for the first time at the earlier grade levels (K–2). Public lessons were an opportunity for parents and families to attend their children's classroom for a period of time and participate in the activities the teachers had prepared for their children. This way, they could see firsthand the way their children were learning and even help them and other kids with their learning through the lesson. During this time, Magnolia also started reflection meetings with the teachers at the school, which concluded with the need to change the teaching methodology, making more sense of the children's experience of their learning. These incipient initiatives had to stop as a result of first, a national teachers' strike, and later, a large-scale social revolt in October 2019 in Chile, which impacted the whole functioning of the educational system.

Magnolia was named interim principal in 2019. Because of her previous experience leading teachers on pedagogical reflection, one of the first steps to start a change in teaching methodologies was the decision to reserve teacher collaborative working hours. These hours were nonexistent before. In Chile, every school has a Teachers Council, which is instantiated as a weekly meeting where teachers, pedagogical leadership, other professionals, and the principal meet. The Teachers Council can be a consultative space, but also a technical one, where teachers can express their professional opinions and resolve technical-pedagogical matters, observing each school's educative project and norms. The Teachers Council should discuss and address what actions are to be taken in order to achieve goals at the national, local, and school levels. Additionally, there is a legal mandate to have teacher preparation time for lesson planning and other teaching-related activities such as communicating with parents and guardians and collaborating with other teachers. However, these hours are not usually used to that end. Assael and colleagues,[8] in the context of understanding how schools do policy, describe two subjective positions about the Teachers Council in two schools: the principalship monologue and the teachers' silence. This might be the case in several schools, and Assael and colleagues express this divide as a manifestation of the impediment of a reflexive dialogue during a Teachers Council. Additionally, during teacher preparation time within the school day, teachers are often called away to cover other classes whose teachers are absent, mostly for being sick. Therefore, having a collective, reflective space as teachers in a school and reserving their preparation time is a very important but hardly usual occurrence in Chile's schools.

Having a collective and reflective teacher space facilitated teachers envisioning change, especially when thinking about how students and their families in the community held negative views about the school. A collective perspective from a teachers' council reaffirmed the value of public lessons or inviting parents and families to participate in their children's classrooms to witness a lesson. Therefore, this reserved time and the public lessons became a kick-starter for other initiatives and launched a process of collaboration among the teachers as a team, learning together through thinking about situated problems they were living by and through their collective reflection. The perception was that the problems of low attendance and low participation was a curricular one.

The COVID-19 pandemic hit the world and Chile at the start of the school year, in March 2020. After only two weeks of classes, the government decided to shut down in-person education in schools. The sanitary crisis consequently took over schools and meant a prolonged closure of schools and many difficulties for their communities and families, particularly low-income families. This historical situation became a spark to think over and again about all the daily work of the school and what needs the school should prioritize. The nature of the problem shifted, requiring parents and families to participate together with teachers. The Teachers Council in El Salitre turned again to pedagogical reflection and action. Despite the chaos and crisis, El Salitre school could maintain an initiative to develop an emergency remote plan and continue its education online. Later, in 2021, Magnolia officially became the principal of the school.

However, when coming back to the school after the pandemic got under control, in the 2021 school year the low attendance issue and lack of student, parental, and family involvement in school resurfaced and became more acute. This happened not only in Chile but in all Latin American countries.[9] Given the prepandemic experience with the kick-starter of public lessons, it was easier to return to these lessons as a way of reconnecting with families.

Step-by-Step Pedagogical Reflection and Action

El Salitre teachers turned to pedagogical reflection to address the growing needs of their community and the call for increasing school attendance. Because of their focus on curriculum as an explanatory framework for low attendance, their reflections pointed to the content and meaningfulness of the activities that filled the school schedule. They had the opportunity to fill in hours for students to participate in workshops that could motivate them regarding their interests, but also regarding school as a whole. Teachers observed that hours outside the mandatory curriculum were usually filled with subject-based activities, such as mathematics and language arts. Using these hours did not produce higher scores on standardized tests and became a focus of critique and conversation. They decided to use these hours differently, and the idea of creating workshops gained momentum. What could these workshops do to foster children's interest in their own learning? This question was passed on to students. Teachers inquired about what were things that interested students and provoked uneasiness.

To address the need for creating these workshops, the school leadership and the community turned to the action of the Barrancas LSE. As mentioned earlier, this institution is in charge of the public management of schools, distributed throughout territorial units. The Barrancas LSE hired the services of "technical educational assistance," or private vendors whose role is to offer services for school improvement or other specific needs. The school requested assistance for learning about project-based learning and it was provided. However, the impact of this assistance did not have the desired effect and El Salitre teachers and the school leadership did not find it particularly useful. That is, the need to take advantage of spaces to mobilize the curriculum was still there. While the teachers, professionals, and leadership in the school kept implementing workshops that were pertinent and addressed children's interests and concerns, there was a perception that more actions were needed to take further steps.

El Salitre's Teacher Council had several opportunities to deepen its pedagogical reflection through conversations with the entire professional team at the school. Each of these instances were a small start toward a higher goal of changing the school experience for motivating children to attend to it. The workshops advanced as the school leadership asked each teacher to think of what kind of workshop they would deliver to develop children's skills. A wide variety of proposals came to the fore: arts, environmental care, crafts, computing, storytelling. This is how the school started initiatives such as the "Ecohuerto," an eco-garden for kindergarten children wanting to learn about plants, and the workshop about "learning through children's movies" in grades 1–7, which addressed student interest in movies. Teachers felt there was a growing need for mobilizing the curriculum to serve the interests and issues that concerned children and their families.

Up to this point, there were several small steps taken in El Salitre school. The first one was to reserve hours for collective pedagogical reflection in the Teachers Council, which sparked several analyses of the situation, defining the problem the school was facing and defining courses of pedagogical action. The second step was to connect with parents and families, creating public lessons that looked to increase a shared understanding of the vision for learning in the school. The third step was to learn together about approaches to address the problem, such as having pedagogical conversations on problem-based learning and ways to use time in the school day. A fourth step was to develop several workshops that addressed students' interests, as a way to mobilize curriculum beyond traditional school subjects.

A SMALL NEW STEP: EXPERIMENTALITY WITH CURRICULUM INTEGRATION

Pedagogical reflection at El Salitre school provided a series of questions regarding the nature of school organization into disciplinary subjects. The drive for these conversations was a search for making sense of children's experiences and having a curriculum that responded to those. That is when the term "curriculum integration" started to surface in the teachers' conversations, understanding that children experience life in an integrated form, while the school teaches subjects separately. As a principal, Magnolia started developing the idea of having a "school with no disciplinary subjects."

Almost by chance, in 2022 the principal reconnected with Ivan, one of the coordinators of the University of Chile's project Escuela-Centro Experimental Carén. This project is an institutional initiative to build a public experimental school in a rural area owned by the university in Pudahuel. Creating a public school meant working side by side with Barrancas LSE, and also working on the experimentality perspective to build shared understandings of its meaning in today's context. Ivan was leading the pedagogy curriculum area of the project, and by that time was organizing an initiative for experimentality self-education and dialogue. The initiative was called *semillero*, or "seedbed" with the idea of gathering educators and community organizers both in the urban and rural territory of Pudahuel. The reason to gather them was to discuss and learn together about what experimentality in education is and what an experimental school for current times should look like. Magnolia opened up El Salitre for organizing the *semillero* in school facilities, and during the second semester of 2022 six joint sessions were carried out, the last being on dependencies of a community garden and education center where one of the *semillero*'s participants worked. Another step was taken in organizing a pedagogical reflection in El Salitre school, this time incorporating University of Chile faculty and community organizers in the Pudahuel territory.

In this step, the interest in addressing El Salitre's school issues and the idea of the University of Chile's project for creating a public experimental school were strongly linked and consistent. The *semillero* gathered eight school educators from the Pudahuel territory, additional educators from El Salitre school and eight community organizers and educators, plus five university faculty and staff. The purpose of *semillero* sessions was to build a shared definition for experimentality in education and to develop an idea for what experimental school schedules should be like and what activities and foci for learning should be. *Semillero* yielded a strong sense of community thinking about transforming schools and highlighted a commitment to continuing collaboration. It also yielded working materials for facilitating pedagogical discussions, and the group became consultative for other initiatives.

After *semillero*, the next step was to advance understanding of curriculum integration. Magnolia and Ivan teamed up to propose for 2023 a learning plan about curriculum integration for the Teachers Council at El Salitre school. The plan consisted of curriculum integration workshops that could provide an example of project-based teaching during the school year. The university team presented a plan to the El Salitre Teachers Council in late April 2023. The plan, called Escuela de Invierno (Winter School), was intended to familiarize teachers with the curriculum integration approach proposed by James Beane.

Beane's curriculum integration approach considers four dimensions of curriculum integration: the integration of experiences, social integration, integration of knowledge and integration as curriculum design.[10] Integrating experiences means looking for new experiences that become part of the "schemes of meaning" we have, and organizing previous experiences in a helpful way for new problem situations. For a curriculum to integrate socially means to have it organized around both personal and social issues, which should be planned collaboratively by teachers and students together. Integrating personal and social issues would open access to knowledge for children and youth and also contribute to creating a democratic classroom arrangement. Integration of knowledge stems from a critique of the subject-based organization of traditional curricula. In drawing knowledge that is useful to addressing personal and social issues, there is a broader spectrum of what knowledge counts in the curriculum, as well as an opening to ways of knowing that go beyond the disciplinary subjects. The integrated curriculum design shares features: it is organized around personal and social problems and issues, learning experiences are planned to integrate pertinent knowledge centered around a named issue, knowledge develops as it is used for addressing and learning about the issue or problem under study rather than for a future test, projects and activities involve applying knowledge and problem-solving, and students participate in curriculum planning.

The Winter School consisted of a set of six working sessions, carried out over a four-month period, facilitated by the university team but organized by the school as part of reflection time in the Teachers Council. To ensure some material conditions for developing the curriculum integration projects, the University of Chile team secured a grant for community outreach.

The start of the curriculum integration process requires gathering children and community concerns, both personal and about the world. Because of one of El Salitre's previous steps, public lessons, the university team managed to take advantage of a planned visit from families of K–2 students and instituted an arrangement for gathering community concerns about the school, its surroundings, and the role these families thought the school should play to address these concerns (figure 4.1). Two main issues

Figure 4.1. A community of parents in El Salitre working on expressing concerns after a public lesson. Ivan Salinas.

were concerns for parents and families: environmental protection and safety at the school and surrounding community.

Right after the public lessons, the work on curriculum integration with the El Salitre Teachers Council began. During the working sessions, teams of teachers engaged in several activities intended to create a curriculum integration project based on the community concerns in different areas of the curriculum. The University of Chile team learned more about what challenges were involved in creating curriculum integration projects, but also in working directly in schools. The El Salitre school team developed a tool for projecting curriculum integration, which was to be implemented as projects during the last part of the 2023 school year and the beginning of 2024.

CURRICULUM INTEGRATION RESULTS

One example of the curriculum integration projects developed in El Salitre school was the initiative "learning with cinema," which was designed and implemented by a team of first-grade teachers. The idea was to encourage teacher collaboration by integrating multiple school subjects. Children chose a theme to develop a project, and they picked cinema out of several options. They then voted on a movie to watch and learn about cinema. A team of six teachers from mathematics, language arts, physical education, technology, plastic arts, and music joined in making cinema a theme of their lessons. The teacher collaborated in planning the lessons in connection with learning goals or curriculum mandates. They focused on having students develop abilities that included reading decoding and comprehension, formulating and answering questions based on a visual and listening experience, or understanding narrative works. Also, the teachers' team proposed that students develop enjoyment of oral and visual narratives and make connections to their own experiences. They also learned to tally votes for the movie selection in the mathematics class. In the physical education class and the music class, students prepared a thematic "flash mob" using the movie theme and performed it during a recess period, dressing up and using makeup for impersonating characters in the movie, while listening to the movie soundtrack. In the arts class, they created masks themed as the movie they chose to watch, as well as other cultural artifacts present in the movie. In math class, again, students learned the geometry of objects, which then was used in the technology class to re-create a model of the main technological objects used in making movies. These are only some of the activities that teachers planned and did in and around a topic chosen by students and a movie chosen by them.

The teachers' plan was a step to break sole disciplinary learning in each subject, by articulating abilities, knowledge, and dispositions dictated by Chile's national curriculum and the contextual knowledge of students, their interests, and their decisions—very much a step forward in curriculum integration.

As this was a small change in terms of teachers' work in the school and incorporating their students' interests and concerns in teaching, it became a transformative experience as well. The team of teachers presented their work at two conferences, a national conference on pedagogical-curricular experimentality (figure 4.2) and a local territorial conference for the Barrancas LSE.

Figure 4.2. A team of El Salitre teachers presenting their curriculum integration work at a national conference on pedagogical-curricular experimentality. Ivan Salinas.

LESSONS LEARNED FOR OTHERS TO KEEP WALKING

We have undertaken a series of small steps over a four- to five-year period in order to create conditions for experimentality with curriculum integration in El Salitre school. This has been a creative process, fueled by conditions that were unimaginable, such as those that resulted from adapting to the COVID-19 pandemic and its aftermath. The reflective stance in the school has yielded a common understanding of what the problem is and how it relates to curriculum as experienced by children and youth. The school leadership understands the power of situated teacher collective pedagogical reflection and collaboration with other institutions, and this is also an important condition to develop further.

In order for other teachers, but mostly for other school leaders, to develop collaborative curriculum integration projects, there are three things to think about. First, create conditions for teachers to engage in collaborative work to kick-start their ideas and to see change as a possible benefit to their students; that is, to form a school community that is concerned and convinced about changing some of their practices and that believe that collaboration among teachers is the avenue to take. A second thing to consider is to ensure that collaborative time is reserved to learn about the curriculum in context and learn about what other teachers do. Teachers should have an enriched and situated opportunity to learn about the connections between school subjects, because that also fosters imagination about how integration will happen and make collaboration tangible. And last, but not least, always keep in mind that these changes can make teaching a better experience, but the final goal is to have students find a meaningful learning experience through school, which is important to care about and participate in.

NOTES

1. K. E. Weick, "Small Wins: Redefining the Scale of Social Problems," *American Psychologist* 39, no. 1, (1984): 43.
2. Camila Pérez-Navarro, *Iniciativas, prácticas y límites de la experimentación pedagógica en la historia de la educación Chilena (1927–1953)* (Bajo la Lupa, Subdirección de Investigación, Servicio Nacional del Patrimonio Cultural, 2020).
3. John Dewey, *Experience and Education* (New York: Simon & Schuster, 1938).
4. James A. Beane, *Curriculum Integration: Designing the Core of Democratic Education* (New York: Teachers College Press, 1997).
5. Biblioteca del Congreso Nacional de Chile (BCN), "Reporte Comunal Pudahuel," BCN, https://www.bcn.cl/siit/reportescomunales/comunas_v.html?anno=2023&idcom=13124 (accessed April 4, 2024).
6. Junta Nacional de Auxilio Escolar y Becas (JUNAEB), "Índice Vulnerabilidad Estudiantil," https://www.junaeb.cl/ive/ (accessed April 4, 2024).
7. Ibid.
8. Jenny Assaél, Felipe Acuña, Paulina Contreras, and Francisca Corbalán, "Transformaciones en la cultura escolar en el marco de la implementación de políticas de accountability en Chile: Un estudio etnográfico en dos escuelas clasificadas en recuperación." *Estudios pedagógicos (Valdivia)* 40, no. 2 (2014): 7–26.
9. United Nations Children's Fund (UNICEF). "Latin America and the Caribbean: Results from the 4th Survey on National Education Responses to COVID-19 School Closures and the Global Education Recovery Tracker." 2023. https://www.unicef.org/media/136626/file/Education%20in%20a%20Post-COVID%20World.pdf.
10. Beane, *Curriculum Integration*.

BIBLIOGRAPHY

Assaél, Jenny, Felipe Acuña, Paulina Contreras, and Francisca Corbalán. "Transformaciones en la cultura escolar en el marco de la implementación de políticas de accountability en Chile: Un estudio etnográfico en dos escuelas clasificadas en recuperación." *Estudios pedagógicos (Valdivia)*, 40, no. 2 (2014): 7–26. DOI: 10.4067/S0718-07052014000300001.

Beane, James A. *Curriculum Integration: Designing the Core of Democratic Education.* New York: Teachers College Press, 1997.

Biblioteca del Congreso Nacional de Chile (BCN). "Reporte Comunal Pudahuel." BCN, n.d. https://www.bcn.cl/siit/reportescomunales/comunas_v.html?anno=2023&idcom=13124. Accessed April 4, 2024.

Dewey, John. *Experience and Education*. New Yor: Simon & Schuster, 1938.

Junta Nacional de Auxilio Escolar y Becas (JUNAEB). "Índice Vulnerabilidad Estudiantil." https://www.junaeb.cl/ive/. Accessed April 4, 2024.

Ministerio de Educación de Chile (MINEDUC). "Portal del Ministerio de Educación de Chile." Gobierno de Chile. https://mi.mineduc.cl/mvc/mime/portada. Accessed 29 Apr. 2024.

Pérez-Navarro, Camila. *Iniciativas, prácticas y límites de la experimentación pedagógica en la historia de la educación Chilena (1927–1953)*. Bajo la Lupa, Subdirección de Investigación, Servicio Nacional del Patrimonio Cultural, 2020.

United Nations Children's Fund (UNICEF). "Latin America and the Caribbean: Results from the 4th Survey on National Education Responses to COVID-19 School Closures and the Global Education Recovery Tracker." 2023. https://www.unicef.org/media/136626/file/Education%20in%20a%20Post-COVID%20World.pdf

Weick, K. E. "Small Wins: Redefining the Scale of Social Problems." *American Psychologist* 39, no. 1, (1984): 40–49. DOI: 10.1037/0003-066X.39.1.40.

Chapter 5

Taking Small Steps toward Inquiry-Based Science Teaching

Zora M. Wolfe

In many urban elementary schools in the United States, science education is, unfortunately, an afterthought. After emphasis on literacy and math, science instruction gets left behind and is often neglected. However, quality science instruction can be the key to motivating students by introducing culturally relevant content to keep them interested in learning and in school. Through the lens of an external university partner, this chapter explores the journey of one K–8 school in urban Philadelphia where a team of educators was interested in emphasizing STEAM (Science, Technology, Engineering, Arts, and Math) instruction as a focus for their school to expose and prepare their students to the wide range of opportunities in STEM-related careers.

The team of teachers and leaders in the school saw an opportunity for their students to gain experience and exposure to science content that could potentially lead to careers in STEM fields, thus opening additional opportunities for their students. By applying for and receiving a small district-sponsored grant, the school was able to support additional professional development time for teachers through additional stipends and worked with a small team of science education experts from a local university to develop and implement a science curriculum.

Unfortunately, before this initiative, science education was an afterthought for the school. Although the district had some science resources available on its website, many teachers lamented that they had very little support, including limited training and minimal science equipment available to share with their students. However, a partnership with university science education faculty was developed using the grant initiative, and we began to engage in professional development with the teachers around science education.

Through a series of professional development sessions we worked with the teachers on the science committee, for a total of eight three-hour after-school sessions to better understand the context within their schools, their goals and objectives. We then determined a plan of action for how to move science instruction forward. During this time, we began the planning stages for the upcoming school year and developed an overarching curriculum scope and sequence plan. Then, using the frameworks of inquiry-based science teaching, the Next Generation Science Standards (NGSS), and Understanding by Design (UbD), we designed four full days of professional development for all teachers in the summer to help the teachers learn and utilize the frameworks to develop individual units. In addition, we planned opportunities for co-teaching and classroom observations to further develop the teachers' ability and comfort level with science teaching, spending two full days in the school building every month.

Using the UbD framework template,[1] which the teachers were already familiar with as their usual school lesson-planning template, we began by thinking about big ideas and essential questions to frame units based around the major science topics. By combining the principles of UbD, which emphasized starting with the end in mind, along with an understanding of NGSS standards, we were able to focus first on defining the understanding, knowledge, and skills we wanted students to acquire before we started thinking about the learning experiences and instruction. This helped to focus lessons on intentional learning of the required science standards, rather than separate, disparate activities that often mark elementary science lessons. Then, we utilized a framework for inquiry-based science teaching (the 5E Instructional Model[2]) to develop activities and lessons within our unit plans to emphasize active exploration and investigation to help students develop deeper understanding of scientific concepts.

Although we had grand plans to develop a fully interdisciplinary, project-based learning curriculum focused on science content, we encountered several obstacles that were not unique to urban schools, such as teacher turnover and lack of resources. Ideally, we wanted to weave other content areas, including literacy, math, and social studies, into science units that were grounded in authentic, real-world problems where students could demonstrate their learning in meaningful projects that demonstrated critical thinking, creativity, and collaboration. However, even though we could not fully design a comprehensive science curriculum within the short time we worked together, we continued to take small steps toward implementing new strategies and ideas within classrooms to start developing excitement and momentum that would move science teaching forward. In this chapter, we use the five Ws (who, what, when, why, where) to explore some of the lessons learned through this experience so other schools can also take small steps forward to improve science education.

WHAT SMALL STEPS DID WE TAKE?

We had grand plans. However, due to some of the challenges that are common in many schools, it was important for us to focus on important principles rather than the specific details around quality science education. For example, one could get into the details of the Next Generation Science Standards[3] and the state science standards, and their rationales; however, because of the pressures teachers had around all the other things they had to do, finding the key ideas and principles was highly impactful. Rather than dissecting each individual standard, we focused on the three dimensions of NGSS: Science and Engineering Practices (SEPs), Disciplinary Core Ideas (DCIs), and Crosscutting Concepts (CCCs). By providing an overview of the SEPs and CCCs, and understanding that they could be threaded throughout the content, teachers were able to identify opportunities to integrate the three dimensions throughout teaching. Just knowing what the SEPs were, why they were a part of the science standards, and how they were connected, allowed teachers to highlight them within lessons they had already been teaching.

Although we had initially wanted to create a complete curriculum around problem-based learning, a simple small-step principle we were able to take away was to begin our science units with a problem or a question that students could explore and then collaborating to brainstorm and generate questions that were broad and relevant to students. Essential questions such as, "Why does it rain instead of snow?" and "Why don't I look like my brother/sister?" helped to frame units around weather and climate and genetics and inheritance. Thus, the teachers were able to incorporate activities and lessons that aligned with students' interests and generated motivation for inquiry.

Specifically, as we were discussing inquiry-based science teaching, a third-grade teacher made the observation that inquiry-based teaching was actually the opposite of the "I do, we do, you do" teaching model that was often utilized in other subject areas. He recognized that in inquiry-based teaching, his role as a teacher was to allow the students to explore under his guidance so that they could make their own scientific discoveries. We coined the phrase, "you explore, I guide, we learn"[4] as a new way of thinking about how to approach science instruction. This overall shift in perspective was transformative for the teachers in the school.

Although we introduced the 5E Instructional Model[5] and tried to create unit plans with the five Es, teachers understood the general principle of allowing students to explore first as a way to transform their lessons. The full 5E Instructional Model provides a framework for designing inquiry-based science lessons by leading students through different phases (engage, explore, explain, elaborate, and evaluate) over a sequence of lessons for each unit. In the first phase, engage, the teacher sparks the students' curiosity and interest to capture their attention and activate prior knowledge. In the next phase, explore, students actively investigate the topics through hands-on experiments, gathering data, making observations, and asking questions. In the third phase, explain, students begin to construct meaning by connecting their observations to scientific concepts; this leads to the elaborate phase, where students are guided to deepen their understanding through application of their knowledge to new situations and making new connections. The framework ends in the final stage, evaluate, where teachers assess their students' learning. These five phases were simplified into the new, "you explore, I guide, we learn" principle, allowing for a small step to be taken toward inquiry-based teaching.

One third-grade teacher was able to take a science experiment lesson that she had always used in her classroom and just shifted the order of how she introduced it so that it could become more inquiry-based. Rather than frontloading the lesson with the scientific concepts and vocabulary (explain) and then letting the students do a hands-on activity (explore), she simply allowed the students to explore first, and then explain. This was much more manageable to her than to have her completely rethink entire unit plans. Specifically, this teacher shared that she always did a bridge-building unit for science where she had her students read books and complete worksheets about how bridges were built and how they were designed with certain shapes to have the strongest structures. After completing the readings and written work, she would allow them to "experiment" and create their own bridges and test them. She realized that by having students do the bridge-building activity first and collect data and make observations on their own, students could then make their own hypotheses and predictions that could be tested. Then, she introduced the readings and workbook activities to reinforce and extend their learning.

Just the simple principle of switching the initial instruction from "I do" to "you explore" opened up a new way of teaching that aligned with inquiry-based science learning. By taking this small step, she was able to change the way that science was viewed by her students and herself, and she was able to apply this principle to future units as well.

WHO SHOULD BE INCLUDED IN MAKING SMALL STEPS?

In taking small steps toward improving science education, it is important to determine the key leaders who can champion the movement. It is important to note that quality science instruction truly depends on the leaders and teachers, on the ground, within a school building. Our initiative started with an interested and motivated science committee of eight teachers representing various grade levels and special education along with the school's principal, who are all personally invested in improving science education.

However, as in many urban schools, personnel turnover became a large obstacle. In our case, nearly half of the teachers who began the professional development series in the spring to develop goals and objectives did not return to the school in the fall to carry the vision. There were also personnel transitions that needed to be accounted for as new teachers were hired throughout the school year and teachers were shifting classrooms and grade levels. In addition, the school principal who championed the STEM school initiative was replaced in the middle of the fall semester, and an interim principal was in place for several months before a permanent replacement could be found.

This situation is not uncommon in urban schools. However, it highlights the importance of finding key personnel who can maintain a consistent presence to keep the momentum for change moving forward. In this particular school, we found a small number of key teachers were very invested in teaching science in their classrooms. As we talked with individual teachers, teacher leaders emerged; specifically, teacher leaders in science surfaced, and became the people who could maintain the momentum even when the administration shifted.

In the case of one grade-level team, the teachers determined that they would divide the core areas and specialize in one specific subject (e.g., math, science, social studies), allowing one teacher, who had a background and interest in science, to be the expert to develop and teach science lessons for all three classes of fifth-grade students. This teacher became a steady, consistent force, able to develop and implement units, and thus began to develop and refine her expertise in science teaching.

By working directly with key personnel such as the grade-level science specialist teacher, we were able to target our work with specific individuals who were motivated and invested in improving their science teaching. As such, one possible strategy for school leaders interested in taking small steps to improve science education is to identify the key personnel most interested in science education and strategically place them in grade bands and grade levels where they want to make the most impact.

In addition, particularly in elementary schools, providing targeted professional development is important because, as generalists, not all teachers have the science background or interest to generate the momentum needed to transform science teaching in the classroom. By providing professional development specific to science, teachers can be supported to develop the necessary content knowledge and pedagogies needed for science teaching. As we engaged teachers as science learners during our professional development workshops, we saw several teachers who initially did not think of themselves as "science teachers" develop their own curiosity and interest in science. Since many teachers remembered science as worksheets and boring lists of vocabulary memorization, engaging them in inquiry-based activities as learners began to transform their conception of what science could look like in their classrooms. Some of these teachers actually became influential teacher leaders who began to champion science teaching initiatives.

WHEN DO YOU "DO SCIENCE"?

Within the many priorities and initiatives introduced in schools, determining a good time to focus on science education is often difficult. However, by focusing only on taking small steps toward improvement, any time could be a good time. Because there never seems to be enough time to tackle all of the improvements we would like to make, taking small steps and reframing the idea of what needs to happen can begin to shift mindsets and practices that could set the stage for larger changes in the future.

Initially, when we conceptualized this project with the principal and science committee, we had grand ideas to develop an all-new interdisciplinary curriculum utilizing project-based learning ideas, aligned to the NGSS standards, with field trips and hands-on experiences for all students. However, in an unexpected development, the district also mandated a new math curriculum and a new reading curriculum that fall. Therefore, within all of the things that the teachers needed to juggle, we decided that even small steps in the area of science would be beneficial, and our original plans had to pivot.

For example, one small step we took was to examine the weekly classroom schedule with our teachers. We noticed that often science instruction was relegated to the end of the day, for only thirty minutes, often on Mondays and Fridays. This small block of time at the end of the day resulted in science instruction being easily dismissed, or compressed and rushed. A small change was to adjust the schedule to create longer blocks of time for science instruction and varying where the science block was placed in the schedule. By making this slight change in the weekly schedule for instruction, we were able to create more opportunities for meaningful instruction and for students to truly have time to engage in science activities.

We also dispelled the notion that science was only done within the science block. We encouraged teachers to think about science throughout the day, weaving in the content throughout the different subject areas. When introducing a literacy topic, could a book or writing assignment connected to the current science unit be used as an example or writing prompt? When teaching a math skill, how could it be applied in science? Teachers were even able to utilize their morning meeting times to connect to science topics and do "mini-lessons" that were related to their curriculum.

WHERE DO YOU "DO SCIENCE"?

Sometimes, resistance to science teaching reform comes in the form of "we can't go outside," "we don't have science labs," or "we don't have any science equipment." Again, these were relatable challenges for the school in this project. The school was located in an urban neighborhood, with no outdoor green space; classrooms were crowded; and previously purchased science kits were scattered and in various states of disarray.

The original idea for our big project was to create a resource center/science lab/classroom area that could be shared among all the teachers in the school by transforming an unused former school library space. Unsurprisingly, this grandiose plan ran into some challenges, and again, taking small steps became easier and more effective. The original library had not been utilized for several years because the librarian position was eliminated several years prior and the room became a general storage space as books and bookcases were displaced by furniture and desks. Upon closer inspection, many of the books and resources that were available were also outdated or in poor condition.

However, we started by taking small steps. As a Saturday work project, we sorted through the bookcases, disposed of unusable furniture, and tidied the space so that one half of the library space was organized for science teaching materials. We curated relevant science resources and grouped them together by topic and grade level so that they could be easily accessible to teachers. We also used a similar concept in gathering, sorting, and curating available science equipment and supplies that had been scattered throughout the school to create a lending library that was accessible for all teachers in the building. Rather than having each teacher have some science materials in their individual classrooms (regardless of whether they were being used or not), we asked all the teachers to bring their science supplies to a central location where they could be sorted and grouped together. Whereas sometimes one classroom had only six magnifying glasses, by pulling together all the supplies, we found that it was easier for a teacher to obtain a full classroom set so that all students in the class could more easily participate in the science activity at the same time. We also organized an area for consumable materials that could be used for science activities, such as paper clips, straws, food coloring, and batteries, and a general supply donation list was shared. With a centralized storage space, teachers and families could donate supplies and they could be organized and stored for easy teacher access.

Finally, we expanded the walls of the school by partnering with local nature centers who could provide topic-specific curricular materials and science educators who could also work with our students. We were able to invite them into classrooms for a science unit, which often culminated in field trips for students to their location. The nature centers provided the school with access to additional resources for the classroom, such as aquaponics tanks and plant growing stations, and sometimes even additional grant funding for transportation and materials.

WHY SHOULD WE TAKE SMALL STEPS?

Although it is intuitive that providing quality science instruction is critical, the idea of transforming science teaching in schools can seem overwhelming. School leaders and teachers may feel like they do not have the expertise or the time to devote to improving science instruction. However, science is an ideal content area for teaching reform to begin because science is all around us and is sparked by children's natural curiosity about the world. Science is a natural place for students to ask questions to better understand the world around them and provides a context in which students can ask questions that are relevant to where they are and who they are in this world.

By taking small steps to initiate change in science education we can begin to generate the momentum needed for larger science education reform. If we do not begin to take the small steps, we may never be able to see the large-scale changes that may be needed. Due to the current landscape of education, there will probably never be an ideal time or enough time to generate all the changes we would like to see. However, by taking small steps we can begin to impact one teacher, one student, one classroom, one grade level, and then that can snowball to create a different culture around science that can generate more excitement and momentum for change to occur throughout the school.

NOTES

1. Grant Wiggins and Jay McTighe, *Understanding by Design* (Washington, DC: ASCD, 2005).
2. Rodger W. Bybee, *The BSCS 5E Instructional Model: Creating Teachable Moments* (Arlington, VA: NSTA Press, 2015).
3. National Research Council, *Next Generation Science Standards: For States, by States*, 2013, https://nap.nationalacademies.org/read/18290/chapter/1#v.
4. Zora M. Wolfe, "'You Explore, I Guide, We Learn!': Developing an Inquiry-Based Teaching Curriculum," *Childhood Education* 95, no. 4 (2019): 30–35.
5. Bybee, *The BSCS 5E Instructional Model*.

BIBLIOGRAPHY

Bybee, Rodger W. *The BSCS 5E Instructional Model: Creating Teachable Moments*. Arlington, VA: NSTA Press, 2015.
National Research Council. *Next Generation Science Standards: For States, by States*. 2013. https://nap.nationalacademies.org/read/18290/chapter/1#v.
Wiggins, Grant, and Jay McTighe. *Understanding by Design*. Washington, DC: ASCD, 2005.
Wolfe, Zora M. "'You Explore, I Guide, We Learn!': Developing an Inquiry-Based Teaching Curriculum." *Childhood Education* 95, no. 4 (2019): 30–35. DOI: 10.1080/00094056.2019.1638710.

Chapter 6

Creating a Discourse-Driven Classroom

Jillian Plum

One of the fastest growing and diverse populations in school settings across the country is that of multilingual learners (ML).[1] The ML can be defined as a student whose first language is one other than English.[2] These students have the beautiful and amazing gift of speaking more than one language. One could describe MLs as linguistically gifted individuals.[3] While being able to speak two or more languages is a talent that greatly increases the intelligence of a student, it can also be a challenge to be multilingual in school settings. On the one hand, speaking two languages does provide multiple benefits for a student's development.[4] On the other hand, having to focus on improving academically and linguistically during daily instruction can be difficult. Therefore, teachers should be mindful of the various needs of MLs and support their academic and linguistic growth throughout the instructional day.

When looking at the linguistic growth of ML students and helping students to reach Fluent English Proficient (FEP) status, two categories are considered: input and output of language. Input of language can be defined as a learner's ability to listen to and read information and process it correctly. Output of language can be defined as a learner's ability to speak and write information after processing it correctly.[5] On average, MLs are more frequently engaged in classroom activities that promote input in a lesson. There are usually fewer opportunities in daily lessons that require output of language. While input is important for ML students and their linguistic growth, teachers need to have a balance and not forget to intentionally teach and promote output of language. Multilingual learners need to practice both input and output. Output of language can increase when a teacher incorporates classroom discourse into daily lessons. Being able to effectively engage students in classroom discourse is a goal that will directly benefit ML students, increase their speaking proficiency scores, and grow their language development. Therefore, creating a discourse-driven classroom is one way to support ML students on their linguistic journey to FEP status.

PICTURE THIS THIRD-GRADE ESTIMATION LESSON

In Classroom A, students are learning about estimation. A teacher has defined and explained estimation. Next, the teacher provided examples of how to estimate on the board. Finally, problems were placed on the board for students to complete. Students raise their hands to share their answers, but not every student has their hand up for each question.

In Classroom B, students are learning about estimation. A teacher has defined and explained estimation with physical movement connected to the word. After the teacher is done, students partner together to explain estimation to each other using the same physical movement the teacher used. The teacher continues by going over an estimation problem on the board and highlights different ways to estimate. The teacher explains what they did and why. Then the students explain what the teacher did and why to their same partner. Students are then put into groups and given an estimation problem to solve together by choosing an estimation strategy they like best. After groups solve their problem, they write an explanation of how they solved the problem and why they chose that strategy. Results for each group are then shared with the class.

If you were a ML in this class, which lesson would be most beneficial to you for promoting your use of the English language? Classroom B is an example of a discourse-driven classroom.

According to Jocuns,[6] classroom discourse includes every type of communication that one encounters in a classroom or school setting. Echevarria and colleagues published widely on effective instruction for MLs, stating that interaction and conversation are key components of ML instruction; in a classroom with high-quality classroom discourse, they noted that it is very important for ML students to have the opportunity to practice language functions and features in conversation to gain FEP status on their ACCESS for ELLs (Assessing Comprehension and Communication in English State-to-State for English Language Learners) exam.[7]

Let's first establish that if you have MLs in your classroom, you are a language teacher. You are a bridge that can support students to successfully understand the content you teach in your room. While there are many areas in the classroom that can be targeted to increase ML success with their use of language and content, one common challenge for many teachers of MLs includes getting students to use classroom discourse. Your ML students benefit greatly when you support them across the bridge to successfully mastering your content.

DEFINITIONS OF TECHNICAL VOCABULARY

- Discourse: The term classroom discourse refers to all forms of talk that teachers and students use to communicate with each other in the classroom. Talking, or conversation, is the medium through which most teaching takes place, so the study of classroom discourse is the study of the process of face-to-face classroom teaching.[8]
- Callback: A chant or group of words that triggers students to respond with the response chant or group of words.

- Procedures: Step-by-step explanations to support students carrying out a task in class.
- ML (Multilingual Learner): students whose first language is one other than English.[9]
- Scaffolds: Intentional instructional items used in education to support and guide students to become competent in an academic area.[10]
- Discourse-Driven Questions: Open-ended questions that encourage students to discuss concepts, defend answers with evidence, and share their thinking with their peers.
- FEP (Fluent English Proficient): A designation that the ML receives upon scoring proficient with the English Language.

SMALL CHANGES

To begin the journey of creating a discourse-driven classroom, consider implementing these small changes to your daily classroom activities:

- Talking procedures
- Discourse-driven questions
- Scaffolds
- Probing statements
- Community that encourages talk

Talking Procedures

Many professionals and experts agree that one of the most important keys to getting your students to succeed with any new idea or concept is to set them up for success with clear and practiced procedures. The same is true when seeking to get your students to use classroom discourse in your daily lessons. Before we ask our students to talk about a concept in class, consider the following options to help students know how and when to talk to their peers.

Assigned Partners: Having an assigned partner takes away the stress of students having to find someone to talk to when you ask a question. This will also cut back on wasted time as students will already know who to turn to and who to engage with. It is also helpful to have visuals for students to see who their partners are when they are asked to talk. Consider also having a follow-up procedure of what to do when a partner is absent. The following are ideas to group students for classroom discourse:

- Partner A and Partner B
- Partner 1 and Partner 2
- Clock buddies: 12:00 Partner, 3:00 Partner, 6:00 Partner, 9:00 Partner

Callback: Another procedure that can assist your students to be prepared to engage in discourse is to have a callback that students can respond to. Implementing a callback is especially great for ML students as it triggers their brain to respond to the callback. There are many types of callbacks teachers can include in their class; a few options are listed in table 6.1.

Table 6.1. Examples of Callbacks to Use with Students

Teacher Says:	Student Responds:
"Turn and talk"	"Okay"
"Let's talk"	"Let's go"
"Ready set"	"You bet"
"Bring it back in 3, 2, 1"	"All done"
"Class class"	"Yes yes"

Body Position: Finally, students should know that when talking with a partner, there is a proper way to set their bodies and be successful with classroom discourse. This type of active listening is beneficial to support students being able to listen and respond to their partners. It might also be helpful to demonstrate the wrong way to set your body when engaging in discourse with a partner. Consider teaching your students to sit:

- Face-to-face
- Knee to knee
- Eyes on partner
- Ears listening

So, before you wonder why your students are not engaging in discourse when you've asked them to, ask yourself, "Did I set up talking procedures for them to be successful?" If not, which of the above steps could be included in your daily lessons?

Discourse-Driven Questions

Now that procedures are in place in your classroom, it is time to consider a change in how we ask students questions in class. Asking certain types of questions can either promote or discourage classroom discourse. The goal is to use discourse-driven questions. These questions are open ended, often have more than one right answer, and promote the need for students to explain or defend their answers. We want to avoid questions that destroy discourse because they lead to one-word answers and/or only have one right answer. Read through the content scenarios in table 6.2 to start seeing how you can change your questioning to be more discourse driven:

Implementing discourse-driven questions takes practice and intentionality. Discourse-driven questions often start with one of the following: why, how, should, describe, what, "tell me about _____," "what do you think about _____?"[11] Using and mastering this skill of questioning will greatly improve the discourse use of the students in your classroom.

Scaffolds

Another small change that can support your students using classroom discourse is the use of scaffolds. Scaffolds are intentional instructional items used in education to support and guide students to become competent in an academic area.[12] Culatta and colleagues stated that classroom discourse can promote comprehension of texts and

Table 6.2. Examples of Discourse-Driven Questions in Various Content Areas

Content	Discourse Destroyers	Discourse-Driven Questions
Language Arts	Who is the main character?	Describe the main character.
Math	What is 6 × 7?	Solve 6 × 7 and explain what strategy you used.
Science	What are the three states of matter?	Tell me about the three states of matter. Which state is better and why?
Social Studies	When was the colony of Jamestown built?	What do you think life was like living in Jamestown as a ten-year-old the year it was built?

content when modified and scaffolded appropriately based on the student's needs and levels.[13] The following scaffolds can be used to promote classroom discourse with your students, especially your ML students:

- Sentence/speaking frames
- Word banks
- Visuals
- Anchor charts

Including scaffolds will support your students using classroom discourse. However, it is important to keep in mind that scaffolds do not always have to stay in use. When students learn the process of using classroom discourse with their peers, scaffolds may not be necessary anymore and therefore you do not have to use them.

Probing Statements: "Are You Sure?"

Students are often very good at picking up on social cues. They can often tell what your emotions are, when they are in trouble, and when they got the right answers based on the physical cues teachers model. Thus, it is beneficial for teachers to become actors to hide and change their social cues so students cannot easily decipher what a teacher means. This forces students to think and process on a deeper level which will then lead to a student engaging in discourse free from pressure and assumptions. For example, whenever I am in a new classroom and I ask students to give me an answer to a content question, I always follow up their response with "Are you sure?" whether their answer was right or wrong. Nine times out of ten, students second-guess themselves thinking they gave the wrong answer, even if they actually had the right answer. I explain that students should feel confident in their responses and defend their answer regardless of what cues the teachers give that indicate they may not be right. Students often thoroughly enjoy engaging with questions and proving why their thinking makes sense. The following statements can be made with a neutral expression.

- Are you sure?
- What else? And what else?
- What comes to mind?

- Tell me more . . .
- Explain yourself.

With any new instructional change that a teacher hopes to include in the classroom, time and practice are important. Give yourself time to use these statements and practice how and when you will use them. Eventually they will become second nature and your students will welcome the chance to engage in discourse and explain their thinking.

Community That Encourages Talk

The last small change that a teacher can make to improve the classroom discourse of their students is to create a community of learners that encourages talk. The affective filter hypothesis, one of the five components of Krashen's second language acquisition theory, discusses the factors that affect the second language acquisition process: motivation, self-confidence, and anxiety.[14] If the goal is to get students to engage in classroom discourse with their peers, it is important to create a safe space for students to take language risks and share their thoughts, even if their line of thinking is wrong. It takes courage and trust for a student to take the risk of fully engaging in classroom discourse, and teachers play a big role in setting up a safe space for students to take speaking risks. This is especially true for ML students. The following considerations should be made to create a community of talk:

- Get to know your students: Getting to know your students on a daily basis is very important for classroom culture. Students are more likely to interact with the teacher and other students if they know the teacher took time to learn something about them. It becomes even more powerful when topics and ideas that students are interested in are integrated into content lessons and academic conversations in class.
- Open space to dialogue: If you do not plan in and plan for opportunities for students to talk in class, they never will have the opportunity to talk. Give your students built-in and planned talking time (table 6.3). This could be done at the beginning of your class time, integrated in portions of your lessons, or placed at the end of the day. Intentionality is key here, rather than just randomly telling students to tell their neighbor what they think. Students will also respond well to being able to freely share and defend their ideas without judgment and criticism.
- Compliments: Complimenting your students by stating specifically what they are doing well is another proven technique to encourage your learners. Highlight those who take speaking risks by providing compliments. This will encourage them to continue to take speaking risks while also encouraging others who are hesitant to try as well. Every student appreciates and benefits from compliments stating what they are doing well.
- Debates: While the concept of a debate might trigger discomfort and discouraging memories for some, debates in class are actually beneficial for preparing students to effectively defend their answers. Set up class norms for how to converse respectfully, how to listen without judgment, and how to disagree when engaged in a debate. Your students will enjoy the opportunity to respectfully share why their point of view makes sense in their eyes.

Table 6.3. Examples of Discourse-Driven Content Ideas

ELA
Read Aloud (kindergarten to fifth grade): Read a picture book aloud to your students. Use sticky notes to write out open-ended questions to ask your students during the reading. Allow students the time to discuss questions and defend answers.
Book Reviews (second to fifth grade): After students finish a book, allow them to write and share a book review with their peers. Students will be allowed to listen to others and get new book ideas.
Theme Generation (third to fifth grade): After reading a text, allow students to discuss what themes they feel connect with the text. Allow students to share and explain why one theme is more powerful than another.

Math
Number Talks (kindergarten to fifth grade): Start each math lesson with a math question that allows for deep thought and multiple avenues to answer the question. Allow students to share how they got the answer and/or why they feel like their avenue toward the solution is ideal for the question at hand.
Math Story Investigations (kindergarten to fifth grade): There are many math-related texts that develop a math concept in the form of a story.* Find texts that develop a math problem that can be solved through brainstorming efforts and investigation.
Math Congress (kindergarten to fifth grade): After students have been given a math assignment, bring the class back together for a math congress. During the math congress students share ideas, offer and receive feedback, and learn from each other.

Science
Science Mysteries (kindergarten to fifth grade): There are texts and online resources that develop science mysteries for students to solve using investigation and classroom discourse with their peers.** Research science topics you will be covering and see if there are any science mysteries that will get your students talking.
Science Question of the Day (kindergarten to fifth grade): Using open-ended questioning terms such as I wonder, why, how, should, describe, what, tell me about and what do you think about . . . ,*** create a "science question of the day" space in your daily science lesson.
Science Showcase (third to fifth grade): At the end of a science unit, divide students into groups to display their learning during the science unit. Students in groups will be able to discuss ideas with their group and then present their learning during a showcase. You can invite parents, other teachers/students in the building, or other community partners.

Social Studies
Would You Rather (kindergarten to fifth grade): Pose various "Would you rather . . ." scenarios to the students that are connected to the social studies unit currently being learned in class.
Social Studies Showcase (third to fifth grade): At the end of a science unit, divide students into groups to display their learning during the science unit. Students in groups will be able to discuss ideas with their group and then present their learning during a showcase. You can invite parents, other teachers/students in the building, or other community partners.

Sources: * L. West, *Empowering Your Students to Thrive* (Metamorphosis Teaching and Learning Communities, 2023); ** K. Schacht and D. Peltz, Mystery Science, https://mysteryscience.com/; *** North Carolina Department of Health and Human Services, "The Art of the Open-Ended Question," April 2019, https://www.ncdhhs.gov/documents/files/dss/training/open-ended-questions.

CONCLUSION

The fact that you are reading this chapter is proof that you care a lot about your students and improving your teaching practice. There are many areas that a teacher can target to support ML students for their second-language acquisition. One important area is using output of language. This includes creating a discourse-driven classroom. Teachers will benefit in their efforts to increase classroom discourse by starting with the small changes described in this chapter: Set up talking procedures so students know what to expect; incorporate discourse-driven questions to stimulate conversation and engagement; use scaffolds to support your ML students to use the language they have and grow to higher levels of discourse; master probing statements to encourage confidence in reluctant speakers; and establish a community that encourages talk by motivating students, reducing their anxiety about discourse, and helping them improve their self-confidence. When you create a discourse-driven classroom, your ML students, and really all the students in your classroom, will grow in their speaking ability and in their confidence to use language every day. This will be a benefit for students long after they leave your classroom.

NOTES

1. J. C. Plum, "A Descriptive Study of Factors That Support and Hinder Classroom Discourse with English Learners" (Doctoral diss., University of South Carolina, 2003); K. Flynn and J. Hill, *English Language Learners: A Growing Population* (Denver: Midcontinent Research for Education and Learning, 2005).

2. Plum, "Descriptive Study of Factors"; D. Freeman, "The Hidden Side of the Work," *Teacher Knowledge and Learning to Teach* 35 (2002): 1–13.

3. J. Urtubey, "How Educators and Communities Can Work Together in Creating Joyous and Just Education Systems," paper presented at the WIDA Annual Conference, Louisville, Kentucky, September 28–30, 2022.

4. R. A. Javier, *The Bilingual Mind: Thinking, Feeling and Speaking in Two Languages* (Berlin: Science + Business Media, 2007).

5. WIDA, WIDA Home Page, https://wida.wisc.edu/ (accessed December 2, 2020).

6. A. Jocuns, "Classroom Discourse," in *The Encyclopedia of Applied Linguistics*, ed. C. A. Chapelle, November 2012.

7. J. Echevarria, C. Richards-Tutor, R. Canges, and D. Francis, "Using the SIOP Model to Promote the Acquisition of Language and Science Concepts with English Learners," *Bilingual Research Journal*, no. 3 (2011): 334–51.

8. C. B. Cazden, C. B. *Discourse: The Language of Teaching and Learning*, second ed. (Portsmouth, NH: Heinemann, 2001); Jocuns, "Classroom Discourse"; G. Nuthall, "Discourse: Classroom Discourse, Cognitive Perspective," State Education.com Education Encyclopedia, n.d., https://education.stateuniversity.com/pages/1916/Discourse.html#:~:text=The (accessed December 15, 2023).

9. "The Hidden Side of the Work."

10. University at Buffalo, "Scaffolding Content," UB Office of Curriculum, Assessment and Teaching Transformation, n.d., https://www.buffalo.edu/catt/develop/build/scaffolding.html#:~:text=Scaffolding%20is%20an%20instructional%20practice,%2C%20processes%2C%20and%20learning%20strategies_(accessed December 15, 2023).

11. North Carolina Department of Health and Human Services, "The Art of the Open-Ended Question," NCDHHS, April 2019, https://www.ncdhhs.gov/documents/files/dss/training/open-ended-questions.

12. University at Buffalo, "Scaffolding Content."

13. B. Culatta, "Talking Things Through: Roles of Instructional Discourse in Children's Processing of Expository Texts," *Topics in Language Disorders* 30, no. 4 (2010): 308–32.

14. S. Krashen, *Principles and Practice in Second Language Acquisition* (Oxford: Pergamon Press, 1982).

BIBLIOGRAPHY

Cazden, C. B. *Classroom Discourse: The Language of Teaching and Learning*, second ed. Portsmouth, NH: Heinemann, 2001.

Culatta, B. "Talking Things Through: Roles of Instructional Discourse in Children's Processing of Expository Texts." *Topics in Language Disorders* 30, no. 4 (2010): 308–32. https://doi.org/10.1097/TLD.0b013e3181ff5a37.

Echevarria, J., C. Richards-Tutor, R. Canges, and D. Francis. "Using the SIOP Model to Promote the Acquisition of Language and Science Concepts with English Learners." *Bilingual Research Journal* , no. 3 (2011): 334–51. https://doi.org/10.1080/15235882.2011.623600.

Flynn, K., and J. Hill. *English Language Learners: A Growing Population*. Denver: Midcontinent Research for Education and Learning, 2005.

Freeman, D. "The Hidden Side of the Work." *Teacher Knowledge and Learning to Teach* 35 (2002): 1–13.

Javier, R. A. *The Bilingual Mind: Thinking, Feeling and Speaking in Two Languages*. Berlin: Science + Business Media, 2007.

Jocuns, A. "Classroom Discourse." In *The Encyclopedia of Applied Linguistics*, edited by C. A. Chapelle. November 2012. https://doi.org/10.1002/9781405198431.wbeal0134.

Krashen, S. *Principles and Practice in Second Language Acquisition*. Oxford: Pergamon Press, 1982.

North Carolina Department of Health and Human Services. "The Art of the Open-Ended Question." NCDHHS, April 2019. https://www.ncdhhs.gov/documents/files/dss/training/open-ended-questions.

Nuthall, G. "Discourse: Classroom Discourse, Cognitive Perspective." State Education.com Education Encyclopedia. n.d. https://education.stateuniversity.com/pages/1916/Discourse.html#:~:text=The. Accessed December 15, 2023.

Plum, J. C. "A Descriptive Study of Factors That Support and Hinder Classroom Discourse with English Learners." Doctoral diss., University of South Carolina, 2003.

Schacht, K., and D. Peltz, Mystery Science. n.d. https://mysteryscience.com/. Accessed December 5, 2023.

University at Buffalo. "Scaffolding Content." UB Office of Curriculum, Assessment and Teaching Transformation, n.d. https://www.buffalo.edu/catt/develop/build/scaffolding.html#:~:text=Scaffolding%20is%20an%20instructional%20practice,%2C%20processes%2C%20and%20learning%20strategies. Accessed December 15, 2023.

Urtubey, J. "How Educators and Communities Can Work Together in Creating Joyous and Just Education Systems." Paper presented at the WIDA Annual Conference, Louisville, Kentucky, September 28–30, 2022.

West, L. *Empowering Your Students to Thrive*. Metamorphosis Teaching and Learning Communities, 2023. https://metamorphosistlc.com/.

WIDA. WIDA home page. https://wida.wisc.edu/. Accessed December 2, 2020.

Chapter 7

Stepping Stones on Mount Project-Based Learning (PBL)

Maggie Demarse and Anne-Lise Halvorsen

"Bats have such a bad reputation! The media presents them as super creepy but they are actually really cute, and even more importantly, they are helpful within an ecosystem!"

In a unit focusing on organisms within an ecosystem through a project-based approach, I (Maggie Demarse) designed a unit titled How Can We as Environmental Stewards Advocate for Our Local Ecosystem?, eliciting the response in the preceding paragraph. Dr. Anne-Lise Halvorsen and I collaborated on this chapter due to our passion for project-based learning (PBL) and our understanding of how challenging PBL implementation can be for teachers. We hope to demonstrate ways to make PBL accessible, doable, and engaging for both teachers and students.

Although a more familiar term in the education world with its growing influence, PBL often exists in a nebulously defined realm. To move toward high levels of impact, our conception of PBL is rooted in a commitment to engaging students in sustained investigation or inquiry on a topic having relevance to the world beyond the confines of school. Our conception of PBL draws on the Framework for High-Quality PBL, comprised of six criteria: intellectual challenge and accomplishment, authenticity, public product, collaboration, project management, and reflection.[1] Coupled with these criteria, we have shaped our beliefs with an attention to the Buck Institute for Education's Gold Standard PBL: Essential Project Design Elements. One can readily see the Buck Institute's emphasis on key knowledge, understanding, and success skills; a challenging problem or question; sustained inquiry, authenticity, student voice, and choice; reflection: critique and revision; and a public product,[2] along with the parallels existing between both philosophies.

Designing and enacting PBL is complex, messy, and challenging work for teachers.[3] The planning is often intense and time-consuming. However, PBL doesn't need to be all or nothing; as Kamps argues, when designing and teaching a PBL unit, teachers can highlight some aspects of PBL while applying a "dimmer switch" to other aspects.[4] For example, in one unit, the dimmer switch may focus on the "bright" aspect of PBL regarding intellectual challenge and accomplishment, authenticity, and a public product; the dimmer switch in this instance is applied to project management. In our chapter for this book on "starting small," we demonstrate ways teachers can revise existing curricula to incorporate some criteria of PBL without completely overhauling their units. Specifically, we describe the teaching methodology for the unit How Can We as Environmental Stewards Advocate for Our Local Ecosystem? through a contextual narrative to explain how two "small changes" were made, share anecdotes about how these changes were enacted, and provide clear advice for teachers who might want to implement these changes in their classroom.

CONTEXT

The unit How Can We as Environmental Stewards Advocate for Our Local Ecosystem? was designed and taught by Maggie Demarse for her fifth-grade classroom. It is a standards-aligned, science-based unit integrating civics and government and citizen involvement. It engages students in studying the interconnections within ecosystems, which is the focus of fifth-grade life sciences. The main learning goals are to understand that organisms perform a variety of roles in an ecosystem and that all processes taking place within organisms require energy. Activities for engaging with these standards include investigations of locally threatened or endangered species, with considerations of the effects of remediation programs and species loss.

The unit is intellectually rigorous and incorporates technical knowledge and skills. We believe children are capable of (as well as interested in) learning the technical lexicon of the content they are learning. However, vocabulary needs to be presented in child-friendly language and with multiple examples and, sometimes, nonexamples. Here we list and define some of the key vocabulary:

- Advocacy: support for a particular policy or change
- Ecosystem: a system in which members are interconnected
- Environmental steward: a person who works to protect the environment

The project began with exploring how organisms perform roles in an ecosystem and how populations can be categorized by how they acquire energy. By creating a food web, students understand the interconnectedness of how energy is acquired in an ecosystem. Utilizing our local ecosystem, we mapped out the consumers, producers, and decomposers within a forest setting. Mapping was done on a classroom board that included images of a forest landscape (e.g., trees, shrubs, grass). We created organism cards, taped them into their habitats, and drew lines to create the web tracking how organisms acquire energy within the ecosystem. Another activity we engaged in was watching videos to observe the interaction of bats and mosquitoes in an ecosystem and how bats sleep in their roosts. This activity helped lead students into the next phase of the project, which involved designing and building a self-sustaining habitat and sharing our work with the community.

TWO SMALL CHANGES

In this section, we describe two small changes implemented to the unit that were different from my (Demarse's) previous instructional approach. First, we provide some background on my professional experiences with PBL. My teaching career began in a small school district in the Midwest. I had a mission of enacting project-based learning (PBL) district-wide. The first two years of implementing PBL in my classroom were challenging, yet rewarding. Going into my third year of teaching, I wanted to hone my practice regarding PBL. The district hosted professional development focusing on Kamps's ideas that PBL is not an on–off switch, but more like a dimmer switch.[5] Teachers do not have to apply all of the criteria for PBL all at once; instead, teachers gradually build skills until they can enact all of the High Quality Project Based Learning (HQPBL) criteria: intellectual challenge and accomplishment, authenticity, public product, collaboration, project management, and reflection; and the PBL Essential Design Elements: key knowledge, understanding, and success skills; a challenging problem or question; sustained inquiry; authenticity; student voice and choice; reflection; critique and revision; and a public product.[6]

Through reflection, I decided to shine a light on two elements of PBL, while "dimming" the others. The two I focused on were student voice and choice, and creating a public product. I knew the importance of drawing on student interest (student voice and choice) and I understood the critical attribute of situating the project in the local community to create the "public product" as I approached the design of the unit; these aspects of PBL guided my intentional design and focus. Student voice and choice is described as, "Students make some decisions about the project, including how they work and what they create, and express their own ideas in their own voice."[7] Situating the project in the local community met the public product description from PBL Works, "Students make their project work public by sharing it with and explaining or presenting it to people beyond the classroom."[8] With these ideas in mind, I was eager for my new assignment of teaching fifth- and sixth-grade science. When examining and deconstructing the fifth-grade life science standards, I saw a strong potential to get my students outside the classroom and center their interests through the aspects of PBL.

Drawing on Student Interest

I immediately began thinking about the potential for teaching and learning in fifth- and sixth-grade science. In particular, fifth-grade life science standards focus on ecosystems, organisms, and the relationship they have with each other and the environment. I looked forward to using some of my summer vacation time to build a relationship with the local nature preserve, and perhaps plan a field trip for the fall. While planning, I thoughtfully balanced how much I planned without the input of students, knowing one of my small changes in approach to PBL involved drawing on student interest and centering on student voice and choice. In response to the concern, I paid attention to what the rising fourth graders were learning about via our school-wide morning news program and spoke with their teachers. At the end of fourth grade, they were learning about bats, spelunking (cave hiking), and "white-nose syndrome," a disease caused by a fungus that affects hibernating bats.

Additionally, I anticipated that not all students wanted to study bats, so I intentionally found other elements to pique student interest. For example, as a class we read the book *Hoot*, which was related to the content of the unit with a focus on owls, their habitat, and the impact of human development on wildlife. Furthermore, I took an interdisciplinary lens when crafting small-group work, providing students opportunities to collect data, make posters, create budgets, work with maps, and use power tools. I hoped each student would tap into one or more of the activities and topics, all related to the focus on bats.

Situating the Project in the Local Community

With the excitement about the potential to learn about bats and their ecosystem, I reached out to the local nature preserve to see if we could collaborate on a field trip to "hook" the students into the project. My collaboration consisted of a few hikes over the summer and one sit-down session before the school year started to talk through logistics. Specifically within the ecosystem standards, we planned to teach symbiotic relationships, endangered species, and invasive species. The naturalists and I planned to hike a path including non-bat-specific activities, such as identifying invasive plant species in our local ecosystem, as well as bat-specific activities, such as identifying roosts (figure 7.1). During the implementation, the naturalist led most of the instruction, and we had parent/guardian volunteers attend the walk to help with organizing our walk from the school to the preserve and back. It was truly a community effort!

Upon our return from the field trip, I planned for a debrief, which included asking the students what they noticed and wondered about, were curious about, and what thoughts they had for continuing their learning journey about bats. In addition to confirming student interest in bats, the debrief introduced the project and established our driving question, How Can We as Environmental Stewards Advocate for Our Local Ecosystem? The debrief helped students engage in reflection, one of the key HQPBL and PBL Works components. Since we were in the Midwest, we studied the Indiana brown bat for our ecosystems unit.

As their science teacher, I was surprised by how well the student interests' aligned with the state standards. For example, the Indiana brown bat is an endangered species; endangered species are one focus of the standard: 5.LS.1: Organisms perform a variety of roles in an ecosystem.[9] Furthermore, white-nose syndrome is a disease in which a parasite lives on bats as their host, exemplifying a symbiotic relationship. To gain an understanding of food webs, mutualism, commensalism, and predator–prey relationships, we explored our local ecosystems as examples. One of my favorite parts of the unit was teaching students how to spot a bat and the times of day people can see them flying around. Bats constantly flap their wings and don't glide like birds. Also, bats are predominantly out at dusk and dawn during certain seasons. Furthermore, student agency and efficacy were built by the sustained inquiry of students tracking local bat sightings on a map of the town.

Last, one of the most engaging aspects of the project is students deciding that we needed to build bat houses to save our local endangered bats: a response demonstrating authenticity (an HQPBL criterion) and a challenging problem or question (a PBL Works element). The students' decision to build houses emerged from a conversation about what we will do with all our newly acquired understanding of bats. Students formed small groups to brainstorm, making great suggestions like making a brochure for the naturalist center. After sharing a few ideas, one student asked about the

Figure 7.1. Field trip, 2018. Maggie Demarse.

resources available to us and brought up the idea of limitations. The student said building a bat house would be fun, but can we do that? I replied, "Sure, we can at least ask!"

Students found a variety of bat house designs online and eventually landed on a design they felt they could accomplish. Additionally, they created a budget for the amount of money they could spend on materials, such as deer netting, wood, screws, and black paint. I worked on getting the funds and contacting parent/guardian volunteers to help students use power tools. To acquire money for the project, I used the remaining funds from my classroom budget and reached out to my principal to ask if he could help find money. Our district had been awarded a Lowe's grant earlier in the year, and he gave my students the money to finish the project. I also needed to find resources to teach power tool safety to my fifth graders! Moreover, I had to get a schedule change approved with my team teachers and principal because we could not accomplish this work in a few class periods. I was fortunate to have many supporters and community members who could come in and help students build bat houses. The construction of the bat houses was an incredible assembly line of local dads, our elementary library, intervention specialist, and other fifth-grade teachers. We set up construction on the stage in the gym and rotated groups of approximately ten students, allowing us to create about eight bat houses. I was a proud teacher, watching students bravely step up to the miter saw and confidently cut the wood they measured twice, never flinching at the loud noise of the saw. Students also walked away feeling they had conquered a fear. The work involved to construct the bat houses not only included students overcoming fear of using heavy machinery, but also aided in their understanding of how bats move within an ecosystem. For example, students were surprised to discover the amount of space inside the bat house was minimal; the width would allow for a human hand to slide in without any wrist rotation. The students were surprised the bats could squeeze into the thin space.

To further situate the project in the local community, we considered the questions: How do we communicate what we have learned about bats within our community? How do we get these bat houses out to the community? Our school expects teachers and students to participate in Exhibition Night, a night when we open our doors to the public to share the work the students have been doing all semester. With a focus from PBL and an awareness of Exhibition Night, students wanted to set up multiple stations to capture the distinct phases of our work from the field trip in September to the building of bat houses in November. Our biggest question was how to get the

Figure 7.2. Exhibition Night, 2018. Maggie Demarse.

bat houses to the community. Some students recommended we have community members buy one. Other students raised equity concerns, like what if a community member can't afford one? Other students recommended giving them away for free, and additional students brought up the point that it may not be fair because we don't have enough for everyone who attends the Exhibition Night. The students landed on creating a raffle, thinking it would be the most equitable option. Students drafted raffle tickets, created guidelines such as only one raffle ticket per person, and asked the principal to use the school intercom to announce winners (figure 7.2). Finally, everything was in place, and we were ready to show the community what we learned and built. Some students worked on drafting invitations, some wrote outlines for how to talk with the public, and others chose to draft a setup/display for our exhibition space in the gym (figure 7.3). Everyone played a key role!

After reflecting on the project, I recognize that two challenges I faced were keeping all stakeholders up to date on our work and managing small groups. For example, I would get approval from the principal to use the gym for constructing bat houses, but I also needed to ask the physical education teacher if we could use the space, then I

Figure 7.3. Exhibition Night, 2018. Maggie Demarse.

needed to let the other fifth-grade teachers know and inform the parent/guardian volunteers. If there was a change in the plan, it was communicated down the same chain. Another challenge was managing small groups. As the project progressed, the small-group needs also changed, morphing to the needs of the project, and it was challenging to keep all students in the loop. We eventually turned our classroom whiteboard into a project log, so each group could see the other groups' progress and tasks. As I reflected on both these challenges, I realized having students take on the role of project managers is a change I would make in future iterations of the unit.

ANECDOTES OF OUTCOMES

Reflecting on this project, it is clear to me that I sturdily footed the stepping stones to Mount PBL, even if the climb was not linear or without setbacks. In the end, it wasn't a perfect run for my first time explicitly focusing on student interest and situating the project in the local community, but I reminded myself there is no such thing as perfection in teaching. Moreover, I could see the positive impact on the outcomes for my students.

For example, I saw students taking on stewardship roles, such as finding trash on the playground and picking it up out of concern for our local ecosystem. I heard students talk about using the power tools, feeling an inspiration to do more woodworking work. I also heard students asking questions like "what about other endangered species?" In summary, students walked away from the project with a stronger awareness of science "in the real world," a sense of agency, and a new understanding of what it means to advocate and serve as environmental stewards.

When reflecting on my goal of centering student interest, I felt it was a win! In this project, there was strong alignment between student interests and the standards, but I realized that even without strong alignment, there are ways to bridge student interest with what they are expected to learn. I have found students make great connections through the learning journey. Also, there were aspects of choice aligning with the standards but also going beyond. For example, I found students stopped being as concerned with their grades and started thinking more about the next steps for the project. Moreover, I found students enjoying the various small-group activities and the opportunities to select which group (e.g., taking on raffle logistics, making posters, painting bat houses, drafting invitations; see figure 7.4) they joined based on their interests.

Considering situating the project within the local community, I saw layers of connections. One layer was the flora and fauna and the organisms living among us, like bats. Another layer was collaborating with a local nature preserve, a walkable distance from the school. Yet another layer was the volunteering by parents/guardians and the community turnout at Exhibition Night. These layers together affirmed both students' learning and engagement while also responding to an authentic problem in the community.

Looking back on the experience, one dilemma I encountered was knowing when to wrap it up. One aspect of PBL my colleagues and I laughed about is a "runaway project"; it just keeps going, and never ends. This can easily happen as students drum up more ideas for how to take a topic further. It's hard as the teacher to keep a big picture

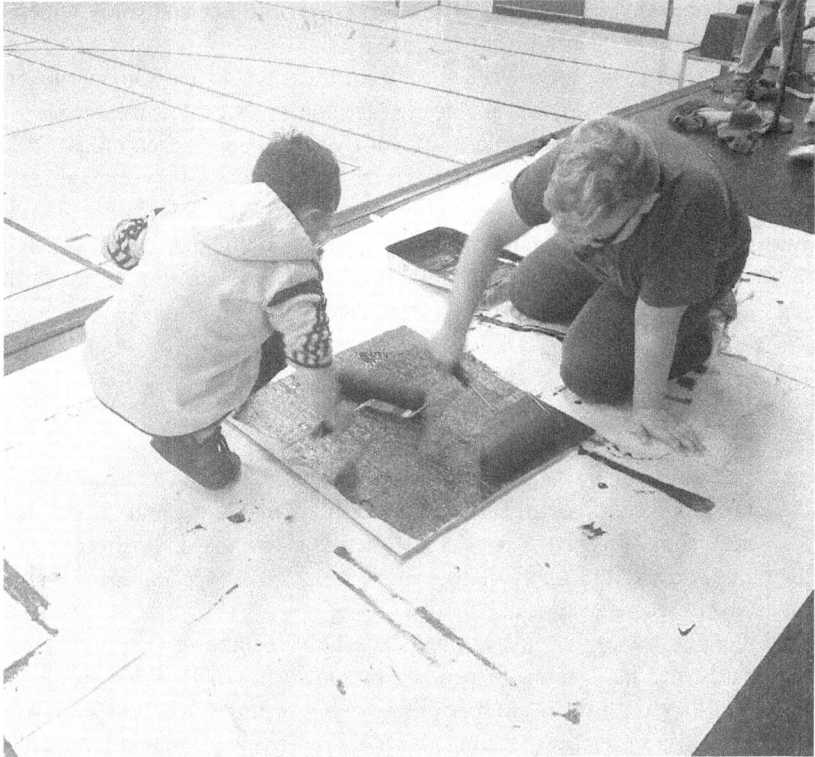

Figure 7.4. Building bat houses, 2018. Maggie Demarse.

focus while honoring the sprouting ideas along the project journey. In these instances, going back to the standards can be helpful—a strategy that keeps me grounded.

STEP-BY-STEP GUIDE TO STARTING SMALL WITH PBL

We hope by providing a glimpse into the process of designing the unit, we have shared both the energy and excitement involved in it as well as the questions and dilemmas that arose. Trying to design, enact, and refine a unit subscribing to all the HQPBL criteria and PBLWorks elements is daunting work. However, by starting small—focusing on components within reach and engaging to you and your students—you can begin to climb Mount PBL. Here we suggest some steps to consider related to drawing on student interest (student voice and choice) and situating the project in the local community (public product).

Drawing on Student Interest

1. Get to know your students as individuals and as a classroom. Consider administering short surveys to ask open-ended questions about their interests and gauge their levels of interest in topics.

2. Read picture books or short articles on a range of topics and study which topics seem to be of greatest interest to students.
3. Engage students in "free writes" or free drawings, when they write or draw about anything they want. Take note of the topics that interest them.
4. Determine which topics would align with your school curriculum or state standards. Think broadly! Like the unit described here, even very specialized topics could be broadened in ways providing alignment and the foci of standards.
5. Narrow down possible topics and invite students to think about ones offering the most interest to them; be sure to only offer topics you are serious about unpacking and exploring.

Situating the Project in the Local Community

1. Begin exploring local community organizations such as nature conservancies, humane societies, literacy coalitions, historical societies, recreation and park associations, libraries, greenway coalitions, museums, and other nonprofit agencies. They often have booths at festivals or events. Leaders in these organizations are excited about partnering with schools. Encourage a mutualistic relationship where everyone benefits.
2. Take the children on a walk around the school community. Provide them with clipboards and have them take notes or make drawings about what they see and what they might want to learn more about or improve. Be careful to use an assets-based approach to valuing the community. Ask students to think about what they could produce that would respond to problems or questions.
3. Connect with students' families to tap into their areas of expertise regarding the local community. Ask if any of them would like to visit the classroom to share their engagement with the community.
4. Find connections between your school/district curriculum and the local community. Think about how partnering with these organizations could deepen students' understanding in meaningful ways.
5. Brainstorm with student products they could design, furthering the missions of these organizations or responding to questions or problems in authentic ways.

CONCLUSION

We hope the chapter has provided some inspiration for how you might "start small" as you climb Mount PBL. In this chapter we focus on two aspects of PBL: drawing on student interest and situating the project in the local community. However, there are many other criteria and elements with which you might like to start. For example, you might begin to establish collaboration and reflection as key practices in your instruction, and once students are comfortable with and skilled at these practices, they can then be used in the service of designing a public product. We urge you to consider Kamps's dimmer switch approach: start by highlighting a small number of criteria or elements and dimming the others until you and your students are ready. Wherever you start, and whatever path you take as you climb Mount PBL, we encourage you to be patient and kind to yourself, to invite student reflection on how to revise units, and to celebrate each step you take.

NOTES

1. HQPBL.org, "A Framework for High Quality Project Based Learning," 2018, https://hqpbl.org/wp-content/uploads/2018/03/FrameworkforHQPBL.pdf.

2. Buck Institute for Education, "Gold Standard PBL: Essential Project Design Elements." PBLWorks, 2023, https://www.pblworks.org/what-is-pbl/gold-standard-project-design.

3. Kristyn Kamps, "Promoting a PBL Mindset: The 'Dimmer Switch' Approach," PBLWorks (January 27, 2021), https://www.pblworks.org/blog/promoting-pbl-mindset-dimmer-switch-approach

4. Ibid.

5. HQPBL.org, "A Framework for High Quality Project Based Learning."

6. HQPBL.org, "A Framework for High Quality Project Based Learning"; Buck Institute for Education, "Gold Standard PBL."

7. Buck Institute for Education, "Gold Standard PBL."

8. Ibid.

9. Ohio Department of Education, *Ohio Learning Standards and Model Curriculum* (Columbus: ODE, 2019), 121, https://education.ohio.gov/getattachment/Topics/Learning-in-Ohio/Science/Ohios-Learning-Standards-and-MC/SciFinalStandardsMC060719.pdf.aspx?lang=en-US. State standard adapted from Next Generation Science Standards (NGSS); see https://www.nextgenscience.org/.

BIBLIOGRAPHY

Buck Institute for Education. "Gold Standard PBL: Essential Project Design Elements." PBLWorks, 2023. https://www.pblworks.org/what-is-pbl/gold-standard-project-design.

HQPBL.org. "A Framework for High Quality Project Based Learning." 2018. https://hqpbl.org/wp-content/uploads/2018/03/FrameworkforHQPBL.pdf.

Kristyn Kamps. "Promoting a PBL Mindset: The 'Dimmer Switch' Approach." PBL Works, January 27, 2021. https://www.pblworks.org/blog/promoting-pbl-mindset-dimmer-switch-approach.

Ohio Department of Education. *Ohio Learning Standards and Model Curriculum*. Columbus: ODE, 2019. https://education.ohio.gov/getattachment/Topics/Learning-in-Ohio/Science/Ohios-Learning-Standards-and-MC/SciFinalStandardsMC060719.pdf.aspx?lang=en-US.

Chapter 8

Stories That Need to Be Told

Clancy Bishop, Tiffany Coleman, Nikki Collins, and Melissa Ewing

There is no greater agony than bearing an untold story inside you.

—Maya Angelou, 2009

Prioritizing student stories can truly revolutionize the landscape of literacy within our educational spaces, benefiting students and teachers alike. This chapter tells the story of the remarkable transformation of literacy spaces through the harnessing of students' personal experiences and storytelling at a Title I elementary school with a high percentage of multilingual learners. It offers practical insights into instructional routines that foster a vibrant culture of critical thinking, reading, and writing across diverse learning communities. You will get a glimpse into the classrooms of Nikki (kindergarten), Clancy (first grade), and Tiffany (fourth grade). We hope to shine a light on the pivotal shift that has amplified students' stories to find their voice, be celebrated and, in turn, ignite excitement and joy among students and teachers ranging from kindergarten to fourth grade.

We embraced a constructivist stance, emphasizing collaboration between teachers and students as they collectively derive meaning from stories.[1] Our aim in transforming our literacy spaces was to cultivate a culture of efficacy[2] among teachers of writing and their students as writers by nurturing the foundational elements of efficacy. To achieve this, we carefully examined instructional routines that foster mastery moments, showcased models of success, provided productive feedback, and ensured a safe and supportive environment.[3] Through the implementation of constructivist principles and a focus on collaboration, we have successfully fostered a culture of efficacy among both teachers and students in our literacy spaces, thereby empowering them to engage meaningfully with stories and develop as writers.

SHIFT HAPPENS: TRANSFORMING LITERACY SPACES

Writing used to evoke a sense of reluctance for many of the teachers in our school. Writing instruction was a topic many often relegated to the background or omitted entirely for the day. However, a change in our perspectives occurred when we embraced a shift in our approach. Relinquishing control, the idea of perfection, and the need for silence marked the transformation necessary to afford students the chance to be inquisitive and write stories holding personal significance. Providing accessible materials allows students to write independently, fostering confidence and joy. Transitioning classrooms into spaces that empowered students as independent writers and thinkers represented a monumental change.

A transformative moment for our school started when a kindergarten teacher, Nikki, read Jennifer Jacobson's book, *No More "I'm Done!"*[4] Nikki read the first part of the book in one night and immediately created space and time for students to write in her classroom. This book prompted a profound shift in our perception of student writing. Nikki and the literacy coach talked almost daily about the stories her students were sharing and writing in their own books. Nikki was constantly seeking professional literature related to teaching writing. She demonstrated a commitment to increasing her specialized knowledge in teaching writing in order to support students in telling their stories.

A struggling student in Nikki's kindergarten class had written two books that supported a powerful mind shift. One was about a mouse that had gotten into the student's house and was chewing on the television wires. The student described the dad's sword fight with the mouse. The student was telling the story; he and Nikki shared the pen to record the words (figure 8.1). The other story was about a bird getting into the house and the mom chasing it out with her broom. The student told stories fueling the motivation Nikki felt to provide more opportunities for student voice in her classroom. Nikki realized she had always thought the students wouldn't have anything to write about because they didn't have many experiences. What she realized was they *do* have many experiences . . . these stories are just different from her own. Conversations about these stories piqued the curiosity of other teachers. The student stories that grew from Nikki's room initiated a curiosity in other teachers and then, engaging students in storytelling and writing spread to other classrooms across the school.

One day, along with a group of fellow teachers, Tiffany reluctantly visited Nikki's classroom, where a group of students engaged in creating these incredible books. Honestly, it seemed a little silly to Tiffany. How could a fourth-grade teacher learn something in a kindergarten class? But, to her surprise, these little authors were diligently telling their very own stories without a seasonal-themed prompt written on the board. And what was even more shocking—they seemed to be enjoying it! After listening to their little voices tell such important ideas about themselves, their lives, or even new adventures of the crazy little pigeon we all know and love from the books, she knew it was time to change her approach! After all, if kindergarten students could tell their stories, her older students definitely had stories to tell. She immediately went back to her classroom to implement changes. She told her students why writing was going to be different from that day forward.

Choice, voice, and engagement were the new normal. Tiffany was amazed at how such a small shift brought out such a variety of writing. Some students chose to research and write informational books. Others chose to write personal narratives. Following students' interests and inquiries led to genres of writing that would not usually be presented until later in the school year. She also saw such creativity in the

Figure 8.1.a. This is the story from the kindergarten student referenced on page 80. The teacher and the student shared the pen to write the student's story. Page One: My dad got the sword and he was sad because the little rat was so fast. It went under the tv. Page Two: My little sister was watching TV. She was sad because a rat bit the wire. The TV wouldn't turn on. Nobody can watch the TV. Ewing, Melissa Renee. "The Power of Story in Developing Cycles of Efficacy for Teachers and Students." EdD diss., University of South Carolina, 2022.

illustrations her students were sharing. These books, created by students for students, turned into points of pride for many of the multilingual students. They were sharing their stories through their art. Each child began experiencing mastery moments where before there was only confusion or a feeling of failure. Everyone became an expert in some area of writing. The shift occurring in these classrooms forever changed how they developed a collaborative classroom community of readers and writers. Students had an authentic purpose for writing. Our writing became who we are, where we have been, and where we are going.

Figure 8.1.b. This is the story from the kindergarten student referenced on page 80. The teacher and the student shared the pen to write the student's story. Page One: My dad got the sword and he was sad because the little rat was so fast. It went under the tv. Page Two: My little sister was watching TV. She was sad because a rat bit the wire. The TV wouldn't turn on. Nobody can watch the TV.Ewing, Melissa Renee. "The Power of Story in Developing Cycles of Efficacy for Teachers and Students." EdD diss., University of South Carolina, 2022.

We transitioned from emphasizing limitations to recognizing and fostering students' capabilities, and it all started with our youngest learners.

JUST SHIFT: PRIORITIZE TIME TO WRITE

Finding the time in your schedule to do something you dread is always a challenge. For many, writing is the dreaded, inevitably skipped, or conveniently forgotten subject. For some, writing serves as nothing more than a *craftivity* used to update bulletin boards where the students' outcomes look very similar.

Many of our students mimicked their teachers' feelings and attitudes toward writing. The announcement of writing time was frequently met with an audible groan of displeasure and dread. However, with a new shift in our writing practices came the realization of writing as a true authentic art, more than a mere activity on a common bulletin board for decoration. It should be meaningful to each unique student author.

All students have stories to tell. It is the teacher's job to create supportive spaces for the development of students as readers, writers, thinkers, and storytellers. Instructional routines for creating spaces like these in our school include a focus lesson, time to write, and time to share.

The first thing needed to make a similar shift in your classroom is simple. START. Allow access to blank paper, pencils, crayons, picture dictionaries, and personal word walls. Whether it is about their favorite science topic, their grandmother's famous empanadas, or a spinoff of their favorite read-aloud, make the shift in your thinking from what your students can't do to what they can do and you will be amazed (and no longer bored and frustrated with the copy-and-paste *craftivities*). Students soon begin requesting extra writing time, and this will be the part of the day prioritized over all times. There is no way to describe the shared joy developed from students telling their own stories through writing.

SUSTAIN THE SHIFT: WRITING TO CREATE CLASSROOM COMMUNITY

Step 1: Focus Lesson

Ask yourself, what you want your students to accomplish in their writing? Do you notice something in one of your students' writing you want to showcase? Maybe a student learned from their own mistake or the mistake of a peer . . . these are what we call "magical mistakes." Mistakes are celebrated and magical when we learn from them. Those magical mistakes are an amazing springboard. By using student work during the mini-lesson, students have immediate buy-in. Many students in first grade write books at the beginning of the year typically following the pattern "I like_____."
By sharing a student's writing with the class and together brainstorming ways to make their writing more interesting, students cannot wait to go back and revise their work. Utilizing student work as illustrative examples facilitates the creation of targeted mini-lessons to teach specific writing skills.

We all know that if you want students to pick up a certain book or author, read it to them! For some reason, a teacher's endorsement is so powerful to students. The same goes for writing. If there is something you want your students to try, you try it first! Yes, you read that right. YOU try it first! Teacher writing can serve as a model of success. Use your own writing to encourage students to try something new in their writing. Dialogue, quotations, the use of similes, transitional words, and spacing are just a few examples of targeted points of focus. Jacobson's book has possible mini-lessons for the entire school year. Teacher modeling is a great place to start; however, don't discount your own knowledge of your students and their needs when creating focus lessons for students.

How is student writing influenced by published authors? There is so much that we can learn from mentor texts. To make writing more intentional, Clancy, a first-grade teacher, incorporated mentor texts and author studies, illustrating to students that they too could be authentic authors like the ones they had studied. Carefully choose stories and authors providing specific opportunities to inspire students to celebrate how and why authors do what they do. Then, encourage students to celebrate what they learned from the specific author or book in their own writing. One of Clancy's favorite author studies focuses on personal narratives from Patricia Polacco. Students are captivated by how the author shares small moments in her life, telling a powerful story of a special person. Students use these same strategies to write their own personal narratives. Clancy's students have written narratives about buying Tic Tacs with their grandpa, celebrating their mom's birthday at their favorite restaurant, traveling to Mexico with their cousins to see their grandparents, and so many other amazing stories that need to be told.

Choosing mentor texts that reflect the students in your class can also increase engagement. We are fortunate to have a beautifully diverse student population at our school, a group of students who are celebrated through their ideas, their expression through writing, and their stories—shared in their books—a set of treasures waiting to be explored in every classroom. In celebration of our multilingual learners, we wanted to expand our exposure to books including more than one language. After seeing their home languages used by published authors, students were inspired to write books in two languages. One mastery moment was when a first-grade student wrote about her cat, Snowflake. The student wrote the book at home with her mother. The student wrote in English and her mother helped her translate it into Russian. One of the most exciting, *and* most rewarding, forms of engagement occurs when students are excited about carrying their new learning home to their families, like a secret they cannot keep. The literacy space has not only moved from the classroom to home, but it has increased in active participants. In this case, the student's enthusiasm to share her story in two languages fueled an efficacy for writing. These small sparks of enthusiasm cause ripples throughout the classroom and beyond, impacting so many.

Some of our best mini-lessons have come from student inquiry. One fourth-grade student noticed some books had an author's note filled with interesting information to provide additional meaning to the story. This led to a deep dive into an author's note study. Through multiple exemplars and peer collaboration, students began creating their own author's notes to enhance their writing. While author's notes was not an intended mini-lesson, following student inquiry led us beyond the standard-based lesson plans. That was just one of the opportunities presenting itself as a result of a small shift in our approach to writing. Engagement is instantly increased when your students have ownership and take action!

Step 2: Independent Writing

For the first ten minutes of your designated writing time, write with your students. During that time, try to incorporate something in your writing you would like for students to try. This small amount of time has a very big impact on the classroom community because students see you as an active participant in the journey. You are providing a model of what a focused writer looks like.

The actual act of writing is one of the most enjoyable parts of the day for both students and teachers. The class DJ, a much sought-after classroom job, is in charge of the soft instrumental music. Teachers set their timers for ten minutes. For the first ten minutes of our writing time, teachers work on their own piece of writing. During this time, students are not allowed to collaborate with their peers or interrupt the teacher's writing time. There are so many purposes your own writing can have. Most importantly, it is vital for students to see you as a writer and a contributing member of the writing community you are creating. This time also has other benefits, such as making common mistakes with the intention of allowing students to help you work through the problems. Students need to see you also make mistakes, and that the classroom and school are safe places for admitting mistakes. After the ten minutes are over, students are free to collaborate with their peers and move around the room for a more comfortable writing place. Students share their ideas, their writing, and meaningful feedback with one another. While students are collaborating, the teacher uses the time to conference with students. The teacher keeps a conference sign-up sheet for students to request a conference, and she also checks in with students who may be more reluctant to request a conference. It is up to the teacher, the day, and the schedule to determine how long the collaboration time lasts. For us, it is usually about twenty to thirty minutes. Putting routines and procedures in place will foster the independence students need to be successful in their literacy spaces.

You may be wondering what a conference should look like. Conferences are different in each classroom. Start small. In the beginning, you observe and notice. You may ask yourself, "What are your students doing? What mistakes are common? What points of pride are you seeing? What little shifts need to be taught to make the most impact for your students?" As difficult as it may be, try not to focus on conventions. Focus more on their ideas and the telling of a story. Once a student feels their story is complete, together, you staple the book. It is very important for our students to have an authentic audience for their stories. Most of our students use a device to record their voice reading the story and a camera to record the pictures. We call this publishing! After publishing, students can now celebrate their stories by sharing them in multiple ways such as sitting in the Authors' Chair, visiting another classroom . . . the possibilities are endless!

Step 3: Daily Share Time

Share time is one of the most important parts of daily writing instruction. Share time happens at the end of independent writing time. It is the time when you pull students together to share what they have written that day. Collective sharing fosters a sense of community and actively contributes to students' learning by allowing them to share their stories with their peers. During this time, students share with their peers and others what they have produced during independent writing time. During share time, students read their writing knee-to-knee and eye-to-eye with a partner on the carpet. These approaches provide a way for all of the students to have the opportunity to

Figure 8.2. The kindergarten teachers work together to constantly refine the writing continuum to support their students as writers. This is an intentional resource that connects all of the students to each other and their writing. It allows all teachers and students the opportunity to provide meaningful feedback based on the success criteria laid out at each level. Ewing, Melissa Renee. "The Power of Story in Developing Cycles of Efficacy for Teachers and Students." EdD diss., University of South Carolina, 2022.

share their hard work. The teacher notices what students are doing during independent writing time and selects a student to present their work either as an exemplar or to highlight areas for improvement. The students' entire story may be read, or just a specific part that highlights a needed shift for many in the class. It is important to relate the noticings to the writing continuum (figure 8.2)[5] for students to be able to set goals for themselves and for the next time to write. For example, students needed to add more details to their stories, so the teacher worked with one student to add more specific examples to create a detailed picture for the reader. The student had written, "I swing on the swings." We collaborated as a class and discussed what could be added to tell more about the story. Then we added "I like to swing high. My friend pushes me on the swing." During share time, the teacher talks with students about how to add more details to create a better image in the reader's mind. As students share with their peers, they use the writing continuum to identify where they are in their writing and what they need to work on to improve as a writer. Share time is a great way for children to learn from each other. During share time, the class engages in identifying the *glows*—their favorite aspects of the student's work—and the *grows*—areas requiring refinement or requiring revisions. Purposeful feedback is then provided to the student, offering valuable insights. Feedback becomes the basis for setting goals for the next day's independent writing, creating a continuous cycle of improvement. Share time stands out as an effective method for students to gain insights from their peers and enhance their writing skills collaboratively. Based on the new learning during share time, students are excited to go back to their writing and practice what they have learned.

ADVICE FOR GETTING STARTED

1. Embrace the Shift: Prioritize student stories, relinquish control, and focus on fostering a vibrant culture of critical thinking, reading, and writing.

2. Learn from Each Other: Nikki's experience with Jennifer Jacobson's book ignited a transformative moment. Share successes and challenges to inspire colleagues and encourage professional growth.
3. Choice, Voice, and Engagement: Allow students the freedom to choose topics, find their voice, and engage in diverse genres. Celebrate creativity and multilingual perspectives.
4. Start Small, Think Big: Initiate the shift in your classroom by providing simple tools like blank paper, pencils, and crayons. Encourage students to tell their unique stories, breaking away from standardized craftivities.
5. Sustain the Shift: Implement focus lessons, learn from student inquiries, and use mentor texts. Create a writing community extending beyond the classroom, involving families and celebrating diverse languages.
6. Write Together: Spend the initial ten minutes of writing time actively participating with your students. Model a focused writing approach, make common mistakes openly, and foster a sense of community.
7. Conferences and Publishing: Conduct conferences focusing on ideas and storytelling. Provide opportunities for students to publish their work, sharing their stories with authentic audiences using technology.
8. Daily Share Time: Make share time a crucial part of daily writing instruction. Foster a sense of community, allow students to showcase their work, and provide constructive feedback for continuous improvement.

Transforming literacy spaces begins with valuing and amplifying student stories. By embracing a shift in perspective, providing choice and voice, and sustaining this approach through collaborative learning, conferences, and daily sharing, you can create vibrant writing communities. The journey from reluctant writers to passionate storytellers is marked by small shifts enacting profound impacts on students' confidence, engagement, and authentic purpose for writing. As Maya Angelou eloquently stated, "There is no greater agony than bearing an untold story inside you." Let's empower our students to share their stories, celebrate their voices, and transform our classrooms into spaces where every story deserves to be told.

NOTES

1. Lev S. Vygotsky, *Mind in Society: The Development of Higher Psychological Process*, eds. M. Cole, V. John-Steiner, S. Scribner, and E. Souberman (Cambridge, MA: Harvard University Press, 1978).
2. Albert Bandura, *Self-Efficacy: The Exercise of Control* (New York: W. H. Freeman and Company, 1997).
3. Paul Bloomberg and Barb Pitchford, *Leading Impact Teams: Building a Culture of Efficacy* Thousand Oaks, CA: Corwin, 2017).
4. Jennifer Jacobson, *No More "I'm Done!": Fostering Independent Writers in the Primary Grades* (New York: Routledge, 2010).
5. M. R. Ewing, "The Power of Story in Developing a Cycle of Efficacy for Teachers and Students" (EdD diss., University of South Carolina, 2022).

BIBLIOGRAPHY

Angelou, Maya. *I Know Why the Caged Bird Sings*. New York: Ballantine Books, 2009.

Bandura, Albert. *Self-Efficacy: The Exercise of Control*. New York: W. H. Freeman and Company, 1997.

Bloomberg, Paul, and Barb Pitchford. *Leading Impact Teams: Building a Culture of Efficacy*. Thousand Oaks, CA: Corwin, 2017.

Ewing, M. R. "The Power of Story in Developing a Cycle of Efficacy for Teachers and Students." EdD diss., University of South Carolina, 2022

Jacobson, Jennifer. *No More "I'm Done!": Fostering Independent Writers in the Primary Grades*. New York: Routledge, 2010.

Vygotsky, Lev S. *Mind in Society: The Development of Higher Psychological Process*. Edited by M. Cole, V. John-Steiner, S. Scribner, and E. Souberman. Cambridge, MA: Harvard University Press, 1978.

Chapter 9

The Naughty List—Time for a Change

Carolyn Davidson Abel and Tingting Xu

A great truth wants to be criticized, not idolized.

—Nietzsche

THE CONTEXT

Oh no! My favorite teaching method is on the National Council on Teacher Quality (NCTQ) naughty list. What should I do?

As my preferred pedagogy materializes on the NCTQ[1] 'Contrary Content' list, I contemplate what response is appropriate. If you teach reading in the early grades, you are well aware of the "scientifically based reading research" (SBRR) that emphasizes the "Big 5" most important skills children must learn to become good readers.[2] It's not that there are no other necessary skills. Recognizing where a word starts and ends and that reading goes from left to right is critical. Of course, there are many others. But the "Big 5," backed by bushels of research and known to predict future reading success, are clearly key. Understandably, educators focus on phonemic awareness, phonics, fluency, vocabulary word meaning, and comprehension.

Additionally, there is a pedagogical side; we now understand that instruction is most effective when clearly stated and taught, systematic and sequential (step by step), and braced with multiple opportunities to not only access, practice, and apply each skill but also to use it in meaningful and creative ways.[3]

This combination of foundational skills and teaching behaviors is often referred to as the " Science of Teaching Reading" (STR) and is based on mountains of supported peer-reviewed, evidence-based studies accumulated over many years. No longer can you hear of a clever idea at the local coffee shop and come to class to try it out on your own students. Teachers are expected to know the research that substantiates their practice and deliver a sound reading education in an accurate, efficient, effective, structured, and systematic (accountable, no gaps) way.

The NCTQ is an organization dedicated to guiding teacher prep programs to include the research base into their teaching of reading. The 2023 *Teacher Prep Reading Foundations Technical Report*[4] states, "Teacher preparation programs (must) ensure that candidates attain the essential knowledge and skills of scientifically based reading instruction." The core concern is that some of our current teaching practices may not be up to standard; this can interfere with the opportunities of some children, especially strugglers, in learning to read.

The report provides a list of "Contrary Content" with warnings against using popular teaching methods such as Guided Reading, Leveled Texts, limited and non-sequential Phonics, Running Records and Miscue Analysis endorsing the three cueing strategies, Balanced Literacy programs that aren't really balanced, and Reading/Writing Workshop.[5]

THE QUESTION

Do we toss out current teaching strategies and automatically adopt something new, starting from scratch again? We think not.

This chapter is about retaining existing popular methods of teaching that appear to have merit while simultaneously considering new information requiring us to make serious adjustments in our thinking and behaviors based on science, now that we know more (figure 9.1).

Let's take a look at a few of the teaching practices on NCTQ's Naughty List and learn some quick adjustments we might make for improvement without *throwing out the baby with the bathwater.*

Figure 9.1. Classroom reading. SFA Charter School.

READING RECOVERY: RUNNING RECORDS, THREE-CUEING SYSTEM, AND MISCUE ANALYSIS

What Is It?

Reading Recovery (RR) endorses the three-cueing system and miscue analysis. RR is an incredibly popular program in most Title 1 low socioeconomic status (SES) schools; its delivery is expensive and comes complete with certified educated master-level teachers who deliver one-on-one instruction to the lowest 20 percent of students in first grade. It was noted quite a few years ago that when students fell behind, something had to be done. Marie Clay saved the day with her Reading Recovery program, which helped these students become independent readers and catch up with their peers. It was a serious but *quick fix* that seemed to work and it provided a good start at the time.

The RR approach utilizes running records (an assessment of reading progress; see figure 9.2) which analyze the child's use of semantic, syntactic, and graphophonic cues to support early reading.[6] It is also known as a method to encourage children to identify a word using a structure/meaning/visual (SMV) system.[7] Although this

Figure 9.2. Taking running records. SFA Charter School.

approach is commonly used among teachers even today, it was found to hinder the development of word recognition skills.[8] Another study found that this approach may not be helpful for word recognition or word prediction, even among fluent readers.[9] This is because it encourages children to "guess" the words, rather than to painstakingly go left to right and "sound out" each word. Yet over time this latter method, based on the new science, is proving to work far better than memorizing whole words and chunks.[10] Emily Hanford explains the important difference in her well-known podcast.[11]

The problem is that if beginning readers are encouraged to guess the words by resorting to semantics, context, and picture clues, they may come to rely on memorizing words, and by second grade, habits die hard; while students will have acquired an impressive sight word vocabulary, it also appears they will begin to max out on memory space to hold all of these words. When presented with a nonsense (novel) word, this problem is telling—they are not easily able to identify it, whereas those who have been tediously "sounding out" decodable words have been improving this skill over the years and by now are more "automatic" when presented with most any word. This allows them to see a new word and decode it almost instantaneously (quick word recognition). While many of these words become recognized by sight, students are no longer dependent upon guessing words based on the three cues to identify it. Quick automatic word recognition fluency is a critical key component (of the Big 5) in learning to read.[12]

Small Changes Can Make a Big Difference

This can actually be an easy fix with a small adjustment. The problem seems to lie in giving equal attention to all three-cueing systems when in fact our newest research supports early emphasis on visual cues when children actually begin reading the print on the page. Directing young children to "guess" at unknown words based on pictures and context can sometimes give them the wrong impression about what reading actually is. For some children, this can become a negative habit that is hard to break. We know young children emulate those around them—teachers should be modeling and "guiding" students to "sound out" words as their primary word attack approach and they should be providing decodable text to read that will give these students multiple opportunities to practice decoding words to become fluent and automatic with their word identification. Semantics and context clues appear more helpful as readers grow older and better at reading complex material, so we are not tossing out the three cueing strategies—just postponing and repositioning the use of all three.

The book offered to the student also matters. The popular patterned, predictable leveled books prevalent in *Marie Clay's Reading Recovery* program are fine for getting our youngest children started on how to hold a book, that reading goes left to right, that there are words and spaces in between—print concepts all of us learn early. But when ready to take the helm—to actually read the text—books that are manageable and decodable and encourage students to "sound out" words can be most helpful. Again, it is an easy adjustment to emphasize the alphabetic principle and basic phonics patterns early when children learn to read, and to save the other cueing strategies that all good readers use until later, once they have mastered using graphophonics as their primary strategy for decoding (and encoding) words.

BALANCED LITERACY MODELS

What Is It?

NCTQ[13] warns that Balanced Literacy (BL) is often framed as a compromise between the "whole-language" and "phonics" approaches to reading instruction, suggesting that each approach has similar value and utility. The approach was later recognized as not systematic or adequate for teaching core elements of reading such as phonemic awareness or phonics.[14] Two popular curricula using balanced literacy were criticized for lacking research-based reading practices—Units of Study from the Teachers College Reading & Writing Projects, and Fountas and Pinnell Classroom. Both did not provide adequate time for the key skills of phonemic awareness and phonics.[15] The Units of Study from the Teachers College Reading & Writing Projects was also found to be problematic in promoting the three-cueing strategies.[16] Moat's popular "Fig Leaf" article best describes the objection.[17] People were calling their programs "balanced," yet they truly leaned significantly to one extreme or the other; while masking their programs with the word "balanced," most were not sincerely balanced.

Small Changes Require Moderation and Thoughtful Synthesis

Balance is key in all that we do, but we can't just use that term to imply we are doing a little of this and that. It must be more intentional and certainly informed. Learning something new is never easy. Change is slow for good reason—we learn something new, integrate it into what we understand, and allow it to marinate into a more informed rich stew, then cautiously move forward with eyes wide open. Little by little, changes are made that truly make a difference, and according to Dewey, this works both ways as extreme views on either side can benefit from a little temperance and thoughtful consideration during continued collegial dialogue from all angles.[18] Fueling the fire with polemic comment only exacerbates the problem, reducing teacher buy-in and ultimately student benefit and learning. How do we move forward when adjusting to the new?

Emphasis must be placed on critical thinking about the decisions made and the criticisms of others that may have some validity. Reading pioneer Dr. Snow states that "the problem is not to achieve a consensus about what works, but rather to ensure that consensus is implemented in such a way that the integration of attention to the different skills required is maintained."[19] That required part stems from the evidence-based information we are learning each day as the research continues to inform us. Let's take a closer look at this one.

One argument often heard refers to the missing explicit systematic sequential delivery of critical foundational skills. It seems a relatively easy adjustment to recognize the importance of intentional and sustained STR teaching methods to best ensure that students grasp important reading (and writing) skills. The workshop framework then easily provides ample time for engagement alone and with others to enjoy practicing what has been newly (and accountably) well taught. It also frees up the teacher to individualize instruction during conferencing.

It is clear students enjoy the freedom to move about the classroom making independent choices of personal relevance, and it encourages self-reliance and offers exciting exploration. But perhaps we can do better when integrating what the research suggests into our current classroom workshop. Distinguished Professor Emeritus Timothy Shanahan comments on reading during workshop time:

> Social interactions about texts tend to sharpen our game: having someone to talk to about a book improves comprehension . . . (yet) the more that the "independent reading" practices are like effective reading instruction, the more powerful they are likely to be. . . . One reason these practices tend not to transfer beyond the classroom is because the student is not trying to find ways to fit reading into their lives.[20]

Teachers can do more beyond teaching students to read with success; they can inspire students to enjoy meaningful, personally relevant texts daily in their own lives. Thoughtful informed adjustments can make a real difference.

GUIDED READING AND READING/WRITING WORKSHOP

What Is It?

According to NCTQ, Guided Reading (GR) is small-group reading instruction using leveled books—an approach to teaching reading made popular by Fountas and Pinnell:

> Students are matched with leveled text of appropriate difficulty and progress into increasingly challenging text. GR teachers teach and prompt students to use (the three cueing systems) . . . word study is embedded in text reading and does not follow a predetermined scope and sequence . . . [it is] part of a primary-grade balanced reading program (which includes Read Alouds, text reading and writing, plus mini-lessons to teach how letters and words work).[21]

According to Denton and colleagues, GR stems from a whole-language philosophy said to be found less effective compared to explicit instruction in terms of students' gain in reading skills, especially the phonological decoding and comprehension.[22] Daily Reading Workshop (RW) provides an opportunity for students to "make your own adventure" during a time designated for deepening reading skills while encouraging young readers to use the cueing systems, often without direct supervision. The NCTQ report notes that while some foundational skills are taught, materials do not sufficiently emphasize explicit systematic teaching and practice of specific skills to support reading and writing success.[23]

Small Changes Can Be Easy to Make

It is still hard to fathom why Guided Reading or Reading/Writing Workshop should be put out to pasture now that "science" has informed us of potential problems associated with the original use of these terms in light of Kilpatrick's orthographic mapping.[24] Again, this can be a small adjustment. We do not need to pitch all of these "well-intended" ideas and start over. If teachers can find a way to be intentional with the Science of Teaching Reading during GR, then RW can provide the time for students to make personal connections for the review of skills taught well.

According to a recent study of 80,000 students, it appears there are three important needs expressed for all students of all ages—success, belonging, and choice.[25] Reading Workshop can offer all three in an accountable, supportive space that effectively monitors student progress. Once systematically taught and supported during GR, where success is virtually guaranteed, students are given choice in selecting activities and books within a nurturing, supportive community. As they grow older and become more competent readers, Shanahan's recommendations can be increasingly helpful.

Unless you reduce class sizes to the size of a family, teachers cannot be with each and every child every minute of every day. Pragmatically speaking, students will need to spend some of their time in class working independently and cooperatively with others. During workshop, fluency development occurs best when students are challenged to read and write using their new (well-taught) skills in activities designed to be a bit more alluring and personalized to student interests and needs. Perhaps the older Reading/Writing workshop model may have pushed kids to practice skills poorly taught, but with the science backing today's explicit direct instruction model that is more sequential and practiced, this problem should be reduced during an adjusted modified workshop time. For additional fluency skill development, teachers can send home activities that parents and guardians can enjoy with their children—activities involving honed skills that blossom further with practice and application that can be done at home during a rich family bonding time. Homework can become the positive experience it should be.

EMBEDDED/IMPLICIT PHONICS

What Is It?

Embedded phonics instruction is usually linked to children's literature or texts that students are engaged with for the purpose of developing meaning.[26] Implicit phonics instruction means to teach sound and spelling with whole words or introduce sound and spelling when students come across the words in texts.[27] Many studies have found that student learning is enhanced from the systematic overembedded phonics instruction[28] and that reading skills are improved from explicit phonics instruction over both embedded and implicit phonics instruction.[29] NCTQ notes the power of explicit systematic sequential phonics instruction and cites numerous studies finding systematic phonics instruction to be more effective in supporting reading and writing skills, overembedded or implicit.[30] In particular, teaching the alphabetic principle and basic phonics patterns in a direct explicit engaging manner seems most effective.

Small Changes Are Manageable and Improve over Time

Yes, it appears early phonics instruction is best delivered in an explicit systematic sequential manner with multiple opportunities to learn, use, and practice applying the alphabetic principle and basic phonics through many reading and writing opportunities.[31] Beck and Beck do the work for you; they offer a list of engaging sequential word building activities to help teach basic phonics to students,[32] but once mastered, there seems no reason why multiple opportunities for review that are more incidental leading to Anita Archer's spaced practice[33] can't be the next best step for helping this learning stick. Again, small changes can make big differences.

FINAL THOUGHTS

Updates and changes happen often in the field of education; teachers will have a favorite teaching strategy and then someone will come along to refute it. These constant changes can be dizzying. Some classroom teachers have been told to simply *close their classroom doors and teach the way they know best*. But what if our best intentions are not best for students?

This chapter has been about teaching strategies long thought to be of the highest standard, now threatened and even called dangerous. Yet teachers can be reluctant to discard what seems to be working—something they have used for years, seemingly with success. Teacher ownership and buy-in play a key role;[34] it may help to salvage parts that can be transformed and modified as teachers work to stay abreast of the changing research in their field. While reflecting on what they are learning and experiencing in their own classrooms, teachers can also find it beneficial to listen to what their colleagues are sharing and to consider new ideas when supported by evidence. Confronted with new information that has potential to improve learning, teachers can begin to appreciate that a few simple changes may easily result in substantial improvement in their teaching. Classroom teachers do not have to pitch their favorite teaching methods, but teachers DO have to critically analyze the new science as it surfaces, and to accommodate it into their teaching with the ultimate goal of demonstrating substantive effectiveness for all students.

NOTES

1. National Council on Teacher Quality (NCTQ), *Teacher Prep Review Reading Foundations Technical Report* (Washington, DC: NCTQ, 2023), 65.

2. National Center on Improving Literacy, *The 5 Big Ideas of Beginning Reading* (Washington, DC: US Department of Education, Office of Elementary and Secondary Education, Office of Special Education Programs, National Center on Improving Literacy, 2023), https://www.improvingliteracy.org.

3. Texas Education Agency, Texas Educator Certification Examination Program, *Science of Teaching Reading Preparation Manual* (Austin, TX: TEA, 2022).

4. NCTQ, *Teacher Prep Review Reading Foundations*, 3.

5. Ibid., 65–68, 70–74.

6. Yaacov Petscher, Sonia Q. Cabell, Hugh W. Catts, Donald L. Compton, Barbara R. Foreman, Sara A. Hart, Christopher J. Lonigan, et al., "How the Science of Reading Informs 21st-Century Education," *Reading Research Quarterly* 55 (2020): S267–S282.

7. Kerry Hempenstall, "What Does Evidence-Based Practice in Education Mean?" *Australian Journal of Learning Disabilities* 11, no 2 (2006), 83–92.

8. Hempenstall, "What Does Evidence-Based Practice in Education Mean?"; Petscher et al., "How the Science of Reading Informs 21st-Century Education."

9. Keith E. Stanovich, "Matthew Effects in Reading: Some Consequences of Individual Differences in the Acquisition of Literacy," *Reading Research Quarterly* 21, no. 4 (1998): 360–407.

10. David A. Kilpatrick, *Essentials of Assessing, Preventing, and Overcoming Reading Difficulties* (New York: John Wiley & Sons, 2015).

11. Liana Loewus, "What Teachers Should Know about the Science of Reading." *Education Week*, March 12, 2019, https://www.edweek.org/teaching-learning/what-teachers-should-know-about-the-science-of-reading-video-and-transcript/2019/03.

12. Linda Farrell, Michael Hunter, Marcia Davidson, and Tina Osenga, "The Simple View of Reading," Reading Rockets, n.d. https://www.readingrockets.org/topics/about-reading/articles/simple-view-reading (accessed January 6, 2024).

13. NCTQ, *Teacher Prep Review Reading Foundations*, 68.

14. Gary E. Bingham and Kendra M. Hall-Kenyon, "Examining Teachers' Beliefs about and Implementation of a Balanced Literacy Framework," *Journal of Research in Reading* 36, no. 1 (2013): 14–28.

15. Marilyn Jager Adams, Lily Wong Fillmore, Claude Goldenberg, Jane Oakhill, David D. Paige, Timothy Rasinski, and Timothy Shanahan, *Comparing Reading Research to Program Design: An Examination of Teachers College Units of Study* (New York: Student Achievement Partners, 2020); Sarah Schwartz, "New Curriculum Review Gives Failing Marks to Two Popular Reading Programs," *Education Week*, November 2011, https://www.edweek.org/teaching-learning/new-curriculum-review-gives-failing-marks-to-popular-early-reading-programs/2021/11.

16. Adams et al., *Comparing Reading Research to Program Design.*

17. Louisa Moats, *Whole-Language High Jinks: How to Tell When "Scientifically-Based Reading Instruction" Isn't*, Reading League, September 2018, https://www.thereadingleague.org/wp-content/uploads/2018/09/Whole-Language-High-Jinks-Moats.pdf.

18. John Dewey, *Democracy and Education: An Introduction to the Philosophy of Education* (New York: MacMillan, 1916).

19. Jill Anderson, "To Weather the 'Literacy Crisis,' Do What Works," Harvard Graduate School of Education Edcast, March 24, 2023, https://www.gse.harvard.edu/ideas/edcast/23/03/weather-literacy-crisis-do-what-works, 10:45.

20. Timothy Shanahan, "How Effective is Independent Reading in Teaching Reading?" *Shanahan on Literacy* (blog), March 25, 2018, https://www.shanahanonliteracy.com/blog/how-effective-is-independent-reading-in-teaching-reading.

21. Irene C. Fountas and Gay Su Pinnell, "Guided Reading: The Romance and the Reality," *Reading Teacher* 66, no. 4 (2012): 70.

22. Carolyn A. Denton, Jack M. Fletcher, W. Pat Taylor, Amy E. Barth, and Sharon Vaughn, "An Experimental Evaluation of Guided Reading And Explicit Interventions for Primary-Grade Students At-Risk for Reading Difficulties," *Journal of Research on Educational Effectiveness* 7, no. 3 (2014): 268–93.

23. NCTQ, *Teacher Prep Review Reading Foundations*, 71.

24. Kilpatrick, *Essentials of Assessing, Preventing, and Overcoming Reading Difficulties.*

25. Jill Barshay, "PROOF POINTS: What Almost 150 Studies Say About How to Motivate Students," *Hechinger Report*, September 27, 2021, https://hechingerreport.org/proof-points-what-almost-150-studies-say-about-how-to-motivate-students/.

26. Theresa A. Roberts and Anne Meiring, "Teaching Phonics in the Context of Children's Literature or Spelling: Influences on First-Grade Reading, Spelling, and Writing and Fifth-Grade Comprehension," *Journal of Educational Psychology* 98, no. 4 (2006): 690–713, https://eric.ed.gov/?id=EJ746474.

27. Read Naturally, "Phonics," July 2022, https://www.readnaturally.com/research/5-components-of-reading/phonics.

28. Yola Center, Louella Freeman, and Gregory Robertson, "The Relative Effect of a Code-Oriented and a Meaning-Oriented Early Literacy Program on Regular and Low Progress Australian Students in Year 1 Classrooms which Implement Reading Recovery," *International Journal of Disability, Development and Education* 48, no. 2 (2001): 207–32; Christensen, Carol A., and Judith A. Bowey, "The Efficacy of Orthographic Rime, Grapheme-Phoneme Correspondence, and Implicit Phonics Approaches to Teaching Decoding Skills," *Scientific Studies of Reading* 9, no. 4 (2005): 327–49.

29. Barbara R. Foreman, David J. Francis, Jack M. Fletcher, Christopher Schatschneider, and Paras Mehta, "The Role of Instruction in Learning to Read: Preventing Reading Failure in At-Risk Children," *Journal of Educational Psychology* 90, no. 1 (1998): 37, https://psycnet.apa.org/record/1998-00166-004

30. NCTQ, *Teacher Prep Review Reading Foundations*, 73.

31. Ibid.

32. Beck, Isabel L., and Mark E. Beck, *Making Sense of Phonics: The Hows and Whys* (New York: Guilford Publications, 2013).

33. Anita Archer and Charles Hughes, *Explicit Instruction: Effective and Efficient Teaching*.

34. T. Xu, Hasbun, T., and C. Abel, "Why Teach? Challenges, Rewards, and Future Considerations for the Profession," *TxEP: Texas Educator Preparation* 7, no. 1 (2023): 35–45.

BIBLIOGRAPHY

Adams, Marilyn Jager, Lily Wong Fillmore, Claude Goldenberg, Jane Oakhill, David D. Paige, Timothy Rasinski, and Timothy Shanahan. *Comparing Reading Research to Program Design: An Examination of Teachers College Units of Study*. New York: Student Achievement Partners, 2020.

Anderson, Jill. "To Weather the 'Literacy Crisis,' Do What Works." Harvard Graduate School of Education Edcast, March 24, 2023. https://www.gse.harvard.edu/ideas/edcast/23/03/weather-literacy-crisis-do-what-works.

Archer, Anita L., and Charles A. Hughes. *Explicit Instruction: Effective and Efficient Teaching*. Guilford Publications, 2010.

Barshay, Jill. "PROOF POINTS: What Almost 150 Studies Say About How to Motivate Students." *Hechinger Report*, September 27, 2021. https://hechingerreport.org/proof-points-what-almost-150-studies-say-about-how-to-motivate-students/.

Beck, Isabel L., and Mark E. Beck. *Making Sense of Phonics: The Hows and Whys*. New York: Guilford Publications, 2013.

Bingham, Gary E., and Kendra M. Hall-Kenyon. "Examining Teachers' Beliefs about and Implementation of a Balanced Literacy Framework." *Journal of Research in Reading* 36, no. 1 (2013): 14–28. https://doi.org/10.1111/j.1467-9817.2010.01483.x.

Center, Yola, Louella Freeman, and Gregory Robertson. "The Relative Effect of a Code-Oriented and a Meaning-Oriented Early Literacy Program on Regular and Low Progress Australian Students in Year 1 Classrooms which Implement Reading Recovery." *International Journal of Disability, Development and Education* 48, no. 2 (2001): 207–32. https://doi.org/10.1080/10349120120053676.

Christensen, Carol A., and Judith A. Bowey. "The Efficacy of Orthographic Rime, Grapheme-Phoneme Correspondence, and Implicit Phonics Approaches to Teaching Decoding Skills." *Scientific Studies of Reading* 9, no. 4 (2005): 327–49. https://doi.org/10.1207/s1532799xssr0904_1.

Denton, Carolyn A., Jack M. Fletcher, W. Pat Taylor, Amy E. Barth, and Sharon Vaughn. "An Experimental Evaluation of Guided Reading and Explicit Interventions for Primary-Grade Students At-Risk for Reading Difficulties." *Journal of Research on Educational Effectiveness* 7, no. 3 (2014): 268–93. https://doi.org/10.1080/19345747.2014.906010.

Dewey, John. *Democracy and Education: An Introduction to the Philosophy of Education.* New York: MacMillan, 1916.

Farrell, Linda, Michael Hunter, Marcia Davidson, and Tina Osenga. "The Simple View of Reading." Reading Rockets, n.d. https://www.readingrockets.org/topics/about-reading/articles/simple-view-reading. Accessed January 6, 2024.

Foreman, Barbara R., David J. Francis, Jack M. Fletcher, Christopher Schatschneider, and Paras Mehta. "The Role of Instruction in Learning to Read: Preventing Reading Failure in At-Risk Children." *Journal of educational Psychology* 90, no. 1(1998): 37. https://psycnet.apa.org/record/1998-00166-004.

Fountas, Irene C., and Gay Su Pinnell. "Guided Reading: The Romance and the Reality." *Reading Teacher* 66, no. 4 (2012): 268–84. https://doi.org/10.1002/TRTR.01123.

Hempenstall, Kerry. "What Does Evidence-Based Practice in Education Mean?" *Australian Journal of Learning Disabilities* 11, no. 2 (2006): 83–92. https://doi.org/10.1080/19404150609546811.

Kilpatrick, David A. *Essentials of Assessing, Preventing, and Overcoming Reading Difficulties.* New York: John Wiley & Sons, 2015.

Loewus, Liana. "What Teachers Should Know About the Science of Reading." *Education Week*, March 12, 2019. https://www.edweek.org/teaching-learning/what-teachers-should-know-about-the-science-of-reading-video-and-transcript/2019/03.

Moats, Louisa. *Whole-Language High Jinks: How to Tell When "Scientifically-Based Reading Instruction" Isn't.* September 2018. https://www.thereadingleague.org/wp-content/uploads/2018/09/Whole-Language-High-Jinks-Moats.pdf.

National Center on Improving Literacy. *The 5 Big Ideas of Beginning Reading.* Washington, DC: US Department of Education, Office of Elementary and Secondary Education, Office of Special Education Programs, National Center on Improving Literacy, 2023. https://www.improvingliteracy.org.

National Council on Teacher Quality (NCTQ). *Teacher Prep Review Reading Foundations Technical Report.* Washington, DC: NCTQ, 2023. https://www.nctq.org/dmsView/Teacher_Prep_Review_Reading_Foundations_Technical_Report.

Petscher, Yaacov, Sonia Q. Cabell, Hugh W. Catts, Donald L. Compton, Barbara R. Foreman, Sara A. Hart, Christopher J. Lonigan, et al. "How the Science of Reading Informs 21st-Century Education." *Reading Research Quarterly* 55 (2020): S267–S282. https://doi.org/10.1002/rrq.352.

Read Naturally. "Phonics." July 2022. https://www.readnaturally.com/research/5-components-of-reading/phonics.

Roberts, Theresa A., and Anne Meiring. "Teaching Phonics in the Context of Children's Literature or Spelling: Influences on First-Grade Reading, Spelling, and Writing and Fifth-Grade

Comprehension." *Journal of Educational Psychology* 98, no. 4 (2006): 690–713. https://eric.ed.gov/?id=EJ746474.

Schwartz, Sarah. "New Curriculum Review Gives Failing Marks to Two Popular Reading Programs." *Education Week*, November 9, 2021. https://www.edweek.org/teaching-learning/new-curriculum-review-gives-failing-marks-to-popular-early-reading-programs/2021/11.

Shanahan, Timothy. "How Effective is Independent Reading in Teaching Reading?" *Shanahan on Literacy* (blog), March 25, 2018. https://www.shanahanonliteracy.com/blog/how-effective-is-independent-reading-in-teaching-reading.

Stanovich, Keith E. "Matthew Effects in Reading: Some Consequences of Individual Differences in the Acquisition of Literacy." *Reading Research Quarterly* 21, no. 4 (1998): 360–407. http://www.jstor.org/stable/747612.

Texas Education Agency, Texas Educator Certification Examination Program. *Science of Teaching Reading Preparation Manual*. Austin, TX: TEA, 2022. https://www.tx.nesinc.com/content/docs/TX293_SciOfTeachingReading_PrepManual.pdf.

Xu, T., T. Hasbun, and C. Abel. "Why Teach? Challenges, Rewards, and Future Considerations for the Profession." *TxEP: Texas Educator Preparation* 7, no. 1 (2023): 35–45. https://doi.org/10.59719/txep.v7i1.6.

Chapter 10

Nurturing the Writer Within

Melissa Ewing, Courtney Kozelski, and Elizabeth Crocker

One of the benefits of ongoing professional study is the opportunity to meet others who sharpen your skills and share your teaching concerns. Thus, the three of us met in a doctoral cohort at the University of South Carolina; we were placed with a wonderful dissertation chair, Dr. Todd Lilly, who helped us to recognize that each of us was conducting research on motivating writing by developing self-efficacy. We were fortunate to collaborate and discover that while we worked with three distinct populations, there were common threads at the heart of our problems of practice. We maintained a deliberate focus on the sources of self-efficacy, drawing from Bandura's social cognitive theory. This is based on the premise that human beings desire control over behavioral, personal, and environmental factors, and the resulting sense of agency leads to self-efficacy.[1] Additionally, we integrated the motivational aspects derived from Ryan and Deci's self-determination theory, including the human need for autonomy, competence, and relatedness.[2] Our intentionality for writing instruction sustained an ongoing cycle of efficacy and motivation, contributing to a dynamic and enriching environment for both teachers and students, particularly in the context of writing.

Melissa Ewing, a literacy coach, was focused on developing teacher self-efficacy for writing instruction in an elementary setting. Courtney Kozelski, a teacher for middle grades students with disabilities, was concerned with customizing literacy instruction to motivate her students, while Elizabeth Crocker, a classroom teacher, was striving to find ways to use social-emotional learning (SEL) strategies to motivate writing among her advanced middle school students in a gifted and talented program. Under the direction of Clinical Assistant Professor Todd Lilly at the University of South Carolina, each of us conducted action research to learn what we could about supporting our developing writers. We discovered that when learners had choice and both social-emotional and instructional support for developing their competency as writers, they became more confident and engaged in meeting their writing goals. In the sections that follow, we'll each share our instructional context and the small changes that made a difference for students.

Melissa: As a literacy coach in a Title I school, I embarked on a collaborative journey with teachers to revitalize our literacy spaces. Our focus was on integrating elements of choice and dedicating time for personal storytelling. The infectious joy that emanated from both students and teachers as they shared their stories marked the beginning of a transformative process. The process of incorporating writing workshops led to multiple positive outcomes. It established classroom communities through the school, fostering a sense of belonging for students in the learning. Additionally, it sparked a genuine enthusiasm for writing, with students discovering authentic joy in the act of putting pen to paper. Inspired by the insights from the book *No More "I'm Done!": Fostering Independent Writers in the Primary Grades*,[3] one kindergarten teacher wasted no time in implementing dedicated writing time the day after she read the book. The impact was immediate, triggering lively conversations among teachers. This shift in perspective prompted teachers to reevaluate their beliefs and see students as more capable writers. They embarked on a journey of collaborative inquiry to refine the art of teaching writing. The ripple effect of this initiative extended beyond individual classrooms, creating a school-wide culture where the power of storytelling became a catalyst for meaningful engagement and learning.

Our approach centered on weaving motivation and efficacy throughout every facet of our storytelling process. Student efficacy plays a pivotal role in enhancing teacher efficacy, creating a symbiotic relationship that keeps the cycle continuously evolving.[4]

Courtney: I teach special education for students with disabilities at a Title I charter middle and high school focused on music. I provide those services in what is sometimes referred to as a resource setting outside of the general education classroom. Additionally, I collaborate in co-taught inclusion services within the general education classroom. The students with whom I worked during this intervention were diagnosed with specific learning disabilities and autism.

I noticed my students' loss of enthusiasm when I reached for the workbooks or scripted curricular programs. Not only that, the strategies they studiously recited and copied in those workbooks didn't seem to transfer to authentic texts, and they continued to struggle to retain information and show understanding when they read. I decided it was time to set aside our textbooks and do a student-selected novel study.

Elizabeth: Although my students were identified as academically gifted seventh graders, I noticed that their enthusiasm for writing had suffered following the pandemic. Despite their advanced reading levels and general motivation for learning, they did not engage in writing tasks with the same energy, particularly the text-dependent writing required for literary analysis in the middle grades. Simultaneously, social-emotional learning (SEL) was gaining new traction, so I wondered how I might apply SEL strategies to my writing instruction.[5] I learned that many of the more traditional writing strategies, including using graphic organizers, were in fact means of SEL and self-regulation for learning, as was goal setting.[6] However, my students taught me that what really mattered most to them was collaboration with the use of the SEL tools.

SMALL CHANGE 1: MAKE TIME TO WRITE

Each of us recognized the need to be intentional in carving out time for writing, which can be challenging because it is a time-consuming process. Although we approached this change within different contexts and different types of writing, each of us maximized instructional time for writing.

Melissa: A powerful shift occurred as teachers in our school made a deliberate choice to prioritize opportunities for students to engage in writing. The impact was profound—students not only embraced writing, but begged for more time to write. The key takeaway is the significance of taking the plunge and establishing a dedicated daily writing routine.

Prior to these transformative shifts, many teachers routinely abandoned their writing time at the slightest disruption to their schedules. The shift involved implementing a daily cycle comprising a focused lesson, dedicated time for writing, and a time to share lasting forty-five minutes to an hour. During the literacy block, students received intentional instruction designed to foster their independence and enhance their skills during the dedicated writing period. Teachers provided paper, pencils, crayons, scissors, glue, word charts, technology, and anchor charts to support student storytelling.

This approach not only elevated the importance of writing in the curriculum but also created an environment where students eagerly anticipated and valued their time to express themselves through writing. Teachers learned so much about their students through their writing. Students knew more about each other. This shift bound them together as a community of writers and thinkers. The success of this model lies in its simplicity—by consistently carving out time for writing, educators witnessed a substantial improvement in students' writing abilities and a heightened enthusiasm for the writing process.

Courtney: My students were, for the most part, reluctant to engage in writing. Traditionally, writing time for them had been focused on creating essays that adhered to specific formats, and navigating through the entire writing process was time-consuming. All that in mind, I needed to lay a solid groundwork for the challenging tasks that were to follow by folding the students into the instructional planning process for the novel study. I gathered four different novels based upon the students' learner profiles, which included their interests, reading levels, and cultural backgrounds. The students previewed each novel and cast their votes to determine which one would be selected for the study. In obtaining student voice and giving them a choice in the planning phase, I intended to increase their sense of ownership in the learning process, thereby enabling us to push the boundaries of their writing abilities.

Annotating text required my students to articulate their comprehension of the reading material in a written format. There were varying levels of enjoyment in writing in the group, but the annotation proved to be a valuable strategy for my students with disabilities because it allowed them to write at their own comfort levels. The flexibility of annotating increased the amount of time we spent writing because it was embedded into our daily reading. The approachability of annotating eliminated the need for me to push for engagement or search for additional writing time. They began doodling symbols in the margins to indicate a mood they felt when reading, writing down questions, or jotting a quick summary of a paragraph by its side.

Annotations themselves are a means of scaffolding, deconstructing complex texts into more manageable pieces. Throughout the intervention, I followed a gradual release of responsibility framework[7] with embedded assessment of student understanding. I was swimming in student annotations in no time! This made it easy to informally and discreetly assess student needs. Notably, this informal assessment approach played a pivotal role in mitigating test anxiety, as students remained unaware of the frequency with which their understanding was informally appraised.

Elizabeth: Just as Courtney scaffolded writing about text through annotation, literature circles[8] turned out to be a powerful tool for developing critical thinking about texts in my classroom. This allowed my students to build on relative strengths, such as talking with peers and an overall enjoyment of reading. I strongly recommend fostering student conversations about text among students of all reading levels before writing about the text. This was a game changer for my students in promoting writing fluency and positive feelings about writing, and it makes sense in terms of the developmental needs of my adolescent learners for peer interaction. Surveys, book passes, and interest inventories can all be used to help find small groups of students who would enjoy reading common titles for a short period of time. The amount of structure needed for productive conversations, including group roles and expectations, will vary according to the needs of the learner and the desired outcomes, but the premise remains true: Students respond well to choice and the opportunity to process what they read with their peers.

Similarly, making time for writing conferences allowed my students to analyze the strengths and opportunities for growth in their writing, as well as to set goals for their writing. I found that small-group writing conferences, using our literature circle groups, were helpful in making this process less intimidating. The writing conference experience built a sense of safety and relationship into the writing process. Before we met, each student prepared a text-dependent writing paragraph about what they had discussed in their literature circle. Typically, they had completed a graphic organizer with the group. As each student read the paragraph they had written aloud, the others offered feedback, noting what stood out about the writing and what questions or connections were inspired by it. This allowed writers to identify key points and strengths in their writing, and it also illuminated any need for clarity, improved word choice, and organization. When this process was completed, the students set a goal for their next writing conference.[9] Because students were sometimes too critical of their own work, I was intentional about noticing strengths and skills I wanted to encourage. As with choosing their own books, setting their own goals was an important tool for empowering the students to take ownership of their writing and view themselves as writers.[10]

Tips to Get Started

As you move forward with making time for writing in your classroom, we offer these suggestions from our experiences.

- Make the task manageable. For example, begin with regular stopping points for annotations that are appropriate for the group or reader. Similarly, start by writing text-dependent analysis paragraphs before moving to extended essays.
- To provide opportunities to gradually release responsibility to students, encourage them to share as they complete their writing. For example, they might share

annotations with the group after reading portions of text together. This gives you the opportunity to provide immediate feedback. Likewise, students may enjoy sharing focused aspects of their writing, such as their topic sentence, transition words, and text evidence.
- Encourage students to write short notes rather than sentences when prewriting, annotating, and note-taking. Shortening the number of words, and thus choosing them wisely, is an excellent writing skill.

SMALL CHANGE 2: MAKE TIME TO NOTICE

We grew in our conviction that providing models for students to notice the writer's craft was essential to students' self-efficacy as readers and writers. We asked ourselves what students could learn from others, as well as what the students were teaching us about themselves as writers.

Melissa: In our school, noticing was practiced when students noticed author style and then emulated it in their own writing; teachers also noticed students' strengths. We discovered the magic of guiding students to notice and analyze the decisions made by published authors in their writing. Author studies emerged as a powerful tool, resonating across all grade levels. Students and teachers observed how and why authors made decisions in their craft. Mentor texts were carefully chosen based on what teachers wanted their students to notice and what action students might take based on the story.

Kindergarteners devoured Mo Willems's books and then infused his style into their writing. Motion lines, speech bubbles, and imaginative stories featuring Willems's characters became the hallmark of their writing. Teachers played a crucial role in this process, taking a moment to notice students' writing strengths and identifying the steps needed to propel their writing. These observations became valuable nuggets of insight, shared on the carpet after the dedicated writing time.

But it didn't end there—students, inspired by mentor texts, became peer mentors themselves. Armed with newfound knowledge about writing gleaned from their favorite authors, they provided thoughtful feedback to their peers. This interactive cycle not only enriched the writing experience but also fostered a supportive writing community. One student was inspired by author Yuyi Morales to include both Spanish and English in her writing. Inspiration from published authors sparked a cascade of creativity and motivation!

Courtney: While Melissa's teachers and students noticed intricacies of the author's craft and written works, I began to notice the quality of annotations produced by my students. Annotations were a strategy that helped my students learn to think and write about texts. All of the students' annotations I had gathered and observed from my students allowed me to make adjustments to how my students made additional annotations. I paid careful attention to students' level of independence when creating an annotation and the quality and quantity of their annotations. Some of the questions that ran through my mind when analyzing their work include:

- Is the student relying on another person to help them know when to pause and make a note?
- Is the student rephrasing the text, including the main idea?
- Is the student noticing how characters' behaviors and values impacted one another and changed over time?

I noticed some students were ready for more challenges, while some needed more guidance. Some of my students were annotating quite independently, identifying and rephrasing main ideas. Partnering them led to the generation of higher quality annotations, the creation of logical inferences and predictions, and the opening up of discussions on themes. On the contrary, another student had significant difficulty with comprehension, and experienced heightened anxiety with tasks that required generating information. The student's sense of self-efficacy with these tasks was very low, so I needed to help them feel more capable if they were to make progress. I was able to give them a routine for creating annotations that made them feel more successful:

- Stop after one paragraph.
- Reread sentence 1.
- Write the most important idea in the first sentence.
- If you know a synonym for the idea, use the synonym instead.

I realized that this strategy wasn't foolproof or perfect. For instance, some paragraphs lack depth, and the main idea isn't consistently in the first sentence. However, this served as a starting point to help this student feel more successful and grasp the text's structure.

Elizabeth: Just as Melissa and her teachers noticed the creative spark generated by mentor texts and Courtney noticed how annotations provided her with insight on scaffolding writing about texts, I noticed the students' perceived confidence and competence in using tools for writing. Because I had taught writing in middle school for many years, I operated on some assumptions about what students would already know and be able to do. For example, I knew they had been introduced to concept mapping, or at the very least "making a web." What I learned was that having been introduced to a practice did not make students see its relevance or feel competent in using it. When they did not feel confident, my students experienced frustration with the tools I wanted them to try, so they needed direct instruction, even for basic writing strategies such as prewriting and planning. Using a gradual release framework,[11] I modeled concept mapping for my own writing, and then we worked together as a whole class to complete a map before moving to working in small groups. When students engaged in mapping in collaborative groups, the changes in their maps were evident.[12] Further, it served the purpose of generating fluency of ideas for writing and organizing those ideas, demonstrating its usefulness as a planning tool.

Figure 10.1 shows a map constructed as prewriting by a student working independently before direct instruction on concept mapping. As I noticed the student's minimal fluency of ideas, I realized students needed more support for planning writing.

After teacher modeling and guided practice in small groups, students constructed the map shown in figure 10.2 electronically using a shared Google Drawing. I noticed

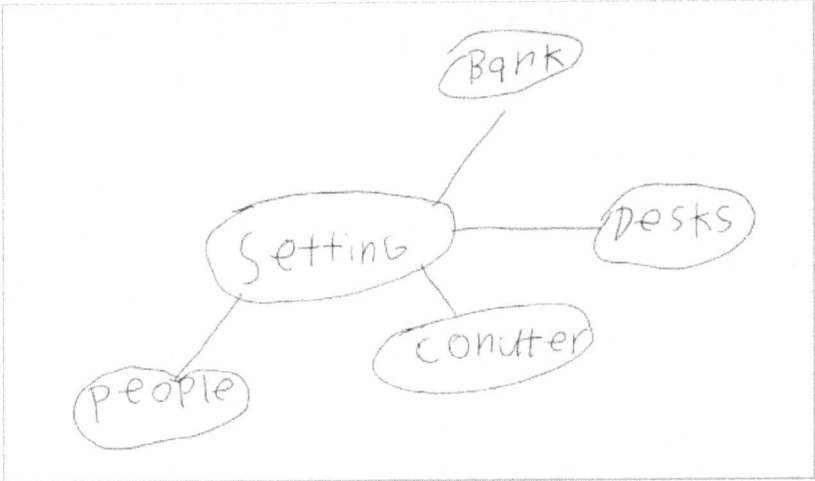

Figure 10.1. "Initial Concept Map." Reproduced with permission from "Exploring the Impact of Social Emotional Learning to Support Motivation and Self-Efficacy in Text-Dependent Analysis Writing" by Elizabeth Nasworthy Crocker. EdD diss., University of South Carolina, 2022.

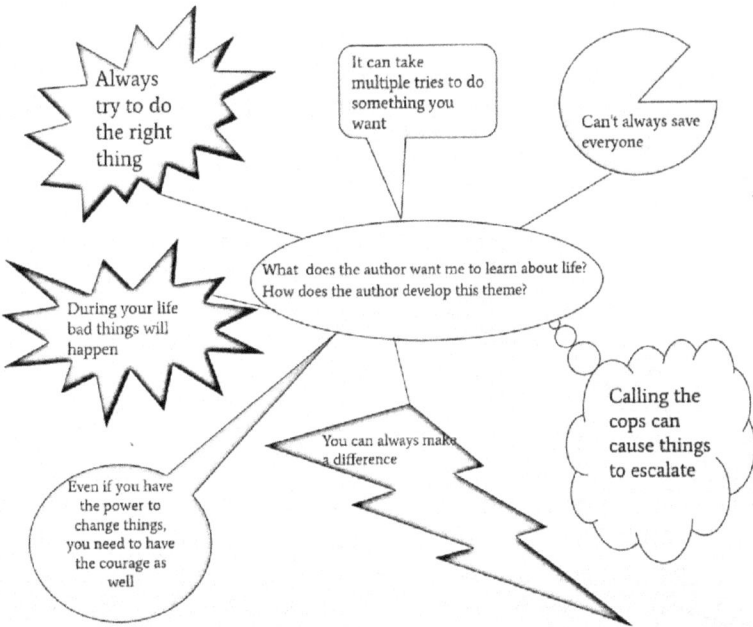

Figure 10.2. "Group Concept Map." Reproduced with permission from "Exploring the Impact of Social Emotional Learning to Support Motivation and Self-Efficacy in Text-Dependent Analysis Writing" by Elizabeth Nasworthy Crocker. EdD diss., University of South Carolina, 2022.

that the students engaged in this collaborative task with more enthusiasm, resulting in critical discussions about text as well as more ideas for writing.

Tips to Get Started

Noticing the writer's craft is an ongoing process that you can achieve with small steps. As you notice writers and their writing, both in published texts and in your classroom, these tips will help.

- Start with a familiar point for you and your students. Introduce new skills alongside more advanced ones. Begin annotation with a skill they're already good at, such as identifying the main idea, and use texts they know well to teach graphic organizers like concept maps.
- Intentionally select mentor texts that support what you want your students to notice. You can share just a page or a selection from a text and collaborate as a class to discover how and why an author did what they did.
- Weave reading and writing together, whether annotating, writing about texts, or writing in a style inspired by another author.

SMALL CHANGE 3: MAKE TIME TO SHARE

One of our major takeaways was the importance of allowing students to share their writing. Achieving this requires building trust within the classroom environment, but it is well worth the effort because it builds relationships that support writing self-efficacy.

Melissa: During classroom visits, a trend caught my attention—not all teachers were incorporating time for sharing at the end of independent writing. However, teachers who did embrace a dedicated share time reported a transformative impact. Much like a vacuum cleaner collects various particles, share time collects and encapsulates the collective reflections, insights, and learning experiences of the writing process. It serves as a container for the richness and diversity of thoughts, allowing for a collective gathering of knowledge and growth for students. Taking the time to share noticings and celebrate students' achievements proved to be a catalyst for encouraging them to take more risks in their writing. For example, a kindergarten student diligently worked on the same book for twenty-eight days! The teacher shared this experience with the class, leaving them in awe. What followed was a ripple effect, with dedicating more time to specific stories rather than rushing to complete a writing piece in a single day.

This shift in approach speaks volumes. When students witness success, understand what it looks and feels like, and are given opportunities to set goals and articulate the actions needed to enhance their writing, the results are truly remarkable.[13] It is a testament to the power of sharing and fostering a supportive environment where students can confidently navigate their writing journeys.

Courtney: Group work was invaluable to student progress. The students collaborated with one another to create more meaning from the text and forge stronger connections with one another. The goal of annotation extended beyond mere text recall; it aimed to offer students supportive tools for active engagement with the material. Rosenblatt's transactional reading theory posits that texts, initially comprising words on a page, come to life when readers, each bringing unique backgrounds to the experience, derive meaning from those words.[14] According to Rosenblatt, students build the most meaning from texts when they discuss them with others because they then hear various perspectives on the same text. Therefore, with the teacher acting as facilitator to guide students in the direction of appropriate interpretation of texts, annotation became a personalized literacy practice,[15] or strategy, to build meaning from the text throughout the novel study.

My students not only completed annotations together, but they also completed a final project in small groups or partners. The project allowed them to demonstrate mastery in multiple personally relevant methods like creating artistic posters and leveraging individual motivations, facilitating deeper connections between themselves and the novel's themes or characters. This approach served as a bridge for students with low self-efficacy, providing them with a comfortable starting point. The elements of autonomy and group work further contributed to the students' enthusiasm, allowing them to dive right into the learning process.

Elizabeth: Like Melissa and Courtney, I wanted to support collaboration for sharing writing, so I participated in writing conferences as a learner, too. I found that sharing my own writing process, as well as inviting students to offer feedback to me about my writing, was important to developing their sense of competency for writing. By describing what I visualized in my writing and was mindful of in my own writing, our relationships as writers and fellow learners grew.[16] When I participated in writing conferences as a writer, not just as a teacher, my think-aloud helped create a more democratic environment in the classroom.[17] Because I was a fellow writer, I could not only model how I visualized myself writing an effective paragraph but also share my process for setting writing goals based on group feedback. This process freed my middle school students to share their own writing, offer feedback to each other, and choose their own writing goals with me using co-constructed rubrics.[18] Their writing showed improvements, not just according to their self-assessments, but also according to my own assessments of their writing. Students did need support in determining criteria for success, but this opened the door for great conversations in writing groups about what makes for effective writing.[19] Table 10.1 is an example of my self-assessment using a simple, co-constructed rubric for my writing goal; using self-assessment prompted meaningful discussions about craft.

Support for writing can and should flow from student to student, teacher to student, and student to teacher!

Table 10.1. Writing Self-Assessment

Name: Mrs. Crocker Date: 4/25/22 **My writing goal:** Use transition words to make the single idea of each sentence clear and focus the sentence on just that one idea. Consider using paraphrasing frames to do this.		
Areas needing attention: Sentences are too wordy and confusing.	**Success indicators: I will see these traits in my writing when I have reached my goal.** Each sentence in my paragraph: • Is clear. • Has an obvious purpose in the paragraph. • Relates a key idea or message concisely. • Develops the central idea in my topic sentence.	**Strengths I can build on:** Use of transition words and paraphrasing frames.

Reproduced with permission from Crocker, "Exploring the Impact of Social Emotional Learning to Support Motivation and Self-Efficacy in Text-Dependent Analysis Writing" (EdD diss., University of South Carolina, 2022).

TIPS TO GET STARTED

We believe that making time to share is one of the most enjoyable parts of writing instruction. It is exciting to engage with students as they develop their writing identity! Here are some lessons we have learned.

- Plan ahead by creating rubrics, timelines, and assessment plans for your unit from the beginning. Build in flexible learning options to offer students choice.
- Create routines and an environment that supports collaboration. Prioritize treating one another in a kind way and viewing mistakes as opportunities for problem-solving.
- Invite students to assess their group skills as well as their writing skills. Posing questions for self-assessment creates opportunities for students to learn and practice social and cognitive skills.

FINAL THOUGHTS

With intentional commitment to making time to write, to notice, and to share, it is possible to take small steps toward nurturing students' self-efficacy as writers. Find a professional partner or two, celebrate progress, and refine your processes as you learn from your experiences. Doing so will help your students discover themselves as writers within your classroom.

NOTES

1. Albert Bandura, *Self-Efficacy: The Exercise of Control* (New York: W. H. Freeman and Company, 1997).

2. Richard M. Ryan and Edward L. Deci, *Self-Determination Theory: Basic Psychological Needs in Motivation, Development, and Wellness* (New York: Guilford, 2017).

3. Jennifer Jacobson, *No More "I'm Done!": Fostering Independent Writers in the Primary Grades* (New York: Routledge, 2023.)

4. Melissa R. Ewing, "The Power of Story in Developing a Cycle of Efficacy for Teachers and Students" (EdD diss., University of South Carolina, 2022).

5. Elizabeth Nasworthy Crocker, "Exploring the Impact of Social Emotional Learning to Support Motivation and Self-Efficacy in Text-Dependent Analysis Writing" (EdD diss., University of South Carolina, 2022).

6. Steve Graham and Dolores Perin, "A Meta-Analysis of Writing Instruction for Adolescent Students," *Journal of Educational Psychology* 99, no. 3 (2007): 445–76; Barry J. Zimmerman, "Becoming a Self-Regulated Learner: An Overview," *Theory Into Practice* 41, no. 2, (2002): 64–70.

7. Douglas Fisher and Nancy Frey, *Engaging the Adolescent Learner: Gradual Release of Responsibility Instructional Framework* (Washington, DC: International Reading Association, 2013).

8. Harvey Daniels, "What's the Next Big Thing with Literature Circles?" *Voices from the Middle* 13, no. 4 (2006): 10–15.

9. Douglas Fisher, Nancy Frey, and John Hattie, *Visible Learning for Literacy: Implementing the Practices that Work Best to Accelerate Student Learning* (Thousand Oaks, CA: Corwin, 2016).

10. Jill Barnes, "Promoting Student Agency in Writing," *The Reading Teacher* 73, no. 6 (2020): 789–95; Barry J. Zimmerman and Albert Bandura, "Impact of Self-Regulatory Influences on Writing Course Attainment," *American Educational Research Journal* 31, no. 4 (1994): 845–62; Barry J. Zimmerman and Anastasia Kitsantas, "Acquiring Writing Revision Skill: Shifting from Process to Outcome Self-Regulatory Goals," *Journal of Educational Psychology* 91, no. 2 (1999): 241–50.

11. Fisher and Frey, *Engaging the Adolescent Learner*.

12. Crocker, "Exploring the Impact of Social Emotional Learning."

13. Paul Bloomberg and Barb Pitchford, *Leading Impact Teams: Building a Culture of Efficacy* (Thousand Oaks, CA: Corwin, 2017).

14. Louise M. Rosenblatt, "Viewpoints: Transaction versus Interaction: A Terminological Rescue Operation," *Research in the Teaching of English* 19, no. 1 (1985): 96–107.

15. Brian V. Street "What's 'New' in New Literacy Studies? Critical Approaches to Literacy in Theory and Practice." *Current Issues in Comparative Education* 5 (2003): 77–91.

16. Ryan and Deci, *Self-Determination Theory*.

17. Fisher et al., *Visible Learning for Literacy*; Barry J. Zimmerman, "Investigating Self-Regulation and Motivation: Historical Background, Methodological Developments, and Future Prospects," *American Educational Research Journal* 45, no. 1 (2008): 166–83.

18. Bloomberg and Pitchford, *Leading Impact Teams*.

19. Elizabeth Crocker, classroom communication, April 25, 2022.

BIBLIOGRAPHY

Bandura, Albert. *Self-Efficacy: The Exercise of Control*. New York: W. H. Freeman and Company, 1997.

Barnes, Jill. "Promoting Student Agency in Writing." *The Reading Teacher* 73, no. 6 (2020): 789–95. https://doi.org/10.1002/trtr.1899.

Bloomberg, Paul, and Barb Pitchford. *Leading Impact Teams: Building a Culture of Efficacy.* Thousand Oaks, CA: Corwin, 2017.

Crocker, Elizabeth Nasworthy. "Exploring the Impact of Social Emotional Learning to Support Motivation and Self-Efficacy in Text-Dependent Analysis Writing." EdD diss., University of South Carolina, 2022.

Daniels, Harvey. "What's the Next Big Thing with Literature Circles?" *Voices from the Middle* 13, no. 4 (2006): 10–15. http://secondaryenglish.pbworks.com/f/smokey_whatsnext.pdf.

Ewing, Melissa R. "The Power of Story in Developing a Cycle of Efficacy for Teachers and Students." EdD diss., University of South Carolina, 2022.

Fisher, Douglas, and Nancy Frey. *Engaging the Adolescent Learner: Gradual Release of Responsibility Instructional Framework.* Washington, DC: International Reading Association, 2013. https://keystoliteracy.com/wp-content/uploads/2017/08/frey_douglas_and_nancy_frey-_gradual_release_of_responsibility_intructional_framework.pdf.

Fisher, Douglas, Nancy Frey, and John Hattie. *Visible Learning for Literacy: Implementing the Practices that Work Best to Accelerate Student Learning.* Thousand Oaks, CA: Corwin, 2016.

Graham, Steve, and Dolores Perrin. "A Meta-Analysis of Writing Instruction for Adolescent Students." *Journal of Educational Psychology* 99, no. 3 (2007): 445–76. https://doi.org/10.1037/1122-0663.99.3.445.

Jacobson, Jennifer. *No More "I'm Done!": Fostering Independent Writers in the Primary Grades.* New York: Routledge, 2023.

Kozelski, C. "A Multiple-Case Study: Motivating Students With Disabilities in Personalized Literacy Instruction." EdD diss., University of South Carolina, 2022.

Rosenblatt, Louise M. "Viewpoints: Transaction versus Interaction: A Terminological Rescue Operation." *Research in the Teaching of English* 19, no. 1 (1985): 96–107. https://www.jstor.org/stable/40171006.

Ryan, Richard M., and Edward L. Deci. *Self-Determination Theory: Basic Psychological Needs in Motivation, Development, and Wellness.* New York: Guilford, 2017.

Street, Brian V. "What's 'New' in New Literacy Studies? Critical Approaches to Literacy in Theory and Practice." *Current Issues in Comparative Education* 5 (2003): 77–91.

Zimmerman, Barry J. "Becoming a Self-Regulated Learner: An Overview." *Theory Into Practice* 41, no. 2, (2002): 64–70. https://doi.org/10.1207/s15430421tip4102_2.

Zimmerman, Barry J. "Investigating Self-Regulation and Motivation: Historical Background, Methodological Developments, and Future Prospects." *American Educational Research Journal* 45, no. 1(2008): 166–83. https://doi.org/10.3102/002831207312909.

Zimmerman, Barry J., and Albert Bandura. "Impact of Self-Regulatory Influences on Writing Course Attainment." *American Educational Research Journal* 31, no. 4 (1994): 845–62. https://doi.org/10.2307/1163397.

Zimmerman, Barry J., and Anastasia Kitsantas. "Acquiring Writing Revision Skill: Shifting from Process to Outcome Self-Regulatory Goals." *Journal of Educational Psychology* 91, no. 2 (1999): 241–50. https://doi.org/10.1037/0022-0663.91.2.241.

Chapter 11

Empowering Middle School English

Small Steps in a Journey of Literacy Transformation

Mona Zignego

CONTEXT

Literacy is best defined as the ability to read, write, speak and listen.[1] Teaching reading is a complex and multifaceted process. There is more research on the science behind how skilled reading works than on any other area of education. Research that supports the science that explains the neurological processes that go into skilled reading has been curated from decades of research from many different disciplines. This research has converged in a preponderance of evidence underpinning an understanding of the elements that are involved in skilled reading.[2] I believe that proficiency in literacy is a skill everyone deserves to possess. It is a civil right. This is my mission and goal in my work. Thus, it was important to me to understand where the schools were in relation to this mission and goal.

In my work as a reading specialist, I go into many schools in my district and engage with K–12 students of all ages to inform, support, and teach the foundational skills needed for skilled reading. I can see within my work that age and economic status are not determinants of literacy proficiency, as students of varying socioeconomic status and age have literacy struggles. Notably, I was assigned to work with eighth-grade middle school teachers in a suburban district. This district had created an English Language Arts (ELA) course for eighth-grade students who were not yet proficient in foundational literacy skills. This course, which was offered for credit, gave special education and general education students who had been identified as needing further skill building in foundational reading skills a chance to receive instruction targeted to specific literacy needs without being pulled for an intervention. Foundational skills in this chapter reflect phonological awareness, phonics, fluency, vocabulary, and comprehension.[3] Students in this course, titled English Essentials, or EE for short, were to be provided with support in varying areas of foundational literacy in order to equip them with the skills to be successful, proficient readers at or above grade level. For the next three years I would work with the seven teachers as they taught the course to special education and general education students to help them reformat and redesign

Table 11.1. English Essentials Ten-Day Cycle

Day 1	Assessment Day: Benchmark or progress monitoring with a digital Reading Standardized Assessment
Day 2	Data Day: Analyze results and debrief with whole class while previewing what the next eight days will bring
Day 3	Reading Day: New reading, recap of previous reading, or continued reading of a novel
Day 4	Group Reading Day: Focus on nonfiction with an emphasis on data obtained from standardized needs assessment to drive instruction of skills while reading
Day 5	Vocabulary Day: Vocabulary work along with presentations by students of words from the reading over the past few days
Day 6	Writing Day: Pre-writing activity
Day 7	Writing Day: Essay writing
Day 8	Reading Day: Pick up the reading from Day 3 again: 20 minutes group reading, 20 minutes independent reading
Day 9	Comprehension Day: Comprehension work
Day 10	Reading Day: Choice reading time

the curriculum with alignment to the Common Core State Standards, build the teachers' literacy content knowledge, and ensure that students were receiving targeted, differentiated support in areas of need. The teachers were comprised of special education and ELA teachers.

Upon stepping into the role of the new reading specialist in this district, my first objective was to ask questions intended to isolate the teaching methods and curriculum then in place, discern the strengths perceived by the teachers within the current program, and identify the challenges that required my support. As I asked questions of the administration and teachers, I learned the course followed a ten-day cycle (table 11.1). Each day, teachers worked on a different skill with students. For example, on day 3 there was either review of previous reading or a new reading task was initiated. The schedule had a heavy emphasis on data collection and analysis in order to determine next steps in instruction. As I studied the ten-day-cycle schedule, I looked to see where each day students could receive targeted, differentiated instruction in foundational reading skills in the area of need. I wondered about the use of grade-level standards and content within the course. I also wondered about the content knowledge teachers possessed on the science behind how skilled reading works.

INITIAL MEETINGS: EXPLANATION OF THE PROBLEM

As I sat in my first meeting with administration, they had almost as many questions as I did. Three main wonderings stood out: Which activities matter the most to students as far as reading improvement? Do we need to add/change/adjust anything? What is most useful moving forward? Administration also wondered how teachers could best use instructional time when working with students, and how we could navigate the boredom teachers and students were experiencing within the EE course. Administration spoke highly of the EE teachers, mentioning teacher expertise and commitment, but were honest about struggles to collect clean data that reflected where students were in the learning process.

I had much to think about as I left the meeting with administration to begin interviewing teachers. While meeting with teachers one-on-one, I asked several questions:

- What is working?
- What is not working?
- How are you differentiating for foundational literacy skill content?
- What standards are you addressing within this course?
- And what literacy content knowledge would be supportive of your work?

Across the board, teachers mentioned a lack of structure within the course alongside their lack of content knowledge within the ten-day cycle as something that was not working. The teachers told me they were given a great deal of autonomy in planning and teaching, but did not have enough literacy content knowledge and resources to navigate creating curriculum that met their students' needs.

The second element that was not supportive of student achievement was the use of a specific digital program for assessing students using standardized data to benchmark and monitor progress. It had no resources for teachers and did not provide students with any digital or face-to-face materials for rehearsal of skills in areas of need. Additionally, the standardized assessment took too long, and students did not take it seriously. Thus, data was not interpretive of student strengths, growth, or areas of struggle.

Last of all, teachers' answers indicated there was a lack of implementation of the Common Core State Standards. This resulted in a lack of guidance on the direction, timing, and methodology for teaching and learning. As a consequence, students were not exposed to grade-level content, and it appeared students were not consistently receiving focused instruction in crucial foundational literacy areas that required additional skill development.

Within this course, elements that were strong were teacher engagement, professionalism, and deep commitment to students attaining literacy proficiency. As I met with each licensed classroom teacher that instructed the EE course, most asked deep and insightful questions, voiced concerns, expressed the desire for more literacy content, and showed care for students' literacy outcomes. One teacher, however, was disengaged with the process and pushed back on what she perceived as yet another district initiative even though she would still have to implement the changes. I chose to focus my efforts on the rest of the teachers who were open to the process. The downside of my decision was that this teacher would not have a voice in how we built the course. I hoped that sooner rather than later, when this teacher saw student outcomes improving, she would willingly work with me.

MY RESPONSE

The teachers and administrators in this school were high quality, caring educators who were deeply invested in student outcomes. All but one willingly engaged with me,

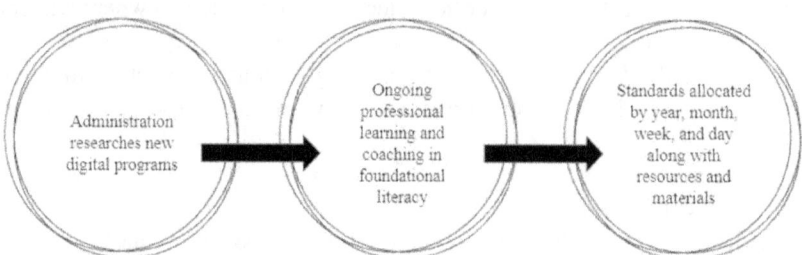

Figure 11.1. Small steps to literacy transformation.

noting strengths, voicing concerns, and contributing to responsive decision-making. After meeting with staff and gathering important information, I was able to formulate a solution-oriented response through tiers of small steps over the next three years that supported teachers and students and answered administrations' questions. A summary of those steps is shown in figure 11.1 and discussed further throughout the rest of this chapter.

Administration Researches New Digital Programs

The educators were clear that the ten-day cycle and the current method of standardized assessing as the sole method of progress monitoring had to go. Educators and students were bored and stressed by the current system, and student outcomes were not where they needed to be. I suggested the administration take the first small step and look at different student assessment measures that would provide more student-centered, clean, and comprehensive data that could be triangulated with classroom data in order to clearly determine next teaching moves. For classroom data, I suggested looking at student strengths and backgrounds to determine areas that were strong and leverage those areas to support elements in need of further skill building. I advocated for cultural responsiveness in looking at who the students were, where they came from, and what the storied elements of their lives consisted of. I also suggested they vet various digital programs to support students and teachers in resources and to provide another data point. The digital program they chose (iReady) had face-to-face and digital resources for providing literacy content to students in foundational reading skills.

Ongoing Professional Learning and Coaching in Foundational Literacy

While the administration addressed these tasks, I focused on delivering ongoing continuous professional learning and coaching in research-aligned models of reading alongside fundamental literacy components of phonics, phonological awareness, fluency, vocabulary, and comprehension. These literacy components adhered with a convergence of peer-reviewed research and encompassed many skills. For example, comprehension included teaching different styles, genres, and types of writing such as narrative writing and summarizing. Within writing instruction, semantics, syntax, and pragmatics content were included.

My approach also involved supporting teachers in conducting whole-group learning sessions with students using grade-level standards, student-centered materials, and high-quality resources while also dedicating class time to individual or small-group support for students to enhance understanding of whole-group content as well as instruct in foundational literacy elements requiring further skill building. All learning was student-centered and was connected to authentic classroom instruction and extension into real-life connections. As part of our work, we additionally included increasing executive functioning skills, engagement, and motivation through our use of materials, resources, and instruction. We were determined not to be part of the "drill and kill" criticism this type of work has been subjected to. "Literacy is for everyone" was our goal, our mantra, and our guiding star.

I actively observed classes providing constructive feedback to teachers. I also co-taught with teachers. Last of all, I modeled teaching or administering assessments when needed. Thus, ongoing professional learning and coaching also encompassed formative and summative assessment measures of classroom learning. These measures were designed to be triangulated with iReady.

As a note, given the eighth-grade middle school students' context, the phonics instruction mentioned above covered not only any early phonics skills that students might be lacking but also involved morphology work. Morphemes are the smallest units of meaning within words, such as prefixes, suffixes, and root words. This small but important step provided students with scaffolded support in sound-letter connections at both the initial phonics as well as multisyllabic and morpheme levels when needed.[4] This instruction involved taking small steps targeted in building a foundation crucial for literacy proficiency. In some instances, this meant incorporating skills typically acquired in the early stages of reading instruction, such as basic phonics skills.

Standards Allocated by Year, Month, Week, and Day along with Resources and Materials

From there, the next step involved working with teachers to plan a scope and sequence for the eighth-grade EE course. I initiated work beginning with dividing up and prioritizing standards. This whole-to-part work then took the next step as I narrowed down and allocated those prioritized standards to each month of the school year and then narrowed even further by week, and last of all by day.

Next, I created a graphic organizer where each month teachers could see the standards allocated by month, week, and day (table 11.2). This graphic organizer also had a space for planning for word work, fluency, vocabulary, and comprehension. Word work was inclusive of phonological awareness, phonics, and morphology. This space contained skills students still needed to acquire in order to be proficient readers and was matched to the standards for that month. Additionally, the foundational skills planning section was consistent with the professional learning teachers had engaged in.

I meticulously curated the resources, exemplars, and other materials needed based on the data we analyzed from students, and through my conversations with teachers to provide targeted, differentiated support for teachers and students in areas that needed skill building. This was done while providing all students with grade-level material during whole group instruction. Differentiated instruction in

Table 11.2. September Eighth-Grade English Essentials Short Example

Standards for the month (abbreviated for space)	Skills: Word work, fluency, comprehension	Resources, exemplars, materials
R.8.1, W.8.1, SL.8.4	**Word Work:** Most common prefixes: un-, re-, in- (im-, ir-, il-), dis-, en- (em-), non-, in- (im-), over, and mis-. **Fluency:** Decoding multisyllabic words using prefixes and rereading strategies **Vocabulary:** Words necessary for understanding the texts for this month would be placed here. **Comprehension:** Citing text evidence Differentiation provided in small group or partner work time.	Materials would be inserted here as links for the teachers. (This includes iReady resources)
Week One **R.8.1** Cite textual evidence that strongly supports an analysis of what the text says explicitly/implicitly and make logical inferences. **W.8.1** Compose reflective, formal, and creative writing, which may happen simultaneously or independently, for a variety of high-stakes and low-stakes purposes **SL.8.4** Present claims and findings, emphasizing significant points in a focused, coherent manner with relevant evidence, sound valid reasoning, and well-chosen details. Communicate clearly and in an engaging manner, considering the audience, purpose, and situation. Explain purpose of language choices.	**Word Work:** un-, re-, in- **Fluency:** rereading non-fiction text **Vocabulary:** Words necessary for understanding the texts for this day would be placed here. **Comprehension:** citing relevant textual evidence	
Monday R.8.1 W.8.1 SL.8.4	Due to space and word restrictions, this is a very brief example of a lesson plan. **10 minutes:** Opener: word work with un-, re-, in- Vocabulary work **10 minutes:** **Learning Intention:** Students are learning how to find evidence in text that clearly supports what the text says. **Success Criteria:** Students will know that they have done this when they can discuss their findings with their partner and write down their answers in the assignment tab in the Google classroom **15 minutes:** Students work with a partner, rereading to find information in the text. Teacher roams the room checking for understanding and reteaching as needed or pulls individuals or small groups for skill building in areas of need. **10 minutes:** Come back together as a group, share out. **5 minutes:** Exit ticket: how did we do? What steps are next for reteaching?	

specific foundational literacy skills happened primarily during small-group time, partner time, and individual work time. Teachers differentiated in various ways during whole-group time as well through, for example, providing talk-to-text or read-aloud features to support students. As I mentioned earlier, the administration agreed on iReady for their digital benchmark and progress monitoring assessments. This program had copious resources that were face-to-face and digital for supporting teachers and students. This program provided teachers with resources that addressed the need for skill building in below-grade-level literacy skills. This was really important as eighth-grade teachers often do not have access to high-quality resources of this nature.

RESULTS

Through this series of small steps, broken down over three years, we were able to achieve favorable outcomes for students. These steps included beginning with interviews with central stakeholders. This involved leadership and teachers being part of the solution and allowing their voices to be heard. This was followed by moving to ongoing professional learning on the science behind how skilled reading works, along with one-on-one coaching, modeling, co-teaching, and classroom observations. Next, grade-level standards were chosen and prioritized specifically for eighth grade. These standards were connected to foundational skills and broken down by month, week, and day. Graphic organizers were created to house all the information for each EE class, and time was spent with teachers planning engaging and evidence-aligned instruction by the month, week, and finally by the day. Curated resources were provided to teachers by me and also through iReady.

We looked at the data at the end of the second year. The result was that 68 percent of students in the course had over a year of growth as defined by iReady and 30 percent of students graduated out of the course. This meant these students no longer needed targeted literacy interventions. As this chapter was being written in the third year, student data was trending in the same direction, and the one teacher who had pushed back on this process was fully engaged, meeting with me consistently, and, as this chapter was going into print, working with me to design a comprehension unit. Students were far more engaged, verbalizing their appreciation for the new iReady program as well as more personalized and student-centered instruction. Instruction provided to students from iReady and through face-to-face classroom instruction was differentiated and based on student literacy needs, thus specific areas of growth varied by student. Students were exited from the course when all areas of literacy were at an eighth-grade level according to triangulation of data with iReady and classroom data along with collaboration among parents, administration, and classroom teachers. In this year (year 3), we tightened up the curriculum and process to support students and teachers more fully, and we continued to bring in teacher and administration input as a valuable and essential part of the process.

Although we obviously have more work to do, we attribute initial successes to a number of factors:

- Teachers were valued as professionals in their field and for their knowledge of their students. They were an integral part of every step of the process.
- We used ongoing professional learning and data analysis to answer initial administrative questions and build strong and comprehensive coursework for students in the process.
- Teachers were provided with foundational literacy content that was aligned with the science behind how skilled reading works and targeted to specific student needs.
- Ongoing professional learning was paired with coaching, co-teaching, modeling, and classroom observations for maximum scaffolding and support for teachers.
- A new standardized assessment program was chosen that provided benchmark assessments, progress monitoring, and foundational literacy work with digital and face-to-face resources.
- Teachers were part of the solution. They were respected as professionals and their institutional knowledge and feedback was solicited and analyzed to design solution-oriented responses.
- Since all but one teacher was on board and excited to move forward with this work, I did not use my valuable time and energy convincing one teacher, but rather let her see the successes of the work we were doing over time. Then I gladly brought her on board when she was ready.
- Coursework was aligned with grade-level common core state standards to ensure students were receiving grade-appropriate content.
- Resources were curated and ongoing professional learning contributed to an environment that was engaging, motivating, and interesting for students.
- The course schedule was remade with time distributed more judiciously and effectively toward the foundational elements of literacy to ensure successful literacy outcomes for students.

Looking back on this process, there are a few things I would have done differently. For one, I would have interviewed students as well as teachers and administration in order to include them in the process of finding solutions and allow their voices to be heard. I also would have included more culturally relevant materials. Moving forward, these elements will play a major role in our work.

HOW TO REPLICATE THESE SMALL STEPS

1. Interview central stakeholders to include them in the process of finding solutions.
2. Provide professional learning for educators and leadership in areas that are in need of further skill building.
3. Pair the professional learning with one-on-one coaching, modeling, co-teaching, and nonevaluative classroom observations.
4. Make sure educators are aware of grade-level standards so that students are being exposed to grade-level materials.
5. Create or become familiar with the scope and sequence of instruction for the year.

6. Break down the learning by month, week, and day in order to see the big picture down to the everyday detail.
7. Organize all information and resources in a way that is accessible to get at and easy to find.
8. Ensure that students are at the center of planning. Personalize and differentiate so that maximum enjoyment of learning can happen along with positive student outcomes.

CONCLUSION

Middle school teachers often struggle to provide support for students in foundational skills. These skills are expected to have already been acquired by this point. Middle school schedules do not easily accommodate learning missed foundational literacy skills. This middle school took deep responsibility for their students and adopted a solution-oriented approach, circumventing barriers and actively working toward providing its students with opportunities to build skills in areas of need alongside grade-level standards and content. As we deepen into this work in the third year, I look back over those last two years at how far we have come with our series of small steps—small steps to empower a middle school ELA course that in turn transformed literacy outcomes for its students.

NOTES

1. Louisa C. Moats, "Creating Confident Readers: How LETRS Supports Teachers—and Their Students," *American Educator* 47, no. 1 (2023): 4.
2. Timothy Shanahan, "What Constitutes a Science of Reading Instruction?" *Reading Research Quarterly* 55 (2020): S235–S247.
3. Bill Honig, Linda Diamond, Linda Gutlohn, Beth Fertig, Harvey Daniel, Steven Zemelman, and Nancy Steineke, *Teaching Reading Sourcebook*, 2nd ed., vol. 3, no. 2 (Washington, DC: Arena Press, 2008).
4. Terezinha Nunes, Peter Bryant, and Rossana Barros, "The Development of Word Recognition and Its Significance for Comprehension and Fluency," *Journal of Educational Psychology* 104, no. 4 (2012): 959.

BIBLIOGRAPHY

Honig, Bill, Linda Diamond, Linda Gutlohn, Beth Fertig, Harvey Daniel, Steven Zemelman, and Nancy Steineke. *Teaching Reading Sourcebook*, Second edition, vol. 3, no. 2. Washington, DC: Arena Press, 2008.

Moats, Louisa C. "Creating Confident Readers: How LETRS Supports Teachers—and Their Students." *American Educator* 47, no. 1 (2023): 4–11.

Nunes, Terezinha, Peter Bryant, and Rossana Barros. "The Development of Word Recognition and Its Significance for Comprehension and Fluency." *Journal of Educational Psychology* 104, no. 4 (2012): 959.

Shanahan, Timothy. "What Constitutes a Science of Reading Instruction?" *Reading Research Quarterly* 55 (2020): S235–S247.

Chapter 12

Beyond Checking Boxes

Enacting Equitable Practices in English Language Arts

Katie F. Whitley, Erin Riley-Lepo, and Ashley Pollitt

Recent diversity, equity, and inclusion (DEI) initiatives across the United States have tasked teachers with rethinking course content and adopting new curricula. Even when teachers are passionate about these initiatives, making changes takes time and requires sustained structural support. Through anecdotes from our classroom experiences, this chapter highlights the actions that secondary English Language Arts teachers take to enact equitable practices that go beyond checking boxes set by district initiatives. Specifically, we discuss ways English Language Arts (ELA) teachers can negotiate power through co-constructed classroom practices, apply critical lenses to canonical texts, and promote student self-regulation while preparing for mandated assessments.

OUR BACKGROUNDS

While we met in a social justice–oriented teacher education PhD program and share common ground in our demographic identities, educational background, and belief systems, there is also variation in our work. We are each nondisabled, cisgender, heterosexual, white women engaged in scholarship grounded in challenging oppressive school structures. However, our areas of specialization diverge. Katie teaches in both a high school and a university setting while remaining active in feminist new literacies research and self-study. Erin began her teaching career, first in Florida and later in New Jersey, in districts that emphasized standardized test scores and Advanced Placement courses. Currently, Erin is a teacher educator in a public college. Ashley was formerly an ELA special education teacher. She is a current teacher educator in a public college. Her research centers practices that provide greater educational equity for historically marginalized students, particularly students labeled with disability/disabled students. In the following sections, we share pedagogical practices designed to create more equitable classroom experiences for students.

POWER SHARING IN KATIE'S ELA CLASSROOM

While broader school and district policies can be punitive in nature, classroom teachers can leverage their power to foster safe and collaborative environments that push back against deficit-based models.[1] Like hooks, I see the classroom as a place where "excitement is generated through collective effort," and this collective effort is only possible when teachers critically examine "the traditional notion that only [teachers] are responsible for classroom dynamics. That responsibility is relative to status."[2] Power sharing with students can begin by negotiating (and renegotiating) class policies. From there, we can build the trust necessary to engage students even more directly in developing units of study, as well as the modes of communication through which they will express what they have learned. Here, I offer suggestions beyond classroom management and teacher-centered designs and describe how I share power with students in my ELA classroom.

Beyond Classroom Management: Co-Constructing our Classroom Community

Classroom communities built on guidelines developed in collaboration with students can bolster students' sense of autonomy over their own learning.[3] While teachers may establish some non-negotiables, students have meaningful opinions about how their ideal classrooms will run. Additionally, the expectations that grow out of student input need to be revisited/revised as needed for the power sharing between teacher and students to be authentic. Luckily, co-constructing community guidelines do not need to be complicated; a straightforward process is likely to work best with K–12 students.

Several years ago, I incorporated a system for co-constructing class norms with students. I prefer to introduce this in the first week of school. I begin with a discussion of what it means to have a classroom community. To establish a group definition of *community* and how a positive class community assists in the learning process, I ask students:

- What is a *community*?
- What does it mean to be part of a *classroom community*?
- Describe a positive experience with a *community* you have been a part of.

Students respond through a Quick Write,[4] where they freewrite ideas inspired by the prompt. Depending on how eager (or reticent) the group is to participating verbally, they may share these thoughts with a neighbor or move right to a full group discussion of their free-writing.

The next phase involves students imagining what their class community should look like, sound like, and feel like; these prompts were inspired by my work with Dr. Monica Taylor and her article with Bohny and colleagues[5] for which students "develop norms, guidelines for behavior, expectations and strategies" by "envision[ing] and articulat[ing] the best and worst visions of the course." Students consider:

1. What would make this the *best* English class you can imagine?
2. What would make this the *worst* English class you can imagine?

Depending on class dynamic, students might tackle these questions individually and/or brainstorm responses in small groups. I limit myself to two sample responses per list to help students get started without overly influencing the norms they develop. I encourage students to include the behaviors and actions they expect of me as the teacher, as well as from themselves and their peers, as they should have the power to hold me to high standards. Finally, we co-construct a set of community standards by pulling wording from the Best Class and Worst Class lists we collaborated to create.

Once our community guidelines are co-constructed, we have to regularly attend to them. For example, before group work, we review the desired norms for working with peers. Students share our norms for collaboration and list them on the board for reference as they work. At this time, we can revise our norms if necessary. The process works best when students take the lead—when reminders come from peers in the class rather than from me. When something is not working, I commit to making time to review and revise our co-constructed community standards; they are adapted as our community evolves.

Beyond Teacher-Centered Design: Co-Constructing Essential Questions and Writing Tasks

In my experience, the trust built through negotiating, revisiting, and revising community norms can promote further opportunities for power sharing with students. While student choice is worked into my curriculum in a number of ways, here, I focused on scaffolding the process of co-constructing units with students. I draw on Wiggins and McTighe's *Understanding by Design* in my curriculum planning; each unit is grounded in a set of essential questions "that are not answerable with finality in a brief statement" but rather are used to "stimulate thought, to provoke inquiry, to spark more questions—including thoughtful student questions."[6] These questions direct the learning goals for a unit, act as the foundation for summative assessments, and can be leveraged to engage students in co-designing unit plans.

Like co-constructing community norms, I developed a process through which students and I could work toward co-development of essential questions and assessments. First, I needed to establish what essential questions are and how they act as a foundation for our learning. Two small changes I made to ground our units in these questions were: (1) naming the units for the ideas we would study (rather than the texts in the unit); and (2) giving students opportunities to return to our essential questions at several points throughout any unit of study. For example, our twelfth-grade unit called *Identity, Power, and the Hero's Downfall* uses Shakespeare's *Othello*[7] and related texts as a vehicle through which we can examine the aforementioned concepts in our lives and the world around us.

I use the first few units of any course I teach to help students become familiar with how essential questions can guide our learning. At the beginning of a course, students and I use essential questions that were designed by me and the teaching partner with whom I developed this curriculum. We begin the unit with an essential questions Quick Write, and we follow these low-stakes writing tasks with a discussion of students' responses and predictions about the upcoming text. A typical Quick Write prompt would read:

Write a response reflecting on your perspective on one of the essential questions above. Make sure to provide explanations and examples (perhaps from your own life, literature that you've read, or movies/tv shows you've seen) to support your perspective.

In order for a unit to authentically center around essential questions, it is critical that we return to them frequently through our informal discussions, formative assessments, and summative assessments. The assessments I design are made up of open-ended questions; students have choices about which topics to address and are encouraged to use their notes along with the texts we are studying to develop their ideas. Rather than looking for *right* answers, students develop ideas using a combination of textual evidence and real-world examples to shape their perspective.

By the third or fourth unit in a course, I more directly engage students in the planning process. For example, in the aforementioned unit *Identity, Power, and the Hero's Downfall*, students and I begin by discussing the unit's title. Then, I provide students with a draft of our essential questions. Students brainstorm in small groups using the following prompt:

> Work with your group to come up with as many questions/ideas as you can about each of the essential questions I provided. You don't need to *answer* the questions. Instead, jot down new questions and/or related ideas.

Students record their brainstorming in shared Google Docs or on poster paper. At the end of our brainstorming session (at least ten minutes), groups decide on their three *most interesting* questions and share them in a Doc. This leads us into negotiating which questions are the most compelling and often involves combining and deleting questions to narrow down to three or four key ideas to explore, as shown in figure 12.1.

As with other units, these questions should be explored in a variety of modes (e.g., class discussions, low-stakes writing, group work) and tied into our summative assessment. This is another area where power-sharing through co-construction is possible.

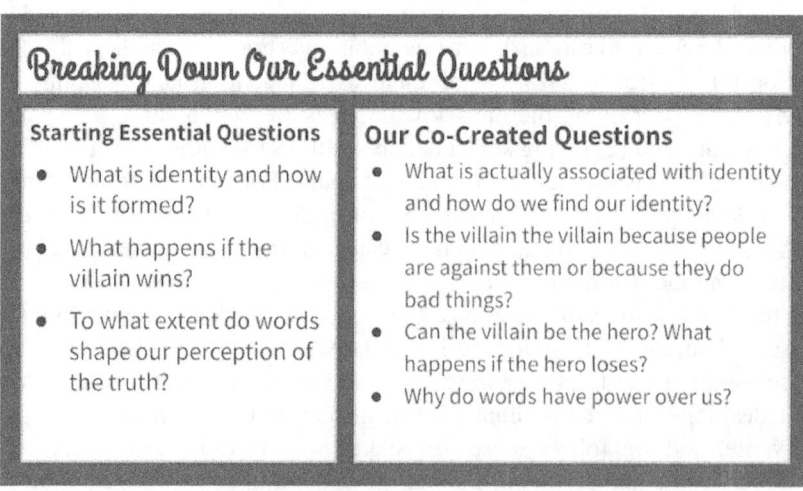

Figure 12.1. Negotiated essential questions.

The unit referenced above culminated in a negotiation of final assessment options. I shared the following general parameters as we returned to brainstorming.

- Create a product that relates to our essential questions.
- Use and cite evidence from the unit's main text(s).
- Offer opportunities for students to express themselves through a combination of words, images, and/or audio.

From there, we developed four project options with a *free choice* that left room for students to propose a different idea. These projects included creating a character history, reimagining the end of *Othello*, interpreting a key scene from the play, and creating/presenting a thematic vision board. For each option, I developed a prompt based on the students' suggestions that encouraged students to connect the play's themes and their own lives and offered submission guidelines. Students' final products, which were assessed using our English department's shared rubrics for creative writing and presentations, varied in modality and represented the wide array of perspectives we explored throughout the unit.

Takeaways

Power sharing with students through co-construction can create opportunities for increased student engagement and autonomy. While we may not be able to change broader school policies, teachers can shift from teacher-centered rules to community norms that represent student voices. When negotiation and co-construction become a consistent pedagogical practice, collaborative class communities can work together to design learning activities that are directly tied to students' strengths and interests.

APPLYING CRITICAL LENSES IN ASHLEY'S ELA CLASSROOM

As a ninth-grade ELA teacher, I taught John Steinbeck's *Of Mice and Men*[8] each year. This text had been implemented into the high school curriculum long before I accepted my teaching position. As a novice, I felt compelled, even excited, to teach it, as I vaguely remembered reading it myself in high school. My colleagues in the ELA department characterized *Of Mice and Men* as a *classic*, a text everyone should read due to powerful messages about friendship and loneliness. Yet, in one department meeting, I recall teachers expressing concern with teaching the book; conversations, however, remained superficial, such as whether to read the written profanity aloud. As a department, we did not interrogate any of the problematic content: the deficit of portrayals of minoritized communities (e.g., Black people, people with disabilities,[9] women, and migrant workers) represented in the text. Only after critical reflection, graduate coursework, and a second read did I recognize a responsibility to teach *Of Mice and Men* differently, if at all.

Ideally, ELA curricula would include culturally responsive texts representing a wide range of human experiences but, like me, some teachers might not have agency to teach such texts. That is, teachers might feel constrained in their text selection due to extenuating circumstances, such as lack of tenure and pre-established curriculum. To enact equitable practices that reflect DEI initiatives, we recommend starting small by applying critical lenses to texts already within curricula, including those considered classics, like *Of Mice and Men*.

BEYOND PERPETUATING SYSTEMS OF OPPRESSION: REIMAGINING APPROACHES TO A CANONICAL TEXT

For context, *Of Mice and Men* follows Lennie and George, two American migrant workers during the Great Depression who dream of owning a farm. While teachers often ground these units in themes of friendship and loneliness, the isolation characters experience is due to systems of oppression. Although never expressly named in the text, Lennie is described as having an intellectual disability; as a result, he is infantilized, compared to animals, and expected to present as nondisabled to maintain his job. Multiple characters experience similar oppression, particularly Curley's wife, who experiences sexism as the only female character; Crooks, who encounters racism and ableism as the sole disabled Black character; and Candy, who faces ageism and ableism as the oldest disabled character. Admittedly, when I first taught the text, I facilitated lessons on the effects of friendship and loneliness without naming the systems of oppression that contribute to each of these characters' isolation.

I now recognize that systems of oppression function at multiple levels: individual, cultural, and institutional. Ableism, for example, refers to the systemic discrimination of disabled people that operates individually, through comments like, "I don't consider you disabled"; culturally, through media representations of disability (or lack thereof); and institutionally, through inaccessible work environments, such as the absence of elevators or interpreters. In *Of Mice and Men*, Steinbeck included several instances of ableism, sexism, racism, and ageism. Rather than ignore social justice issues by examining themes of friendship or opting out of teaching the text altogether, my co-teacher and I developed an interdisciplinary project for students to apply critical lenses to *Of Mice and Men*.

To illuminate social justice issues in *Of Mice and Men*, ELA students in my co-taught ninth-grade class self-selected one form of discrimination represented in the text to examine. Students traced how the issue is still not remedied today, decades after Steinbeck wrote the text, by defining the issue, creating a timeline with five to seven related major US cultural events or laws, and ending the timeline with recent statistics and news stories connected to the issue. For students to address intersectionality, or the ways in which people can experience multiple forms of discrimination based on different elements of their identity,[10] my co-teacher and I requested students comment on the events' potential impacts on multiply marginalized people (e.g., Crooks and Candy). For instance, the group that examined ableism reflected on how the COVID-19 pandemic disproportionately affected people with disabilities and racial and ethnic minorities,[11] commenting on the pandemic's impact on disabled people of color.

From there, my co-teacher and I partnered with eleventh-grade US history teachers whose students were studying the Progressive Era, a period of widespread social activism in the United States. Like the ELA students, US history students formed groups based on the aforementioned social justice issues. First, the ELA student groups met their US history counterparts to share their research findings. Next, the history students brainstormed strategies to reform their assigned issue: They considered their main goal, the reform level necessary (e.g., individual, municipal, state, federal), short-term and long-term plans, actionable steps, and potential challenges. To raise awareness, US history students also created visual representations to share through media as well as letters to politicians or other stakeholders interested in the issue. Ultimately, the history students presented their work to the entire ELA class, who then voted on the most convincing reform strategy.

Since this project occurred early in the school year, I noticed the ELA students apply critical lenses to other texts we read with the language to name forms of discrimination. Students called out sexism in William Shakespeare's *Romeo and Juliet*[12] and ageism apparent in Elie Wiesel's *Night*.[13] By prioritizing critical consciousness over themes of friendship and loneliness in *Of Mice and Men*, my co-teacher and I decided to go beyond simplistic interpretations of characters to explore systems of oppression that contribute to isolation.

Takeaways

When planning whether and how to teach a canonical text, we propose that ELA teachers not entirely discard it from the curriculum or reproduce lessons that perpetuate systems of oppression. Specifically, teachers can approach texts like *Of Mice and Men* in ways that prompt students to address the absence of diversity, equity, and inclusion, both in texts and in their own lives. My co-teacher and I used the approach of collaborating with colleagues in a different grade level and subject area in order to demonstrate that social justice issues transcend ninth-grade ELA classrooms. Further, we emphasized the ongoing nature of critical work; students should not expect a resolution but, instead, develop skills to work toward a freer and more just society.

NAVIGATING PREPARATION FOR STANDARDIZED ASSESSMENTS IN ERIN'S ELA CLASSROOM

When selected by my administration to teach Advanced Placement Language and Composition (AP Lang) courses, I was honored, but conflicted. While excited to be selected, I recognized that there is a false narrative that teaching AP courses reflects one's competence as an educator. I also have a complex relationship with standardized assessments. I perceive them as a necessary means to an end for students who need to pass these tests to graduate and, perhaps, to gain acceptance to a college, but I also acknowledge that these tests do not accurately measure student learning.[14] Furthermore, culturally responsive and sustaining teaching calls for variety in the ways we assess our students;[15] I feared that I would be encouraged to teach to the test to ensure students' success on the AP Lang exam. Ultimately, I enjoy teaching writing and this particular AP course emphasizes writing development, so I accepted. In this portion of the chapter, I offer suggestions beyond checking the box of standardized test preparation.

In my first year of teaching AP Lang, I used the curriculum crafted by my well-respected predecessor, Roberta Schilling. The readings were *classics* (e.g., Plato's "Allegory of a Cave"[16] and Thoreau's *Walden*[17]) and there was a heavy emphasis on testing skills, such as identifying distractors on multiple-choice questions and formulaic essay writing. Students reported enjoying the class[18] and did well on the AP exam, but the class did not reflect my ethos as an educator. Each subsequent year, my goal became to revise my curriculum in equitable ways. Thankfully, my school administrators supported my efforts.

Changes began with my course materials. I asked myself questions inspired by Emily Style[19] such as:

- Who are the students in my classroom and are they represented in our readings?
- Am I selecting readings that help my students examine perspectives and experiences outside of their own?

Although more comfortable with my revised materials, I still felt disingenuous: my readings were more culturally responsive, but I was still teaching to the AP test in standardized ways (e.g., multiple-choice practice questions, essay writing with teacher-centered feedback). I wanted to rethink this part of my class as well, but felt beholden to preparing my students for the AP test and struggled to change my teacher-centered test preparation instruction.

During this time, I was taking graduate-level classes, many of which focused on culturally responsive and sustaining teaching and educational psychology. These classes began to inform the way I taught for the AP exam. I made explicit choices that gave my students more agency in their test preparation practices, such as fostering metacognitive practices and student autonomy.

Metacognition and Multiple Choice

Metacognition is thinking about one's thinking. Facilitating students' metacognition not only supports them on standardized assessments, but also supports their self-regulation and critical thinking in other activities.[20]

In my first year of teaching AP Lang, I gave many multiple-choice assessments that were one-and-done experiences: students took the assessment and received their results without any reflection. To foster metacognition, students reflected on their multiple-choice results. First, after students took a formative multiple-choice practice assessment (often the ones provided by the College Board), I would examine the results and select one or two questions on which students struggled. Then, students revisited the passage and corresponding multiple-choice question. Through this activity, students had the correct answer—as identified by the College Board—ahead of time, as the focus of this activity was not to get the correct answer but to discern *why* the answer was considered correct and to examine the types of questions they would encounter on the AP test. I also encouraged students to discuss not only the correct answer in their reflection, but also to consider why the other answers were identified as incorrect.

One important factor in this process was that the multiple-choice portion of this activity was ungraded. Because AP exams can cause deep anxiety in students, which affects their performance on the test itself,[21] I hoped to take pressure off of the multiple-choice practice and, instead, focus on the reflection portion of this assignment, the only graded portion. This sort of reflection was new to many students, so I created models and a rubric for their reflection (textbox 12.1).

TEXTBOX 12.1. A MODEL MULTIPLE-CHOICE TEMPLATE AND SAMPLE PROVIDED TO STUDENTS

Think About Your Thinking Template

The College Board-selected answer to number ___ is ___. My original answer was ___. I understand now that [provide evidence of the correct answer according to the College Board here]. It states in the text that [provide support for the correct answer here]. This is different from my original answer because [provide your new thinking here].

Other Sentence Stem Suggestions

The other choices are labeled as incorrect because . . .
I am still confused about (provide questions here).

Think About Your Thinking Model

The College Board selected answer to question 7 is B. My original answer was D. The reason B is correct is because the sentence is about "quartering large bodies of troops." The "bodies of troops" would be the antecedent. The sentence states that they are quartering the large bodies of troops. The next line "for protecting them," <u>them</u> is the pronoun replacing bodies.

This specific example quotes the text and uses the correct terminology (pronoun/antecedent).

Autonomy in Assessment

Multiple choice is an inevitability for many teachers who teach AP courses or other courses that culminate in a standardized test, but it does not have to be the only way we assess students. Research indicates that fostering student autonomy is an important way to be responsive to students' needs and perspectives.[22] Making room for choice in assessments can benefit both students and teachers. For teachers, providing students with options to demonstrate their learning can help us better understand and, perhaps, even be more responsive to individual students. Additionally, when students have choice in their assessments, they may be more intrinsically motivated to complete the assessment well.[23] One of the changes I made in the AP course was to add a variety of assessments, formative and summative, that fostered student autonomy. One specific assessment that fostered this autonomy was the Individualized Learning Plan (ILP), an assignment passed down to me by Mrs. Schilling.

Approximately eight weeks before the exam, students began their ILP. The purpose of this plan was for students to prepare for the exam based upon their own assessment of their learning. While our shared coursework continued in the classroom, students were engaged in this individualized work at home. To make space for students to enact their ILP, I refrained from assigning other homework during this time.

The first step in this process was for students to review their portfolio of writing and other assessments (e.g., multiple-choice practice, projects, group assignments) and to list "areas of strength" and "areas in need of improvement." After the list was made, students examined their areas in need of improvement and created goals for their ILP. Once the goals were made, students developed a study plan. This plan was specific, but also iterative. Each week, students decided what to focus on and described how they planned on reaching their selected goals. I encouraged students not to reinvent the wheel and take *more* multiple-choice assessments or write *more* essays, but, instead, to use the eight weeks to reflect on their growth and consider ways to improve. For example, if they felt they needed to work on analysis writing, they might reread an already completed essay and reflect on the peer and teacher feedback they received. Then, they could rewrite a portion of the essay. I continuously emphasized the iterative nature of the work; in other words, if students felt that they had reached a goal they set ahead of their self-selected schedule, they could create a new goal and revise their ILP.

My role in this process was facilitator and cheerleader. Every week, for accountability (and for school-mandated grading purposes), students wrote a short reflection on their progress detailing what they did, how much time they spent on tasks, and their revised plan for the next week. I would give process-type feedback on these documents—adding questions, suggestions, and encouragement—and enter a weekly completion grade into my gradebook. My district allotted time in our schedule for office hours during homeroom. Students could build conferencing time into their ILP (or use it as they discovered it was necessary); in my ILP feedback, I would occasionally encourage a student to conference with me if I felt they needed one-on-one support, particularly if I sensed they were experiencing test anxiety or self-doubt. In the days leading up to the AP exam, I refrained from teaching new material and instead tailored my instruction to what students identified were their ongoing areas of need.

Takeaways

The practices I used in my AP Lang classroom may support teachers who feel beholden to teaching standardized test preparation; however, I encourage teachers to continue to further challenge the constructs of standardized testing. Supporting students to problematize multiple-choice questions—asking them to consider the fixed idea of *rightness* or encouraging them to brainstorm other, valid responses—could foster their metacognitive practices and disrupt the authority of such assessments. Another practice could be asking students to examine the readings on the standardized assessment and consider points of view, perspectives, and/or life experiences not captured.

FINAL THOUGHTS

In this chapter, we have suggested three ways that high school ELA teachers can enact equitable practices in their classrooms. We would like to emphasize that these small changes did not occur overnight. This work originated from reflection on our practice and remains ongoing, as there is always room for growth. However, these seemingly small changes have the power to foster more equitable practices for their students.

NOTES

1. bell hooks, *Teaching to Transgress: Education as the Practice of Freedom* (New York: Routledge, 1994); Bettina L. Love, *We Want to Do More Than Survive: Abolitionist Teaching and the Pursuit of Educational Freedom* (Boston: Beacon Press, 2019).

2. hooks, *Teaching to Transgress*, 8.

3. Brenna Bohny, Monica Taylor, Sa Qwona S. Clark, Susan D'Elia, Graziela Lobato-Creekmur, Stephanie Brown Tarnowski, and Sara Wasserman, "What Happens in Vegas Doesn't Always Stay in Vegas: Negotiating the Curriculum Leads to Agency and Change," *Studying Teacher Education* 12, no. 3 (2016): 284–301; hooks, *Teaching to Transgress*; Love, *We Want to Do More Than Survive*.

4. I use the term Quick Write for low-stakes writing tasks that invite students to work out a preliminary idea, engage in self-reflection, or share a point of view.

5. Bohny et al., "What Happens in Vegas Doesn't Always Stay in Vegas," 288.

6. Grant Wiggins and Jay McTighe, *Understanding by Design,* Second edition (Brunswick, NJ: Pearson, 2005), 106.

7. William Shakespeare, *Othello*, eds. Barbara Mowat, Paul Werstine, Michael Poston, and Rebecca Niles (Washington, DC: Folger Shakespeare Library, 2004).

8. John Steinbeck. *Of Mice and Men* (London: Penguin, 1994).

9. To honor and represent diverse preferences within the disability community, we use person-first language (e.g., people with disabilities) and identity-first language (e.g., disabled people) interchangeably; see "Disability Language Style Guide," https://ncdj.org/style-guide/.

10. Sumi Cho, Kimberlé Williams Crenshaw, and Leslie McCall, "Toward a Field of Intersectionality Studies: Theory, Applications, and Praxis," *Signs: Journal of Women in Culture and Society* 38, no. 4 (2013): 785–810.

11. Divya Goyal, Xanthe Hunt, Hannah Kuper, Tom Shakespeare, and Lena Morgon Banks, "Impact of the COVID-19 Pandemic on People with Disabilities and Implications for Health Services Research." *Journal of Health Services Research & Policy*, April 2023; Don Bambino Tai, Irene G. Sia, Chyke A. Doubeni, and Mark L. Wieland, "Disproportionate Impact of COVID-19 on Racial and Ethnic Minority Groups in the United States: A 2021 Update," *Journal of Racial and Ethnic Health Disparities* 9, no. 6 (2021): 2334–39.

12. William Shakespeare, *Romeo and Juliet*, eds. Barbara Mowat, Paul Werstine, Michael Poston, Rebecca Niles (Washington, DC: Folger Shakespeare Library, 2004).

13. Elie Wiesel and Marion Wiesel, *Night* (London: Penguin Books, 2006).

14. Wayne Au, "Can We Test for Liberation? Moving from Retributive to Restorative and Transformative Assessment in Schools," *Critical Education* 8, no. 13 (2017): 3.

15. Geneva Gay, "The What, Why, and How of Culturally Responsive Teaching: International Mandates, Challenges, and Opportunities," *Multicultural Education Review* 7, no. 3 (2015): 135.

16. Plato, *The Allegory of the Cave* (Brea: P & L Publication, 2010).

17. Henry David Thoreau, *Walden* (New Haven, CT: Yale University Press, 2006).

18. To monitor student satisfaction with the course, I gave mid-year and end-of-year surveys.

19. Emily Style, "Curriculum as Window and Mirror," *Social Science Record* 33, no. 2 (1996): 21–28.

20. Philip Adey and Michael Shayer, "An Exploration of Long-Term Far-Transfer Effects Following an Extended Intervention Program in the High School Science Curriculum," *Cognition and Instruction* 11, no. 1 (1993): 1–29.

21. Nathaniel von der Embse and Ramzi Hasson, "Test Anxiety and High-Stakes Test Performance Between School Settings: Implications for Educators," *Preventing School Failure* 56, no. 3 (2012): 180–87.

22. Richard M. Ryan and Edward L. Deci, "Intrinsic and Extrinsic Motivation from a Self-Determination Theory Perspective: Definitions, Theory, Practices, and Future Directions," *Contemporary Educational Psychology* 61 (2020): 101860.

23. Ibid.

BIBLIOGRAPHY

Adey, Philip, and Michael Shayer. "An Exploration of Long-Term Far-Transfer Effects Following an Extended Intervention Program in the High School Science Curriculum." *Cognition and Instruction* 11, no. 1 (1993): 1–29.

Au, Wayne. "Can We Test for Liberation? Moving from Retributive to Restorative and Transformative Assessment in Schools." *Critical Education* 8, no. 13 (2017).

Bohny, Brenna, Monica Taylor, Sa Qwona S. Clark, Susan D'Elia, Graziela Lobato-Creekmur, Stephanie Brown Tarnowski, and Sara Wasserman. "What Happens in Vegas Doesn't Always Stay in Vegas: Negotiating the Curriculum Leads to Agency and Change." *Studying Teacher Education* 12, no. 3 (2016): 284–301.

Cho, Sumi, Kimberlé Williams Crenshaw, and Leslie McCall. "Toward a Field of Intersectionality Studies: Theory, Applications, and Praxis." *Signs: Journal of Women in Culture and Society* 38, no. 4 (2013): 785–810. https://doi.org/10.1086/669608.

Gay, Geneva. "The What, Why, and How of Culturally Responsive Teaching: International Mandates, Challenges, and Opportunities." *Multicultural Education Review* 7, no. 3 (2015): 123–39.

Goyal, Divya, Xanthe Hunt, Hannah Kuper, Tom Shakespeare, and Lena Morgon Banks. "Impact of the COVID-19 Pandemic on People with Disabilities and Implications for Health Services Research." *Journal of Health Services Research & Policy* (April 2023). https://doi.org/10.1177/13558196231160047.

hooks, bell. *Teaching to Transgress: Education as the Practice of Freedom*. New York: Routledge, 1994.

Love, Bettina. *We Want to Do More Than Survive: Abolitionist Teaching and the Pursuit of Educational Freedom*. Boston: Beacon Press, 2019.

Plato. *The Allegory of the Cave*. Brea: P & L Publication, 2010.

Ryan, Richard M., and Edward L. Deci. "Intrinsic and Extrinsic Motivation from a Self-Determination Theory Perspective: Definitions, Theory, Practices, and Future Directions." *Contemporary Educational Psychology* 61 (2020): 101860.

Shakespeare, William. *Othello*. Edited by Barbara Mowat, Paul Werstine, Michael Poston, and Rebecca Niles. Washington, DC: Folger Shakespeare Library, 2004.

Shakespeare, William. *Romeo and Juliet*. Edited by Barbara Mowat, Paul Werstine, Michael Poston, and Rebecca Niles. Washington, DC: Folger Shakespeare Library, 2004.

Style, Emily. "Curriculum as Window and Mirror." *Social Science Record* 33, no. 2 (1996): 21–28.

Tai, Don Bambino, Irene G. Sia, Chyke A. Doubeni, and Mark L. Wieland. "Disproportionate Impact of COVID-19 on Racial and Ethnic Minority Groups in the United States: A 2021 Update." *Journal of Racial and Ethnic Health Disparities* 9, no. 6 (2021): 2334–39.

Thoreau, Henry David. *Walden*. New Haven, CT: Yale University Press, 2006.

von der Embse, Nathaniel, and Ramzi Hasson. "Test Anxiety and High-Stakes Test Performance Between School Settings: Implications for Educators." *Preventing School Failure: Alternative Education for Children and Youth* 56, no. 3 (2012): 180–87.

Wiesel, Elie, and Marion Wiesel. *Night*. London: Penguin Books, 2006.

Wiggins, Grant, and Jay McTighe. *Understanding by Design*, Second edition. New Brunswick, NJ: Pearson, 2005.

Chapter 13

Conferencing in the High School STEM Classroom

Lauren Bsales and Tanner Huffman

Finding time to work one-on-one with students in a high school setting can be challenging. With limited classroom time and a large curriculum to complete, high school science, technology, engineering, and math (STEM) teachers can feel they have little to no time to work with their students individually. However, all students benefit from one-on-one attention from their teachers, with high school STEM subjects being no exception. Conferencing, a tool often used in elementary school writing instruction,[1] has been long shown to be an effective differentiation aid, and this chapter will work to introduce the strategy in a secondary school STEM context.[2] Conferencing can be adapted from effective elementary techniques to be applied to high school STEM subjects using activities teachers are already using in their classrooms. By applying the principles of elementary school writing conferences to high school STEM subjects, teachers can foster skills for independence, provide opportunities for one-on-one and small-group instruction, and show students that teachers are invested in their learning and care about them. This chapter introduces conferencing techniques and strategies that can be used in high school STEM subject areas to address students' needs in the classroom.

WHAT IS CONFERENCING?

Conferencing is a small-group instructional technique often used in elementary writing instruction and can be adapted to meet the needs of different learners at all levels and within all subject areas.

When a teacher *confers*, they are taking the time to work with students individually to make the student a better mathematician, scientist, engineer, or learner. Meeting with students one-on-one helps build rapport, differentiates instruction, and provides opportunities for assessment. When conferencing, teachers allow students to guide the learning objective of the conference to meet students' needs and enhance their learning outcomes. To establish the goal of a conference, teachers begin by asking questions about a student's work. The teacher will also observe the student's work and listen to the student to find an area of improvement for the conference session. After discussing the strategy, concept, or technique to practice, the teacher will invite the student to try this on their own.

For example, teachers may identify organization as a need for students working on solving algebraic equations. The teacher may then create an example with a student showing organized solving of an equation. The teacher could also model referencing a mentor question where the steps are written out clearly for the student to follow. During this process, the teacher is showing the student how to engage in a new technique while also demonstrating how to do the task on their own. Through this process, students learn what questions to ask themselves to help scaffold their own learning.

Conferencing is a highly effective instructional technique that can be implemented in the classroom by making small changes to activities that teachers are already engaging in. Educators often use classroom time to circulate among students and provide individualized help as needed. By changing the format of these conversations and ensuring teachers see all students, teachers can pivot the classroom structure from answering student questions to conferencing, where students learn how to explore and answer their own questions. As teachers and students become more confident and comfortable with conferencing, this instructional technique can make for peaceful independent work time where students take charge of their learning and instructors can use the time to enhance student thinking and achievement.

HOW TO CONFERENCE

Conferences should have a predictable structure (figure 13.1). As teachers become more confident in conferencing techniques, a natural structure will emerge that works best in different classrooms.

INVITE STUDENTS TO CONFER

All conferences start with the teacher inviting the student to conference. This can be a consistent question or the teacher can ask the student if it is a good time to conference about their work. When used consistently and followed up with deeper questioning, "How's it going?" can be a highly effective conference opener.[3] At first, this opening question will likely need follow-up questions to get productive answers from the students. However, as conferencing becomes more natural for students, they will begin to answer this question in a productive way. Sometimes, students are not ready to confer with you. They may want more time to complete work and find their own questions they can confer with you about. When this occurs, you can set a designated time when you will return to confer. This could look like inviting the student to confer, the student expressing a desire for extra independent time, and you replying with, "Okay, I will return to confer with you in ten minutes" or "Okay, I will confer with two other students and then circle back to you."

Conferencing in the High School STEM Classroom 139

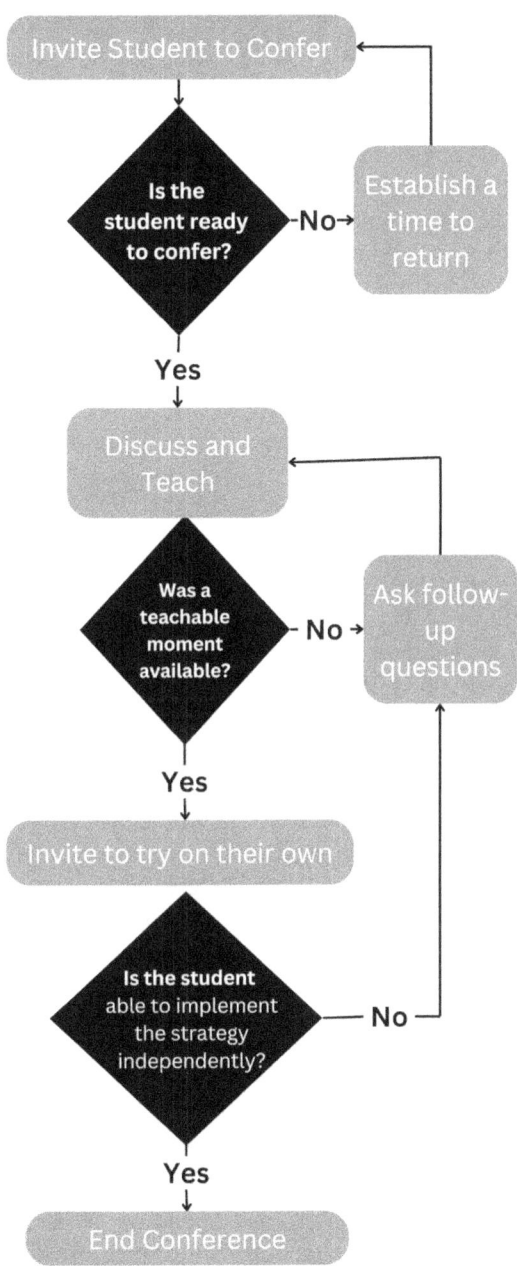

Figure 13.1. Conferencing flowchart. Bsales, L. & Huffman T.

Discuss and Teach

After initiating the conference with students, teachers will engage in exploratory questions to assess their student's understanding. The discussion can center around a previous strategy you have taught, or reference work or a strategy they are engaging in. The discussion should be student-led. It is during this discussion time that the teacher is building rapport, assessing the student's needs, and finding out more about the work the student is engaging in.

Through the discussion with the student, the teacher will identify a teachable moment. As the content area expert, the teacher has knowledge of many more strategies, techniques, and topics than the student has. By engaging in discussion with students, teachers can use their judgment to discern a topic the student could benefit from learning. This can include organization strategies, new techniques, or additional information and resources the student may benefit from. As teachers become more skilled at conferencing, identifying these small teachable moments will become easier. Teachers should keep in mind that conferencing is not the time to review the entire lesson that was taught to students. This is also not the time for an editing session of the students' work. By identifying one area you can teach a student about, conferencing can stay manageable for both the teacher and the student.

Invitation to Try on Their Own

After engaging the student in their teachable moment, teachers should invite the student to try the strategy on their own and move on to the next conference. This is the conclusion of conferencing when the teacher ensures that the student feels confident in attempting to implement the strategy on their own. Before moving on, the teacher should ask the student, "Do you think you can try that on your own?" If the student is not confident with the strategy, the teacher can spend more time with the student on another example. The teacher can also provide encouragement to the student, letting them know that they have seen their skills and know they can do it on their own. Moreover, the student will have confidence that the teacher will conference with them again and provide more support if needed. Inviting the student to try strategies on their own helps transfer skills taught during conferencing to the student's independent work time. This emboldens students to use skills taught in conferences all the time, not just during conferences. By ending conferences with an invitation to try on their own, teachers are ensuring they do not leave a student too soon and instilling confidence in the student that they can use this skill independently.

GOALS

Conferencing with students can have many lesson- and unit-specific goals, but every conference has three goals in common: metacognition, building independence, and building rapport. The topic of conferencing will change every time you conference with a student, but the overarching teaching and learning goals remain the same. Educators want students to know that we care about them, their lives, and their learning. Conferencing teaches students how to solve problems they encounter when teachers are not available to them. And, it gets them to think about their strategies and how they are engaging with the content. All of these teaching and learning goals are happening as educators assess student understanding and address their needs on an individual level.

Metacognition

Metacognition is an essential goal of conferencing with STEM students. Through conferencing, students learn how to think and talk about their strategies and the way they approach the content. By providing guidance, modeling thinking, and asking follow-up questions to help students say more about their strategies, we can uncover student thought processes. Through these lines of questioning, teachers can often find the source of misconceptions, help students expand their number sense, and guide students in becoming effective mathematicians, scientists, and engineers.

Rapport

Conferring with students helps build classroom rapport between the teacher and students. By conferencing with every student one-on-one, we show students that we care about each of them individually. Individualized instruction can show the teacher's engagement with the way the student thinks, completes their work, and participates in the class and their interests outside of the classroom. When conferring with the student and showing interest in their work, the teacher shows that every student is an important member of the classroom community. As the teacher conferences with students, questions such as "I am curious about this, can you tell me more about what you did here?" can show your personal interest in how the student thinks and participates in the classroom community. Additionally, by complimenting student work and strategies you see in every conference, students gain confidence and know that a conferencing session is not a time for the teacher to correct or grade them, but a time for the teacher to learn more about each student and guide students to do their best. Conferencing creates outstanding relationships with teachers, especially when teachers ensure that they conference with all students.

Teach Students Independence

When conferencing with students, the teacher needs to teach and foster skills for independence. A common teacher question about conferencing is "what are the other students doing while I am conferencing with a student?" The simple answer is that they should be doing the same thing that the student you are conferencing with is doing. As we conference with students, we are teaching them skills such as identifying where they have questions, referencing their resources, and using model samples. While you conference with a student about their work, the other students will be working on their assignment and using the skills you have taught them during conferencing to keep themselves on task.

STEM teachers can also provide resources around the room that will help the students check their work during conferencing. One example of this is during an around-the-room activity in a math classroom. During this activity, various questions are posted around the room, and students move between stations to answer the questions. The teacher can have the solutions placed on another paper taped to the wall facing backward. By expecting students to show their work, and only listing the answer, teachers can provide feedback to the student while they conference with another student. Students can use the solutions, previous work, classroom resources, and previous lessons taught in conferencing to remain independent while the teacher conferences with others.

SAMPLE CONFERENCE TOPICS

When conferencing with students, teachers will ask exploratory questions to find out more about the student's work and thought process. Through this exploration, a conferencing topic may become apparent based on the student's needs and where the student is guiding the conference. However, it is helpful to have a conferencing topic preplanned as students and teachers learn how to engage in the conferencing process. The conferencing topics described below are commonly used in STEM conferencing and can be applied to various subject areas.

Using a Mentor Text

Similar to elementary writers referencing a book in the classroom library for inspiration, high school STEM students can reference example problems to help answer questions, solve problems, graph formulas, or write proofs or open-ended answers, among other tasks. In a conference, the teacher can model referencing a mentor question for students and invite the student to try it as they move forward.

A good example of using mentor texts is during math and science problem sets. As teachers conference with students, they may notice an incorrect step in their solving strategy or students not knowing what the next step is. Teachers can model identifying where confusion occurred and thinking about where they can find a correct example of the problem. It is more than likely that an example has been shown during class, in notes, completed for homework, or is on the board. Model referencing the example for the student, and encourage them to try it together on the next example and then independently.

During this conferencing topic, be careful not to explicitly tell the student the answer, but guide their attention toward their mistake and ask prompting questions to help the student correct the mistake. By focusing on asking questions of the student, you are modeling the metacognition and independence strategies the student can use on their own while you are conferring with other students. This makes the strategy applicable to not only this question, but to future questions and tasks in your class.

Using Reference Materials

Classroom notes and materials are a powerful tool for students to build understanding. Many students do not know how to properly use their notes to find answers, or would default to asking the teacher rather than looking through their notes. Conferencing is a great place to help guide students to using their notes and textbooks effectively. At first it may seem more effective to simply answer a question the student has, rather than guiding them through their reference materials to find the answer. However over the long term, this strategy will save time for the teacher in the classroom and help students answer their own questions when you are not available. When students are completing homework, studying for an exam, or during conferencing, you are not always available to the student. When students begin to realize that the teacher will expect them to find the answer to their questions, the students will reduce the number of questions they ask. When you confer with a student and help them build the techniques needed to answer their own questions, they will not feel abandoned to their questions, but empowered to identify their misunderstanding and find answers using their resources.

New Strategy

Conferencing can be a great time to introduce a new technique, skill, or challenge to students. This can be a differentiated approach for many different levels of learners. When conferring with a student, the teacher may notice a more efficient way to achieve the student's goal. The teacher may also know of a mathematical technique that aligns more with the student's way of thinking that may help the student. Teaching this technique to the class may not be necessary or there might not be enough time, and teaching it during a conference, or introducing it to the student early, might help them. One example of this might be commands in a computer program such as AutoCAD, which is taught in engineering classes. Programs such as AutoCAD for engineering and even Photoshop have many more commands than can be taught quickly before having students start on projects and activities. When conferring with students about their project or design, teachers may come across a situation where students are creating more work for themselves because they do not know a command exists in the program. One such example was when a student was creating a rectangular pattern to mimic the design on a garage door. In this case, the student was working in AutoCAD and was using the copy/paste function to create the pattern. Rather than copy/paste twenty rectangles, the teacher taught the student the array tool, allowing the student to duplicate the rectangle into the pattern more easily and quickly. This tool would not be taught to the class for another week, but it was helpful to the student in the moment. It also helped the student understand that the program had many additional helpful functionalities that they may not be aware of. This encouraged the student to explore the program more and ask themselves, "could there be a faster or easier way to do this in the program?" This led to additional conference opportunities where the student would tell the teacher the task they wanted to complete, and ask if there was a more efficient way to do that in the program. Later, the student was confident enough to explore the program on their own and found additional commands without the teacher explicitly teaching them.

Organization Techniques

Individualized instruction about organizational techniques can be very helpful for students in STEM settings. Great examples of this can be seen in the beginning stages of algebraic equations. When students are setting equations equal to each other and solving for a variable, students struggle with the mathematical concepts more when their spatial organization of the problem is not set up properly. During conferences, teachers can provide a variety of techniques that can help students to organize their work in a more effective way. For this specific example, teachers can introduce the use of graph paper, encourage larger handwriting, and model organization of equation solving.

Organization techniques can range outside of the way a student writes their problems to other organization techniques. For example, if the teacher is conferencing during homework review and a student often forgets the assigned homework, the teacher can model an organization technique for the student. In this context, the teacher can use the conference time to get to the root of the missing homework problem with the student. Is the problem forgetting homework is assigned, not knowing what was assigned, not knowing how to use their resources to complete the assignments at home independently, or something else? The teacher can then introduce organization skills to help the student solve their individual difficulty. One example might be placing a Post-it in their notebook on important notes that could help with the homework, writing down a note in their phone or a planner of the assigned tasks, or setting a reminder for after school to complete their homework. By building rapport with the student through conferencing, teachers can more effectively address the cause of student confusion or missed assignments and address those during conferencing time.

WHEN TO CONFERENCE

Conferencing is an instructional technique that can be integrated into your classroom's daily routine through activities students are already doing. STEM classrooms have activities that are unique to their field including labs, problem sets, and design projects. These activities are great opportunities to confer with students as they complete their work. Below are conferencing examples that can be done during various STEM classroom activities.

Labs

During science and engineering labs, teachers can circulate between groups to conference with students. In these contexts, teachers can conference with students individually or in small groups. While conferencing during lab activities, the teacher can engage in several content- or procedural-based lines of inquiry. Lab procedures can be a challenging area for students, so this is a good opportunity for conferencing with groups to ensure they understand procedures and have strategies in place to effectively follow the correct lab procedures. One strategy that can be taught to help enhance student understanding of lab procedures is annotating the laboratory procedures. This can be done in several ways to help the students understand the steps they need to take when following the provided directions. Laboratory annotations can include separate paper notes, highlighting important information, and writing notes in the margins. Helping students find a strategy that helps them follow procedures at the beginning of the year will help the students thoroughly read the laboratory procedures. As students become more proficient with the procedures, they may not need the notes as a support. By conferring with students and helping them find a reading and annotation strategy that helps them follow the procedures, students become stronger in executing the labs and can do so without teacher support.

Independent Work

A great time to conference is while students are working independently on worksheets, activities, or online math activities such as Desmos or Albert.io. During this time the teacher can circulate to students' desks and engage them in conferences. The teacher can elicit student metacognition about their problem-solving process. While conferring with students, avoid turning the session into a review-and-edit session. Work with the student on one problem, explore their strategies and thought processes, and offer one teachable moment. Then invite the student to continue to use the strategy on their own as they continue. If a student indicates needing more help, take note of it, but do not use your conferencing time to correct every mistake they have. Guide them to a resource that can help them such as notes, a Google Classroom post, previous examples, or the textbook, and encourage the student to use this resource as a mentor text. You can model using the material for the student, use it together, then invite the student to try on their own and allow them space to try without your support.

Group Projects

Group projects can be a great time to conference with students. Conferencing with students during group work activities can help keep groups on track and guide students through effectively working with their peers. Group projects that are completed in class provide students with a large amount of time that can feel unstructured and unmonitored. By conferencing with students and giving effective strategies for self-monitoring and time management, teachers can help students work more effectively in groups and use time productively. Conferences with groups should continue to be guided by the students' needs, similar to individual conferences, but these conferences can center more around group work strategies. Some conferencing topics can be about strategies for separating work, how group members will keep each other accountable, and where to find information needed to complete the project. Teachers can also encourage the group members to use one another as a resource during the project; when one student does not know the answer to a question, a group member might and can be asked before the teacher.

Around-the-Room Activities

During around-the-room activities the teacher can meet with a larger number of students within a given class period. When activities are posted around the classroom or hallway for students to travel to and complete, the teacher can station themselves strategically around the room. The teacher can circulate to many students as they travel between questions, or stay at one question that may be challenging or pose a good opportunity for a specific teachable moment. When students circulate, they can work at vertical nonpermanent surfaces such as the whiteboard or on the classroom windows. This allows the teacher to see the work of the students as they circulate and quickly identify students that may benefit from a conference. Additionally, students circulating the room can help teachers new to conferencing pace their conferences to better confer with all of their students. This can be done in several ways. First, by requiring students to answer all posted questions and stationing yourself at one question, you guarantee that every student has the opportunity to confer with you when they are at that question. Additionally, the conference can only last as long as it takes the student to complete the question you are stationed at. This helps keep your conferences short and sweet, avoiding using the conferencing session to reteach the full lesson you have taught on the topic. This around-the-room activity is highly engaging to the students and, because similar questions are posted around the room for students to complete, they can use your conferencing teachable moment as they continue to work around the room.

Conference Notes

Student Name: GS   Project: 3D Pen Design   Period: 2

Date: 2/5	Date: 2/7	Date: 2/8	Date: 2/15
Brainstorming - how to think of many ideas - stuck on "not good" ideas - how to expand	follow up on brainstorm - build confidence	Adding Material - extrude	Tapering Extrude
Date: 2/21	Date: 2/23	Date: 2/27	Date: 3/1
Revolve - what is an axis of rotation?	Placement of axis of rotation why is that important	What is a "profile"/ 2D closed snaps	Lofting - order of selection of profiles
Date: 3/3	Date: 3/8	Date: 3/12	Date: 3/15
Changing units in Inventor	Coil tool - size of profile	Coil parameters height, pitch, revolutions, when to use	thread vs coil
Date: 3/26	Date: 3/28	Date: 4/8	Date: 4/10
why changing units is important * potential mini lesson for full class	wrap up pre-spring break goals for when they return	To Do - goals check in post-break	not ready to confer -- creating coil
Date: 4/15	Date: 4/18	Date: 4/22	Date: 4/23
Adding color/material	dimension lines as a constraint	Assembly - flush mate	Assembly - regular mate
Date: 4/25	Date:	Date:	Date:
Solving Mate error message thought process			

Figure 13.2. Sample conferencing documentation.

Conference Notes

Date: Project: Period:

Student: ____________
Student: ____________
Student: ____________
Student: ____________
Student: ____________
Student: ____________

Conference Notes

Student: Project: Period:

Date: ____________
Date: ____________
Date: ____________
Date: ____________
Date: ____________
Date: ____________

Figure 13.3. Sample conferencing documentation.

Conference Notes

Student Name: Project: Period:

Date: ________	Date: ________	Date: ________	Date: ________
Date: ________	Date: ________	Date: ________	Date: ________
Date: ________	Date: ________	Date: ________	Date: ________
Date: ________	Date: ________	Date: ________	Date: ________
Date: ________	Date: ________	Date: ________	Date: ________
Date: ________	Date: ________	Date: ________	Date: ________

Conference Notes

Date: Project: Period:

Student: ________	Student: ________	Student: ________	Student: ________
Student: ________	Student: ________	Student: ________	Student: ________
Student: ________	Student: ________	Student: ________	Student: ________
Student: ________	Student: ________	Student: ________	Student: ________
Student: ________	Student: ________	Student: ________	Student: ________
Student: ________	Student: ________	Student: ________	Student: ________

Figure 13.4. Conferences spreadsheet.

DOCUMENTATION

Documentation is an important part of conferencing but should not overshadow time spent conferring with students. There are a variety of ways to document conferencing that will work for different teachers, subjects and grade levels, and student dynamics. Documenting conferences holds two main benefits. First, it keeps a record of the topics and strategies you have taught students. When you document, educators have recorded and can remember what has been taught to a student in the past and refer back to it during other conferences.[4] This also helps ensure teachers do not reteach a strategy to a student. Second, recording conferences helps you ensure that you confer with all students. Often in our classrooms the students that we spend the most time with may be the students who struggle or are the most vocal about needing help. When conferencing is not documented, there may be students whom teachers have been missing without noticing. By documenting conferences, teachers can see which students are not visited often enough and ensure they receive conferencing instruction. When teachers confer with students, it is important that all students know that the teacher will conference with them. When the students know that the teacher will get to them and help them with their questions at some point, they are less likely to interrupt while the teacher is conferring with another student. Documenting which students teachers have conferenced with, when the conference took place, and what it was about can help ensure you get to every student.

Documentation can be short or robust depending on what works for your classroom. Figures 13.2 and 13.3 are some examples of conference documentation that works for different teachers.

CONCLUSION

Conferencing can be used across grade levels in STEM settings to differentiate instruction, build rapport with students, and encourage student independence. By conferencing with all students, educators can scaffold learning across levels to meet all students' needs. Through the implementation of small changes in activities that are already happening in STEM classrooms, teachers can address students' individual needs and build student confidence in STEM fields. Conferencing can happen naturally and organically within lessons as teachers and students become more comfortable and confident in the approach. By conferring with their students, STEM teachers can increase student confidence, increase skill level, assess student understanding, and create meaningful connections with their students.

NOTES

1. Julie Learned, Michael Dowd, and Joseph R. Jenkins, "Instructional Conferencing," *Teaching Exceptional Children* 41, no. 5 (2009): 46–51.

2. Carl Anderson, *How's It Going? A Practical Guide to Conferring with Student Writers* (Portsmouth, NH: Heinemann, 2000); Steve Graham, Charles A. MacArthur, and Jill

Fitzgerald (eds.), *Best Practices in Writing Instruction* (New York: Guilford Press, 2007), 1–30; Donald H. Graves, "Six Guideposts to a Successful Writing Conference," *Learning* 11, no. 7 (1982): 76–77.

3. Anderson, *How's It Going?*
4. Ibid.

BIBLIOGRAPHY

Anderson, Carl. *How's It Going?: A Practical Guide to Conferring with Student Writers*. Portsmouth, NH: Heinemann, 2000.

Graham, S., Charles MacArthur, and Jill Fitzgerald. (Eds.). *Best Practices in Writing Instruction*. New York: Guilford Press, 2007.

Graves, D. "Six Guideposts to a Successful Writing Conference." *Learning* 11, no. 4 (1982): 76–77.

Learned, Julie, Michael Dowd, and Joseph R. Jenkins. "Instructional Conferencing: Helping Students Succeed on Independent Assignments in Inclusive Settings." *Teaching Exceptional Children* 41, no. 5 (2009): 46–51. https://doi.org/10.1177/004005990904100505.

Chapter 14

Creating Multiple Pathways for Outcomes and Unit Themes through Standards

Samantha Shane

Sunday afternoon around 3:00 p.m. is when the sinking feeling would start. I would make myself a cup of coffee and sit at the dining room table and think about my lesson plans. The Sunday Scaries filled more time than I cared to admit before I had a better system in place for lesson planning. I would spend hours thinking about what activities I thought students needed to engage in while reading the class novel. This would always include some type of writing, usually a literary analysis, vocabulary practice, and grammar. I spent so much time creating vocabulary lists, reading comprehension questions, and essays based on the book at the center of the unit. For example, when teaching *Lord of the Flies*, I would center the essay, project, and lessons around the book. I would read similar responses in the assigned essay on the characters in the novel. I would then randomly select standards that I thought fit and then I would feel accomplished. I thought I was preparing my students to be strong readers and writers.

As a high school English teacher, I feel strongly about how well students need to write, read, and think. I firmly believe that students should learn new vocabulary, routinely write, and critically think about the readings. For the majority of my career, I've been working in a career technical high school where students studied a specific career cluster like business, biotechnology, education, culinary ats, and more. My students would come in buzzing about the projects they were completing in those classes. I loved hearing about their projects, like growing algae, creating new recipes for an upcoming lunch, or student teaching to preschool students. Then, I would make students write a five-paragraph essay because that's what I thought was best. I felt jealous that my students weren't buzzing about the essays or as deeply engaged as I wanted them to be in class. This started my journey into looking at how to better improve my practice. It started with examining my grading practices. What types of assignments was I giving? What were the unit standards? Why did I grade the handing in of the signed syllabus? I quickly realized my grades and assignments started with the standards and how I grouped them to create multiple pathways for my students. It also allowed me to create strong themes that related to students and the world around them.

Standards create a road map for the teacher. It may seem overwhelming to look at the standards that need to be covered in a single year. Standards are learning targets that are established for each grade level and subject. That map can give the teacher numerous options for projects, lessons, and essays. A demand for common standards among schools started in 1892 when the National Education Association advocated for a system. Many organizations created loose frameworks and, through many reforms over the years, this led to national standards being passed in 2010. Since 2010, there have been many revisions to the standards and varying opinions.[1] States have the option to create their own learning standards or use the national Common Core Standards. While the standards provide guidance to teachers and can improve learning outcomes, teachers should focus on strong teaching practices in addition to the standards. The goal of this chapter is to better understand how a teacher can map out standards to create authentic assessments, connect students to the world around them, and provide choices.

With artificial intelligence (AI) becoming increasingly integrated in our lives and preparing our students for jobs that don't exist yet, educators need to shift what types of assignments we give our students. In a recent study, the top skills needed in the next ten years are digital literacy, data literacy, critical thinking, creativity, emotional intelligence, collaboration, curiosity, and collaboration.[2] As educators, it is our role to provide students with an education that can prepare them successfully for the future. As I reflected more on these skills, I found myself wondering how my essay assignment for *Lord of the Flies* did this. Could students just copy from the internet? How did my essay prepare students for the next steps? In college, students will need to write research papers, read and write about literature, and participate in discussions. I further reflected, are my assignments just "Googleable"? My first step was to understand my standards. If I understood what the standards were focusing on, my assignments would reflect that skill and concept.

Your first task when unpacking and picking your standards is to create a mind map of the standards. By visually grouping the standards, you can make strong connections, and group like standards from the various categories. I usually complete this on a big anchor chart or whiteboard. I like being able to visualize the standards and language in front of me. It also allows me to easily move things around and consider new connections.

When I first completed a mind map of my standards, I found similarities between standards, standards that complemented each other, and the versatility of standards. I asked myself what connections made the most sense. What connections did I miss? I selected standards that have commonalities based on the language and task (table 14.1). For students to be strong writers, they need to practice identifying and analyzing pieces of informative texts. Moreover, the reading informational standard focuses on analyzing perspectives as presented in different mediums directly related to the speaking standards about evaluating a speaker's point of view. After a teacher groups together like standards, they can engage in determining the desired results.

As a teacher groups the standards, consider the following questions to help guide the unit planning process:

- How will I provide multiple pathways for my students to achieve the standards?
- What are the desired results?
- How will I provide opportunities for students to apply their knowledge?
- What assessments are key to measuring student learning?

Table 14.1. New Jersey Learning Standards

Reading Standard	Writing Standard	Speaking Standard
RI.9-10.1. Accurately **cite strong and thorough textual evidence** (e.g., via discussion, written response, etc.) and make relevant connections, to **support analysis of what the text says explicitly** as well as inferentially, including determining where the text leaves matters uncertain.	NJSLSA.W2. **Write informative/ explanatory texts to examine and convey complex ideas** and information clearly and accurately through the effective selection, organization, and analysis of content.	NJSLSA.SL3. **Evaluate a speaker's point of view**, reasoning, and use of evidence and rhetoric
RI.9-10.7. **Analyze various perspectives as presented in different mediums** (e.g., a person's life story in both print and multimedia), determining which details are emphasized in each account.	NJSLSA.W6. **Use technology, including the internet, to produce and publish writing** and to interact and collaborate with others.	

Consider how the standards in table 14.1 can function together and support one another. What themes and patterns emerge from the language? How can the specific standards support one another? The next step is identifying the connection between the standards. In looking at the bolded language, there seems to be a shared theme. The "evaluate a speaker's point of view" speaking standard directly relates to the reading standard "analyze various perspectives as presented in different mediums."[3] An example of an assignment that would cover both standards is reading a story about someone's life and then listening to a podcast or video describing the same person's life. Students can compare and contrast which details are important and use rhetoric throughout. When creating the assignment directions, I always use the language of the standards. This helps me not only ensure that I am covering the standard, but also equipping the students with the language. I want them to use the same terminology so they also know what exactly I'm measuring. The language also helps guide what grades are going to "count" for that marking period. Table 14.2 gives an example.

If the assignment does not cover a standard, it does not count toward the marking period grade. I made the shift to giving feedback and tracking student progress, but these assignments don't impact the final marking period grade. These are often defined as formative assessments. As I map out my standards, I usually have a list of possible formative and summative assessments I might use throughout the unit. I later finalize this list after I identify the desired results for each unit.

After looking at the language of the standards, determine the desired results and what the end of the unit looks like for the students. The writing standard has "look fors" like examining complex ideas and conveying them accurately. It provides room to plan an authentic assessment. Authentic assessments mirror the real world and challenge students to use the skills they learned throughout the unit.[4] Three aspects make an authentic assessment: it integrates the skills of the unit, includes a real audience,

Table 14.2. Example of an Assignment Based on a Standard

New Jersey Learning Standard	Directions I Give Students
R4. Interpret words and phrases as they are used in a text, including determining technical, connotative, and figurative meanings, and analyze how specific word choices shape meaning or tone	Task: As you read the next set of pages in *Long Way Down* by Jason Reynolds, choose 2–3 phrases. On the graphic organizer, interpret • The technical definition • The connotative definition • Figurative meanings • How the word or phrase shapes the meaning

and connects to the real world.[5] While traditional tests can be beneficial, they often have students regurgitate the information and not extend it. If we want our students to become independent thinkers, we need our assessments to reflect this. Once students leave traditional school, they are not taking multiple-choice assessments daily.[6] Determining the desired results will create a sense of purpose and direction when starting the unit.

A benefit of mapping out the standards ensures that all standards are covered. As an English teacher, I found myself favoring the reading literature standard about determining themes. In mapping out the standards, each unit has clearly defined goals. Understanding by Design (UbD) is a framework that should be used to plan meaningful units for students and focuses on transferring knowledge. The theme of the framework is to plan with the end in mind. In the framework, teachers follow three steps in determining their units, identifying desired results, determining assessment evidence, and planning learning experiences. The framework defines effective curriculum as planned, long-term, desired results that help deepen student understanding.[7] Table 14.3 from UbD's framework serves as a guide for teachers as they move through the curriculum process.

Using the UbD framework, brainstorm the various ways a standard can be measured, and provide students with a rigorous classroom experience. As a brainstorming exercise, take a standard that involves multiple days for students to learn. Write it down and brainstorm the numerous different projects that relate (table 14.4). While you may not use these projects, it helps be creative and generate new ideas.

Each project listed in the table represents an authentic learning project. Students should be active participants in their learning. In Erin Nerlino's "Making Curriculum Matter to Students," the main goals of creating a curriculum are relevant and timely themes, making purpose explicit, centering student agency, and scaffolding skills.[8] Each project allows for student agency. For example, I had students read informational texts about a local issue that relevant to many of them, the drowning of the New Jersey shore. While reading this article, we looked at how the author developed the argument through the use of data and emotion. Afterward, students identified a local issue they cared about. We discussed what data they needed to make their argument, how to convey emotion, and how to structure their letter. Through this process, each student worked toward the common goal of writing an effective argument, but focused

Table 14.3. Understanding by Design at Glance

Stage 1: Desired Results What goals are specific and targeted? What essential questions can students grapple with? What are the goals of the unit?	Tenets of the UbD Framework Purposeful curricular planning leads to enhanced learning. The framework is founded on student understanding and how they apply the learning. Indicators of understanding are key in knowing if a student can transfer their learning.
Stage 2: Evidence What products will clearly define the evidence? How are the assessments aligned to the standards? What other evidence is key to measuring student understanding?	Authentic assessments demonstrate student mastery. Planning backward avoids treating the textbook as the guide. Teachers are facilitators of the curriculum. Working on continual improvement allows for increased student learning.
Stage 3: Learning Plan What learning activities will lead students to success? How will the plan help students with understanding and transferring knowledge? How will the teacher measure each step of the goal?	

Source: Jay McTighe, "Understanding by Design Framework Introduction: What Is UbD Framework?" in Jay McTighe and Grant Wiggins, *Understanding by Design Framework* (Washington, DC: ASCD, 2012).

Table 14.4. Examples of Projects Related to a Standard

Standard	Project Options
NJSLSA.W1. Write arguments to support claims in an analysis of substantive topics or texts, using valid reasoning and relevant and sufficient evidence. (from "New Jersey Student Learning Standards for English Language Arts Grade 9–10," n.d.)	Letter to local officials arguing for a change and solutions Reviewing a product online Op-ed for a newspaper or online platform Business proposal asking for funding Petition for a certain issue or event

on their topic. The topics varied from river pollution, access to free menstruation products, food stamps, and access to fair education. While we worked on this project, the class read *Frankenstein* and found similarities in how the monster conveys his argument for a wife. Thus, when students engage in reading the novel, they are making connections between current events and the book. The students have a purpose while reading, and I center our assessments around that skill set.

When looking at your desired results and thinking about the possible assignments, think about how the assignments will be specific to the standards yet allow for student choice. How can you elicit student thinking and have students apply the information? I often make a list of real-world tasks students might need to engage in. This includes writing emails, advocating for a cause, proposals for work, social media content, and creating a website. I then consider how I can re-create this for students and ensure they are applying the skills from the standards.

One exercise I engaged in when I first started to examine my standards was looking at my previous projects. As teachers, we know that time is scarce, so creating a new project may seem overwhelming. Look at your previous projects and think about the following:

- What choices do students have within this project?
- What skills are being measured?
- How can I add an authentic learning component to this project?

Once a teacher groups like standards, consider what themes emerge that are timely for students. Some examples of themes for a unit based on standards are shown in table 14.5.

In this unit, teachers have the option to include classic texts like *Frankenstein* by Mary Shelley, or *The Tragedy of Macbeth*. Based on the standards, students have the opportunity to engage in reading and reflect on the reading, critical thinking about characters, and examining language. The goal of the unit allows students to participate in traditional English activities but challenges the students to connect the literature to their own lives. As a teacher, think about what topics and themes are timeless for students yet capture the current state of the world around them. In looking at the language standard, it is important to avoid just creating a vocabulary list. The purpose

Table 14.5. Unit Ideas Based on New Jersey ELA Standards

Unit Theme	Standards	Possible Ideas for Assessments
Reflections of Our Past: In this unit, students will explore how the past has shaped who they are today. What actions influence the decisions we make today?	Determine a theme or central idea of a text and analyze in detail its development over the course of the text. Analyze how complex characters develop over the course of a text, interact with other characters, and advance the plot. Determine the meaning of words and phrases as they are used in the text, including figurative and connotative meanings. Write arguments to support claims in analysis of substantive topics or texts, using valid reasoning and relevant and sufficient evidence.	• Writing an argument analyzing the characters • Creating a playlist to reflect one of the complex characters • Writing an argument on how a certain character would react to an event today • Comparing the theme to today's world • Looking at how certain phrases change over the course of a text

is to provide students with tools to determine unknown words instead of memorizing them. Thus, practicing strategies would be more effective than a list. A teacher can assess this by giving students a timely article and having them identify words after practicing with words from the core novel. This skill will benefit students in the real world when they encounter unknown words in their careers or college. The goal is to think about what activities and assessments a teacher can plan that allow for student agency, relevancy, and critical thinking. How can the assignments created support the standards and skills that are needed to be successful after high school?

While I no longer give vocabulary lists, I do provide students with various resources for each whole-class novel. Each book that we read includes reading comprehension questions for students to use as they read. I do not collect their responses or require them, but it provides support to the students. We always have class discussions based on the questions, but I only assess what my standards are asking. I also provide an audiobook, author background, and character chart. Scaffolding and providing support for the students helps set the foundation for students to critically think about the unit and transfer their knowledge. The resources help students develop the habits they need to be strong readers and writers. Additionally, students build confidence in the choices they have to be prepared and successful in the class. Not every student finds the questions helpful, but many love the audiobook and graphic organizers. Students develop routines and patterns so they can transfer these skills beyond my classroom. After doing the work of identifying and analyzing the standards and assessments, I know where my students are going intellectually. I can turn my attention to the day-to-day engagement.

There are several examples of projects for writing informative texts and using technology to publish work, including the following:

- Reports for a newspaper: Students can explore the editorial process by looking at examples of investigative reporting in various areas like science, business, and more. The focus would be on informing readers without adding an opinion and conveying complex ideas.
- Blog posts: Students can create a blog to inform their readers about a certain topic, event, or idea. Routinely writing over time will help students practice their informational skills.
- Infographic: Infographics combine images and words to create important visuals for people to digest information. An example project of this would be creating an infographic on a historical event, scientific phenomenon, or concept in literature.
- TikTok: While TikTok may seem like a fun content form, the planning and writing that goes into TikTok directly relates to the writing standard. Students would use the quick, video-style content to write a script for an informational video. Videos could be on a topic of choice or even a grammar concept.

After, consider the theme of the unit and what enduring understandings emerge. A theme provides direction and clarity for the teacher and students. Some example themes I have used include:

- Reactions of Our Past
- How We See Things
- Chaos and Order
- Response to Change

As a teacher designing the curriculum, consider what themes can be timely yet relevant for students. Try to avoid narrow themes that force one side or issue. I like to frame units as questions so students can create their answers to the questions. Many of the assignments and readings will allow students to explore multiple aspects and perspectives of that question while learning skills.

While mapping out standards and exploring what themes to create, it is essential to keep in mind the purpose of school. While each subject area is important for children to be exposed to, what skill set can your classroom help develop? The ASCD Whole Child Framework centers around preparing students for life beyond school. The five tenets of the framework are healthy, safe, engaged, supported, and challenged. The main themes of the framework promote students being critical thinkers while being safe and supported. The framework provides the foundation support for successful schools, and the tenets engaged and challenged directly relate to creating multiple pathways for our students.[9] The main focus of the framework is on using active learning strategies, promoting students' understanding of the real world, and creating high expectations for students. I like to keep the ASCD tenets in mind when looking at the standards and thinking about what I want my students to learn and do after a year in my classroom. I always ask myself three questions when I am mapping out standards and designing with the end in mind:

1. What skills will my students use?
2. Is this assessment the best use of their time?
3. What knowledge are they transferring to other tasks?

Teachers know their content and students best. Finding comfort in lesson planning and standards to create a comprehensive unit will leave teachers and students energized. Starting small, just mapping out the standards, can lead to big changes in assignments, student choice, and grading. Teachers should no longer be tied to outdated practices. Standards serve as a road map, and the texts a teacher chooses serve as a vehicle. The road map contains many different routes for students and teachers to take. Think about the themes that are relevant and timely. Then, create authentic assessments that provide students choice and allow students to engage with real-world tasks.

If a teacher feels ready to dive deeper into the world of redesigning their curriculum, there are several suggested books, authors, and resources.

- *Understanding by Design* by Jay McTighe and Grant Wiggins
- ASCD (Association for Supervision and Curriculum Development) publishes numerous books, and many articles in the *EL* magazine offer curriculum guidance
- Edutopia website's sections for Student Engagement and Project-Based Learning
- Myron Dueck's *Grading Smarter Not Harder* and *Giving Students a Say*

As one looks to the standards and starts small, a world of possibilities will open. The Sunday Scaries went away as I dove deeper into better understanding my standards. I love being creative and seeing students make English meaningful for them. However, redesigning standards and lessons takes a lot of time. As the educator in the room, you have the knowledge and power to make the changes best for your students. Start one step at a time!

NOTES

1. Will Greer, "The 50 Year History of the Common Core," *Journal of Educational Foundations* 31, nos. 3–4 (2018): 115.
2. Bernard Marr, "The Top 10 Most In-Demand Skills for the Next 10 Years," *Forbes*, February 20, 2024, https://www.forbes.com/sites/bernardmarr/2022/08/22/the-top-10-most-in-demand-skills-for-the-next-10-years/?sh=2794d86e17be.
3. State of New Jersey, "New Jersey Student Learning Standards for English Language Arts Grade 9–10," n.d., https://www.nj.gov/education/standards/ela/Docs/2016NJSLS-ELA_Grades9-10.pdf (accessed January 11, 2024).
4. Edutopia, "Grant Wiggins, Defining Assessment," January 2002, https://www.edutopia.org/grant-wiggins-assessment.
5. Ibid.
6. Ibid.
7. Jay McTighe, "Introduction: What Is UbD Framework?" in Jay McTighe and Grant Wiggins, *Understanding by Design Framework* (Washington, DC: ASCD, 2012), https://files.ascd.org/staticfiles/ascd/pdf/siteASCD/publications/UbD_WhitePaper0312.pdf.
8. Erin Nerlino, "Making Curriculum Matter to Students," *EL Magazine*, no. 5 (February 2023): 68.
9. ASCD, "The Whole Child Approach to Education," n.d., https://www.ascd.org/whole-child (accessed January 15, 2024).

BIBLIOGRAPHY

ASCD. "The Whole Child Approach to Education." n.d. https://www.ascd.org/whole-child. Accessed January 15, 2024.
Edutopia. "Grant Wiggins: Defining Assessment." January 2002. https://www.edutopia.org/grant-wiggins-assessment.
Greer, Will. "The 50 Year History of the Common Core." *Journal of Educational Foundations* 31, nos. 3–4 (2018): 100–17.
Marr, Bernard. "The Top 10 Most In-Demand Skills for the Next 10 Years." *Forbes*, February 20, 2024. https://www.forbes.com/sites/bernardmarr/2022/08/22/the-top-10-most-in-demand-skills-for-the-next-10-years/?sh=2794d86e17be.
McTighe, Jay. "Introduction: What Is UbD Framework?" In Jay McTighe and Grant Wiggins, *Understanding by Design Framework*. Washington, DC: ASCD, 2012. https://files.ascd.org/staticfiles/ascd/pdf/siteASCD/publications/UbD_WhitePaper0312.pdf.
Nerlino, Erin. "Making Curriculum Matter to Students." *EL Magazine*, no. 5 (February 2023): 68–72.
State of New Jersey. "New Jersey Student Learning Standards for English Language Arts Grade 9–10." n.d. https://www.nj.gov/education/standards/ela/Docs/2016NJSLS-ELA_Grades9-10.pdf. Accessed January 11, 2024.

Chapter 15

Small Steps toward Amplifying More Voices in Your Social Studies Classroom

An Exercise in Critical Literacy

Ashley Wright

CONTEXT

As the United States continues to grow as a more diverse and multicultural society, it's more essential than ever that our teachers respond to this change and incorporate more culturally responsive instructional practices into their classrooms. Students come into our classrooms with more diverse social identities, and our school environments should celebrate and teach our students how to navigate these diversities. As this demographic change occurs, a teacher's ultimate goal should be to create a safe environment that fosters inclusion, educational curiosity, and a love of learning for their students. However, cultivating and maintaining this endeavor requires constant work, education, and reflection. And within an educational system that continues to ask so much of our educators, finding a place to start building these practices can feel overwhelming, especially at the hectic start of the school year. However, small incremental changes to our classroom practices can make building these spaces more manageable for educators interested in this work.

This was where I found myself in 2020, amid conversations on social justice in education sparked by the Black Lives Matter protests. The movement pushed me to significantly reflect on my instructional practice and come back with the intent to refocus my curriculum with social justice outcomes in mind. Throughout my reflection, I identified how much I defaulted to predominantly White male perspectives when choosing supplemental sources for my government classes. I aligned my curriculum to the course standards and incorporated foundational readings from my college experiences as a political science and history student. I was focused on providing my students with what I considered "foundational" information for my subject area in US government, but in doing so, I intentionally silenced knowledge, narratives, and experiences from other perspectives. My curriculum lacked diversity from individuals of different genders, sexual orientations, social classes, racial and ethnic backgrounds, and intersectionalities that my students are exposed to daily living in a diverse, multicultural society. I did not realize how much knowledge and how many voices I was silencing with the choices I had made in my course, and after this self-reflection, I was committed to reapproaching my craft in a transformative way. This chapter will examine the steps I took to start diversifying my course curriculum in my twelfth-grade US government classes through exercises in critical literacy. Hopefully, it will provide insights and guidance for other educators looking to do this work in their educational spaces.

While any classroom can benefit from these practices, the social studies classroom is uniquely suited to make efforts toward multicultural and culturally responsive education—that is, teaching that responds to the experiences of our student population and actively shapes their understanding of the world they live in.[1] Efforts toward multicultural education can foster classroom equality, justice, and equity, creating opportunities for teachers to teach for and to all learners.[2] Courses in the discipline of social studies provide a tremendous amount of opportunity for culturally relevant teaching practices and cultivating inclusive learning environments. Overall, education in the humanities allows students to explore their social nature critically, gives them basic knowledge regarding their social, economic, and political backgrounds and interrelationships, and can help them commit to transforming their communities and society as a whole. Social studies educators have a unique opportunity to provide students with a curriculum that guides them in making social, economic, political, and historical decisions in a complex and diverse world, but this work has applications across disciplines.[3]

However, even with the opportunity for change in how teachers implement their instructional practices, research regarding social studies education has documented how social studies standards, teaching, and textbooks reflect predominantly White male perspectives.[4] A lack of a diversified curriculum in schools contributes to minority student groups feeling unwelcome, insignificant, and alienated within their school communities and classrooms.[5] This one-size-fits-all curriculum style also tends to perpetuate more mainstream-based ideologies, which can marginalize students who do not typically fit into the White middle-class, heterosexual, English-speaking model. The content of textbooks, selected literature, and class lessons without diversity make students perceive the educational material as irrelevant, possibly leading to a lack of student engagement in and beyond the classroom. The lack of voice and perspectives from women, people of color, and traditionally marginalized groups does our student population a disservice. By diversifying their curricula, teachers can cultivate an environment that encourages students to consider opinions beyond their own and prepare them to engage in a diverse society. Students' work in the classroom allows them to recognize inequities and use space in school to discuss real problems. However, as I began this journey, I noticed how difficult it was to locate specific methodologies I could translate to my classroom and navigate the resources available to produce more culturally responsive learning communities.

CRITICAL CHANGES IN MY CLASSROOM

In my research, instructional approaches based on critical literacy practices seemed best suited to meet my goals of providing my students with course content that helped them relate to perspectives outside of traditional narratives and empowered them to engage in more civic-based practices. Lewison, Flint, and Van Sluys identified "four dimensions" of critical literacy in their definition: (1) disrupting the commonplace, (2) interrogating multiple viewpoints, (3) focusing on sociopolitical issues, and 4) taking action and promoting social justice."[6] With these dimensions in mind, I set up a reading intervention for my government classes that focused on three main components during the intervention (figure 15.1): (1) content integration and knowledge construction, where I would focus on adapting the supplemental source materials I brought into my class to address more diverse perspectives and concepts related to social justice; (2) student engagement and action, where I would provide and create space for the students to engage with the source material and each other; and (3) a continuous loop of reflection, where I would focus on what components were successful or needed work before I moved on or adapted the cycle again.

The first literacy intervention occurred during a spring semester in my senior US government classes. For background, the US government course itself consists of five central units of study: constitutional foundations, institutions of government, civil rights and civil liberties, political behavior, and linkage institutions, during an eighteen-week-long semester. I started small, prioritizing higher-quality readings and time for engagement rather than an abundance of sources thrown at my students throughout the semester. The goal was to allow my students to develop higher-order critical literacy skills and ways of thinking without adding a workload burden on my

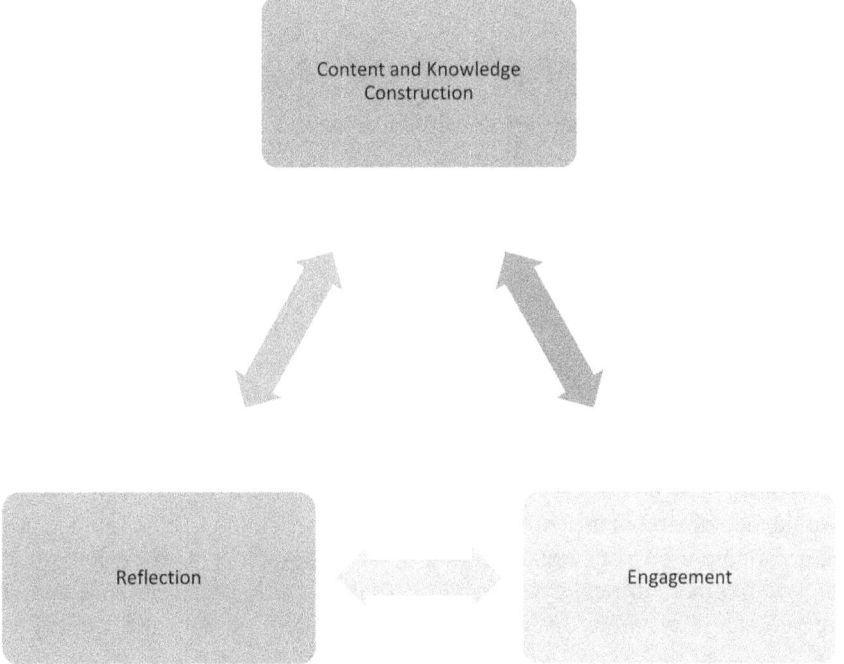

Figure 15.1. Following a critical approach, each phase informs the next to build the intervention, focusing on building knowledge, providing engagement, and reflecting on the cycle.

second-semester seniors, prioritizing the quality of the readings and authentic student engagement over sheer quantity.

I organized my literacy interventions on three major topics aligned with the curriculum, focusing on themes relating to citizenship and social justice perspectives. I researched supplemental materials during the content construction phase to incorporate more diverse narratives and perspectives into my curriculum. I paired two supplemental reading sources alongside three foundational concepts for the course: one in the first unit associated with foundational understandings of American democracy paired alongside the Declaration of Independence, the second within a discussion on the topic of federalism—divided state and federal powers—and last, readings in the section covering civil rights and civic participation.[7]

I felt that each location within my curriculum was appropriate for meaningful conversations on social justice and the theme of citizenship in American democracy through different perspectives. Following each literacy exposure, I built space and assessments for my students to engage beyond just reading the sources. For my first intervention cycle, this came in the form of providing students with the opportunity to write open-thought reflections on the readings and giving them dedicated class discussion time. Finally, throughout each phase, I took the time to reflect on the process with my students before tackling the next phase in the cycle. To more accurately measure the impact of this intervention, I incorporated student surveys, informal interviews, and my class discussion observations. These data points were used to help guide my practice (table 15.1), but this process could look much more informal in your classroom.[8]

Step 1: Content Integration and Knowledge Construction

Content integration and knowledge construction are some of the most accessible ways for educators to begin diversifying their curriculum. Banks states, "Content integration deals with the extent to which teachers use examples, data, and information from various cultures and groups to illustrate the key concepts, principles, generalizations, and theories in their subject area or discipline."[9] In considering content, educators need to consider whether the learning materials used in their classrooms reflect the diversity of their students. Textbooks, literature, and media should include diverse authors, characters, and perspectives representing our students' diverse world. However, this can be more easily said than done. When tackling this in my classroom, I was at a loss for how to start. The amount of sources and materials available via the internet was more than a tad overwhelming, and as a White educator, I was worried about "getting it wrong."

I would recommend first examining your course curriculum to ease into the process. Get comfortable with your standards and objectives, then start to explore your curriculum with a more critical eye. Pay close attention to locations in your curriculum where you can insert more diverse voices into the story. Ask yourself if any voices are missing from the content you're teaching; if so, consider how you can provide access to those narratives for your students. One example that comes to mind is the history of the United States, where much of the curriculum provides opportunities to include indigenous people's voices. Consider pairing foundational concepts like the

Table 15.1. Sample Literacy Intervention Timeline

Prior to First Day of Class	**Curricular Review:** Evaluate the course objectives and standards and identify locations for the inclusion of diverse sources. Reflect on the sources you currently use in your classes; where is there room for improvement or new perspectives? Are there any social concepts or perspectives you've noticed students struggle with? These could be sources for intervention.
	Selection of Sources: Use databases like the Library of Congress to find source materials in US history or government.
	For sources related to courses in world or European history, international relations, economics, and law, use databases like the Avalon Project, World Digital Library, HathiTrust Digital Library, and the British Library.
First Week of Classes	**Reflect and Assess:** Take time during the early weeks of your course to reflect with your students on their experiences in social studies classrooms and assess their needs in terms of what source material would be appropriate. This could be achieved formally or informally through any of the following means: • Course surveys • Class discussions or conversations • Student interviews • Practice document analyses

Throughout the Course	**Implement Critical Literacy Intervention:**
	1. Provide students with the proper background, context, and course knowledge they need to engage with your selected supplemental sources.
	2. Present the sources. This could be independent or guided practice, depending on your grade level or instructional style.
	3. Give students space and support as they read or analyze your selected sources. Ensure you give students appropriate time and assistance as they work through the sources.
	4. Dedicate time for reflection and engagement. Allow your students to consider the sources they've been exposed to independently or as a class.
	   a. Written reflections
	   b. Class discussions
	   c. Civic action projects
	   d. Additional research and education on the perspective
	   e. Critical questioning
	   f. Guided inquiry projects
	5. Reflect on the process. Assess what worked or didn't. Can you take additional steps to make this more effective, or do you need to do something different?
	6. Prepare to start the cycle again. Do you have another round of interventions planned, or did you complete the course? How can you improve moving into the cycle?

establishment of government under the Articles of Confederation or the Constitution with the Haudenosaunee (Iroquois) Confederacy in addition to the traditional Western Enlightenment influences that we typically use. The Smithsonian National Museum of the American Indian and the blog *American Indians in Children's Literature* (*AICL*) are accessible sites for instructional resources and education for those looking for a place to start.

Or, if that's still too much, consider diversifying your content with a general theme in mind. I found this approach easier to wrap my head around than the former in my US government classes, as I could incorporate so much potential content into each unit. Instead, I focused on the central theme of citizenship across my course curriculum because I realized most of my students could not relate to conversations surrounding the denial of civil rights or civic participation. With that in mind, I considered the appropriate locations in my curriculum to incorporate discussions on citizenship using primary sources from traditionally marginalized groups. One example from my first intervention cycle included pairing the analysis of concepts from the Declaration of Independence with Fredrick Douglass's speech, "What to the Slave Is the Fourth of July?" and Abigail Adams's "Remember the Ladies" letter to her husband John Adams.

When adapting new materials to your classroom, there are also a few tips to consider. First, assess where your students are in terms of their content or skill level and meet them there. When tackling this instructional change in my classroom, I was determined to provide my students with rigorous sources, especially since I was teaching high school seniors. Before my intervention, I decided to survey the students to see what their reading and source material experience had been like throughout high school, and I am so glad I did. Their responses were enlightening. Most seniors that year couldn't recall reading many primary sources throughout their high school history classes, let alone sources from women, people of color, or individuals from varying socioeconomic classes. This meant that the sources I could use in my classes needed to be more foundational, and that I would need to provide more context for some concepts and historical backgrounds they might be unfamiliar with. This is also beneficial and best practice for assessing your students' level before conducting an intervention; this way, you can provide sources and materials appropriate for their learning level. Additionally, this exercise gives you and your students an insight into their personal experiences within their journey of social studies education.

Secondly, use primary sources when possible. I've conducted this intervention cycle over the years, rotating through different sources to see what impacts the students more. One observation I've seen consistently in the student data from the reflection phase is that students overwhelmingly reported and demonstrated more preference for primary sources when comparing primary and secondary sources. My students reported that the nature and voice of the primary sources "personalized" historical events for them, making it easier to conceptualize outside of the textbook or some event of the distant past. Students expressed that the speeches I used, in particular, made them feel more "in the moment" than other text-based sources I had used. Students expressed how the tone of speeches allowed them to imagine the speaker conversing with themselves as members of the audience, which seemed to have a lasting impression on how they thought about those sources. Having students recognize and express this in their reflections and across our class discussions showed me how not all primary documents are created equally.

Do not forget that sources can be multimodal; incorporate print, visual, and auditory materials for your students when possible. I was guilty of this during my first intervention attempt when I defaulted and selected all print sources. I opted for different writing styles, including speeches, letters, and published works. I failed to realize how impactful and thought-provoking imagery can be alongside traditional print sources for our students. Visuals and auditory sources are also beneficial for building media literacy, providing accessible options for students who may struggle with the reading level necessary for some print document sources.

Step 2: Engagement

In many school districts and popular writings, attempts toward multicultural education are viewed only, or primarily, as content integration; however, it is critical to provide students with the opportunity to work deeply with the content we've integrated into our classes.[10] It is not enough to give the students access to these sources and hope the only impact comes from exposure to these materials. Critical engagement prioritizes students using their learning in service of their own "academic, personal, social, and political lives," which means that students should be given the opportunities to personalize the curriculum they are exposed to in their classes.[11]

Phase two of my critical literacy intervention focused on student engagement with the supplemental source materials I added to my US government curriculum. The first time I implemented the intervention, these engagement exercises included reading the source material, completing a short written reflection, and a class discussion period structured similar to a Socratic seminar. Students would have a week to work through the readings and their written reflections alongside the other materials for that course section. The class discussion would occur at the culmination of the instructional objectives for that section as a way for students to tie all the content and perspectives together.

Students' freedom of choice is an essential piece of the puzzle when attempting to promote equity and literacy efforts in the classroom. Student choice could include choosing to participate in various activities, choosing the direction when analyzing text, or choosing the themes or concepts to reflect on, and was at the heart of my instructional design for this intervention.[12] My students were always given two sources from different perspectives with similar messaging or themes to analyze during this intervention phase. They could decide to read both or just one depending on their preference. Having two sources meant students could adapt the process to their needs. Did one source resonate more with the student? Was another presented in a way that made reading more accessible for the student? If the students were interested in gaining more insights on the topic, they could continue reading. These choices made it more likely they would participate authentically in this process.

The written reflection portion of the intervention was also designed with the same choice-driven intent in mind. The reflection prompt instructed the students to write a one-page document about their thoughts while engaging with the readings and provided only open-ended guiding questions to help them if they were at a loss for a place to begin. The directions to the students prioritized the inclusion of their perspectives, opinions, and thoughts while reading, and avoided having them summarize the documents unless it helped make their point more straightforward. Students were not required to answer any direct questions, but I included guiding personal questions such as: (1) Can you make any connections to the class from these readings? (2) what did you learn about yourself as a reader, writer, learner, or citizen by reading this?

(3) if you've read the text before, has your view of it changed after this reading? I also included some standard critical literacy questions, including having the students consider the audience, author, and perspectives included and excluded from the source. Designing the written reflections this way allowed my students to discuss any interesting or important topic in the documents they read.

Finally, having a space for written and in-person reflections through the journaling assignment and class discussion allowed students to choose how to express their thoughts. The written reflections could be a judgment-free place for students to practice organizing their thoughts and opinions, especially for students who could be uncomfortable expressing themselves in an open forum. The class discussions allowed students to speak comfortably and engage further in these conversations with their classmates. While these choices may feel inconsequential to us as teachers, for students, they provide the opportunity to take ownership of the learning process, making for a more authentic and personalized student experience.

Step 3: Reflection

We do not learn from experience. We learn from reflecting on experience.

—John Dewey (1933)

Reflection. I'm not going to preach the importance of reflection to educators. We understand that it's one of the most crucial steps in the educational process but tends to fall by the wayside because of time constraints or other obstacles we face as educators. Instead, I will ask that reflection becomes prioritized and reconceptualized as you navigate your practice. The quote from John Dewey at the beginning of the paragraph emphasizes reflection as an active and continuous process. Reflection should not be considered the final step in a process, but rather the framework that guides educators in instructional inquiry and problem-solving. When evaluating the literacy intervention I did with my government students, we can peel back layers of reflection embedded in its design. The intervention itself was born out of reflection.

I identified a problem relating to my instructional methods and the state of social studies education at my organization. I sought ways I could address that problem to transform my practice. I used student interviews and survey responses to encourage students to reconsider their social studies education experience before, during, and after my class. The engagement phase of the intervention emphasized creating and guiding students on their personal journey of reflection with diverse historical sources. Finally, student feedback and my observations guided how I would work through the cycle each time I conducted the intervention. I could make changes or adjustments before the end of an intervention because reflection was an embedded process. By engaging in continuous active reflection and incorporating it into our instructional practices, we can commit to transforming our classrooms to meet our students' diverse needs.[13] It's important to remember that transformative educational efforts are continuous efforts that require continued reflection and adjustments. We won't always get it perfect or get in on the first try, but there is always room for growth and new understandings. All it takes is that first small step.

On that note, the study of history and social studies is rooted in inquiry-driven reflection. Research in social studies and history tends to be seen as a completed process. To the public, this means that when historians, political scientists, sociologists, or other discipline experts conclude on an event or concept when studying the human experience, that becomes the final version accepted in our history books. However, this is a fundamental misunderstanding of the work done in social studies education and academia. Social studies students should reflect and revisit their learning because our present constantly changes. New tools, materials, resources, and perspectives always come to light and can reshape how we understand human history. No matter how often we teach an event or concept, a new perspective can always enlighten and guide our instruction.

OUTCOMES

"This document was especially eye-opening for me." "I learned that I, too, am very passionate about modern social issues and will fight and make it known that these things must change." "These documents help me realize and reaffirm that there is still so much work to be done in society. It is crazy to think about how long our world has been dealing with issues like these."[14] These quotes are just snippets of the responses from students across their written reflections, highlighting what I believe is the goal of social studies education. Providing our students with multiple and diverse perspectives to critically engage with the multicultural society they live in and with interventions like these are two of the many tools educators can utilize in their classrooms to make that a reality. The reflections, instructional practices, and conversations in my classroom have evolved due to these continued interventions for me and my students. However, I'm astonished by the more prominent effect these classroom efforts have had on my department. When I implemented these changes, I was focused on addressing a problem within the scope of my teaching practice; since then, the social studies department at my school has grown and adapted what I've learned in this undertaking to two new elective courses, African American History and Holocaust History, both designed with the intent of teaching historical events with personal narratives at the forefront. In the short time since our school began offering these electives, we've seen their popularity rise within our student population. The general sentiment is that by intentionally designing the courses to focus on the personal perspectives and experiences of the individuals involved in the content, our students are gaining a new appreciation for studying social studies, and all it takes is a step in the right direction.

NOTES

1. Geneva Gay, *Culturally Responsive Teaching: Theory, Research, and Practice* (New York: Teachers College Press, 2018).
2. National Association for Multicultural Education, "Definitions of Multicultural Education," n.d., https://www.nameorg.org/definitions_of_multicultural_e.php, (accessed April 15, 2024).

3. John P. Myers, "Rethinking the Social Studies Curriculum in the Context of Globalization: Education for Global Citizenship in the U.S," *Theory & Research in Social Education* 34, no. 3 (2006): 370–94.

4. William B., Russell (ed.), *Contemporary Social Studies: An Essential Reader* (Charlotte, NC: IAP, 2012).

5. Gay, *Culturally Responsive Teaching.*

6. Mitzi Lewison, Amy Seely Flint, and Katie Van Sluys, "Taking on Critical Literacy: The Journey of Newcomers and Novices," *Language Arts* 79, no. 5 (2002): 382.

7. Ashley Kristen Wright, "There's Action in Silence: An Action Research Study on the Impacts of Diverse Narratives in an Advanced Placement United States Government Class" (PhD diss., University of South Carolina, 2022).

8. Wright, "There's Action in Silence."

9. James A. Banks, "Multicultural Education: Historical Development, Dimensions, and Practice," *Review of Research in Education* 19 (1993): 3–49.

10. Banks, "Multicultural Education."

11. Learning for Justice Staff, "Critical Engagement with Materials," Learning for Justice, May 23, 2023, https://www.learningforjustice.org/magazine/publications/critical-practices-for-social-justice-education/curriculum-and-instruction/critical-engagement-with-materials.

12. Lynette Pretorius, Greg P. van Mourik, and Catherine Barratt, "Student Choice and Higher-Order Thinking: Using a Novel Flexible Assessment Regime Combined with Critical Thinking Activities to Encourage the Development of Higher Order Thinking," *International Journal of Teaching and Learning in Higher Education* 29, no. 2 (2017): 389–401.

13. Laura Saunders and Melissa A. Wong, "Practicing Reflective Teaching," in *Instruction in Libraries and Information Centers* (Champaign, IL: OPN Textbooks, 2020).

14. Wright, "There's Action in Silence."

BIBLIOGRAPHY

Banks, James A. "Multicultural Education: Historical Development, Dimensions, and Practice." *Review of Research in Education* 19 (1993): 3–49.

Gay, Geneva. *Culturally Responsive Teaching: Theory, Research, and Practice*. New York: Teachers College Press, 2018.

Learning for Justice Staff. "Critical Engagement with Materials." Learning for Justice, May 23, 2023. https://www.learningforjustice.org/magazine/publications/critical-practices-for-social-justice-education/curriculum-and-instruction/critical-engagement-with-materials.

Lewison, Mitzi, Amy Seely Flint, and Katie Van Sluys. "Taking on Critical Literacy: The Journey of Newcomers and Novices." *Language Arts* 79, no. 5 (2002): 382–92.

Myers, John P. "Rethinking the Social Studies Curriculum in the Context of Globalization: Education for Global Citizenship in the U.S." *Theory & Research in Social Education* 34, no. 3 (2006): 370–94. https://doi.org/10.1080/00933104.2006.10473313.

National Association for Multicultural Education. "Definitions of Multicultural Education." n.d. https://www.nameorg.org/definitions_of_multicultural_e.php. Accessed April 15, 2024.

Pretorius, Lynette, Greg P. van Mourik, and Catherine Barratt. "Student Choice and Higher-Order Thinking: Using a Novel Flexible Assessment Regime Combined with Critical Thinking Activities to Encourage the Development of Higher Order Thinking." *International Journal of Teaching and Learning in Higher Education* 29, no. 2 (2017): 389–401.

Russell, William B. (Ed.). *Contemporary Social Studies: An Essential Reader*. Charlotte, NC: IAP, 2012.

Saunders, Laura, and Melissa A. Wong. "Practicing Reflective Teaching." Chapter 14 in *Instruction in Libraries and Information Centers*. Champaign, IL: OPN Textbooks, 2020. DOI: 10.21900/wd.12.

Wright, Ashley Kristen. "There's Action in Silence: An Action Research Study on the Impacts of Diverse Narratives in an Advanced Placement United States Government Class." PhD diss., University of South Carolina, 2022.

Chapter 16

Think Big, Start Small

A Story with Strategies for Curriculum Change

Emily S. Meixner and Rachel Scupp-Jorge

In the undergraduate reading and writing methods courses Emily teaches, students regularly ask how curricular change happens. Who decides what students are supposed to do and what teachers are supposed to teach? How much autonomy do teachers have to change the curriculum if and when they recognize it is not meeting students' needs, developing their skills, or igniting their passions and that it is perhaps even doing harm?

This chapter is both a response to these questions and a story about an experience we shared that resulted in curricular change in the school district where Rachel currently works. As we tell our story, we recognize that it is just that—*our story*—however, we hope our process will provide inspiration as well as a possible road map for teachers like us who want to make school curriculum more relevant and inclusive.

We have known each other for over a decade. Rachel is a graduate of the secondary English education program in suburban New Jersey that Emily coordinates, and following Rachel's graduation we kept in touch. We are both white, educated, native-English-speaking, cisgender women. Rachel identifies as straight, Emily as pansexual. Because of our shared commitments to student-centered methods and inclusive, culturally relevant and sustaining pedagogies, we began attending and then presenting together at local and national conferences.[1]

This particular story began as a conversation at a conference in 2016 when Emily mentioned to Rachel that she had been thinking about the dearth of LGBTQ+ content in middle school English/Language Arts curriculum.[2] In addition to secondary reading and writing methods courses, Emily also regularly teaches courses on children's and young adult (YA) literature, and had been teaching a seminar in research and theory specifically on LGBTQ+ YA literature. As she mused out loud about the possibility of developing LGBTQ+ middle-grade ELA content, Rachel leaned in and her eyes began to twinkle. "What I need," Emily said, "is a middle school teacher and some students."

"What about me?" Rachel replied. "And how about my students?"

And we were off and running. Sort of.

In *We Got This*, Cornelius Minor argues that teachers perpetuate ineffective teaching practices for several reasons, the most important being that they underestimate their own agency.[3] They have difficulty imagining how, given the procedures and power dynamics in their various school settings, they might shift thinking, school culture, or instruction in any significant way. As a result, teachers constantly "surf the tension between what should be and what is," often maintaining the status quo by not challenging well-intentioned curricular mandates and/or outdated instructional practices, even when they recognize that these run counter to what students actually need:[4]

- More diverse texts[5]
- More opportunities to engage in student-centered supported and immersive reading and writing practices[6]
- More emphasis on literacy as a human right and fundamental to students' identity development and collective, community activism[7]
- More creative play that fosters engagement, critical thinking, appreciation for aesthetic beauty, and joy[8]

Refusing to address ineffective practices, contends Minor, is dangerous. "Fail to fight an oppressive thing long enough," he warns, "and you become it."[9]

To help teachers remedy what's not working in their specific schools and classrooms, Minor offers a five-part inquiry-based "blueprint" for effecting change that's manageable and local, that starts "small": (1) imagine what this change will look like, he recommends, then (2) plan and implement it, developing explicit assessments you can use to (3) study students and (4) measure the plan's impact. Finally, (5) share your findings.[10]

Despite the fact that Minor's book was published in 2019, three years after we started working on this project, we want to highlight it here because his perspective and blueprint align so closely with our own process. Reading his work enabled us to name, organize, and narrate the story we want to tell. Here's how thinking big, but starting small, led to the district-wide adoption of an eighth-grade LGBTQ+ book club unit in the two middle schools in Rachel's school district[11] (figure 16.1).

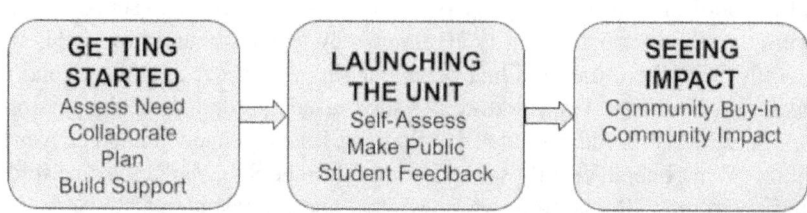

Figure 16.1. Our process for book club curriculum development, implementation, and impact.

I. GETTING STARTED: IMAGINING THE POSSIBLE

Assess Need

The absence of LGBTQ+ middle-grade content was not specific to Rachel's district, an affluent suburban community in central New Jersey with a diverse, upper-middle-class, majority Asian (primarily Indian) student population. Nationally, if teachers were integrating LGBTQ+ literature into their teaching, very few were writing about it despite NCTE's 2007 "Resolution on Strengthening Teacher Knowledge of Lesbian, Gay, Bisexual, and Transgender (LGBT) Issues" and the findings of GLSEN's *National School Climate Surveys* which indicate middle schools are hostile spaces for LGBTQ+ youth. With the exception of Wood, Kissel, and Miller's work using LGBTQ+ content in a social justice unit to build empathy and create "safe zones" for their LGBTQ+ students, there were very few published examples of middle-grade LGBTQ+ inclusive curriculum.[12] Most of the models, if they existed, were situated in high school classrooms.[13]

In terms of Rachel's eighth-grade curriculum, while it focused broadly on human rights and students were reading, writing, and talking about racism, classism, sexism, violence, prejudice, inequity, power, and privilege, it did not engage with heteronormativity, sexual orientation, gender expression, or gender nonconformity. As a result, we saw an immediate need for this work to address both omissions—the absence of an explicit LGBTQ+ presence in the eighth-grade curriculum and the national silence around LGBTQ+ middle-grade content.

Collaborate

As Emily contemplated this work, she recognized this wasn't simply a thinking exercise; she needed hands-on engagement with middle school teachers and students. Rachel knew she had the teaching experience and insight to help shape the methods and materials, but she wasn't as knowledgeable about the texts or the theory Emily believed middle school students would be able to analyze and apply. As mentioned previously, what we shared was a similar orientation to teaching: a deep commitment to cultivating English classrooms in which students engage in learning tasks that are meaningful, relevant, and socially aware. Our experience presenting at conferences together multiple times solidified the mutual respect and trust co-teaching this unit would require.

Plan

The planning of the unit began in the summer of 2017. Since Emily was already familiar with most of the middle-grade titles, she made the initial recommendations. Rachel then read the books with which she wasn't familiar and we began to develop questions to use to evaluate them:

- Were characters who identified as LGBTQ+ central to the story?
- What kind of diverse representation was possible among authors and protagonists?

- Did the narratives offer hope as well as demonstrate struggle?
- Would the students be able to apply the conceptual lenses we were considering?
- Would discussions across the books complicate students' thinking?

Given the texts available at the time (2016–2017), we eventually landed on six: Lisa Bunker's *Felix YZ*, Barbara Dee's *Star-Crossed*, Donna Gephardt's *Lily and Dunkin*, James Howe's *The Misfits*, Ami Polonsky's *Gracefully Grayson*, and Alex Sanchez's *So Hard To Say*.[14] To this list we added Raina Telgemeier's *Drama*, which we used as a mentor text, as well as Nicole Melleby's *Hurricane Season* when it was published in 2019.[15] We recognized this list was not as racially diverse as we'd hoped, so as books like Aida Salazar's *The Moon Within* and Kacen Callender's *Hurricane Child* became available, we introduced them to the students using excerpts or via book talks.[16]

Similar types of questions guided our thinking about the concepts we wanted to teach.

- What domain-specific vocabulary terms would students need to know to access these texts?
- What concepts would help students understand not just what was happening to the characters in the book, but why it was happening?
- Which concepts might also help move students from understanding to action? From recognizing prejudice to combating it?

We realized immediately that we would need to address LGBTQ+ vocabulary. It was essential to us that students knew and felt comfortable using terminology they would encounter in the books. Emily then suggested several additional theoretical concepts that had been valuable to her college students: heteronormativity, internalized homophobia, and the closet.[17] Because we wanted students thinking critically about characters' (and their own) agency as they read, to this list we added resilience, which also included these subcategories: resistance, self-advocacy, and support/advocacy (ally behavior).[18] From these beginnings, the shape of the unit began to emerge (table 16.1).

Build Support

Our next step was to reach out to Rachel's supervisor to see if we might teach this unit in the upcoming school year. Thankfully, she was enthusiastic about the idea and discussed it with the school principal and district superintendent, who also agreed to let us run the unit as a pilot with Rachel's classes. Rachel's supervisor's only caveat was that the unit be framed as a close reading unit, a request that dovetailed beautifully with our desire to have students reading the texts using theoretical conceptual lenses. Rachel's supervisor also asked us to create a budget because the district would need to purchase sets of our recommended book club books.

We are deeply appreciative that Rachel's supervisor, principal, and superintendent were all on board and indicated they understood the value of this work for the students and in the district. We recognize that any of them could have dismissed our request or pulled the plug on this project at any point. They didn't. What we believe helped and

Table 16.1. LGBTQ+ Book Club Unit, Stage 1 Outcomes

Essential Questions
1. What impact does heteronormativity have on our lives and the lives of LGBTQ teens (real and fictional)?
2. How can we deepen our reading experiences by applying critical lenses to our reading?
3. How can we apply critical lenses to unfamiliar texts?
4. How can we use what we've learned to positively impact our community?

Transfer Goals
- Communicate effectively
- Use discipline/topic specific vocabulary
- Read and respond to print and digital texts in multiple ways
- Collaborate and work effectively with others
- Empathize with people whose experiences and beliefs are different from ours
- Act to cultivate equity and justice in our communities

Knowledge and Skills
- To define heteronormativity
- To analyze a variety of print and digital texts using heteronormativity as a critical lens
- To accurately use LGBTQ vocabulary
- To define internalized homophobia and recognize examples of it in book club books and other texts
- To explain why "the closet" is an important metaphor and to identify examples of it in book club books and other texts
- To explain the role agency, resistance, advocacy and support play in critiquing heteronormativity and to provide examples from their book club books
- To apply close reading lenses to an unfamiliar text and compare and contrast it with a book club book
- To develop and defend a project that teaches others about heteronormativity and its effects

Meaning-Making
- Heteronormative expectations are embedded in all aspects of our lives and impact how we see ourselves and others.
- Heteronormativity is an ideology that can oppress groups of people, including children and teens.
- Reading literature using heteronormativity as a critical lens can help us to understand its impact in the real world.
- Reading in this way can also lead us toward solutions and ideas for valuing all people equally. These solutions can be interpersonal as well as institutional.

ultimately worked in our favor were three specific moves we made as we considered what might make them more amenable to our idea and more likely to offer support:

1. Approaching Rachel's supervisor with a fully formed, well-researched idea that reflected the district's current eighth-grade human rights–centered curriculum and could be substituted for a unit on close reading that Rachel was already teaching.
2. Suggesting this curriculum as a pilot and inviting Rachel's administrators to visit her classes to witness how it was working.
3. Emphasizing the benefits of co-teaching this unit and connecting our work to Emily's college-level content and curriculum-building expertise, something

Rachel believed would be both pedagogically reassuring and status-enhancing in her district.

Once we received approval from Rachel's administrators and Rachel's supervisor placed the book order, we went into planning mode again. How would we put the unit into practice? What would the lessons and our co-teaching actually look like?

II. LAUNCHING THE UNIT

On the first day of the unit, the students entered Rachel's classroom to find a museum-style "LGBTQ+ Gallery Walk" prepared for them to build context through discovery. Several students nodded as they scanned the quotes, images, cartoons, and statistics affixed to the walls, recognizing their importance. Others were nervous, a little reluctant, or unsure. One student loudly exclaimed, "Yes! I LOVE this topic!"

The room was silent as students studied each artifact, jotting down their observations and reactions. Following the gallery walk, students were asked to select an artifact that resonated the most with them, and to share their reflections. Many students were taken aback by statistical information about the experiences of LGBTQ+ youth, or the realities captured in school climate data. Others were indignant about the laws banning the mention of LGBTQ+ information in schools. Some students found solace in the examples of allyship that were portrayed, and wondered how they might create similarly inclusive spaces in their own district.

Building on their energy and curiosity, Rachel introduced the students to the Universal Declaration of Human Rights, a document they would return to throughout the year, asking them to consider how this unit might reflect its intentions.[19]

Self-Assess

Over the next four weeks as the students read, mastered the vocabulary, acquired the conceptual theoretical lenses, and met in their book club groups, we communicated nearly every day. For each lens mini-lesson, Emily initially drafted lesson content, which Rachel amended based on her knowledge of her students. Together we designed accompanying activities, creating models of the work we wanted the students to produce. Additionally, after each lesson we would debrief, evaluating our approach and reflecting on student understanding and engagement to make adjustments for Rachel's afternoon classes, which she taught herself.

Given Emily's college schedule, she was able to co-teach in Rachel's school two or three mornings a week, so we decided those would be the days in which we introduced the students to the conceptual lenses they would use to analyze their books. On the days Emily wasn't there, Rachel deepened students' understanding of the lenses using selected mentor texts and facilitating in-class reading and writing activities designed to help us assess students' comprehension (see figure 16.2).

Although most of the unit progressed smoothly, there were, of course, snags along the way. We quickly realized that when copying articles into a Google Doc from sources that would typically be blocked by school algorithms, we needed to remove

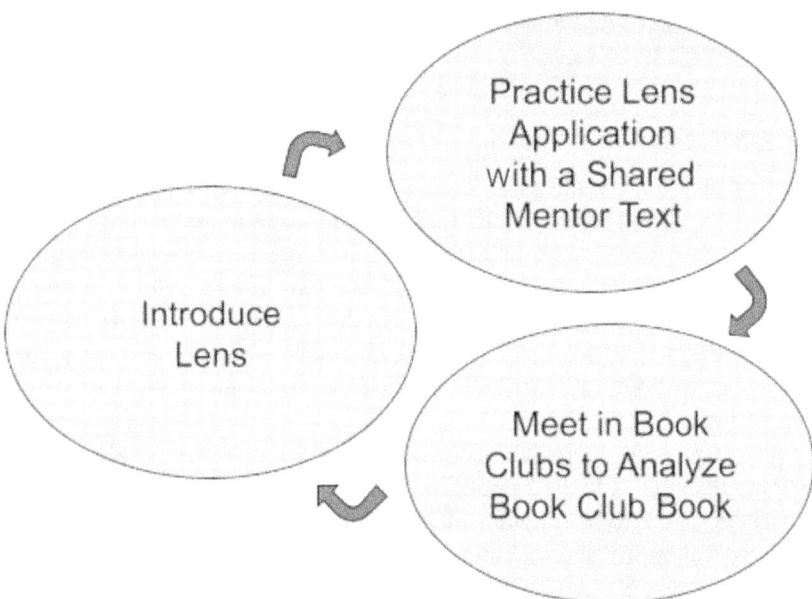

Figure 16.2. Unit instructional cycles for our book club curriculum.

internal hyperlinks from those sources to provide students (and parents) with an added level of protection. When a parent accessed one of these articles on her own, non-school-issued, unregulated device and complained about hyperlinked content, Rachel's supervisor was quick to reassure her that this content was not approved curriculum and that at school students did not have access to it.

Another snag occurred when one administrator encouraged us to provide a "balanced" depiction of LGBTQ+ acceptance in order to avoid potentially "indoctrinating students." "You would like for us to show examples of LGBTQ individuals being discriminated against as a means of promoting balance?" Rachel asked. Rethinking his recommendation, this administrator agreed that a curriculum promoting human rights, allyship, kindness, and acceptance was in the best interest of the students.

Make It Public

Because we proposed this unit as a pilot, we invited school and district administrators to observe Rachel's students (and us) at work. As a result, they came. Grade-level and subject supervisors, school principals and vice principals, and even the superintendent in the district stopped by Rachel's room. Typically they listened as students applied the lenses to their book club books, but they also observed students analyzing a short film, drafting literary letters about their books, and developing their advocacy projects (see Community Impact below).

Each time an administrator dropped in, they remarked on the thoughtfulness and maturity of the students and how impressed they were with eighth graders' ability to process complex concepts, navigate differing perspectives, and make connections between the unit topic and the human rights theme. We didn't convince them that the unit worked—the students did.

Student Feedback

At the end of the unit, we surveyed Rachel's students to help us evaluate the efficacy of the unit and procure recommendations for future modifications. In *We Got This*, Minor encourages teachers to collect formal and informal feedback from students as a foundation of equitable practice.[20] While we didn't hold official class meetings, which is one of Minor's recommendations, we did touch base regularly in discussion, via literary letters and, as we concluded, with a formal survey. In general, the students were enthusiastic about the texts (several students read more than one), but wanted more nonfiction.

They also expressed appreciation for the unit vocabulary and the way the lenses were helping them analyze their books, people's experiences, and their own thinking. "[The unit] taught me to be more aware of the assumptions I make (especially 'cause you know what they say about assumptions) that I didn't realize *were* assumptions," reflected one student. Similarly, wrote a second, "I think that [the unit] opened me up to more of a world and to a new genre of books. It made me realize things we take for granted such as being accepted and feeling the gender we were born into."

Mostly they shared their thanks for the opportunity to learn about a topic that felt timely and relevant to them. "As a learner, I always wanted to learn about LGBTQ but couldn't do it until now. I feel like I am educated more about the world," a student shared, while another commented, "I will remember that there is heteronormativity in everything because I see it everywhere I go."

III. SEEING IMPACT

Community Buy-In

Our pilot experience included numerous positive moments in which students were able to share their thinking in mature and impactful ways, and unit content sparked an interest in creating a more inclusive space for LGBTQ+ youth at Rachel's school. These reactions, the affirmations of the district administrators, and the open-mindedness of Rachel's grade-level colleagues ultimately resulted in a successful pitch to the teachers and the school board that the unit be integrated into the eighth-grade curriculum. The school committed funds to purchasing more books, and Rachel facilitated a professional development session for her colleagues on the unit, sharing all of our lessons, materials, and assignments.

Community Impact

This unit has impacted students, teachers, community leaders, and Rachel's school district more than we expected. At the end of the pilot unit, we offered students an opportunity to develop an advocacy project to pay their learning forward. Several book club groups created bulletin boards that informed younger peers about heteronormativity and LGBTQ+ vocabulary, whereas others researched LGBTQ+-inclusive picture books that could be recommended to local elementary schools. Some students developed curricula for younger students in the district, and others wrote a letter advocating for the presence of a Gay Straight Alliance (GSA) at Rachel's middle school (which was subsequently created).

Colleagues in disciplines like physical education have consulted with Rachel about more inclusive LGBTQ+ content. And, the guidance counselor in Rachel's building decided to audit one of Rachel's class periods in order to learn more about the curriculum and to enrich her own understanding of LGBTQ+ youth. Having the counselor in the classroom learning and talking along with the eighth graders was a remarkable experience. The students could see that their school, their district, and beloved adults in the community were also supportive.

Since 2017, students have continued their advocacy work, successfully advocating for gender-neutral restrooms in all schools throughout the district and all-inclusive signage on single-stall teacher restrooms. Rachel's school even held the first-ever New Jersey GSA (Gay Straight Alliance) conference to be hosted at a middle school. This conference also prompted Rachel's larger school community to develop an EdCamp for Equity and Inclusivity that was co-sponsored by the New Jersey Trans Alliance.[21]

Lastly, we collaborated with Rachel's students on a *Nerdy Book Club* blog post about the impact of the unit.[22] In a world that is so often riddled with stories of hate, this unit offered hope to students, teachers, leaders, and the larger community.

FINAL THOUGHTS

Over the past seven years, as Rachel's students and the world changed, so has the unit. During the pandemic, some of Rachel's colleagues worried about potential parent backlash because of online instruction. Luckily, those concerns were unfounded and the curriculum was appreciated for its focus on human rights. One parent even sat off-camera during Rachel's class so they could become more informed. Post-pandemic, some of Rachel's colleagues have integrated the LGBTQ+ texts into a larger social justice–themed book club unit, whereas for others, the unit has remained a separate entity in order to maintain the integrity of the LGBTQ+ close reading lenses.

Although the unit from its inception has organically changed, one constant remains: this life-affirming work is essential because this curriculum shows students they matter, they have a voice, and that we, as educators, care. "Thinking big, but starting small" enabled us to create change in Rachel's school community. We hope this process and our story helps you do the same.

NOTES

1. Django Paris and H. Samy Alim, *Culturally Sustaining Pedagogies: Teaching and Learning for Justice in a Changing World* (New York: Teachers College Press, 2017); Lorena Germán, *Textured Teaching: A Framework for Culturally Sustaining Practices* (Portsmouth,

NH: Heinemann, 2021); Gloria Ladson-Billings, *The Dreamkeepers: Successful Teachers of African American Children*, 2nd ed. (Hoboken, NJ: Wiley, 2022).

2. Emily S. Meixner, "Book Talk: Finding Just the Right Story: Motivating Readers with Middle Level LGBTQ-Themed Literature," *Voices from the Middle* 23, no.1 (September 2015): 80–82.

3. Cornelius Minor, *We Got This: Equity, Access, and the Quest to Be Who Our Students Need Us to Be* (Portsmouth, NH: Heinemann, 2018).

4. Ibid., xvi.

5. Rudine Sims Bishop, "Windows, Mirrors, and Sliding Glass Doors," *Perspectives: Using and Choosing Books for the Classroom* 6, no. 3 (1990).

6. Kylene Beers, *When Kids Can't Read, What Teachers Can Do: A Guide for Teachers 4–12*, 2nd ed. (Portsmouth, NH: Heinemann, 2023); Penny Kittle, *Book Love: Developing Depth, Stamina, and Passion in Adolescent Readers* (Portsmouth, NH; Heinemann, 2012); Kelly Gallagher and Penny Kittle, *180 Days: Two Teachers and the Quest to Engage and Empower Adolescents* (Portsmouth, NH: Heinemann, 2018); Maryann Wolf, *Reader Come Home: The Reading Brain in a Digital World* (New York: HarperCollins, 2018).

7. Gholdy Muhammad, *Cultivating Genius: An Equity Framework for Culturally and Historically Responsive Literacy* (New York: Scholastic Professional, 2020).

8. Gholdy Muhammad, *Unearthing Joy: A Guide to Culturally and Historically Responsive Curriculum and Instruction* (New York, NY: Scholastic Professional, 2023).

9. Minor, *We Got This*, 49.

10. Ibid., 52–53.

11. Harvey Daniels, *Literature Circles: Voice and Choice in Book Clubs and Reading Groups* (Portland, ME: Stenhouse Publishers, 2002); Harvey Daniels and Nancy Steineke, *Mini-Lessons for Literature Circles* (Portsmouth, NH: Heinemann, 2004); Sonja Cherry-Paul and Dana Johansen, *Breathing New Life in Book Clubs* (Portsmouth, NH: Heinemann, 2019).

12. National Council of Teachers of English. "Resolution on Strengthening Teacher Knowledge of Lesbian, Gay, Bisexual, and Transgender (LGBT) Issues," November 30, 2017, http://www.ncte.org/positions/statements/teacherknowledgelgbt; GLSEN, "School Climate Survey," 2021. https://www.glsen.org/school-climate-survey; Karen Wood, Brian Kissel, and Erin Miller, "Safe Zones: Supporting LGBTQ Youth Through Literature," *Voices from the Middle* 23, no. 4 (May 2016): 46–54.

13. Mollie V. Blackburn and J. F. Buckley, "Teaching Queer-Inclusive English Language Arts," *Journal of Adolescent and Adult Literacy* 49, no. 3 (2005): 202–12; Caroline Clark and Mollie Blackburn, "Reading LGBT-Themed Literature with Young People: What's Possible?" *English Journal* 98, no. 4 (2009): 25–32; Cammie Kim Lin, "Queering Literature in the secondary English classroom," *ALAN Review* 42, no.1 (2014): 44–51.

14. Lisa Bunker, *Felix Yz* (New York: Penguin Young Readers Group, 2017); Barbara Dee, *Star-Crossed.* (New York: Aladdin, 2017); Donna Gephart. *Lily and Dunkin* (New York: Delacorte Books for Young Readers, 2016); James Howe, *The Misfits* (New York: Atheneum Books for Young Readers, 2021); Ami Polonsky, *Gracefully Grayson* (New York: Disney-Hyperion, 2014); Alex Sanchez, *Hard to Say* (New York: Simon & Schuster Books for Young Readers, 2004).

15. Nicole Melleby, *Hurricane Season* (New York: Algonquin Young Readers, 2019); Raina Telgemeier, *Drama* (New York: Graphix/Scholastic, 2012).

16. Kacen Callender, *Hurricane Child* (New York: Scholastic Press, 2018); Aida Salazar, *The Moon Within* (New York: Arthur A. Levine Books, 2019).

17. Emily S. Meixner, "Theory as Method: Queer Theory, LGBTQ Literature, and a Path to Professional Development," *English Leadership Quarterly* 39, no. 1 (August 2016): 9–13; Adrienne Rich, "Compulsory Heterosexuality and Lesbian Experience," *Journal of Women's*

History 15, no. 3 (1980): 11–48; Eve K. Sedgwick, *Epistemology of the Closet* (Oakland: University of California Press, 2008).

18. Rich Savin-Williams, *The New Gay Teenager* (Cambridge, MA: Harvard University Press, 2006).

19. UN General Assembly, "Universal Declaration of Human Rights," United Nations, 1948, http://www.un.org/en/universal-declaration-human-rights/.

20. Minor, *We Got This*, 77–100.

21. An EdCamp is a free, participant-driven conference in which participants collectively and collaboratively determine topics to be discussed as well as share resources and experiences.

22. Emily Meixner, Rachel Scupp, and Rachel's 8th-grade students. "Eight Reasons We're Ready: Human Rights, Social Justice, and LGBTQ Book Clubs," *Nerdy Book Club* (blog), June 23, 2018, https://nerdybookclub.wordpress.com/2018/06/23/eight-reasons-were-ready-human-rights-social-justice-and-lgbtq-book-clubs-by-emily-meixner-rachel-scupp-and-rachels-8th-grade-students-at-grover-middle-school/.

BIBLIOGRAPHY

Beers, Kylene. *When Kids Can't Read—What Teachers Can Do: A Guide for Teachers 4–12*. 2nd ed. Portsmouth, NH: Heinemann, 2023.

Bishop, Rudine Sims. "Windows, Mirrors, and Sliding Glass Doors." *Perspectives: Using and Choosing Books for the Classroom* 6, no 3 (1990).

Blackburn, Mollie V., and J. F. Buckley. "Teaching Queer-Inclusive English Language Arts." *Journal of Adolescent and Adult Literacy* 49, no. 3 (2005): 202–12.

Bunker, Lisa. *Felix Yz*. New York: Penguin Young Readers Group, 2017.

Callender, Kacen. *Hurricane Child*. New York: Scholastic Press, 2018.

Cherry-Paul, Sonja, and Dana Johansen. *Breathing New Life in Book Clubs*. Portsmouth, NH: Heinemann, 2019.

Clark, Caroline, and Mollie V. Blackburn. "Reading LGBT-Themed Literature with Young People: What's Possible?" *English Journal* 98, no. 4 (2009): 25–32.

Daniels, Harvey. *Literature Circles: Voice and Choice in Book Clubs and Reading Groups*. Portland, ME: Stenhouse Publishers, 2002.

Daniels, Harvey, and Nancy Steineke. *Mini-Lessons for Literature Circles*. Portsmouth, NH: Heinemann, 2004.

Dee, Barbara. *Star-Crossed*. New York: Aladdin, 2017.

Gallagher, Kelly, and Penny Kittle. *180 Days: Two Teachers and the Quest to Engage and Empower Adolescents*. Portsmouth, NH: Heinemann, 2018.

Gephart, Donna. *Lily and Dunkin*. New York: Delacorte Books for Young Readers, 2016.

Germán, Lorena. *Textured Teaching: A Framework for Culturally Sustaining Practices*. Portsmouth, NH: Heinemann, 2021.

GLSEN. "School Climate Survey." 2021. https://www.glsen.org/school-climate-survey.

Howe, James. *The Misfits*. New York: Atheneum Books for Young Readers, 2021.

Kittle, Penny. *Book Love: Developing Depth, Stamina, and Passion in Adolescent Readers*. Portsmouth, NH; Heinemann, 2012.

Ladson-Billings, Gloria. *The Dreamkeepers: Successful Teachers of African American Children*. 2nd ed. Hoboken, NJ: Wiley, 2022.

Lin, Cammie Kim. "Queering Literature in the Secondary English Classroom." *ALAN Review* 42, no.1 (2014): 44–51.

Meixner, Emily S. "Book Talk: Finding Just the Right Story. Motivating Readers with Middle Level LGBTQ-Themed Literature." *Voices from the Middle* 23, no.1 (September 2015): 80–82.

Meixner, Emily S. "Theory as Method: Queer Theory, LGBTQ literature, and a path to professional development." *English Leadership Quarterly* 39, no. 1 (August 2016): 9–13.

Meixner, Emily, Rachel Scupp, and Rachel's 8th-grade students. "Eight Reasons We're Ready: Human Rights, Social Justice, and LGBTQ Book Clubs," *Nerdy Book Club* (blog), June 23, 2018. https://nerdybookclub.wordpress.com/2018/06/23/eight-reasons-were-ready-human-rights-social-justice-and-lgbtq-book-clubs-by-emily-meixner-rachel-scupp-and-rachels-8th-grade-students-at-grover-middle-school/.

Melleby, Nicole. *Hurricane Season.* New York: Algonquin Young Readers, 2019.

Minor, Cornelius. *We Got This: Equity, Access, and the Quest to Be Who Our Students Need Us to Be.* Portsmouth, NH: Heinemann, 2018.

Muhammad, Gholdy. *Cultivating Genius: An Equity Framework for Culturally and Historically Responsive Literacy.* New York: Scholastic Professional, 2020.

Muhammad, Gholdy. *Unearthing Joy: A Guide to Culturally and Historically Responsive Curriculum and Instruction.* New York: Scholastic Professional, 2023.

National Council of Teachers of English. "Resolution on Strengthening Teacher Knowledge of Lesbian, Gay, Bisexual, And Transgender (LGBT) Issues." NCTE, November 30, 2017. http://www.ncte.org/positions/statements/teacherknowledgelgbt.

Paris, Django, and H. Samy Alim. (Eds.). *Culturally Sustaining Pedagogies: Teaching and Learning for Justice in a Changing World.* New York: Teachers College Press, 2017.

Polonsky, Ami. *Gracefully Grayson.* New York: Disney-Hyperion, 2014.

Rich, Adrienne. "Compulsory Heterosexuality and Lesbian Experience." *Journal of Women's History* 15, no. 3 (1980): 11–48. DOI. 10.1353/jowh.2003.0079.

Salazar, Aida. *The Moon Within.* New York: Arthur A. Levine Books, 2019.

Sanchez, Alex. *So Hard to Say.* New York: Simon & Schuster Books for Young Readers, 2004.

Savin-Williams, Rich. *The New Gay Teenager.* Cambridge, MA: Harvard University Press, 2006.

Sedgwick, Eve K. *Epistemology of the Closet.* Oakland: University of California Press, 2008.

Telgemeier, Raina. *Drama.* New York: Graphix/Scholastic, 2012.

UN General Assembly. "Universal Declaration of Human Rights." United Nations, 1948. http://www.un.org/en/universal-declaration-human-rights/.

Wolf, Maryann. *Reader Come Home: The Reading Brain in a Digital World.* New York: HarperCollins, 2018.

Wood, Karen, Brian Kissel, and Erin Miller. "Safe Zones: Supporting LGBTQ Youth through Literature." *Voices from the Middle* 23, no. 4 (May 2016): 46–54.

Chapter 17

A Simulation Activity

Supporting Preservice Teachers through the Response-to-Intervention Process

Molly D. Keough

In 2019, Georgia's governor signed Senate Bill 48 into law. This law requires elementary schools to identify and support students showing signs of dyslexia in kindergarten through third grade.[1] Starting January 1, 2024, teacher education programs that lead to certification in Georgia must demonstrate teacher candidates' proficiency using the Multi-Tiered System of Supports framework to support student learning deficits in reading, writing, mathematics, and behavior. This requirement includes applying knowledge of universal screening, evidence-based interventions, tools for progress monitoring, and utilizing student data as part of the response-to-intervention (RTI) process.[2]

The rationale for requiring the RTI process in teacher preparation programs will allow our preservice teachers (PSTs) to support their cooperating teachers in the field and better prepare them to use the process as beginning teachers. The RTI process is essential for our PSTs to know, understand, and implement because it emphasizes early identification and intervention for students struggling academically, behaviorally, or socially/emotionally. Preservice teachers knowledgeable about RTI can proactively recognize signs of difficulties and implement targeted interventions early in their teaching careers. Preservice teachers who can analyze data to adapt instructional strategies and target individual learning needs can support their cooperating teachers in their field placements and directly impact student success. Knowledge and understanding of RTI enhance the professional readiness of preservice teachers, preparing them to navigate the complexities of the classroom quickly and confidently.

NEW STATE REQUIREMENTS FOR EDUCATION PREPARATION PROVIDERS

To address this new requirement, our department identified which courses would include aspects of the new dyslexia law. As the course coordinator of our Classroom Assessments for Elementary Teachers class, I was assigned to incorporate the Response to Intervention (RTI) process in my course content. As the RTI process has multiple components to address various student needs, we would need to include RTI multiple times throughout the program. The Classroom Assessment course would provide curriculum and instruction to introduce and apply understanding of RTI. However, to assess our PSTs' competency in the RTI process for accreditation purposes, we plan to review the content again at the end-of-the-program seminar, allowing our students a full year of student teaching to apply their knowledge and understanding of the RTI process under the guidance of a certified teacher.

The PSTs taking the Classroom Assessment course are second-semester juniors previously admitted into our Elementary Childhood Education program. Program completers earn a Bachelor of Science degree in Elementary Education and are certified to teach prekindergarten through fifth-grade students. Only students in our program may take this course. The Classroom Assessment course is part of our Block II semester. It includes four other courses: Teaching Reading and Writing in Elementary Grades 3–5, Improving Learning with Technology in Elementary Classrooms, Teaching Mathematics in Grades 3–5, and Elementary Classroom Management and Learning Environments. Additionally, students must complete twenty-five hours of classroom fieldwork. All Block II courses must be completed successfully to move into the year-long clinical experience.

The rationale for including the RTI process in the Classroom Assessments course included the need for our PSTs to have an emerging understanding of the components of RTI and how these components help identify students needing additional support. Additionally, adding the RTI process to this course enhances course content by introducing our PSTs to RTI vocabulary, including universal screeners, interventions, and progress monitoring before starting their clinical year. Introducing RTI in Block II aims to provide background knowledge and understanding of the process early, allowing our PSTs to support their cooperating teachers and students quickly and effectively.

USING A SIMULATED-BASED LEARNING EXPERIENCE

My goal for adding the topic of Response to Intervention to our Classroom Assessment course required me to simplify this process to make the content reachable for PSTs who have little knowledge of or experience in implementing the RTI process. Introducing and creating practical, real-life experiences required a more comprehensive learning tool. I wanted this learning environment to mimic each step of the RTI process from analyzing screener data to identifying appropriate research-based interventions to administering and analyzing progress monitoring data, all while working in mock data teams.

I selected a simulation-based learning approach because this format best allows our PSTs to role-play general education teacher roles in the RTI process. Using a simulation allows our PSTs to analyze data, identify different interventions and progress-monitoring tools, and identify ways to provide more appropriate support before working with real students in the field. Using a simulation allows me to design practice opportunities to examine universal screener data to identify next steps and create data team experiences, similar to how general education teachers collaborate to support students receiving Tier 2 supports. Throughout the simulation, the instructor, serving in the role of a building administrator, can provide targeted and appropriate feedback to foster understanding and learning. All the sections of the simulation allow our PSTs to engage in group discussions, sharing their experiences, insights, and challenges from the RTI simulation.

DESIGNING A SIMULATION-BASED LEARNING EXPERIENCE

This simulation-based experience was designed to familiarize our PSTs with the RTI process before they start their yearlong clinical field experiences. Preservice teachers in the final semester of their yearlong clinicals will participate in a second simulation that is similarly structured but more in-depth, including students with a variety of academic, behavioral, and social-emotional concerns.

By engaging in this simulation, our PSTs will gain practical experience in specific RTI components such as early identification of struggling students, tiered interventions, and data-driven decision-making. The simulation allows our PSTs to apply theory from their coursework to a real-world RTI scenario. The simulation structure provides similar experiences that general elementary educators face when implementing the RTI process in their classrooms. Specifically, through this simulation, our preservice teachers practice analyzing screener data, identifying appropriate interventions and progress monitoring tools, and planning the following steps to support specific students' academic needs.

SIMULATION EXAMPLE

In this simulation, the course instructor takes on the role of a building-level administrator, responsible for guiding and facilitating various activities. The building-level administrator collaborates with participants, who play the roles of second-grade general education elementary teachers working in grade-level data teams. Each PST is given a participant's guide to assist them throughout the simulation.

The simulation is structured similar to the RTI framework. It is divided into three main sections, corresponding to the tiers within the RTI structure: Tier 1, Tier 2, and Tier 3, which is also known as the Student Support Team. Each section of the simulation will include instructional videos, explanations provided by the instructor, and student data for analysis. Furthermore, each section will present specific tasks and tools tailored to the requirements of each level within the RTI process, making it a comprehensive learning experience for state certification.

Simulation Introduction

The simulation begins by introducing the Multi-Tiered System of Supports (MTSS), drawing on definitions and resources available on the Georgia Department of Education website. It is worth noting that the Georgia Department of Education has adopted its MTSS definition from the National Center on Response to Intervention, which defines MTSS as a "tiered system of supports aiming to integrate assessment and interventions across the entire school, offering a multi-level prevention system that seeks to enhance student achievement while curbing behavioral issues"[3]

Within this simulation, our PSTs examine the five programs under the MTSS umbrella. These programs include RTI, Positive Behavioral Interventions and Supports, Student Support Team, Student Mental Health, and Wrap-Around Services. PSTs engage with these topics through video content and discussions, which prompt them to connect key MTSS programs with their observations in real-world field placements.

Following the introduction to MTSS, our PSTs explore the RTI Pyramid, which provides an overview of all three levels within this multilevel framework. Additionally, the simulation covers the various steps integral to the RTI process. These steps encompass conducting and analyzing universal screeners, identifying students needing additional support, implementing targeted interventions, monitoring progress, and making informed decisions about possible next steps to support students receiving Tier 2 supports.

Section 1: Tier 1

To start the Tier 1 segment of this simulation, PSTs begin by examining the specific universal screener tool utilized by the school district where they are conducting their field hours. It is important to note that PSTs were actively engaged in classroom settings across six distinct school districts within the metro Atlanta area during the first simulation. This activity is important to ensure this simulation aligns with the specific tools our PSTs observe being implemented in their placements. It is also important to note that all the universal screening tools PSTs evaluate for this activity are sourced from the Georgia Department of Education's Qualified Dyslexia Screening Tools.[4]

Once PSTs familiarize themselves with their district's chosen universal screener tool, they use the iReady Reading Diagnostic to analyze student data. The purpose for using one universal screener for this simulation is to make sure all participants are using the same framework and data.

Following an introductory overview of Tier 1, our PSTs complete the necessary steps to identify students eligible for talented and gifted (TAG) evaluations or Tier 2 interventions. PSTs collaborate within data teams to follow a structured protocol for analyzing iReady diagnostic reading and math data. They also examine data derived from Fountas and Pinnell's Benchmark Assessment System.[5] This protocol is similar to protocols used to analyze data in elementary schools today. For a visual representation of this process, you can refer to figures 17.1 and 17.2, which provide a comprehensive snapshot of the protocol, data, and the corresponding section in the RTI Participant's Guide that PSTs work through collaboratively in their data teams.

Section 2: Tier 2

Upon identifying students needing Tier 2 support, participants transition into the Tier 2 phase of this simulation. In the Classroom Assessment course context, this section takes center stage because it focuses on the pivotal role elementary general educators

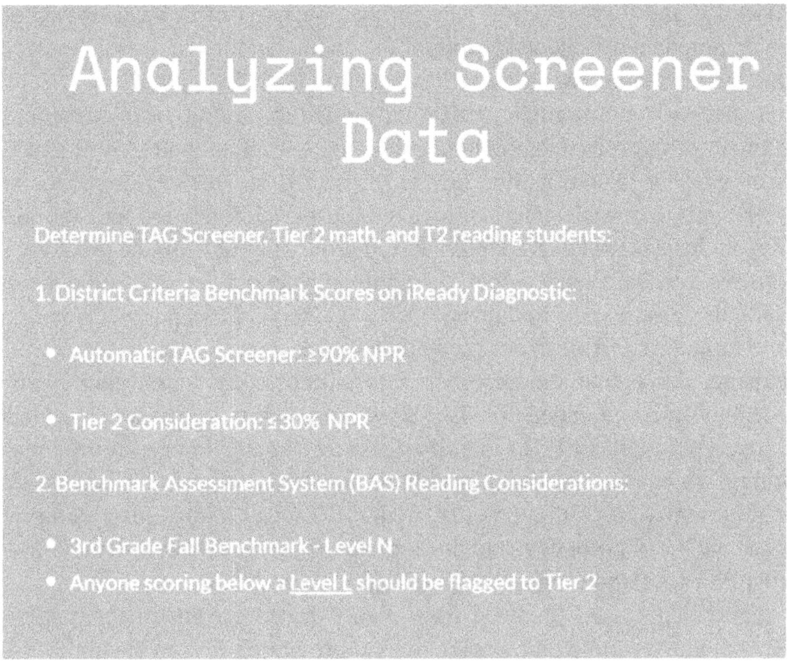

A Simulation Activity   189

Analyzing Screener Data

Determine TAG Screener, Tier 2 math, and T2 reading students:

1. District Criteria Benchmark Scores on iReady Diagnostic:
   - Automatic TAG Screener: ≥90% NPR
   - Tier 2 Consideration: ≤30% NPR

2. Benchmark Assessment System (BAS) Reading Considerations:
   - 3rd Grade Fall Benchmark - Level N
   - Anyone scoring below a Level L should be flagged to Tier 2

Figure 17.1. Tier 1 protocol.

MTSS – RTI Tiers 1 and 2 Data Cycles
Participant's Guide

Tier 1 Universal Screener Data – Fall Window

Based on district criteria, identify who qualifies for:

Grade	First Name	Reading NPR	Fall BAS	Math NPR	TAG Screener	T2 Reading	T2 Math
3	Natalie	67	N	86			
3	Demauveil	92	Q	99			
3	Jasmine	68	M	78			
3	Yen	87	O	94			
3	Mark**	37	K	21			
3	Isabelle	26	L	72			
3	Claire	13	P	98			
3	Zeporia	75	N	99			
3	Jeffrey	6	E	61			
3	Carlos	54	N	42			

**SPED

CODING GUIDE						
BAS Gr.	KG	1st	2nd	3rd	4th	5th
Level	Pre-A – D	E-J	K-M	N-P	Q-S	T-V
Universal Screeners		0-24	25-49	50-74	75-100	

Figure 17.2. Universal screener data.

play in Tier 2 of the RTI process. The primary objective of this phase is twofold: first, to gain a comprehensive understanding of the characteristics of Tier 2, and second, to determine the next steps for students identified for Tier 2 support.

To initiate the Tier 2 segment, PSTs are guided through a video presentation and provided with an overview that includes defining the target instructions and progress monitoring concept. Additionally, they are informed of state requirements about the number of hours per week interventions should be administered and the maximum number of students allowed in an intervention group. In line with the practical requirements observed in field placements, the simulation mandates that students receiving Tier 2 support receive sixty minutes of targeted interventions per week and complete a progress monitoring assessment every other week.

Participants delve into the screener data, strategically identifying break points where students recommended for Tier 2 support exhibit skill deficits. Once these deficits are pinpointed, our PSTs identify district-mandated interventions and progress monitoring tools to craft individualized plans for Tier 2 support for each student. For a visual representation of this process, figures 17.3 and 17.4 offer a comprehensive snapshot of the break point data and the corresponding section in the RTI Participant's Guide that PSTs collaboratively navigate within their data teams.

Once participants have finalized their plans, the course instructor, taking on the role of a building administrator, conducts a thorough review to ensure the accuracy and appropriateness of the selected tools to address the unique needs of each student requiring Tier 2 support. Our PSTs come to understand that following the initial data team meeting, it is the responsibility of the general education teacher to implement these interventions and administer progress monitoring assessments in alignment with Tier 2 requirements and each student's personalized plan. In the context of this

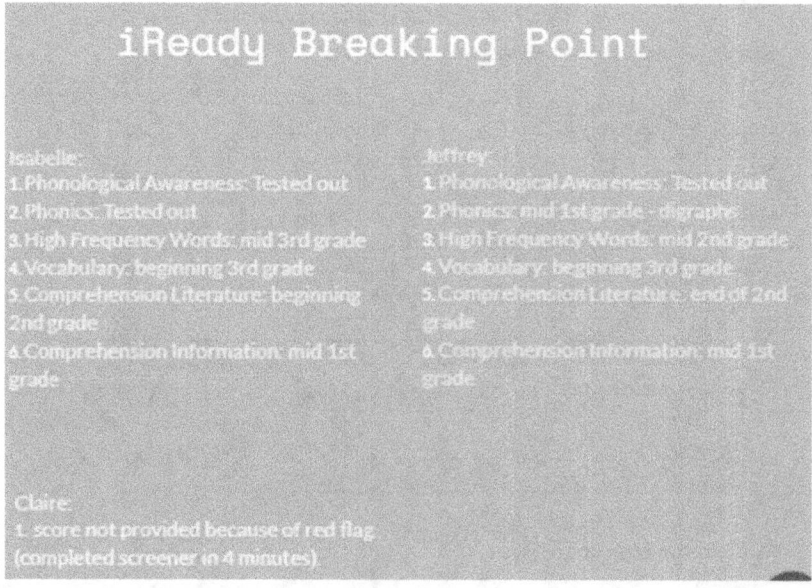

Figure 17.3. Break point data and intervention.

Tier 2 Initial Data Team Meeting – Reviewing Fall Screener Data

First Name	Reading NPR	Fall BAS	Math NPR	TAG Screener (met criteria)	T2 Reading	T2 Math	Area of Concern	Interventions computer-based	teacher-based	Progress Monitoring (PM) EasyCBM
Isabelle	26	L	72		x		Reading Comprehension			
Claire	13	P	98	x	x		Basic Reading			
Jeffrey	6	E	61		x		Basic Reading			

rushing red flag on iReady Reading Diagnostic. student spent less than 11 seconds on average per item on the reading diagnostic. recommendation to retake the iReady diagnostic.

District-Selected Interventions and Progress Monitoring Tools

AREA	Computer-Based Intervention	Teacher-Based Intervention	Progress Monitoring EasyCBM
Basic Reading	iReady Reading	Digraph Roll a Word	Word Reading Fluency
Reading Fluency	iReady Reading	Repeated Reading	Passage Reading Fluency
Reading Comprehension	iReady Reading	Question Cards	Proficient Reading

Figure 17.4. Progress monitoring planning guide.

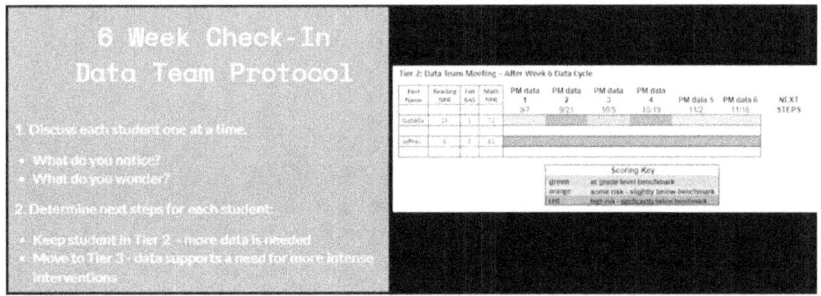

Figure 17.5. Six-week data team protocol and student data set. Mary (Molly) Keogh

simulation, we engage in role-playing where, during the subsequent data team meeting, participants will assess the first six data sets collected for each student.

Within this data team meeting, the team follows a structured protocol for each student benefiting from Tier 2 support. The discussion encompasses questions related to the presented data, offering an opportunity for participants to delve into data analysis. Additionally, participants discuss observed patterns while identifying any additional questions that may arise regarding the progress monitoring data. During this meeting, the course instructor is actively engaged, addressing any notices, inquiries, or the need to clarify confusion or misconceptions. Following this discourse, the teams are tasked with determining the next steps to support students who are receiving Tier 2 support. To visually grasp this process, figure 17.5 provides a comprehensive representation of the six-week data team protocol and the student data included in the RTI Participant's Guide, which PSTs collaboratively navigate within their data teams.

After the six-week data team meeting, our PSTs understand their ongoing responsibility for implementing interventions and conducting progress monitoring assessments as per Tier 2 requirements and the individualized plans of each student. During the subsequent data team meeting to review Week 12 data, participants evaluate the next six sets of data collected for each student. With a total of twelve data sets to analyze, participants are able to gain valuable insights into the impact of interventions on each student's progress.

Within their data teams, participants discuss their observations and questions regarding the progress monitoring results and collaboratively devise plans to determine the most appropriate next steps for supporting each student. For each student, the team will collectively choose one of three options based on the data. They can opt to move a student back down to Tier 1 if the data indicates that Tier 2 support is no longer necessary. Alternatively, if the data appears inconsistent, they may decide that the student would benefit from continuing to receive Tier 2 interventions. Lastly, they can request to advance students within the RTI framework to receive Tier 3 support.

In this simulation, the instructor provides guidance on the most suitable plan for each student. For Isabella, the plan is to continue providing Tier 2 support, while for Jeffrey, the plan involves requesting advancement within the RTI process to receive Tier 3 interventions and progress monitoring assessments. To gain a visual understanding of this process, figures 17.6 and 17.7 offer a comprehensive representation of the twelve-week data team protocol and the student data included in the RTI Participant's Guide, which PSTs collaboratively navigate within their data teams.

12 Week Check-in Data Team Protocol

1. Discuss each student one at a time.
   - What do you notice?
   - What do you wonder?

2. Determine next steps for each student:
   - Keep student in Tier 2 – more data is needed
   - Move to Tier 3 – data supports a need for more intense interventions
   - Add another intervention or identify another data source
   - Move to Tier 1

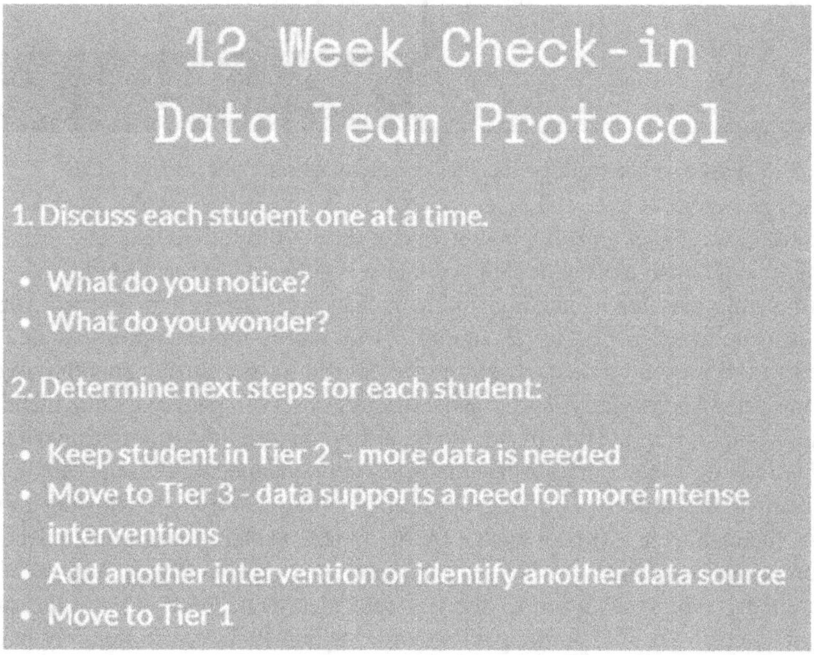

Figure 17.6. Twelve-week data team protocol. Mary (Molly) Keogh

Tier 2: Data Team Meeting – After Week 6 Data Cycle

First Name	Reading NPR	Fall BAS	Math NPR	PM data 1 9/7	PM data 2 9/21	PM data 3 10/5	PM data 4 10/19	PM data 5 11/2	PM data 6 11/16	NEXT STEPS
Isabella	26	L	72							
Jeffrey	6	E	61							

Scoring Key	
green	at grade level benchmark
orange	some risk - slightly below benchmark
red	high risk - signficantly below benchmark

Tier 2: Data Team Meeting – After Week 12 Data Cycle

Name	Reading NPR	Fall BAS	Math NPR	PM data 7 12/7	PM data 8 12/17	PM data 9 1/11	PM data 10 1/25	PM data 11 2/8	NEXT STEPS
Isabelle	26	L	72						
Jeffrey	6	E	61						

Figure 17.7. Student data set.

Section 3: Tier 3

The concluding section of this simulation uses an open discussion format where participants learn how students advance to the next level within the RTI framework and explore the role of the general education teacher at this stage. Specifically, PSTs gain insights into the steps involved when a grade-level data team determines that a student requires more intensive targeted interventions and progress monitoring assessments. In such cases, it is critical to communicate these concerns to the building-level RTI chair. Participants learn that once the RTI chair approves the student for Tier 3 support, the RTI chair begins to oversee the student's Tier 3 support plan. This plan includes scheduling hearing and vision testing and contacting the student's parents or guardians to inform them about the change in support.

Moreover, participants learn the RTI chair also arranges an initial Student Support Team (SST) meeting to review concerns and all the data collected. In this first meeting, the RTI chair, parents or guardians, and the student's classroom teacher meet to discuss the data findings and determine the subsequent course of action. If the plan involves the student receiving Tier 3 support, the classroom teacher may be required to provide the mandated 120 minutes of intense, targeted instruction to the student. Additionally, the teacher may be required to administer a weekly progress monitoring assessment to gauge the effectiveness of the additional intervention time.

During this phase, PSTs collaborate with other PSTs who are completing field hours in the same school district. They are prompted to engage in discussions about how interventions and progress monitoring assessments are executed for students receiving Tier 3 support. From our initial simulation, we discovered that districts implement the RTI process in various ways. Some have dedicated intervention time in which students receiving Tier 3 support are pulled out of their classrooms for these interventions. Some districts incorporate an intervention block in which students requiring different interventions meet with other teachers on that grade level. Finally, certain districts mandate that each classroom teacher administers all Tier 2 and Tier 3 interventions and progress monitoring assessments to their own students. This discussion serves to enrich our PSTs' understanding of the diverse approaches to RTI implementation across the state and helps bridge course content with their field placements.

It is important to emphasize that the primary goal of this simulation is to introduce our PSTs to the RTI process prior to commencing their yearlong clinical experiences. In one of their clinical seminars, they will engage in a more comprehensive simulation that delves deeper into Student Support Teams and eligibility meetings. This second simulation is intentionally designed to learn how informed our PSTs are regarding the RTI process from their observations and experiences supporting their cooperating teachers in their yearlong clinicals. This initial simulation described in this chapter has been purposely designed to equip our PSTs with a practical understanding, enabling them to better support their cooperating teachers and be aware of how the RTI process is executed within their respective host schools and districts.

REFLECTION

While I attempted to simplify the RTI to focus on the basics of each component, the PSTs seemed overwhelmed at times.. Specifically, having only one intervention and one progress monitoring tool for each academic concern glossed over the process each data team goes through to select appropriate resources. The RTI process is intricate, with several components that are hard to expose students to in a single three-hour simulation. Shortening the time typically spent by teachers to identify interventions and progress monitoring tools devalued this critical task for the data team. In the future iterations of this simulation, I will include time to explore more than one intervention and progress monitoring tool to better align with real-word data team meetings.

Another observation that needs to be revisited before revising the next iteration of this simulation is to better acknowledge where our PSTs are in their program. Most of our PSTs had not completed their twenty-five hours of fieldwork before participating in the simulation. In most cases, the schools in which our PSTs complete their hours have a scheduled intervention block to work with students receiving tiered supports. Many of our PSTs reported not being present during these intervention blocks, causing them to have limited knowledge of the structure or vocabulary used by teachers to discuss components of the RTI process.

To address this concern, I will revise the Classroom Assessment course to include technical vocabulary needed to effectively access the activities. Introducing terms like universal screeners, interventions, and progress monitoring while simultaneously asking students to apply their understanding of these terms caused some confusion. Not only will this benefit our PSTs in Block II and completing this simulation, but it will also familiarize PSTs with key RTI vocabulary before they start the field placement.

One positive observation from the simulation was how quickly our PSTs were able to interpret, analyze, and determine the next steps for the students in our simulation. Our PSTs were able to use district guidelines to identify which students qualified to take the talented and gifted screener and which students should be moved into Tier 2. Not only were they able to discuss the results from the initial universal screeners, but they were also making connections to students they work with in their field placements. Moreover, in their Tier 2 data teams, they were able to successfully and collaboratively complete the data team protocols where they analyzed progress monitoring data and the impact of targeted interventions. Finally, our PSTs were able to correctly provide the next steps for each of our students. This included continuing to provide Tier 2 supports to one student and moving another student up the RTI framework to increase intervention time and the frequency of completing progress monitoring assessments.

ADVICE

When incorporating a simulation into a teacher education course, focus on using real-world experiences, keeping students engaged, and allowing time for reflection and feedback. When planning:

1. Define the simulation's learning outcomes and highlight its real-world applicability.
2. Ensure presented scenario closely mirrors the challenges and situations they may face in classrooms.
3. Cultivate a collaborative learning environment that encourages PSTs to collaborate, share perspectives, and learn from one another's experiences.
4. Deliver timely and constructive feedback to enhance their decision-making abilities.
5. Integrate reflective components that encourage preservice teachers to critically assess their actions, pinpoint strengths, and acknowledge areas for improvement.
6. Balance theoretical knowledge and hands-on experiences, enabling PSTs to apply pedagogical concepts in a simulated yet more realistic setting.

Considerations for Various Classrooms

Adapting simulations to diverse educational settings demands careful consideration. Start by:

1. Acknowledging the variety of learning environments and available resources in different classrooms.
2. Customizing the simulation scenario to match the grade level, subject matter, and context specific to each educational setting.
3. Offering flexibility in learning styles, allowing for individual and group participation based on the classroom's dynamics.
4. Encouraging feedback from participants to continually improve the simulations for various educational settings and students.

EVALUATION

The evaluation and assessment of student comprehension and knowledge gained from a simulation are pivotal components of the efficacy of simulation-based learning experience. These assessments give educators insights into whether the educational objectives have been met, spotlighting areas that might require enhancement or refinement. Moreover, assessments enable educators to gauge the depth of students' comprehension, practical application of theoretical insights within real-world scenarios, and enhance critical competencies. Regarding feedback, these evaluative processes provide informed instructional purposes and the development of future teaching strategies. A post-simulation assessment can provide thoughtful and thorough feedback on the value and success of the simulation, giving the simulation designer the opportunity to examine strengths and limitations of the format. This data can also support planning and revising of the next iteration of the simulation.

CONCLUSION

Incorporating simulations into teacher education programs signifies a revolutionary approach with purposeful implications. Key features of simulations allow for a unique capacity to bridge theory and practice, offering immersive learning to PSTs. Simulations create a secure environment for grappling with real-world challenges, nurturing the development of critical competencies like decision-making, collaboration, and problem-solving. The impact on preservice teachers is multifaceted, influencing their knowledge, attitudes, and readiness for the intricate classroom landscape.

Simulations provide a structured pathway for reflective practitioners who translate pedagogical theories into instructional methods. Knowledge, understanding, and confidence is built through role-playing before students step into classrooms to work with real students. In essence, simulations within teacher education support the shift toward experiential learning, priming preservice teachers to navigate the challenges of today's classrooms with poise, proficiency, and a solid understanding of their roles as educators.

NOTES

1. Georgia Department of Education, "Dyslexia," n.d., www.gadoe.org/Curriculum-Instruction-and-Assessment/Curriculum-and-Instruction/Pages/Dyslexia.aspx (accessed January 16, 2024).

2. Georgia Professional Standards Commission, "505-3-.01: Requirements and Standards for Approving Educator Preparation Providers," June 15, 2024, www.gapsc.com/Rules/Current/EducatorPreparation/505-3-.01.pdf.

3. Georgia Department of Education, "Multi-Tiered System of Supports," n.d., https://gadoe.org/whole-child-supports/gatss/ (accessed January 20, 2024).

4. Georgia Department of Education, "State Board of Education Approved Qualified Dyslexia Screeners," updated May 21, 2023, https://lor2.gadoe.org/gadoe/file/51c2c724-114a-4a4c-b748-9d0660b027f7/1/SBOE%20Qualified%20Dyslexia%20Screening%20Tools.pdf.

5. Fountas and Pinnell Literacy, "What Is the Benchmark Assessment System (BAS) and How Is BAS Used?" n.d., www.fountasandpinnell.com/bas (accessed January 20, 2024).

BIBLIOGRAPHY

Fountas and Pinnell Literacy. "What Is Benchmark Assessment System (BAS) and How Is BAS Used?" n.d. www.fountasandpinnell.com/bas. Accessed January 20, 2024.

Georgia Department of Education. "Dyslexia." n.d. nwww.gadoe.org/Curriculum-Instruction-and-Assessment/Curriculum-and-Instruction/Pages/Dyslexia.aspx. Accessed January 16, 2024.

Georgia Department of Education. "January 2024 State Board of Education Meeting." https://simbli.eboardsolutions.com/Meetings/Attachment.aspx?S=1262&AID=1523705&MID=109380. Accessed January 20, 2024.

Georgia Department of Education. "Multi-Tiered System of Supports." n.d. https://gadoe.org/whole-child-supports/gatss/. Accessed January 20, 2024.

Georgia Department of Education, "State Board of Education Approved Qualified Dyslexia Screeners." Updated May 21, 2023. https://lor2.gadoe.org/gadoe/file/51c2c724-114a-4a4c-b748-9d0660b027f7/1/SBOE%20Qualified%20Dyslexia%20Screening%20Tools.pdf.

Georgia Professional Standards Commission. "505-3-.01. Requirements and Standards for Approving Educator Preparation Providers and Educator Preparation Programs." June 15, 2024. www.gapsc.com/Rules/Current/EducatorPreparation/505-3-.01.pdf.

Chapter 18

A "Small but Meaningful" Framework for Improving Postsecondary Courses

Amy L. Clay

For the great doesn't happen through impulse alone, and is a succession of little things that are brought together.

—Vincent van Gogh[1]

This chapter presents a framework for making "small but meaningful" changes to pursue teaching excellence. The framework is focused on postsecondary teaching, but contains parallels for other contexts. It includes a series of "small but meaningful" changes that can be introduced individually or combined. The goal is to support the pursuit of teaching excellence, all the while recognizing the limited availability of individual resources (time and energy) and the related mental and physical health risks for faculty members.

Faculty members in institutes of higher education balance competing demands on their personal resources: time and mental/emotional energy. They work in roles beyond the traditional categories of research and teaching. They do student-centered work like curricular revisions, writing recommendation letters, and organizing study-abroad programs. They also serve the profession by giving presentations, serving as editors and reviewers, providing their professional knowledge to the media or general public, and serving on committees.[2] Their work may include administrative appointments such as program directors, advisors, or course supervisors (figure 18.1).[3] Despite the wide variety of work done, most faculty members' professional evaluations are heavily focused on research productivity, with a secondary focus on the quality of their teaching. With one's attention divided in this way, faculty must carefully balance innovations in teaching with their other professional requirements.

The most visible, and oftentimes personally rewarding work, is teaching. Faculty members lead courses with large groups of students, multiple times per week. In these classes, they receive immediate gratification as they see students learning new concepts and skills. Faculty may heavily focus on preparing for these courses, in search of that visible, immediate reward. The upside of this focus is instructional excellence.

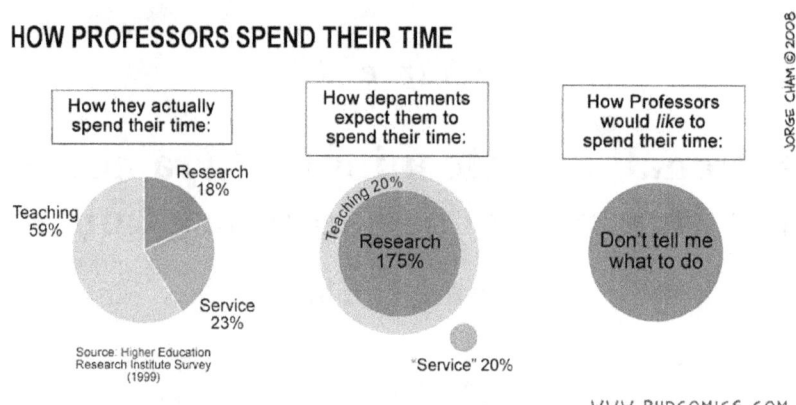

Figure 18.1. "How Professors Spend Their Time." Reproduced with permission from *Piled Higher and Deeper (PhD)* by Jorge Cham www.phdcomics.com.

The downside, however, occurs when an individual puts too much time and energy toward instruction and does not spend sufficient time on research or other professional expectations.

Burnout is another major concern for educators across domains. Research on teacher burnout in higher education highlights contributing factors, like an imbalance in research, teaching, and service, excessive task-switching and (perceived or real) values mismatches between educators and institutions.[4] As memorialized in the PhD Comic shown in figure 18.1, faculty manage perceived or real conflicts in personal and organizational values with respect to time and resources allocated teaching.[5] Taking on innovations that put a heavy demand on an individual's resources can put one's emotional and mental well-being at risk. However, approaching innovation and improvement in "small but meaningful" ways can help to avoid some of these burnout risks, while still leading to a sense of accomplishment when improvements and innovations are successful.

Through a series of small changes and careful assessment of resources, you can improve your instructional practices and students' learning outcomes and avoid burnout related to overcommitment. By freeing up some time and mental or emotional energy, you can divert those resources to accomplish meaningful innovations in the future or, perhaps, to better balance teaching with other professional expectations. Thinking small does not mean doing the minimum or avoiding big projects. It means assessing your resources and priorities and doing the best work you can within those limitations. In a "small but meaningful" frame, faculty members make meaningful changes that improve their overall teaching effectiveness and efficiency. By doing this, they are making time for more time-intensive teaching innovations in their future. This framework, when thinking about teaching innovations, includes a series of small changes and a resource analysis tailored to assessing potential teaching innovations.

SMALL CHANGES TO FREE UP RESOURCES FOR FUTURE INNOVATIONS

Small Changes to Course Policies and Procedures

Do you find yourself shaking your head in vociferous agreement with every "Read the Syllabus" meme? Maybe the students are the problem, or—stay with me here for a moment—maybe making a few small changes to policies and practices will reduce the personal resources that you expend to explain and enforce policies. Try these three small changes to simplify your policies and improve student retention of the information.

Review Course Policies

Spend one hour reviewing course policies before the term starts to save a future version of yourself a great deal of time and mental and emotional energy. Consider these questions to assess both the efficiency and effectiveness of your existing course policies:

- Does the policy help students reach the learning outcomes in this course?
- Is the policy assessing compliance or learning outcomes?
- What are the negative consequences of removing or simplifying this policy? How do the consequences balance with the resources needed to explain and enforce the policy?

For policies that support student learning, the simplest version is the one that requires the least future interactions and mental energy from you and your students. Revise or omit policies that are compliance-focused, with no clear relationship to student learning outcomes. This frees instructors from using time and energy to enforce policies or review potential exceptions, for example, deciding if a student's emergency situation warrants an exception to the late work and absence policies.

Take, for example, a "small but meaningful" late work policy shift in the introductory language course sequence that I supervise. Late work that does not impede the ability to participate and learn in class is not penalized if it is submitted within two weeks of the original due date. This means that summative assignments like papers and recordings are accepted late without any consequences or documentation. This system is more efficient than requesting documentation to excuse late work in emergencies or other special circumstances. Instructors grade the submitted assignments after the due date and check for any late submissions at the close of the two-week grace period. This policy is also better for students. It is respectful of their needs and their privacy around personal circumstances and it does not penalize otherwise successful learners for personal and family issues.

Implement Course Information Sessions and a Syllabus Quiz

"Syllabus day" gained Urban Dictionary status in 2012, where it suggests that students attend the first day of class in subpar states of mind because professors do nothing more than read through the syllabus with students.[6] While instructors may assume that they have done their due diligence of explaining the course policies, many students choose not to attend, and those that do attend do not retain the information. Instead of starting off your term with a dull course policies review, divide course policies into two weeks of course information sessions (i.e., six sessions for a course that meets three days a week) and share only the minimal information that students need to get started on the first day. By offering the information in smaller chunks over the first two weeks of class, students have time to understand and formulate questions. They also learn better by seeking out answers themselves. At the end of those two weeks, offer a syllabus quiz to confirm retention of key information. As an alternative to "syllabus day," opt for community building, collaborating on learning objectives, or getting to know your students' needs and expectations.[7]

In the language classes I teach, our first day begins with a community-building activity in French. Students use level-appropriate French to greet each other and exchange information about themselves. They report back on what they learned about their peers, register for the e-book platform, and identify what to prepare for the next class session. Subsequent sessions include ten-minute course information sessions to introduce course policies (absence policy, translators and AI policy, late work policy) and procedures (best practices for completing work in the e-book, studying for quizzes and exams, contacting the instructor, and using the course website). At the end of the two weeks, students complete a syllabus quiz to confirm they have retained the information. They must earn 100 percent on the syllabus quiz and may retake it as many times as needed. A perk for quizzes completed is that instructors can take class time to review items that had frequent incorrect responses.

Create Template Emails

Despite the syllabus quiz and information sessions, students may still seek guidance or request exceptions to course policies. In these cases, template emails are a simple way to reduce the time and mental energy required to individually address frequently asked student questions. To learn how to create and send template emails, search "template email" followed by your email service (e.g., Gmail or Outlook) in a search engine to find tutorials. In addition to addressing exception requests or questions, template emails can also be used to gently redirect students to find information that is already available on your course site or in your syllabus. Barrett-Fox in her blog *Any Good Thing* recommends sending a message asking the student to take a screen capture of the part of the materials (e.g., assignment instructions, syllabus section, or rubric) that they have a question about and send it back with the specifics of their question.[8] By doing this with a template email, you offer the student a chance to learn how to find information for themselves with minimal commitment of personal resources.

Small Changes for More Effective and Efficient Grading and Feedback for Students

Consider the Value of Different Types of Rubrics

If you do not already use rubrics for most assignments, consider integrating them into your teaching. If you already use rubrics, consider how to make your rubrics work better for you by considering affordances and best practices with analytic and holistic rubrics. Analytic rubrics contain a list of criteria, each with a series of rating levels.[9] They are best used to provide clear feedback to students on formative assignments, including providing clear feedback on how to improve first drafts of assignments or projects. Analytic rubrics contain various amounts of descriptive information for the criteria and levels, but the ideal rubric contains simple titles for the criteria and detailed descriptions. In this way, the qualities for each feature and level are clarified for graders and students, and instructors and course supervisors spend less time clarifying expectations. Overall subjectivity in grading is also reduced. A holistic rubric contains a complete description of what earns each grade.[10] They give an overall assessment of the quality of the work, rather than detailed information about the various areas of assessment. This type of rubric works well when detailed feedback is not useful for students (*e.g.*, short assignments with a completion-focus and summative assessments). The main advantage of using a holistic rubric is for instructors and materials creators: it takes less time.

Grading rubrics, particularly those that are used appropriately, set expectations and provide key feedback to students.[11] Remember that rubrics can be used to more efficiently grade portions of an assessment, like a rubric for a short answer or essay section of an exam, in addition to being used to grade whole assignments.

Quiz Corrections with Explanations

Self-corrections on formative assessments promote student self-regulation and increase uptake of the feedback.[12] To take advantage of this, instructors can assign students to complete self-corrections with written explanations of the corrections outside of class. The written error identification along with the corrected responses provide evidence of student learning, the goal of formative assessments. In order to motivate students to complete corrections, instructors may opt to allow students to earn credit if they show that the skill or knowledge has been acquired. For example, in the courses I supervise, students may earn up to 50 percent of missed points back on formative quizzes. Self-corrections with explanations are more effective than instructor-provided feedback because students' attention is brought to the error and its correction. Moreover, this process is more efficient for instructors who can more quickly grade a quiz or exam and only provide feedback on students' self-corrections.

A SMALL FRAMEWORK FOR DECISION-MAKING

After implementing some of these small changes to improve efficiency without sacrificing effective teaching, instructors might consider how to use some of the newfound time to innovate or improve their teaching. To improve your success with future innovations, start by getting better feedback from students and insights from peers about what will be valuable. Then, review the balance between available resources, required resources, and the potential impact when deciding what to pursue.

Get Better Information

Systematic Self-Reflection

Instructor self-reflection helps identify areas of need for innovation and improvement. In single-instructor courses, this self-reflection happens individually. For courses with multiple instructors or discussion and lab instructors, include collaborative self-reflections in one-on-one or course meetings. The goal of this once-per-semester self-reflection is to identify and separate out needs and desires. Set a twenty-minute timer and prepare typed notes. Use the following questions to guide your reflection:

- Are students meeting the learning objectives? Who isn't? What might help them?
- What am I spending the most time on as a teacher? Am I spending too much or too little time in any specific areas?
- How do I want (or need) to evolve as a teacher?[13]

Use this reflection to consider instructional practices, effective use of time, feedback practices, DEI (diversity, equity, and inclusion) goals, and the appropriateness of course materials.[14] Ideas generated through this reflection can be used to identify innovations to consider for implementation. You can also refer back to your reflections in order to document your teaching activities for future annual reports, promotion files, and teaching statements.

Improve Student Feedback

Student feedback is primarily collected through university-wide end-of-semester course evaluations. On these forms, questions that target what you want to learn about student experiences in your classes, along with open-ended comments from students, provide one information point for triangulating areas for improvement and innovation. However, this is only one information point. In fact, relying solely on these evaluations might lead instructors to make a course easy and fun, without a focus on effective teaching practices.[15] To improve on what many consider a broken system of student evaluations, consider a few small changes that will give more information points and allow you to triangulate what matters most from students' perspectives.

Start by incorporating student self-reflection into written course evaluations and reframing open-ended comments using "I like . . . , I wish . . . , I wonder . . . "[16] First, student self-reflection questions help instructors to better understand why students perceive the course the way they do. Self-reflection should include questions about the amount of time they spend on different course components, their goals in the class, whether they expect to meet those goals, what they want to continue to do, and what they want to do differently to improve their learning in the class. Second, framing open-ended comment questions with a requirement to use the "I like . . . , I wish . . . , I wonder . . . " format guides students to identify something they like about the course, something they wish was different, and something that they wonder about or do not fully understand. While "I" statements may no longer be in vogue for family therapy, the framing above can help direct students to comment from their own perspective instead of from a perspective of knowing what is best for teaching and learning, information that is easier for teachers to critically interpret.

In addition to written course evaluations, incorporate informal focus groups to discuss students' evaluations of the course or to seek student perspectives on potential course changes. To do this, take a small amount of class time to discuss any feedback you collected or to share your goals for the course, and listen to students' ideas about what will (or will not) work for them. Use the time to better understand student experiences in the course and to collaboratively generate ideas for how to address any concerns that students brought up in their evaluations. You can also use some of this time to help students consider how to balance your teaching knowledge, the learning objectives, and their ideal learning settings.

Center Students in Peer Observations

Peer feedback through classroom observations and reviews of course materials can provide yet another set of information to use to triangulate which improvements or innovations are most appropriate for your teaching context. While most peer observations lead to productive discussions about teaching practices and student learning, feedback from peer observers are sometimes limited by subjective standards of excellence and teaching styles that differ for the teacher and observer.[17] One way to improve the feedback that peer observers offer is to ask the observer to move their focus from the teacher to the students in the classroom. Start by providing the peer observer with a list of objectives and other specific areas of interest (e.g., student engagement through oral and written participation and evidence of critical thinking about the topic). Then, the observer takes notes that focus on how and when students meet—or do not meet—the instructor's objectives. The observer focuses on how the instruction and materials facilitated or distracted from the intended outcomes and provides the teacher with insights into the ways that the class functions for learners. This student-focused approach is inspired by the "lesson study" approach to professional development, wherein teachers collaborate to identify an objective, collaborate on a lesson to address the objective, and evaluate its success by observing student thinking during the lesson.[18]

Identifying Constraints and Impacts

After completing self-reflections and collecting feedback from students and peers, evaluate the resources needed for any potential innovations. Consider available resources (yours and others), required resources, and the potential impact of the innovation. What can I and others offer in terms of time, energy, and knowledge? What do I need to do, learn, or teach others to do? How much will this positively impact the target audience? Are there any potential negative impacts?

Assess Available and Required Resources

As a first step, consider the resources available to you and the resources required for the innovation, including time commitments, the necessary knowledge or skills, the mental/emotional energy, and the extent to which those involved may need to shift their attention from one topic to another. Note also that innovations in teaching materials and practices may require resources from individuals other than the instructor. As you use the guiding questions in table 18.1, consider the course supervisor, current and future instructors, and current and future students.

Assess Potential Impact

How much does this improvement or innovation matter for those involved? Considering the balance of constraints and affordances alone is not enough to make a decision. Do we have enough resources to overhaul the structure of a course? The answer might be yes, but would it be an effective use of the resources? Consider the potential impact of such a change, paying special attention to course objectives and student learning outcomes. Is my existing curriculum already effectively helping students to meet the learning outcomes for this course? If the answer is yes, and the student learning outcomes are appropriate for the course, I would typically consider how small changes

Table 18.1. Resource Assessment Questionnaire

Resources	Questions
Time	What time constraints do I and others currently have? Consider professional workload and any potential impact of current/upcoming personal life on the ability to take on additional time at work.
	How much time is required to learn about, develop, implement, evaluate, and improve the innovation? Consider the time required to manage team members or student questions and learning related to the innovation.
Knowledge or Skills	What knowledge or skills do we already have or need to learn?
	What knowledge or skills do the students involved already have or need to learn?
Mental/Emotional Energy	What else is demanding mental/emotional energy from myself and others involved (e.g., supervisors, teachers, students)?
	What mental/emotional energy will be generated through innovation?
	What mental/emotional energy will be required in the implementation stage?
Attention	How often will I and others need to change focus in order to accomplish this innovation?
	To what extent can I and others shift between tasks without it impacting our ability to complete required tasks?
Monetary Costs	What costs or cost savings are associated with this change for the teaching team or for students?
	What financial resources are available to me currently and what resources can I seek out for additional support (e.g., grant funding, salary, or stipends for team members)?

might have an impact on specific areas, such as student engagement, collaborative learning, or real-world connections. I would also consider whether or not substantive changes would improve the overall teaching and learning environment, for example, accepting a diversity and inclusion project to improve student and instructor experiences in a course or program.

Throughout this book, you will find an abundance of small teaching innovations. To decide how to start, gather feedback to evaluate your needs and identify a way to address those needs. Consider how the available and required resources balance with the potential outcomes to select the most effective balance for your circumstances.

NOTES

1. Vincent van Gogh, "Letters to Theo," no. 274, 1882, Van Gogh Museum, https://www.vangoghmuseum.nl/en/highlights/letters/274.

2. American Association of University Professors, "What Do Faculty Do?," AAUP, July 27, 2006, https://www.aaup.org/issues/faculty-work-workload/what-do-faculty-do.

3. Jorge Cham, "How Professors Spend Their Time," PHD Comics, August 25, 2018, August 25, 2018, https://phdcomics.com/comics/archive.php?comicid=1060.

4. Wilmar B. Schaufeli, Michael P. Leiter, and Christina Maslach, "Burnout: 35 Years of Research and Practice," *Career Development International* 14, no. 3 (January 1, 2009): 206–7; Zaynab Sabagh, Nathan C. Hall, and Alenoush Saroyan, "Antecedents, Correlates and Consequences of Faculty Burnout," *Educational Research* 60, no. 2 (April 3, 2018): 137–39; Tiffany Coyle, Erica Miller, and Christa Rivera Cotto, "Burnout: Why Are Teacher Educators Reaching Their Limits?" *Excelsior: Leadership in Teaching and Learning* 13, no. 1 (October 26, 2020): 64–66.

5. Schaufeli, Leiter, and Maslach, "Burnout."

6. @steveo2, "Syllabus Day," in Urban Dictionary, May 13, 2012, https://www.urbandictionary.com/define.php?term=Syllabus%20Day.

7. Robert Vavala, "It's Only Syllabus Day—Who Cares?" University of Nebraska, 2021, https://engineering.unl.edu/downloads/files/First%20Day%20of%20Class-EITS_Fall%202021_4.pdf; Des Robinson, "Engaging Students on the First Day of Class: Student-Generated Questions Promote Positive Course Expectations.," *Scholarship of Teaching and Learning in Psychology* 5, no. 3 (September 2019): 183–88.

8. Rebecca Barrett-Fox, "What to Say When You Want to Say 'It's on the Syllabus,'" Rebecca Barrett-Fox, January 12, 2024, https://anygoodthing.com/2018/12/10/what-to-say-when-you-want-to-say-its-on-the-syllabus/.

9. Jennifer Gonzalez, "Know Your Terms: Holistic, Analytic, and Single-Point Rubrics," Cult of Pedagogy, May 1, 2014, https://www.cultofpedagogy.com/holistic-analytic-single-point-rubrics/.

10. Ibid.

11. Heidi Goodrich Andrade, "Teaching with Rubrics: The Good, the Bad, and the Ugly," *College Teaching* 53, no. 1 (n.d.): 27–28.

12. Wenli Guo and Vazgen Shekoyan, "Facilitation of Student-Centered Formative Assessment Using Reflective Quiz Self-Corrections in a Calculus Physics Course," ASEE Peer (June 2014): 10–11, https://peer.asee.org/facilitation-of-student-centered-formative-assessment-using-reflective-quiz-self-corrections-in-a-calculus-physics-course; Dawn E. McCormick and Mary Lou Vercellotti, "Examining the Impact of Self-Correction Notes on Grammatical

Accuracy in Speaking," *TESOL Quarterly* 47, no. 2 (2013): 410–20; Ángela Zamora, José Manuel Suárez, and Diego Ardura, "Error Detection and Self-Assessment as Mechanisms to Promote Self-Regulation of Learning among Secondary Education Students," *Journal of Educational Research* 111, no. 2 (March 4, 2018): 175–85.

13. Amy Clay, "A Small But Meaningful Mindset for Improving Your Teaching" (Presentation, Art of Teaching Series, University of Illinois Urbana-Champaign, October 25, 2023), https://mediaspace.illinois.edu/media/t/1_ffswbljd.

14. Nicole Kirpalani, "Developing Self-Reflective Practices to Improve Teaching Effectiveness," *Journal of Higher Education Theory and Practice* 17, no. 8 (2017): 73–80.

15. Shana K. Carpenter, Amber E. Witherby, and Sarah K. Tauber, "On Students' (Mis) Judgments of Learning and Teaching Effectiveness.," *Journal of Applied Research in Memory and Cognition* 9, no. 2 (June 2020): 137–51.

16. Rebeca Elizabeth Alvarado Ramírez, "Move Student Communication from Passive to Active Using 'I Like, I Wish, I Wonder,'" *Times Higher Education*, August 31, 2023, https://www.timeshighereducation.com/campus/move-student-communication-passive-active-using-i-i-wish-i-wonder.

17. Joe Bandy, "Peer Review of Teaching," Vanderbilt University Center for Teaching, 2015, https://cft.vanderbilt.edu/guides-sub-pages/peer-review-of-teaching/.

18. Aki Murata, "Introduction: Conceptual Overview of Lesson Study," in *Lesson Study Research and Practice in Mathematics Education*, ed. Lynn C. Hart, Alice S. Alston, and Aki Murata (Springer Link, 2011), 1–12, https://link.springer.com/chapter/10.1007/978-90-481-9941-9_1.

BIBLIOGRAPHY

Alvarado Ramírez, Rebeca Elizabeth. "Move Student Communication from Passive to Active Using 'I Like, I Wish, I Wonder.'" *Times Higher Education*, August 31, 2023. https://www.timeshighereducation.com/campus/move-student-communication-passive-active-using-i-i-wish-i-wonder.

American Association of University Professors. "What Do Faculty Do?" AAUP, July 27, 2006. https://www.aaup.org/issues/faculty-work-workload/what-do-faculty-do.

Andrade, Heidi Goodrich. "Teaching with Rubrics: The Good, the Bad, and the Ugly." *College Teaching* 53, no. 1 2005): 27–31.

Bandy, Joe. "Peer Review of Teaching." Vanderbilt University Center for Teaching, 2015. https://cft.vanderbilt.edu/guides-sub-pages/peer-review-of-teaching/.

Barrett-Fox, Rebecca. "What to Say When You Want to Say 'It's on the Syllabus.'" Rebecca Barrett-Fox, January 12, 2024. https://anygoodthing.com/2018/12/10/what-to-say-when-you-want-to-say-its-on-the-syllabus/.

Carpenter, Shana K., Amber E. Witherby, and Sarah K. Tauber. "On Students' (Mis)Judgments of Learning and Teaching Effectiveness." *Journal of Applied Research in Memory and Cognition* 9, no. 2 (June 2020): 137–51. https://doi.org/10.1016/j.jarmac.2019.12.009.

Cham, Jorge. "How Professors Spend Their Time." PHD Comics, August 25, 2018. https://phdcomics.com/comics/archive.php?comicid=1060.

Clay, Amy. "A Small But Meaningful Mindset for Improving Your Teaching." Presentation at the Art of Teaching Series, University of Illinois Urbana–Champaign, October 25, 2023. https://mediaspace.illinois.edu/media/t/1_ffswbljd.

Coyle, Tiffany, Erica Miller, and Christa Rivera Cotto. "Burnout: Why Are Teacher Educators Reaching Their Limits?" *Excelsior: Leadership in Teaching and Learning* 13, no. 1 (October 26, 2020). https://doi.org/10.14305/jn.19440413.2020.13.1.04.

Gonzalez, Jennifer. "Know Your Terms: Holistic, Analytic, and Single-Point Rubrics." Cult of Pedagogy, May 1, 2014. https://www.cultofpedagogy.com/holistic-analytic-single-point-rubrics/.

Guo, Wenli, and Vazgen Shekoyan. "Facilitation of Student-Centered Formative Assessment Using Reflective Quiz Self-Corrections in a Calculus Physics Course." ASEE Peer, June 2014. https://peer.asee.org/facilitation-of-student-centered-formative-assessment-using-reflective-quiz-self-corrections-in-a-calculus-physics-course.

Kirpalani, Nicole. "Developing Self-Reflective Practices to Improve Teaching Effectiveness." *Journal of Higher Education Theory and Practice* 17, no. 8 (2017): 73–80.

McCormick, Dawn E., and Mary Lou Vercellotti. "Examining the Impact of Self-Correction Notes on Grammatical Accuracy in Speaking." *TESOL Quarterly* 47, no. 2 (2013): 410–20.

Murata, Aki. "Introduction: Conceptual Overview of Lesson Study." In *Lesson Study Research and Practice in Mathematics Education*, edited by Lynn C. Hart, Alice S. Alston, and Aki Murata, 1–12. Springer Link, 2011. https://link.springer.com/chapter/10.1007/978-90-481-9941-9_1.

Robinson, Des. "Engaging Students on the First Day of Class: Student-Generated Questions Promote Positive Course Expectations." *Scholarship of Teaching and Learning in Psychology* 5, no. 3 (September 2019): 183–88. https://doi.org/10.1037/stl0000139.

Sabagh, Zaynab, Nathan C. Hall, and Alenoush Saroyan. "Antecedents, Correlates and Consequences of Faculty Burnout." *Educational Research* 60, no. 2 (April 3, 2018): 131–56. https://doi.org/10.1080/00131881.2018.1461573.

Schaufeli, Wilmar B., Michael P. Leiter, and Christina Maslach. "Burnout: 35 Years of Research and Practice." *Career Development International* 14, no. 3 (January 1, 2009): 204–20. https://doi.org/10.1108/13620430910966406.

@steveo2. "Syllabus Day." Urban Dictionary, May 13, 2012. https://www.urbandictionary.com/define.php?term=Syllabus%20Day.

van Gogh, Vincent. "Letters to Theo," No. 274. 1882. Van Gogh Museum. https://www.vangoghmuseum.nl/en/highlights/letters/274.

Vavala, Robert. "It's Only Syllabus Day—Who Cares?" University of Nebraska, 2021. https://engineering.unl.edu/downloads/files/First%20Day%20of%20Class-EITS_Fall%202021_4.pdf.

Zamora, Ángela, José Manuel Suárez, and Diego Ardura. "Error Detection and Self-Assessment as Mechanisms to Promote Self-Regulation of Learning among Secondary Education Students." *Journal of Educational Research* 111, no. 2 (March 4, 2018): 175–85. https://doi.org/10.1080/00220671.2016.1225657.

Chapter 19

Exploring Cosmopolitan and Critical Perspectives in a Writing Course

Grace Y. Kang

BACKGROUND

Teacher candidates from the United States and Argentina participated in a global intercultural exchange around the teaching of writing. After developing relationships, reading multiple articles and books about diverse perspectives, and collaborating on various projects, they said it expanded their view of global perspectives. Figure 19.1 shows a word cloud created when these teacher candidates (TCs) added three keywords/phrases about their intercultural exchange.

This intercultural writing course was taught at a midwestern public state university. The university is the largest producer of teachers in the state. The majority of TCs are white females enrolled in the elementary education program. The course explored

Figure 19.1. Word cloud from teacher candidates' big takeaways from their global intercultural exchange.

critical perspectives, culturally sustaining pedagogies, and antiracist lenses in teaching writing. It was built on the National Writing Project (NWP) model, where teachers of writing become writers themselves and also grow in practices of teaching writing. This course was purposefully 100 percent asynchronous to support TCs' clinical, course, and work schedules. TCs worked on their course at their own pace and schedule, and because of the asynchronous nature of the course, the instructor tried to ensure there was high engagement and collaboration throughout the semester. This usually meant TCs were actively engaged on various digital platforms and tools. Digital forms of collaboration were how TCs worked with each other and with the TCs participating in the virtual global intercultural exchange.

Kang and Kline[1] describe the negotiation of teaching practices in an online undergraduate writing course. The overarching purpose was to disrupt dominant discourses of writing and illuminate critical perspectives, specifically intentional shifts around tenets of critical literacy and some instructional moves to enact humanizing and critical writing pedagogies. This course was revised to focus on humanizing and critical perspectives[2] and culturally sustaining pedagogies;[3] however, courses are always in process and global perspectives were absent.

I investigated various theoretical frameworks and saw that cosmopolitanism aligned with both the critical perspectives described earlier and illuminated a global perspective. Cosmopolitanism[4] encompasses a standpoint that delves into students' roles and agency as global citizens. A cosmopolitan perspective may be understood as developing a humanistic approach for twenty-first-century education: learning from each other through the intersection of individual and cultural funds of knowledge.[5]

As a critical antiracist educator focusing on global education, I investigated a cosmopolitan, global-centric stance to widen and deepen students' perspectives as global citizens. Often educators talk about a surface-level notion of celebrating diversity; however, a cosmopolitan perspective deeply considers local cultural literacies and funds of knowledge with a global community.[6] Choo reveals that in a cosmopolitan framework, "competencies are tied to human capabilities, involving the provision of opportunities, freedom, and agency, and these should ultimately serve to cultivate cosmopolitan capacities involving ethical engagement with and responsibility to multiple and marginalized others in our world."[7]

ENACTMENTS OF SMALL SHIFTS

First, TCs read several readings about cosmopolitanism paired with critical perspectives (see appendix A at the end of this chapter). We discussed the readings through discussion posts and Flips. The readings set the foundation for the critical and global frameworks we drew from. The TCs applied these readings by engaging in several activities. One of the main avenues through which we explored global issues was a global partnership through iEARN (www.iearn.org) with a teaching university in Argentina. Through iEARN, we participated in a global project, Knowing Our Students, Knowing Ourselves (KOSKO), in three phases: (1) group introductions, (2) a collaborative small group activity involving TCs from both classes, and (3) final reflections. Both professors collaboratively crafted the projects and themes to best

Cultural X-Rays of Personal Cultural Identity, Alejandro and Natali, Fifth Grade

Figure. 19.2. Short's (334) Cultural X-ray examples. Kathy Short

serve the needs of TCs from both classes/contexts. Throughout the semester, my TCs met, collaborated, and engaged in various activities with the TCs from Argentina.

The first activity we engaged in was Short's Cultural X-rays (see figure 19.2). Cultural X-rays provide an opportunity for students to recognize their various cultural identities, develop varied understandings of culture, and raise awareness of how and why culture matters to them.[8]

I modeled the introductory Cultural X-ray activity for my students. Then the TCs created their own Cultural X-rays and exchanged videos via Flip with the TCs in Argentina. The TCs got to know each other using digital tools like Flip (https://info.flip.com/en-us.html) and Padlet (https://padlet.com).

SHARED CONTEXT AND UNDERSTANDING: THE GLOBAL READ ALOUD

Additionally, TCs engaged in the Global Read Aloud (www.theglobalreadaloud.com). The Global Read Aloud (GRA) was created with one simple goal, "One book to connect the world." A book/author is selected, and the classroom teacher reads aloud the book to their students during a six-week period; during that time, the students make as many global connections as possible. Each classroom makes these connections in different ways, the scope and the depth of the project is up to the classroom teacher and students. Some classrooms make connections through digital tools (e.g., Zoom, Padlet, Flip), social media (e.g., Facebook, X), or as pen pals using snail mail. I read

Table 19.1. Book List and Reading Schedule

Week 1	You Matter by Christian Robinson
Week 2	Another by Christian Robinson
Week 3	Milo Imagines the World by Matt de la Peña, illustrated by Christian Robinson
Week 4	The Smallest Girl in the Smallest Grade by Justin Roberts, illustrated by Christian Robinson
Week 5	Last Stop on Market Street by Matt de la Peña, illustrated by Christian Robinson

aloud a GRA picture book each week (see table 19.1), and the TCs from the United States and Argentina would respond to prompting questions via Padlet.

After TCs posted their initial response on Padlet, they would interact with each other by responding to their peers. The GRA provided a meaningful shared context where all the TCs had read the same texts by the selected author, Christian Robinson. They could delve deeply into discussion and reflection through this shared context and understanding. Some reflections after completing the GRA included:

> The GRA allows students to interact with other students from around the world, I learned about a new culture and diverse books I have not read before. These stories may help students feel more seen and express their feelings and ideas that can be shared with other students. The GRA can also be a safe place. Students can think critically about the text in each book and grow to be more diverse and creative in and out of the classroom, even in their writing.

And

> The GRA offers students the opportunity to connect with others worldwide. Through this program, students can develop empathy and understanding for other cultures and perspectives while improving their reading and writing skills. By participating in the GRA, students are introduced to a diverse range of authors and books, which expands their understanding of the world.

As they engaged in the GRA exchange, the TCs from Argentina wanted to share about intercultural norms and things that were unique to their culture. They made videos about how to make a special drink, campus life, and things that were special to them. My students responded by creating intercultural videos about their lives. The TCs enjoyed having this organic space to share informally about their favorite food or drink, their hobbies, and their families and friends.

CRAFTING WRITING MINI-LESSONS

After the TCs established a relationship and learned some of the various norms around their cultures, TCs interacted by creating a writing mini-lesson using one of the GRA picture books. I created a template of a writing mini-lesson for TCs to use as a starting point, and I modeled an example of a writing mini-lesson (see appendix B). Then TCs from both countries crafted a writing mini-lesson using one of the Christian Robinson texts as a mentor text.

TCs chose a teaching point, part of the mentor text, and the context of how they would teach this (e.g., genre, grade level, standards). I modeled this for students, and the TCs posted their mini-lessons to Padlet and then discussed the similarities and differences of their lessons on Padlet (e.g., What are some similarities/differences? What did you learn and perhaps want to try out in your future writing instruction?). Students learned how to craft writing mini-lessons in their contexts, but also considered how lesson plans vary depending on different cultures and contexts.

REFLECTIONS

Lastly, via Flip, the TCs engaged in reflecting on their growth and learning from this intercultural experience and on the experience of collaborating internationally with TCs in another country. They returned to the Cultural X-rays, GRA Padlet and reflections, intercultural Flips, and writing mini-lessons on Padlet. Then they considered what they learned and gleaned from their international partners using prompting questions, such as:

- What are your big takeaways from this intercultural exchange?
- Did you have any shifts in how you will teach writing in the future?
- Did you see any growth in your own identity development as a teacher of writing?
- Did you notice ethnocentrism and how you can see outside your cultural norms and language?

TCs said they appreciated the perspectives and ideas of TCs from the other country. One student shared in a Flip, "I would like to thank all of you for being a part of this experience, it was fantastic—your stories and your lesson plans. I realized that we have differing perspectives, ways of thinking, and it's fascinating. Your ideas helped me a lot, they helped me with inspiration, to bring different and new ideas into my classes, and I am very grateful for that." TCs from both countries consistently repeated this sentiment in their reflections. Their values, beliefs, and cultural norms were challenged through this experience, and another TC shared, "This experience helped me to see how important it is to include different perspectives and make students feel comfortable in their writing, and that they can use their own voice and bring out their own culture and identity."

NEXT STEPS

Teachers are constantly making shifts and revisions to their instruction. They are able to think on their feet, and daily and weekly lesson plans change minute by minute. However, when we notice a gap or missing aspects in our teaching, we can make critical changes, sometimes small or, often, large shifts. There is no recipe or one way to make revisions to teach from a global perspective. It is context-specific and must be appropriated for specific classrooms and particular students. However, when we consider moving to a critical global lens, here are a few steps to follow:

1. Consider a theoretical framework to draw from and select critical readings.
2. Consider your platform (e.g., face-to-face, hybrid, asynchronous) and various digital tools or technologies to utilize (e.g., Flip, Padlet, Google Docs).
3. Perhaps find a global partner (www.iearn.org or www.ePals.com).
4. Create a project or assignment to collaborate on together (e.g., Cultural X-ray, Global Read Aloud, mini-lessons, reflections).
5. Make sure to give yourself time and space to collaborate with your global partner(s).

CONCLUSION

Teaching is in constant revision, and pedagogy is always in process. I have revised this course too many times to count, and I am sure I will continue to make shifts and changes every time I teach it. However, each time I teach a class, it offers new opportunities for improvement and makes it more relevant and meaningful to TCs and their future classrooms. This shift in drawing from a global cosmopolitan perspective responded to a missing element. Because global perspectives were absent from this course, this revision provided a transformative global experience in how students viewed larger society and the world through writing.

NOTES

1. Grace Kang and Sonia Kline, "Critical Literacy as a Tool for Social Change: Negotiating Tensions in a Pre-Service Teacher Education Writing Course." *Journal of Language and Literacy Education* 16, no. 2 (2020): 4.

2. Amy Flint, "'See, That's Me. I'm Proud': Manifestations of a Humanizing and Culturally Sustaining Writing Pedagogy for Young Writers," *Language Arts* 100, no. 2 (November 2022): 85; Sonia Kline and Grace Kang, "Reflect, Reimagine, Revisit: A Framework for Centering Critical Writing Pedagogy," *Language Arts* 99, no. 5 (May 2022): 302.

3. Django Paris, H. Samy Alim, Valerie Kinloch, Mary Bucholtz, Dolores Inés Casillas, Jin-Sook Lee, Tiffany S. Lee, et al., *Culturally Sustaining Pedagogies: Teaching and Learning for Justice in a Changing World* (New York: Teachers College Press, 2017), 10; Rebecca Woodard, Andrea Vaughan, and Emily Machado, "Exploring Culturally Sustaining Writing Pedagogy in Urban Classrooms," *Literacy Research: Theory, Method, and Practice* 66, no. 1 (August 2017): 221.

4. Lenny Sánchez and Tami Ensore, "Stepping beyond the Shadow to Engage a Globalized World," *Talking Points* 34, no. 2 (May 2023): 5.

5. Suzanne Choo, "Approaching Twenty-First Century Education from a Cosmopolitan Perspective," *Journal of Curriculum Studies* 50, no. 2 (April 2017): 170; Luis C. Moll, Cathy Amanti, Deborah Neff, and Norma Gonzalez, "Funds of Knowledge for Teaching: Using a Qualitative Approach to Connect Homes and Classrooms," *Theory Into Practice* 31, no. 2 (March 1992): 134.

6. Glynda Hull and Amy Stornaiuolo, "Literate Arts in a Global World: Reframing Social Networking as Cosmopolitan Practice," *Journal of Adolescent & Adult Literacy: A Journal from the International Reading Association* 54, no. 2 (October 2010): 87.

7. Choo, "Approaching Twenty-First Century Education from a Cosmopolitan Perspective," 178.

8. Kathy Short, Deanna Day, and Jean Schroeder, *Teaching Globally: Reading the World through Literature* (New York: Routledge, 2016), 333–34.

9. Ralph Fletcher and Joann Portalupi, *Craft Lessons: Teaching Writing K–8* (New York: Routledge, 2007).

APPENDIX A: READINGS

Critical and Humanizing Perspectives Readings:

Bomer, Katherine. *Hidden Gems*. Portsmouth, NH: Heinemann Educational Books, 2010.
Fletcher, Ralph, and Joann Portalupi. *Craft Lessons: Teaching Writing K–8*. New York: Routledge, 2007.
Flint, Amy. S. "'See, That's Me. I'm Proud': Manifestations of a Humanizing and Culturally Sustaining Writing Pedagogy for Young Writers." *Language Arts* 100, no. 2 (November 2022): 83–95.
Kline, Sonia, and Grace Kang. "Reflect, Reimagine, Revisit: A Framework for Centering Critical Writing Pedagogy." *Language Arts* 99, no. 5 (May 2022): 300–11.
Lewison, Mitzi et al. *Creating Critical Classrooms: Reading and Writing with an Edge*, Second ed. New York: Routledge, 2015.

Cosmopolitanism and Global Perspectives Readings:

Asia Society, and Organisation for Economic Co-operation and Development. *Teaching for Global Competence in a Rapidly Changing World*. Paris: OECD, 2018. https://doi.org/10.1787/9789264289024-en.
Choo, S. S. *Teaching Ethics through Literature: The Significance of Ethical Criticism in a Global Age*. New York: Routledge, 2021.
Short, K. "The Dangers of Reading Globally." *Bookbird* 57, no. 2 (2019), 1–11.
Short, K., Deanna Day, and Jean Schroeder. *Teaching Globally: Reading the World through Literature*. New York: Routledge, 2016.

APPENDIX B: CRAFT A MINI-LESSON

As one of the last pieces of your portfolio, you will create a mini-lesson around an craft/area of writing. Please use Fletcher and Portalupi's *Craft Lessons*[9] as a guide, as well as your own craft lesson you tried out in your narrative writing. Consider the various crafts of writing we have discussed in various forms of writing:

> Crafts of writing by Subject (pp. vii–xi in *Craft Lessons*): Character, Details, Dialogue, Endings, Focus, Ideas, Imagery, Irony, Leads, Paragraphing, Point of View, Pacing, Repetition, Scene, Sentences, Setting, Story Structure, Symbolism, Time, Titles, Voice, Word Choice

Here's what you will do:

1. Pick a craft of writing that you would like to focus on. Flip through the *Craft Lessons* book—it will help you narrow and hone in on a craft of writing.
2. Create a mini-lesson using the template (table 19.2).
3. Pick a mentor text (you can pick any of the Christian Robinson texts from the GRA or any text with diverse characters or themes).
4. Use the mentor text in your mini-lesson to teach a specific craft of writing.
5. Remember a mini-lesson is meant to be a "mini." It should only take you 8–12 minutes to teach this lesson, so that your students have TIME TO WRITE!

Table 19.2. Mini-Lesson Template with Descriptions and Examples

Mini-lesson title: This should tell us what your mini-lesson is about—get to the heart of it.
"Use Your Voice When You Write"
Grade level: This should tell us what grade level you plan to teach this lesson in.
Fourth grade
Form of writing (e.g., narrative, poetry, expository, persuasive): This should tell us what form of writing your students will be working on when you teach this mini-lesson.
Personal narrative
Mentor text(s): This section lists the title(s) of your mentor texts and author(s).
The Day You Begin by Jacqueline Woodson
Discussion: This section goes into detail about WHY this mini-lesson is necessary and how it will support your students' writing. Set the stage for us on WHY this is an important and vital mini-lesson.
"Good writing needs voice, and the idea of using voice scares kids to death. Writing teachers must support students to take risks and use their voice in their writing. This craft lesson builds on the natural link between spoken and written language. It gives children an introduction to the idea of using their own voice in their writing."
How to teach it : This section walks students through HOW to teach this mini-lesson and may incorporate your own quotes and use THINK ALOUDS from the mentor texts (include page numbers). Show examples of this craft of writing you are focusing on.
"When we think about the way we speak out loud and the way we write words on paper, sometimes they are really different and sometimes they can be pretty similar. Today we are going to talk about the writing craft of using your voice when you write. Famous published authors use their voice when they write all of the time. Most of you know the book, *The Day You Begin* by Jacqueline Woodson. We have read this together; I am going to reread a few pages and highlight a few sentences. Listen carefully because I want you to notice how it sounds as if the author is talking to us. You can hear her speaking. [Read a few pages and discuss; MAKE SURE TO HIGHLIGHT THE PAGES] On page 15, Woodson writes: "'What's in there, anyway?' And you'll wonder how she doesn't see the rice beneath the meat and kimchi. You'll wonder why she doesn't remember that rice is the most popular food in the world." And on page 18, she writes: "I don't want him on our team. You can watch. Maybe you can have a turn later." Lastly, on page 27, she writes: "This is the day you begin to find the places inside your laughter and your lunches, your books, your travel and your stories." You can hear Woodson's voice in these examples. When you write, consider how you can see the link between your spoken and written language. Jacqueline Woodson shows us how to do this!"
Final words for your students to apply the mini-lesson to their writing: This section is your final charge and challenge for students to practice in their own writing.
"Today when you write in your writers' notebooks, try to use your own talking/speaking voice when you're writing words. You may even whisper words out loud as you write your own words."

BIBLIOGRAPHY

Choo, Suzanne S. "Approaching Twenty-First Century Education from a Cosmopolitan Perspective." *Journal of Curriculum Studies* 50, no. 2 (April 20, 2017): 162–81. https://doi.org/10.1080/00220272.2017.1313316.

Flint, Amy Seely. "'See, That's Me. I'm Proud': Manifestations of a Humanizing and Culturally Sustaining Writing Pedagogy for Young Writers." *Language Arts* 100, no. 2 (November 2022): 83–95. https://doi.org/10.58680/la202232136.

Hull, Glynda A., and Amy Stornaiuolo. "Literate Arts in a Global World: Reframing Social Networking as Cosmopolitan Practice." *Journal of Adolescent & Adult Literacy: A Journal from the International Reading Association* 54, no. 2 (October 2010): 85–97. https://doi.org/10.1598/jaal.54.2.1.

Kang, Grace Y., and Sonia Kline. "Critical Literacy as a Tool for Social Change: Negotiating Tensions in a Pre-Service Teacher Education Writing Course." *Journal of Language and Literacy Education* 16, no. 2 (2020): 1–16.

Kline, Sonia, and Grace Kang. "Reflect, Reimagine, Revisit: A Framework for Centering Critical Writing Pedagogy." *Language Arts* 99, no. 5 (May 2022): 300–11. https://doi.org/10.58680/la202231790.

Moll, Luis C., Cathy Amanti, Deborah Neff, and Norma Gonzalez. "Funds of Knowledge for Teaching: Using a Qualitative Approach to Connect Homes and Classrooms." *Theory Into Practice* 31, no. 2 (March 1992): 132–41. https://doi.org/10.1080/00405849209543534.

Paris, Django, H. Samy Alim, Valerie Kinloch, Mary Bucholtz, Dolores Inés Casillas, Jin-Sook Lee, Tiffany S. Lee, et al. *Culturally Sustaining Pedagogies: Teaching and Learning for Justice in a Changing World.* New York: Teachers College Press, 2017.

Sánchez, Lenny, and Tami Ensor. "Stepping beyond the Shadow to Engage a Globalized World." *Talking Points* 34, no. 2 (May 1, 2023): 2–9. https://doi.org/10.58680/tp202332464.

Short, Kathy, Deanna Day, and Jean Schroeder. *Teaching Globally: Reading the World through Literature.* New York: Routledge, 2016.

Woodard, Rebecca, Andrea Vaughan, and Emily Machado. "Exploring Culturally Sustaining Writing Pedagogy in Urban Classrooms." *Literacy Research: Theory, Method, and Practice* 66, no. 1 (August 2017): 215–31. https://doi.org/10.1177/2381336917719440.

Chapter 20

Flip, Switch, Reverse

A New Faculty Member Tackling a New Course and Content Area

Abby C. Emerson

As a first-year faculty member I was handed a course new to me in a content area outside my expertise: elementary literacy methods for undergraduate education majors. With limited time to prepare and limited background knowledge, I needed to make the course work for me. This course had a bit of social studies tucked into it, which previous instructors have tacked onto the end. However, being adept with social studies methods, I flipped the course around, frontloading the social studies and using that arc to help me approach the literacy content. In this proposed chapter I would like to reflect on how making a switch such as this one can shape the narrative of a course, giving it meaning for us, which in turn improves our teaching.

THE CONTEXT

My last fifth-grade classroom sat on the fourth floor of a large public school building in New York City. I taught elementary grades in public schools for ten years, working with colleagues and grade team partners to revise and create curricula that would meet students' needs and be relevant to their backgrounds. We worked to make both the content and teaching methods relevant to them, their lives, and their academic needs. It was in these experiences as an elementary school teacher that I developed the capacity to adapt the provided curriculum and make it a living curriculum for me and my students to work with and through.[1]

Recently I started as a first-year faculty member in an elementary special education department working with undergraduates majoring in education. One of the key reasons I was hired was to support the development of a new social studies methods course for these future teachers. Due to the common combination of schedule limitations and being a new hire, I was asked to teach an upper elementary literacy methods course. This was an area I did not feel very confident in, despite teaching English Language Arts to fifth graders for years. I was not up on the research and I was hesitant about my capacity to support students who entered my class seeking information on how to teach reading and writing to children. Sure, I could explain what I experienced and did in the schools in which I had worked, but it was my responsibility to know more about the field to teach this course. I knew that there had been some recent shifts in language arts, as balanced literacy models were under scrutiny and the Science of Reading was finding a home in districts implementing new curricula, but I was not incredibly familiar with those conversations.[2] That ignorance made me unsure about my ability to teach a literacy methods course.

The methods course had been taught for many years in the department and emphasized language arts teaching in grades 3–6. Additionally, there was a small amount of social studies content tucked in at the end, making the course approximately one-third on reading methods, one-third writing methods, and one-third social studies methods. Since my new social studies methods course had not yet been rolled out by the college, the social studies portion of this class was the only social studies methods those current students would be receiving during their teacher education program.

Given my interest in social studies teaching and methods, it was important to me that my students get exposed to critical understandings of social studies. It could not just be an add-on at the end. Social studies had been a central focus of much of my elementary school classroom teaching and an area I considered a strength. I wanted my teaching to introduce my students to social studies with a critical lens that sought to "provid[e] elementary school students opportunities to engage critically in the world around them."[3]

I ultimately found myself juggling a few concerns and considerations. First, I was teaching a literacy methods course and I was not confident in literacy methods. Second, my main interest in social studies was currently framed as a mere add-on to the literacy focus of the class. Third, I was, like all educators, short on time and didn't have unlimited capacity for syllabus revisions. Fourth, I was new to my institution and unfamiliar with the students and setting. As any educator knows, starting in a new institution or even just starting a new school year, no matter how experienced you are, can bring about some anxiety as you find your footing. Thankfully, my background in revising curricula could come to my assistance as I maneuvered the semester.

THE CHANGE

The summer before I started, I inherited a few versions of the course syllabus from previous instructors and faculty. During this time I started researching and learning about the current debates in literacy instruction, particularly what was currently happening in the state where I was starting my new position. I also spent time reading the literacy methods textbook, which I chose not to change. Changing the textbook felt like too big a shift in this new content area. I wouldn't have even known what other textbook I might select! As I made sense of the reading and writing content I would be teaching my students, I contemplated how to make the course work for me. Were there any small changes I could make that seemed feasible? Were there tweaks that could be made so that the course really felt like my own? Whenever I teach, it is important to me that I have a command of the structure and organization. If I feel confident in that area, the rest tends to fall into place.

Accordingly, I decided to flip the course content around and move social studies from the back end to the front. So the first third of the class focused on social studies, and then we transitioned into literacy for the remainder. Most of the literacy content stayed the same from the syllabi that I had inherited. I also used very similar course assignments to what had been used in the past. Yet, by moving social studies up front, I was able to have a consistent thread that connected the assignments to each other such that they scaffolded intentionally. I was also able to lead with what I was confident in. I was new at my institution, and while I had a good deal of teaching experience both in elementary schools and in higher education, I wanted to start on the right foot, which for me would be social studies. By flipping the content, it not only helped the course start smoothly, but it helped me take the social studies themes and threads from the initial portion and weave them throughout the remaining ELA sections of the course. Overall, I just switched the order of the course and then edited some of the existing assignments to reflect that shift. This way of starting small in the course felt attainable for me as a new faculty member at my college. It was a small shift, but one that had a big impact.

THE RESULTS OF THE CHANGE

One of the best ways I can demonstrate what this small switch of content chronology accomplished is by demonstrating what students did in their assignments. Below, I highlight two students' work and share a bit about how they approached the three key assignments of the course—one in social studies, one in reading, and one in writing. I organized the three key assignments by having students first select a social studies inquiry topic. At the beginning of the semester, I encouraged them to select a topic that they either did not know much about (e.g., Claudette Colvin) or a topic that is commonly covered but one they would like to revisit in a more critical way, perhaps examining the perspectives of the nondominant groups (e.g., women's suffrage, but with an emphasis on Black women's voting rights).

Before sharing examples of how two students undertook the assignments, I will describe the three assignments. In the first portion of the semester, the students did an inquiry into their selected topic and created a multimodal project that reflected what they learned. They had to do a bit of research and become familiar enough with the topic that they felt they could plan a unit around it for elementary-age students. The second project entailed reading an upper-elementary-level text that was directly related to that inquiry topic. Students then created a series of three reading lessons that went with that text. In this particular class of students, half of the texts they selected were realistic or historical fiction, and half were nonfiction. Students could create their three reading lessons targeted toward any objectives that aligned with the standards for their selected grade level and matched well with the text. Students selected teaching points that ranged from identifying how character point of view influences a story's events to comparing and contrasting different authors' approaches to topics. The third key assignment of the course was to develop a writing assignment that elementary-age students might take up in response to the book used for the reading assignment. The preservice teachers wrote a corresponding writing assignment in student-friendly language, formulated a rubric, and then created a mentor text that could support them in their teaching of writing. For example, the students constructed writing assignments that spanned various genres, inviting elementary children into poetry, persuasive writing, and reading responses. As you can see, these three assignments built on each other sequentially, deepening students' social studies inquiries while maintaining a strong focus on developing their literacy instruction skills.

Annie: The Young Lords

The first student whose work I would like to highlight here is Annie, who studied the Young Lords, a community-based organization active in Chicago and New York City.[4] Annie wrote in a reflection:

> The Young Lords were a social activist group during the 1960s that fought for the civil rights of Puerto Ricans, but their story is frequently forgotten. There are so many other activist groups which are overlooked in our history books which students should learn about, instead of only focusing on specific heroes. Even when learning about these "heroes" in our history, their stories are often misconstrued.

In an effort to fill this knowledge gap, Annie researched the group and their work because she had never heard of them and wanted to learn about a narrative of history that was not the dominant narrative.[5] For the social studies multimodal project, she created a website detailing what she learned about the group (figure 20.1). On her website, Annie included contextual information, Puerto Rican history, connections

Figure 20.1. The Young Lords Organization website created by Annie.

to the Black Panthers, timelines, the group's 13 Points, and references (https://ahlady1234.wixsite.com/theyounglordsorganiz).

For her second assignment, Annie read a book called *The Revolution of Evelyn Serrano* by Sonia Manzano and created a series of three reading lessons for sixth graders that related to the text and topic. Her first reading lesson's objective was related to identifying genre. She understood that a fictional character based in a historical time period with the inclusion of historical facts might be slightly confusing to students, and wanted to set them up for success with handling the genre of text. In her second lesson, Annie created a lesson focused on vocabulary and using context clues to help understand the Spanish words interwoven throughout the text. Her third reading lesson focused on the skill of identifying theme or the central message of the text. Across these lessons, Annie demonstrated so many wonderful teaching pedagogies for developing elementary school students' literacy skills. For example, she created a Heads Up! style game for vocabulary development, cards with potential themes pre-written out as a differentiation support for certain students, centers for students to engage with theme in multiple ways, and engaging PowerPoints that used visuals to ensure different learning styles were supported[6] (figure 20.2). Further, Annie pulled the idea of having an "engaging hook" at the start of a lesson from our week on culturally responsive literacy teaching and used memes to bring students into the learning.[7]

When it came to the writing assignment, Annie created a task where the sixth graders could create poems about their own cultures or from the perspective of the main character. To support students around expectations, she created a rubric that touched on several important parts of sixth-grade writing, including poetic elements such as imagery; content related to culture; word choice, including vocabulary that would evoke emotions; and of course, the writing conventions for sixth graders. At the end of the course, Annie reflected on her learning across these three assignments:

> I was able to dive deep into my own inquiry with a topic which I knew nothing about: The Young Lords Organization. Not only did I enjoy learning about this topic, I feel that students would as well. In my own classroom, I plan to incorporate this type of guided inquiry when it comes to social studies. Students will be able to choose their own topic based on what we are learning and investigate themselves. A great feature about this type of learning is that they not only learn themselves, but through their peers as well. On the last day of class, I was able to hear about the rest of the class's topics and learn something from my classmates. Learning this way promotes a classroom environment where the students are learning from one another and not just from the teacher.

Annie's work that fall semester demonstrated what a small shift did for a course. By using social studies to power the course, we were able to drive toward meaningful interdisciplinary literacy teaching in the upper elementary grades. Annie demonstrated a meaningful engagement with the sixth-grade literacy standards, applying an understanding of how to unpack the standards for students of diverse abilities in ways that would be both memorable and effective.

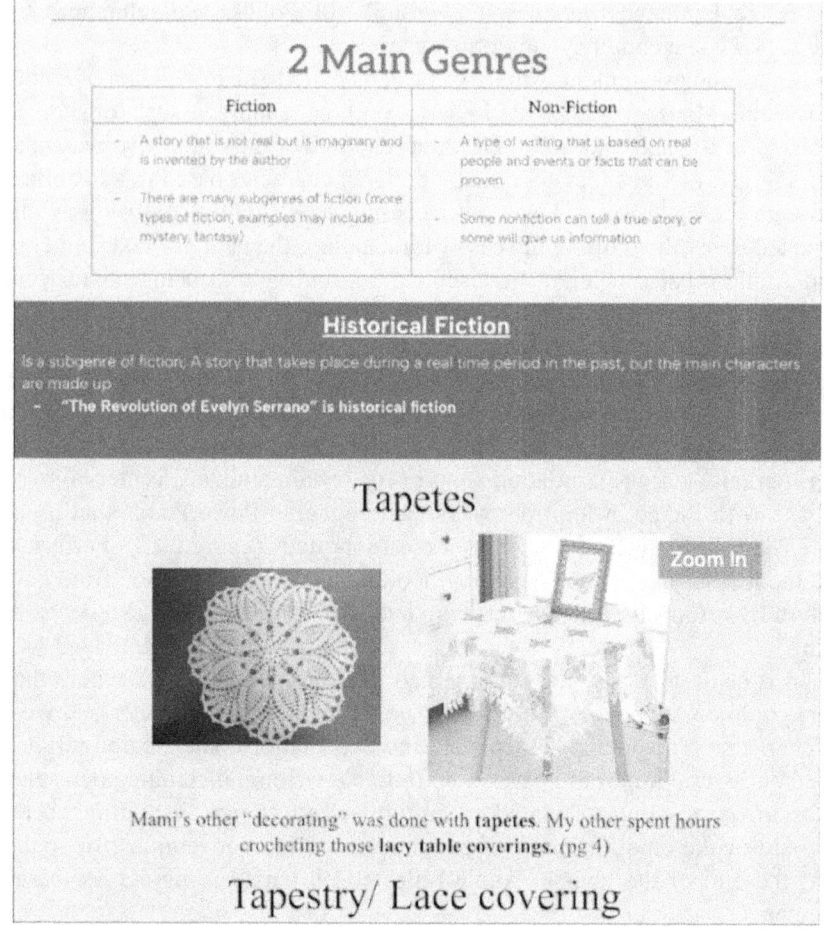

Figure 20.2. Sample of Annie's PowerPoint slides.

Laney: Police Brutality

The second student whose work demonstrates how the small shift to the course structure played out was Laney. For her inquiry across the semester, she selected the topic of police brutality. She explained:

> When choosing between inquiry topics, I first wanted to choose something I was genuinely interested in learning more about. I have had the privilege of not being forced to be super aware of the plague of police brutality in our country until the pandemic, more specifically the murder of George Floyd. The era of the Black Lives Matter protests was what initially ignited my desire to learn more about the racial injustices in our country and during this time period I did learn a lot about the current climate of racism in the United States. However, I still had never researched the in-depth history of police brutality and how it developed over time, so I decided to take the opportunity that this project offered to do so.

This was exactly the type of critical inquiry into our social world that I hoped students would take up across the course's assignments. Laney was considering some of her own identities in relation to the world around her and seeking out information to better understand the broader context.

For her first assignment, Laney created a magazine detailing her research, critically examining the role that policing has in people's lives in the United States (figure 20.3). In her magazine, she drew connections between policing and enslavement, considering how the Thirteenth Amendment existed as a loophole to continue the "targeted violent behavior" directed at Black people even after the end of slavery. Laney then examined key events throughout police brutality history, such as the beating of Rodney King and the murder of George Floyd.

After building her foundation of understanding about the topic, Laney moved to creating upper-elementary reading lesson plans. When creating her three lessons,

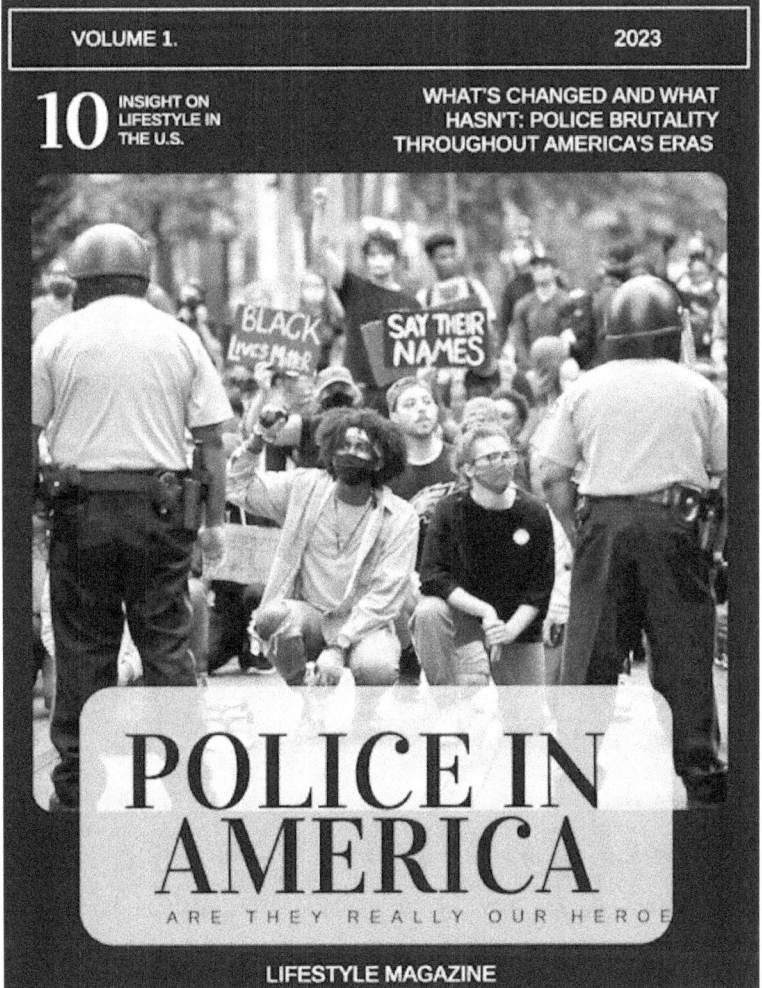

Figure 20.3. Laney's magazine inquiring into police brutality.

Laney focused on the text *All American Boys* by Jason Reynolds,[8] which is a young adult novel about racism and police brutality within a community. Laney imagined this text would work with a "high-level sixth grade" group of students and set up her lessons to follow a book club format where students engaged in questions and activities collaboratively. Her first lesson's objective consisted of analyzing point of view, both how it is developed and the impact it has on the storytelling. The second objective emphasized literacy devices with a focus on figurative language. The third lesson's objective focused on analyzing key events and character behavior to understand the main theme of the text. Throughout her lessons, Laney attended to important environmental factors like room configuration as a way to foster collaboration between the youth learners. She also mapped out preplanned questions for the explicit instruction parts of her teaching. Laney had key points and lesson vocabulary (e.g., point of view) translated into accessible language so students could fully participate. Her lessons guided elementary learners toward specific parts of the text, asking them to elaborate on their ideas with evidence. The lessons concluded with some sort of assessment that were directly related to the teaching point of the day. Many of the strong upper-elementary literacy practices we talked about during our class sessions were reflected in her work.

Laney's writing assignment to accompany *All American Boys* was a response to reading (figure 20.4). She provided a key quote from the text, directed students to a certain section of pages, and asked them to state a claim and give text evidence to support it. This sort of writing is a main focus of the upper-elementary grades and it is clear that Laney has a handle on what is expected. She maintained high expectations, but also created a writing rubric outlining how to meet those expectations in areas such as organization/purpose, evidence/elaboration, and language conventions. From the

Writing Assignment:

On page 215, Quinn writes, "*The Invisible Man* at Central High: Rashad." How do the authors develop the idea that Rashad is treated like he is "invisible"? Identify 1 way they do this and write a paragraph with a claim, strong evidence from pages 186–203, and an explanation.

Mentor text:

One way that the authors of *All American Boys* develop the idea that Rashad is invisible is through the interview with Roger Stuckey who is the cab driver. Stuckey, who has never even met Rashad, admits that if he saw Rashad on the street and it was dark outside he would not pick him up. Stuckey doesn't see Rashad as a person, shown when he says, "I mean, listen, I've been robbed before. Right around here. And I just...I don't ever want to be robbed again. And he looks like the guy who robbed me. He was dressed just like him'" (187). Stuckey sees Rashad as just another black boy who are "crazy these days"(187), instead of an individual. This interview shows the idea that instead of really seeing Rashad, many people only see his clothing and skin color and make assumptions about him. Through Stuckey's interview, the authors show that biases against young Black men have made individual people, like Rashad, invisible to people who don't know him.

Figure 20.4. Laney's writing task for sixth graders.

initial social studies inquiry to the final writing assignment, the integration of social studies and literacy was consistent. Gholdy Muhammad argues that "students need spaces to name and critique injustice and ultimately have the agency to build a better world for all."[9] That orientation toward not just social studies, but learning broadly, was one I tried to convey through readings and activities in our course together. Laney took up those considerations and reflected on the need for critical engagements with the social world as demonstrated in her three key assignments:

> Besides my personal desire to learn more about police brutality, I was also motivated to choose this topic because I think it needs to be discussed and taught in schools. Police brutality is a pressing issue in our country and originates in the racism that we pass along through generations and the racist biases that we teach our children. Racism needs to be actively combated against starting at a younger age and directly addressed in the curriculum.

By flipping the course content around, I was able to make this literacy-heavy course work for me. My past experiences with social studies were able to give me the structure so that I could tackle the language arts content. It was a small change that had a big impact on how the students and I navigated the semester.

CONSIDERATIONS

There are three considerations that I pull from this experience of teaching a class and content area that is new to me. The first is inspired by the words of the abolitionist Mariame Kaba when she talks about "a million different experiments."[10] She cautions against seeking perfection and argues that we should try out different ventures, even when we're unsure how they will go. This small change to the course felt like that. There were years of the class being taught one way before me, and I had little except an intuitive feeling that my change might just work backing me up. I was not sure how my small curricular design change would work upon implementation. Perhaps the assignments wouldn't connect as much as I imagined. Perhaps it would lead to an overemphasis on social studies at the expense of quality literacy teaching. However, that proved not to be the case. This experience made me feel confident to try out other small changes in future courses.

The second consideration has to do with the mechanics of the change I made. As I stated, I kept the content for the course largely the same, but just organized it in a different order. Like many, I am in agreement with Picower when she says that "Teachers are busy and don't have time to reinvent the wheel."[11] By being strategic about the small change, we can preserve much of the strong work that exists and update it for a new context, a new educator, or a new group of students. It does not have to be a large change to have a large impact.

The final consideration I am taking away from this experience pertains to my choice to start with social studies. Starting with what I knew helped me build the confidence so that when it was time to tackle the new content, I felt comfortable. Further, I spent the first third of the semester building relationships with students that helped set a positive tone for the remaining portions. In those first few weeks I was getting to know the new school in multiple ways: how to make copies, how much students would be emailing me, how to schedule a van for a field trip. By the time I got to the literacy methods, I was feeling comfortable in the space. That confidence also helped me recognize that I *did* know quite a bit about literacy methods. I had worked at three different public schools and was therefore familiar with three very different literacy curricular approaches. All of those helped inform the teaching I did with my students. While of course I had to refamiliarize myself with some of the content over the summer, I was actually pleasantly surprised how little there was that was new to me. My lived experience as a classroom teacher was able to come to the fore once I was feeling confident and comfortable.

Being able to make a small change to our teaching and curricula is an important step in a world where the demands on educators are extremely high. Oftentimes we feel compelled to make large, sweeping changes, but that is not always realistic due to limited time and resources. As I sought to demonstrate here, a small change was a way for me to take on a new content area while maintaining my own goals and orientations toward teaching and learning.

NOTES

1. Gholdy Muhammad, *Cultivating Genius: An Equity Framework for Culturally and Historically Responsive Literacy* (New York: Scholastic, 2020); Christine Sleeter, *Un-Standardizing Curriculum: Multicultural Teaching in the Standards-Based Classroom* (New York: Teachers College Press, 2005).

2. Emily Hanford, *Sold a Story* (podcast, American Public Media, 2022), https://features.apmreports.org/sold-a-story/.

3. Bree Picower, "Using Their Words: Six Elements of Social Justice Curriculum Design for the Elementary Classroom," *International Journal of Multicultural Education* 14 no. 1 (2012): 1–17.

4. Library of Congress, *1968: The Young Lord's Organization/Party*, special resource guide, Library of Congress, n.d., https://guides.loc.gov/latinx-civil-rights/young-lords-organization (accessed January 16, 2024).

5. Paul Gorski, "Stages of Multicultural Curriculum Transformation," EdChange.org, n.d., http://www.edchange.org/multicultural/curriculum/steps.html (accessed January 17, 2024).

6. CAST, "Universal Design for Learning Guidelines version 2.2," 2018, http://udlguidelines.cast.org.

7. Zaretta Hammond, *Culturally Responsive Teaching and the Brain* (Thousand Oaks, CA: Corwin, 2015).

8. Jason Reynolds, *All American Boys* (New York: Atheneum, 2015).

9. Muhammad, *Cultivating Genius,* 120.

10. Mariame Kaba, *We Do This 'Til We Free Us: Abolitionist Organizing and Transforming Justice* (Chicago: Haymarket Books, 2021), 166.

11. Picower, "Using Their Words," 14.

BIBLIOGRAPHY

CAST. Universal Design for Learning Guidelines, version 2.2. 2018. http://udlguidelines.cast.org.

Gorski, Paul. *Stages of Multicultural Curriculum Transformation.* EdChange.org, n.d. http://www.edchange.org/multicultural/curriculum/steps.html. Accessed January 17, 2024.

Hammond, Zaretta. *Culturally Responsive Teaching and the Brain.* Thousand Oaks, CA: Corwin, 2015.

Hanford, Emily. *Sold a Story.* Podcast produced by American Public Media. 2022. https://features.apmreports.org/sold-a-story/.

Kaba, Mariame. *We Do This 'Til We Free Us: Abolitionist Organizing and Transforming Justice.* Chicago: Haymarket Books, 2021.

Library of Congress. *1968:The Young Lord's Organization/Party.* Special resource guide, Library of Congress, n.d. https://guides.loc.gov/latinx-civil-rights/young-lords-organization. Accessed January 16, 2024.

Muhammad, Gholdy. *Cultivating Genius: An Equity Framework for Culturally and Historically Responsive Literacy.* New York: Scholastic, 2020.

Picower, Bree. "Using Their Words: Six Elements of Social Justice Curriculum Design for the Elementary Classroom." *International Journal of Multicultural Education* 14, no. 1 (2012): 1–17.

Reynolds, Jason. *All American Boys.* New York: Atheneum, 2015.

Sleeter, Christine. *Un-Standardizing Curriculum: Multicultural Teaching in the Standards-Based Classroom.* New York: Teachers College Press, 2005.

Chapter 21

Incorporating Lesson Study

An Improvement Process for Elementary Social Studies Teacher Candidates

Alexander S. Butler

This chapter looks at the introduction of a form of lesson study to design, experiment, observe, and revise lesson plans in an undergraduate social studies methods course. It reviews the concept of lesson study and how I have implemented it, providing anecdotal responses from current teacher candidates participating in the implementation. The inclusion of lesson study in my methods class has transformed teacher candidates' learning and preparedness to teach inquiry-based social studies lessons.

Brenda: What do you think?

Me: It is awesome! These students are doing a great job.

Brenda: This is their third time teaching this lesson.

Me: Wow. When do they start student teaching?

Brenda: What?

Me: When do they start student teaching?

Brenda: Not anytime soon. These are freshmen.

Me: What?! No way! I thought these were seniors getting ready for the field.

Brenda: No. . . . Why would you think that?

Me: Their lesson was better than most of my seniors' lessons. Your students produced an inquiry-based lesson. My teacher candidates are still building teacher-centered lessons. How did you do this?

The dialogue above is a re-creation of a conversation I had with a colleague while watching a group of freshmen teacher candidates (TC) teach a middle school social studies lesson to their peers. I had been invited to the last class of a course to watch TCs teach their final lesson of the semester. The only context I had for the course was that these TCs were middle- and secondary-level social studies teacher candidates. I walked in and sat in the back of the university classroom. There were probably twenty or so teacher candidates in the class, and one of them went up to teach. The TC passed out materials and then started teaching. I was so impressed. I thought I was observing an upper-level undergraduate TC teach their final lesson before student teaching. The lesson had a clear, compelling question. The tasks/activities were student-centered. Their peers were engaged using a variety of primary and secondary sources to build an argument in response to the compelling question. As seen in the dialogue above, I was shocked to find out that the TCs in the room were all freshmen. The lesson I watched was better than most of the seniors' lessons in my elementary social studies methods course. I needed to know how my colleagues had taught their TCs how to build and implement an inquiry-based lesson so well.

The foundational structure that supported these TC products was lesson study (LS). This chapter describes LS, how I implemented LS to improve the learning outcomes of my elementary TCs in a social studies methods course, how my TCs' learning and preparedness to teach inquiry-based social studies improved, and what difficulties and suggestions I have for implementing LS in a methods course.

CONTEXT

This story and the changes associated with this innovation took place in an Inclusive Early Childhood teacher education program's senior-level social studies methods course. The methods block for seniors is half a semester of seven or eight four-hour classes. At the midway point of the semester, TCs stop all their methods courses and start student teaching. There were thirty-five TCs registered for the class. This group of TCs had spent much of their freshman and sophomore years of college taking online courses due to the COVID-19 pandemic. Therefore, they had not spent as much time as pre-COVID-19 cohorts completing field observations and practicing teaching with students. Additionally, their K–5 experience and their field observations were shaped by the consistent marginalization that social studies has faced in public elementary school curriculum since at least the 1980s.[1] The result of this marginalization has impacted my senior TCs in three ways. First, my course is the only explicit social studies course in their teacher education program. Second, very few have seen a social studies lesson taught in their placements. Third, few TCs have memories of elementary social studies instruction.

The cumulative effect of this impact has led many of my TCs to express that social studies is their least favorite subject when I ask at the beginning of a semester, "What worries you about this class?" When I follow up to ask why social studies is/was their least favorite, they respond that social studies is/was boring. When I ask why it was boring, they generally mention they did not like memorizing a bunch of dates and names. Though I point out that their ire seems to be at the way they were taught rather than the field of social studies, many are unmoved. Frankly, I cannot blame them for this opinion. I vividly remember sitting in classes filling out worksheets, taking multiple-choice quizzes, and memorizing facts (e.g., state capitals or the Preamble to the Constitution) throughout my social studies experiences. Most social studies lessons were boring or not meaningful. Teachers' emphasis on facts contributed more to my success at trivia night than to any improvement in my daily life.

Based on my own and my TCs' experiences, I set out to create an elementary social studies methods course that helped TCs see the importance of social studies and how to make it engaging, empowering, challenging, and relevant to their future students' lives.[2] Therefore, I built an elementary social studies methods course for the fall of 2022 emphasizing inquiry-based practices.[3] Unfortunately, the course did not achieve my goals by the end of the eight weeks. I had used our eight four-hour class sessions to teach about inquiry-based lessons using the inquiry design model[4] coupled with backward design.[5] I also modeled inquiry-based lessons for the students. Despite my modeling and teaching, many TCs struggled to build inquiry-based lessons. Rather than start by building a compelling question and assessment as I had taught and modeled, TCs often started by building "fun" activities. This often led to a disconnect in their lesson plan between their objectives and what students did. For example, if they wanted students to learn about important symbols and practices of the United States (a kindergarten standard), they would read a book to students about the symbols on the flag. Then, they would have students color in the flag. Students never had the chance to engage with multiple sources, including primary sources, to draw conclusions and explore what the different parts of the flag meant or why we and others consider flags important. TCs struggled to build lessons that gave students opportunities to use higher-order thinking skills. TCs consistently did not see the issue with these types of lessons. They felt like their peers had engaged well in the activity because they had produced something—a colored-in map. It was clear from my perspective they were struggling to assess the learning of students related to their objectives and reflect on what they did well and what they needed to improve upon.

I believe they struggled to build an aligned inquiry-based lesson for two major reasons. First, it was a result of the way I structured the course curriculum. I tried to do too much. The course met once a week for four hours. Teacher candidates in the course had four other methods courses that met for the same length of time once a week. Additionally, they were in the field one day a week. I felt pressure to squeeze as much social studies into the eight weeks as possible, while also knowing they were being stretched thin. Since they had never had an elementary-focused social studies class before, I used the first four classes to introduce the teacher candidates to social studies as a field, the importance of representation, inquiry-based social studies, and source work. During these weeks I modeled several short inquiry-based lessons and gave TCs significant time in the first four weeks in class to work in groups practicing the methods and skills they learned about in their weekly resources. The second half of the course was used to plan a unit of three lessons focused on one of the four social studies disciplines (history, geography, civics, economics) covered in the state's standards, and then teach one lesson from the unit. I planned for them to spend two classes planning their unit and then one class teaching one of the lessons. The last class was for TCs to debrief, work on and submit revisions, and write a justification for their lesson, explaining how it was inquiry-based. Their grade was based primarily on their initial plan and their teaching. Though they had time to reflect on and revise their plans, these were not worth as much for their grade. Additionally, they never had time to implement the revisions and find out if the revisions led to better student outcomes.

Second, TCs taught their lesson together in a large group. Due to the size of the course's enrollment, I had TCs join groups based on the grade they were student teaching. There were six groups of six TCs in the class. Though the groups worked well together, the group size and length of the lesson limited the ability for everyone to teach. In some groups, a dominant TC did most or all of the teaching. A handful of TCs even refused to stand in front of a large group of their peers and teach. When I asked why they had not participated in the teaching portion of the lesson, they said it caused them too much anxiety. In other groups, the teaching load was more equally shared. In both instances, it was clear the TCs did not have enough opportunities or a safe space for all of them to teach. Frankly, most of the lessons felt more like a group presentation than a lesson.

When these issues were combined, the groups were only able to teach their lesson once, and never saw their revisions in practice. The result was that teacher candidates in the course could build a "fun" social studies lesson plan, but not one consistently aligned between questions, tasks, and sources and fully inquiry-based. In the fall of 2022, I did not give them enough time to practice teaching. If I wanted TCs to be able to plan and teach engaging, empowering, challenging, and relevant inquiry-based social studies lessons to their future students, then I needed to make some changes.

SMALL CHANGES

Lesson Study

After observing my colleagues' course, I decided to restructure my course to use a modified lesson study (LS) framework. LS is an approach to instructional improvement. Participants, generally teachers but in this case TCs, work collaboratively through iterations of four steps.

1. Formulate goals for student learning
2. Plan a lesson using these goals
3. Teach and observe the lesson
4. Reflect on the lesson[6]

These steps are probably familiar to many educators. I follow this process when planning lessons. However, the difference in LS is that educators are doing these steps collaboratively and iteratively. They must come to consensus, a democratic process,[7] when moving through the steps. When they teach the revised lesson, a new team member teaches, and the initial teacher becomes an observer. One other difference I have found in the process is when the team observes the lesson. The team members observing the lesson are asked to observe the students' learning processes, not the teacher. For example, the observers monitor how a student's learning progresses and how their learning was supported or hindered during the lesson. The teacher's delivery of the lesson might be one of these supports or hindrances, but observers are supposed to discuss this related to students' learning. They might make observations based to the following questions: did the task allow students to engage the compelling question?

How did students interact with the sources? Did students understand the instructions? This is an important observational shift to recognize, and is why I incorporated an observation protocol to help TCs focus their observation.

The LS framework then calls for the team to repeat steps 2–4 by revising the lesson, having another teacher in the group teach the revised lesson while the team observes, and then the group spends time reflecting on the second lesson. This process of revising and reteaching "increases opportunities for teachers to learn from one another" and "teaches valuable skills of lesson observation, discussion, and adaptation that are fundamental to improvement of teaching."[8] Essentially, lesson study is a teach, reteach framework.

Jigsaw Lesson Study

In the fall of 2023, I faced the same context I had in the fall of 2022, but this time I had one less class session due to fall holidays. In response to the shortening of the course and aforementioned issues, I modified the LS process for my teacher candidates using the Jigsaw Lesson Study process.[9] This adaptation of LS was built for teacher candidates who were practicing their teaching in their university classroom. I had TCs separate themselves into six elementary grade–based LS teams of three or four members each. There were eleven groups, with nine groups of three and two groups of four. Each team then collaboratively developed a twenty-minute inquiry-based lesson plan for the next class when they would teach three iterations of their lesson. LS teams completed steps 1 and 2 outside of class for their initial lesson.

The next class began by having one TC teach their team's lesson to another team. Team members of the TC teaching would each complete a PASS (Powerful Authentic Social Studies) protocol (figure 21.1) observing students' learning while their team member taught. After the TC finished teaching, the two teams would reflect on the lesson. Then the team that had been students would have one of their team members teach (figure 21.2). Once both teams had taught and shared feedback, teams had

PASS Element	Evidence from Lesson and Rationale	Rating (circle)	Suggestions for Future Teaching
Meaningful? (How was this connected to students' lives?)		• Emerging • Acceptable • Target	
Active? (Identify instructional Strategies used)		• Emerging • Acceptable • Target	
Challenging? (evaluate alignment of stated OLS, Objectives and instruction/assessments)		• Emerging • Acceptable • Target	
Integrative? (evaluate the source analysis/literacy components)		• Emerging • Acceptable • Target	
Value-based? (students practice building arguments/voice)		• Emerging • Acceptable • Target	

Figure 21.1. PASS Protocol used by TCs to evaluate learning of peers during teaching.

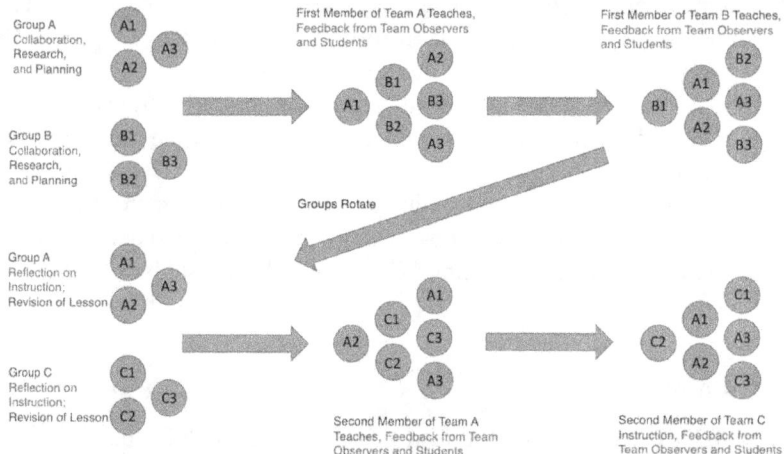

Figure 21.2. Example of LS structure. Figure is adapted from Weaver and Matney, "Adapting Lesson Study for Preservice Teachers' Instruction and Learning," 185.

twenty minutes to revise their lesson. When the teams finished their revisions, the groups rotated and a new TC would teach their team's revised lesson to another team. The cycle of teaching, reflecting, and revising occurred three times in each class. TCs in a three-member team each had the opportunity to teach once and observe twice per class. Each time the lesson was taught, it was taught to a new team of TC peers.

Incorporating Jigsaw Lesson Study as my instructional framework in the fall of 2023 not only improved TC learning, but addressed the largest challenges I encountered in the previous fall. These conclusions are drawn from my analysis of a two-page final reflection that TCs submitted at the end of the course and my observations of their learning demonstrated in their teaching. First, from my perspective, the course's curriculum was focused and did not try to do too much. The simplified curriculum helped me and the TCs focus on their teaching. Every TC who submitted the final reflection described the benefits of the LS process. For example, one TC reflected that being taught a lesson I helped build was "helpful because I could hear how other people were teaching it and it made it easier to reflect on the lesson during the revisions" (TD). Even when TCs suggested I make a change to the structure, they focused on group dynamics. For example, several students commented that they wished they could have changed groups because some group members did not contribute equally.

Second, every TC taught multiple lessons. This was a significant issue in the fall of 2022, because groups only taught one lesson. Some TCs did not even participate in the teaching. In the fall of 2023, I made the groups smaller, and the LS process dictated everyone have an opportunity to teach. TCs valued the opportunity to teach and watch their lesson taught, as this TC described:

> The teach, revise, re-teach process allowed us to . . . critique one another, and . . . learn from one another. . . . I was able to teach a lesson and gain experience, make my lesson better through feedback, and re-teach an even more beneficial lesson. This process was

vital to our success, because we got to ensure we were teaching the best lesson that would reach our students and the standards/content meant to be taught or learned. (CS)

Other TCs emphasized how the intentional iterations of the process built their confidence and how they could see their lessons improving:

The first lesson my group and I created was a struggle, . . . we did not know what we were doing. This is where the revision process was very beneficial. . . . It gave us a chance to go back and look at what ideas were good, but could be built on, and what ideas did not promote inquiry and could be removed from our lesson. Doing this process three times allowed us to build a better understanding of the process and how to create an inquiry-based lesson. Repeating this process . . . has made me feel more comfortable when creating an inquiry-based lesson plan. (MA)

And

I loved the idea of teaching, revising what we did correctly and what we can change, and then re-teaching. I think as college students, the lesson plans we create are never going to go as well as we think. . . . When the professor allows us to make mistakes and not put extra pressure on us for being right and wrong, we are able to revise the lesson to make it better. (HL)

It is clear from responses like these that the TCs were engaged and saw the benefit of the process. Additionally, TCs felt safe to make mistakes and try things out because they could revise their work. The framework's iterative process inherently emphasized that there was always room for improvement. The LS process seemed to lessen their anxiety. These were important change in TCs' outcomes.

Third, TCs were able to reflect and gather feedback to implement revisions. The instant feedback helped TCs see how their lessons might not be aligned to their goals and how their peers were not learning what they wanted them to learn. They were then able to brainstorm revisions to build better lessons. For example, one student reflected on how feedback helped them realize that some of their resources were redundant and could be cut from the lesson (AC). Many TCs highlighted the importance of having feedback from their team and peers acting as students, and the professor.

Even when TCs called the process "overwhelming at first," they later commented "how helpful it was for all of us . . . because we were able to not only get feedback from our peers that we were teaching to but we also [received] good feedback from Dr. Butler" (CA). Comments emphasizing the importance feedback from their peers and myself were consistent throughout TCs' reflections. From an instructor standpoint, being able to see their teaching was a result of TCs teaching four lessons three times each. In the fall of 2022, I only had the chance to see a lesson once and, because the groups were larger, they had to be spread across separate rooms. This meant that I had a small window to observe each TC teaching. Using the Jigsaw LS gave me more opportunities to see each TC teach. It was clear from their written reflections that they valued their peers' and my feedback.

DIFFICULTIES AND SUGGESTIONS

Even though I think fall 2023 was a success based on student feedback and my own observations, there were difficulties the teams and I faced. One difficulty, previously mentioned, was that some teams struggled to work together. TCs in the two teams of four specifically mentioned the difficulty of working in groups. Frustration stemmed from having difficult teammates and not everyone being able to teach each lesson they created. The latter frustration excites me, because the TCs expressed a desire to teach. They wanted the opportunity to practice and receive feedback. While the LS process solved the issue I had in the fall of 2022 with some TCs hiding within their group so they did not have to teach, I would put TCs in a team of two before a team of four next time. Related to the construction of the teams, some TCs suggested rotating groups or allowing them to reconstitute grade-based groups so they could teach other grades since they were not sure which grade they wanted to teach. Whether or not one takes up this suggestion should be more about the TCs in their specific class. I like both ideas and will try them in future semesters.

Another issue we faced was that all the teaching took place in the same classroom. Several TCs mentioned how loud it was in class when four other people were teaching small groups of students. One TC wrote, "You should continue to do this for future classes as it taught me so much," followed with "There were a lot of times where I felt like nobody was paying attention to the lesson I was teaching because they were focused on the group across the room singing or they were whispering to their friend in the next group over" (BE). I need to figure out how to space out the groups more effectively. From a practical standpoint this will be difficult if other rooms are not free during my teaching block. However, putting groups in other classes may make it more difficult for me to observe all the groups. One way to possibly address this issue is by having the TC teams only teach twice each class. While this reduces the number of times TCs will teach over the course of the semester, it would allow me to ensure fewer teams are teaching at the same time. It would also allow me to put three teams together so that the teaching team will have more students for feedback. Grouping three teams together would address an issue that a TC raised about having only six people felt too small and not like teaching a class. Adding extra "students" to each teaching session may help it feel more like their future classrooms.

Lastly, I had one TC make an excellent suggestion about creating a repository for all the lessons created. They felt like this "would be a good resource to refer back to in the future when planning lessons for different grades" (MI). From this type of statement, I concluded that TCs found the LS process valuable and helped them produce inquiry-based lessons. This conclusion is confirmed by TCs' final reflections. Every student who submitted a final reflection felt like they had experienced and taught inquiry-based lessons.

CONCLUSION

It is clear to me that LS positively impacted my TCs. This was affirmed after reading through their final reflections. 2023 TCs were able to build and implement inquiry-based lessons more effectively than TCs in the fall of 2022. Not only did the 2023 cohort build better plans, but they also felt more confident in their teaching. Though it might seem like a large change to shift the whole framework of a course, it was really a small change because it was easy to implement. Additionally, it simplified my curriculum. The impact of lesson study and the teach, reflect, revise, and reteach process was huge for my TCs in 2023.

NOTES

1. Paul G. Fitchett and Tina L. Heafner, "A National Perspective on the Effects of High-Stakes Testing and Standardization on Elementary Social Studies Marginalization," *Theory & Research in Social Education* 38, no. 1 (2010): 115; Council of Chief State School Offices, *The Marginalization of Social Studies* (Washington DC: CCSSO, 2018), https://ccsso.org/sites/default/files/2018-11/Elementary%20SS%20Brief%2045%20Minute%20Version_0.pdf.

2. Gholdy Muhammad, *Cultivating Genius: An Equity Framework for Culturally and Historically Responsive Literacy* (New York: Scholastic, 2020); Joanna Weaver and Gabriel Matney, "Adapting Lesson Study for Preservice Teachers' Instruction and Learning," in *Lesson Study with Mathematics and Science Preservice Teachers*, ed. Sharon Dotger, Gabriel Matney, Jennifer Heckathorn, Kelly Chandler-Olcott, and Miranda Fox (New York: Routledge, 2024).

3. S. G. Grant, Kathy Swan, and John Kelly Lee, *Inquiry-Based Practice in Social Studies Education: Understanding the Inquiry Design Model* (New York: Routledge, 2017), 13–14.

4. Ibid., 25.

5. Carol Ann Tomlinson and Jay McTighe, *Integrating Differentiated Instruction and Understanding by Design* (Alexandria, VA: Association for Supervision and Curriculum, 2006).

6. Catherine C. Lewis and Jacqueline Hurd, *Lesson Study Step by Step: How Teacher Learning Communities Improve Instruction* (Portsmouth, NH: Heinemann, 2011), 19–23.

7. Jongsung Kim and Kazuhiro Kusahara, "Democratic Characteristics of Social Studies Lesson Study: A Case Study in Japan," *Journal of Field-based Lesson Studies* 2, no. 1 (2021): 25.

8. Lewis and Hurd, "Lesson Study Step by Step," 63. This is found in the inset called "A Closer Look." It is written by Makoto Yoshida, PhD; Dr. Yoshida is a lesson study researcher.

9. Weaver and Matney, "Adapting Lesson Study for Preservice Teachers' Instruction and Learning," 183.

BIBLIOGRAPHY

Council of Chief State School Offices. *The Marginalization of Social Studies.* Washington DC: CCSSO, 2018. https://ccsso.org/sites/default/files/2018-11/Elementary%20SS%20Brief%2045%20Minute%20Version_0.pdf.

Fitchett, Paul G., and Tina L. Heafner. "A National Perspective on the Effects of High-Stakes Testing and Standardization on Elementary Social Studies Marginalization." *Theory & Research in Social Education* 38 no. 1 (2010): 114–30. https://doi.org/10.1080/00933104.2010.10473418.

Grant, S. G., Kathy Swan, and John Kelly Lee. *Inquiry-Based Practice in Social Studies Education: Understanding the Inquiry Design Model.* New York: Routledge, 2017.

Kim, Jongsung, and Kazuhiro Kusahara. "Democratic Characteristics of Social Studies Lesson Study: A Case Study in Japan." *Journal of Field-Based Lesson Studies* 2, no. 1 (2021): 23–46.

Lewis, Catherine C., and Jacqueline Hurd. *Lesson Study Step by Step: How Teacher Learning Communities Improve Instruction.* Portsmouth, NH: Heinemann, 2011.

Muhammad, Gholdy. *Cultivating Genius: An Equity Framework for Culturally and Historically Responsive Literacy.* New York: Scholastic, 2020.

Tomlinson, Carol Ann, and McTighe, Jay. *Integrating Differentiated Instruction and Understanding by Design.* Alexandria, VA: Association for Supervision and Curriculum, 2006.

Weaver, Joanna, and Gabriel Matney. "Adapting Lesson Study for Preservice Teachers' Instruction and Learning." In *Lesson Study with Mathematics and Science Preservice Teachers*, edited by Sharon Dotger, Gabriel Matney, Jennifer Heckathorn, Kelly Chandler-Olcott, and Miranda Fox, 182–91. New York: Routledge, 2024.

Chapter 22

Collaborate with Librarians
How Adding New and Relevant Materials Matters
Ewa Dziedzic-Elliott

I spent over a decade working in public schools as a school librarian and I loved it. I loved igniting passion for reading, watching my students developing their literacy skills and becoming their own people. School librarianship has many challenges: shortage of staff, money, and time; lack of support as well as understanding the school library profession, and so much more. In the presence of a highly motivated and passionate school librarian there is no shortage of willingness to grow, learn, and stay current.

A good school librarian needs to be connected to the library community, attend conferences and workshops, follow current literary trends and, most importantly—read, read, read! I remember my days in elementary school when every couple of weeks, or during holidays and long breaks, I would take home a stack of books and say: I have to work this weekend.

Years later as a high school librarian, I decided to code newly arrived books by genres and add appropriate stickers to book spines and make the shelf browsing easier for my students (I never genre-fied the collection, intentionally, but that's a different story). Sometimes reading the back of the book, its endorsements, or summary would be enough to identify the genre, but sometimes I would have to read a few pages to assign the genre. In many cases my preliminary reading would get me hooked and I would end up with a tall stack of young adult (YA) books to read.

As an academic librarian I still read professional reviews, attend conferences and workshops that highlight current publishing trends, follow the prestigious book awards, and read newly published books to stay up to date with my professional practice.

American English is a live language, continually changing and evolving. When I pick up an older book for children I notice that the vocabulary is different, the sentence structure is not the same, and it is often much longer. Our daily lives are so different from the ones represented in the books from just a while ago. Our students, for the most part, don't know how to operate an old-fashioned phone or printer, and have probably never heard of a fax machine. So why would we ask them to read books that they cannot relate to technologically unless to use it as a historical fact?

In this chapter I will give a few recommendations for educators on how to most effectively collaborate with your school librarian using their professional expertise. School librarians are the only group of educators trained to support state standards, a district's curricula, and a school's lesson plans, regardless of the subject and content area. I will also write about educational resources and/or strategies librarians use to be better literacy specialists.

SMALL RECOMMENDATION #1: ATTEND EVENTS WITH AUTHORS AND ILLUSTRATORS

My appreciation for book authors and illustrators grew even more after seeing many of them present and hold tables at various professional conferences. Knowing their creative process adds to the level of understanding of individual styles, perspectives, or formats, which translates later on into unique ways to use their work in your classroom.

Very often we focus on authors digesting, analyzing, and taking apart the written words using illustrations as accompaniment to the text. It wasn't until I listened to some illustrators that I understood the level of involvement and comprehension of the text that it takes for them to create art for books. We take the visuals for granted, assuming that this is just it, the one, only, and final complement to the text. But the story is much deeper. There is an ongoing and nuanced conversation happening between the text and images. They can complement each other, provide additional information, or create a completely new layer of looking at the book as a whole.

During a conference, I attended a panel of authors and illustrators. A moderator asked about their creative process: What comes first: text or illustrations? Do the authors suggest or request certain images? Do the authors choose illustrators? They talked about whether they actually know each other during the process of writing, whether they are in touch, or whether the editor assigned the work for the illustrator. One of the authors said that they had no contact with the illustrator and when the work came to them for approval they were very surprised by the final result: the main character looked like nothing they imagined.

You don't have to go far to see great presentations or workshops led by authors or illustrators. Most states have their teachers' union lead conferences, and many have various library organizations that put together annual events. Being in New Jersey, I can say that we have an amazing selection of conventions, conferences and workshops led by the New Jersey Education Association (NJEA, https://njeaconvention.njea.org/), New Jersey Association of School Librarians (NJASL, https://www.njasl.org/), and New Jersey Library Association (NJLA, https://njlaconference.info/). We can use the attendance at one of these special events as an inspiration that can be used later on in the classroom.

SMALL RECOMMENDATION #2: FOLLOW BOOK CREATORS ON SOCIAL MEDIA

In the past, to learn about rising literary stars and their publications, we had to read professional magazines and journals such as *School Library Journal* (https://www.slj.com/), *Booklist* (https://www.booklistonline.com/), *Kirkus Reviews* (https://www.kirkusreviews.com/), *The Horn Book Magazine* (https://www.hbook.com/), or *Horn Book Guide* (currently titled the Guide/Reviews Database, https://www.hornbook-guide.com/site/www.hornbookguide.com/site/?page=about-the-horn-book-guide). Right now we have many new ways to learn about literary trends for our youngest readers. One of my favorite ways is following authors and illustrators on their social media pages. They provide updates on their current projects, add information about school visits, share about creative ways to use their materials for student learning opportunities, post videos about their writing or drawing techniques, strategies, and tips. To interact with their audiences many of them ask for feedback, recommendations, and opinions, making the process of creating books even more exciting and interactive.

Exercise 1: Read the Book but Don't Show the Illustrations

Read a picture book to your students but don't show them the illustrations. Ask them what they think the main character looks like. Is it a person, an animal, maybe neither? Ask your students to become illustrators and see how many details of the book they can capture on the paper without being influenced by the original work. Have them pair and share their creations and discuss their final work.

Exercise 2: "Read" a Wordless Book and Have Students Write the Text

Use a wordless book and ask students to write the stories to accompany the images. This would be a wonderful challenge for students whose first language isn't English. Instead of decoding the words, students would be decoding illustrations to create the text. There are some amazing books that, even with no text, are as complex as they can be, and can become an amazing canvas for students to exercise their vocabulary. Think how this exercise can be paired up with practicing students' new vocabulary words and spelling.

SMALL RECOMMENDATION #3: FOLLOW ANNUAL BOOK AWARDS

American book awards for children's and YA literature have changed so much over the past couple of decades. We all are familiar with Rudine Sims Bishop's concept of windows, mirrors, and sliding glass doors,[1] an idea that guides modern education and librarianship in believing that children need to be able to see someone else's experiences, see themselves, or be able to step in and empathize with the protagonists. Whenever you read a book to your students, or recommend one to them, please ask yourself if the book you are presenting meets any of these concepts. If not, there is a great way to learn about modern children and YA literature. Just follow the American Library Association's annual book awards.[2] When you follow the awards, you will notice many current publication trends, learn about new authors, and learn about new writing and narration styles and innovative illustration techniques and book formats.

Exercise 1: Classroom Book Awards

Read a few selected books, set up ground rules, and create classroom book awards. Create appropriate categories, such as best animal book, best book on friendship, best illustrations, most surprising ending. Students can participate in creating the categories. Have your students discuss the books and decide who wins which award. Great March Madness idea, right?

Exercise 2: Follow a Selected Book Award

Choose one annual book award, for example the Newbery Award (https://www.ala.org/ala/alsc/awardsscholarships/literaryawds/newberymedal/newberyhonors/newberymedal.htm), and with your students, follow the process from announcement of the contestants to the results. Read a few nominated books and have your students vote on their favorites. When ALA reveals the award winners, discuss with your students if they agree with those selections. It is really fun to anticipate whether our favorite books win.

Within the publishing world there has been a strong push for representation and diversification in literature for children. The latest book-banning wave attempted to instill the chill/fear factor and force publishers to move away from uncomfortable or controversial subjects. Older students can discuss whether the latest award winners submit to the censors or whether the selected winners stand strong against it.

SMALL RECOMMENDATION #4: PARTNER UP WITH A LIBRARIAN

If following book creators on social media or following annual book awards is not for you, there is another way to stay in touch with the current children's and YA literature: partner up with a librarian. In an ideal world, I would have said to partner up with your school librarian, but this might not be the case in the absence of a school librarian and/or library program in your building or even in your school district.[3] There are three types of librarianship I would like to mention here: school, public, and academic. In the pages that follow, you will find a few recommendations on how to best partner with them as an educator.

School Librarian—Your Classroom Collaborator

Your school librarian has a teaching certification or has taken classes that pertain to education, children and youth development, and state teaching requirements, such as state standards,[4] in order to receive a state's certification. Like any other educator, they are obligated to continue their professional growth and attend/complete professional development events that are specific to their job. That often includes attending local or national conferences, workshops, and webinars that provide information on current publications and literary trends. Those latest trends include: adding diverse literature to children and YA collections, bilingual and foreign language books, wordless books with different levels of complexity of the illustrations, and graphic novels. By supporting students' access to academic and leisure reading materials and collaborating with school librarians, educators have an opportunity to increase and/or support students' school achievement and literacy scores.[5]

Opportunity 1: Collaborative Research Project

Set the parameters of the project with the librarian. As an educator, you can introduce the research project from the perspective of your academic focus and allow the school librarian to be your partner that focuses on resources. The librarian can take the lead in providing instruction on the appropriateness of resources, their academic value, and the academic integrity of the resources, even formatting, which allows you to focus on the merit of the project and the craftsmanship of the writing.

Public Libraries—Leisure Reading Collaborator

Generally speaking public libraries and their programs focus on leisure resources. They provide access to materials that a typical school library might not be allowed to have. I have seen school libraries where the main part of the collection was nonfiction books and databases that directly support state standards and school districts' curricula. Their collections would often be missing popular fiction, especially graphic novels or manga. By partnering with a local public library you may be able to get access to materials that are not readily available in your school building. Unfortunately for many school districts, in the absence of a school library program the public library becomes the only source of any research and non-research materials for K–12 students.[6]

Opportunity 2: Bring Your Public Librarians to Your School

Not everyone knows that public library cards are free (in some countries there is a fee that comes with access to a public library). Invite your public library to your school building during the school's community events, such as back-to-school night, your school's open house, or parent–teacher conferences. Allow the public librarians to share with your community what kind of programs they offer to their patrons of different ages. Give them space and time to provide free public library cards. When I was a high school librarian, I would invite the public library to host a table with brochures about their programs, events, museum passes, and requirements to obtain a card. I also had them come during faculty meetings so teachers could get public library cards.

Opportunity 3: Public Library Cards for K–12 Students and Educators

Getting a public library card for young readers can be challenging. Usually public library cards can be given after official documents establishing residency or employment are provided. To make things easier for the local families, develop a partnership between your school district and the local public library. Maybe the public library can use students' ID numbers to issue library cards? What if parents can give consent to issue a library card using the district's management system/portal?

Opportunity 4: Collaborative Events with Public Librarians

When I was an elementary school librarian, we would have meetings with public librarians at the beginning of every school year to decide on our theme and joint programs. The school would host children's librarians during Read Across America and have them lead storytimes with puppets and other activities. If we had special events such as pajama storytime, public librarians would be among the guest readers. Closer to the summer, we would have an assembly with public librarians who would come over to introduce their summer reading programs. None of this happened overnight; it took years and years to arrive at this level of collaboration.

Academic Librarians—Taking School Research to the Next Level

Some of us are fortunate enough to be surrounded by higher education institutions. In the school district in which I live we have a private university, public state college, and a two-year college, all within a few miles' radius. Some of these institutions often have an outreach librarian who is responsible for developing partnerships with other institutions in the area. For some it is a form of soft advertisement: selling the academic institution to the students and community members through the library programs. Marks and colleagues write about partnerships developed between William Paterson University and local school districts in New Jersey.[7] Authors write about providing professional development for their neighboring school districts, as well as providing academic level research resources for students.

Opportunity 5: Collaborative Research Project

When I was a high school librarian, I had developed a partnership with a couple of local higher education institutions regarding my students' research projects. Twice a year I would organize research trips to one of the colleges nearby. In stage 1 of the project I would collaborate with the teachers setting up the guidelines for the project: What do we want the students to learn? What kind of research skills do we want to exercise? What did we want to achieve by bringing our students to the college library? What was our focus? Usually the main goal was to access digital and print resources that were not available to our students at school, such as microfilms or higher-level and more expensive, databases. Another goal was to give students a glimpse of college-level research, research strategies, and resources. Very often the visits would take a different path: high schoolers who never considered attending college would start envisioning themselves as college students for the first time, especially those who would be first in their families to even consider college. Academic librarians would be flooded with questions that typically would be asked of school counselors or college admissions officers regarding the institution, their programs, student life on campus, or the admissions process.

During the college visits, or by developing partnerships with academic librarians, K–12 educators have an opportunity to learn more about college readiness and the type of skills that should be practiced. When I started my collaborative work with academic librarians I began to pay more attention to research about college readiness, inquiry and research skills, source evaluation, and helpful tools and strategies.

Opportunity 6: Higher Education Librarian-Led Professional Development

If it is not possible to bring your students to college campus, invite local higher ed librarians to provide professional development (PD) for your educators. These can be done in person or virtually. The subject of the PD can depend on the librarian's specializations, for example a librarian who specializes in information literacy can conduct a workshop around academic-level research strategies and tools, resource evaluation, using critical thinking skills when reading professional materials, and so much more.[8]

CONCLUSION

The world of education is changing faster than ever. Evolution of technology, changes to the workforce, and other factors force us to stay current on educational trends. In education we often talk about lifelong learning and reading. We are to raise our students to understand the importance of always being current, staying on top of the latest new additions to our worlds. But first we have to focus on ourselves and our own development. Are we doing what we expect our students to be doing? Do we understand the changes in the education world around us? Are we flexible enough to recognize the need for those changes?

In order to stay relevant and on top of all of those challenging changes, we need to surround ourselves with a community of educators who will continue to inspire us and help us grow and become even better facilitators of knowledge and information.

NOTES

1. R. Sims Bishop, "Mirrors, Windows and Sliding Glass Doors," *Perspectives: Choosing and Using Books in Classroom* 6, no 3 (1990).

2. ALA awards list for children's and teens' books and other materials: https://www.ala.org/news/mediapresscenter/presskits/youthmediaawards/alayouthmediaawards.

3. To learn more about the state of school librarianship, visit the website of one of the most comprehensive national school library studies, the SLIDE study: https://libslide.org/.

4. In the state of New Jersey, school librarians have been trained to use New Jersey Student Learning Standards from various disciplines when teaching, such as English or Social Studies. As of Spring 2024, the New Jersey Department of Education is working on the Information Literacy Student Learning Standard.

5. Debra E. Kachel, "Advocating for Collaboration," *Teacher Librarian* 46, no. 4 (2019): 48–50.

6. Check if your state library organization provides free statewide educational resources. In New Jersey, we have a program called Jersey Clicks (https://www.njstatelib.org/services_for_libraries/statewide_services/jerseyclicks/) that provides access to all New Jersey residents, students, and employees.

7. Gary Marks Jr., Neil Grimes, and Bonnie Lafazan, "Academic and School Library Partnerships: An Organization-Led Collaboration," in *Cases on Establishing Effective Collaborations in Academic Libraries* (IGI Global, 2023), 46–67.

8. Ibid.

BIBLIOGRAPHY

Bishop, R. Sims. "Mirrors, Windows and Sliding Glass Doors." *Perspectives: Choosing and Using Books in Classroom* 6, no. 3 (1990). www.readingrockets.org/sites/default/files/migrated/Mirrors-Windows-and-Sliding-Glass-Doors.pdf.

Kachel, Debra E. "Advocating for Collaboration." *Teacher Librarian* 46, no. 4 (2019): 48–50.

Marks, Gary, Jr., Neil Grimes, and Bonnie Lafazan. "Academic and School Library Partnerships: An Organization-Led Collaboration." In *Cases on Establishing Effective Collaborations in Academic Libraries*, 46–67. Hershey, PA: IGI Global, 2023.

Chapter 23

Jagged Learning Profiles for Culturally Responsive Classrooms

Serena Morales

Learners are complex, and teachers are limited. The schooling context requires responding to many needs at once: teaching, testing, social-emotional learning, and supporting struggling learners. What if teachers had a visual anchor of self-identified characteristics for students to reference, respond to, reflect on, and readjust during a school year, semester, or learning cycle? Jagged learning profiles make learning needs visual; they lead to meaningful reflection of students' perceptions of their capabilities before, during, and after a learning cycle.

WHAT IS A JAGGED LEARNING PROFILE?

In the book *The End of Average*,[1] Todd Rose challenges the traditional metrics that measure skills and abilities against an average and presents an alternative to understanding abilities based on an average. Rose explains the importance of a *jaggedness principle*,[2] which asserts that individual talent is jagged and fixed traits are a myth. Rose suggests that teachers can best discover how to leverage their students' strengths and address learning gaps if they understand the ways their students' abilities are uneven across a variety of abilities. A jagged learning profile (JLP) is a visual representation of how students perceive their own learning abilities based on self-identified characteristics. The profile includes a sketched silhouette of the individual, self-selected learning characteristics, and a form of "score" that helps individuals identify how they perceive their learning traits. Creating a JLP image helps students reflect on and identify their unique learning traits as well as note how their capabilities change over time.

In public education, we often use grades as a one-dimensional ranking system that fixes students and their learning into categories they carry through their learning journey—sometimes as a badge, often as a label. This type of objective system leaves out talent and pigeonholes capabilities. A JLP rejects static preferences like a one-dimensional ranking system or learning style. Instead, a JLP visualizes multiple dimensions of learning and asserts that learning is fluid and changes over time and across developmental stages, both biologically and academically. A JLP takes cultural and linguistic diversity into account, demonstrating how students—and their learning abilities—change along a continuum of skills and talents. Uncovering the JLP of each student peels back layers of learning and capabilities defined by that student's own definition.

Creating a jagged learning profile benefits students across all content areas in upper-elementary, middle school, high school, and higher education, as well as benefiting in-service teachers and administrators. The focus of the JLP highlights the process of learning, helping students name and describe their learning processes and applying their profile to specific learning contexts; the profile process is fluid and flexible for a variety of learning settings. It is a powerful, continuously reflective process.

THE SMALL CHANGE

Creating jagged learning profiles can be incorporated into lessons at any time of the school year, semester, or unit. In addition to building a culture for learning and collaboration, the process gives instructors the chance to teach and reinforce classroom procedures and protocols for individual, paired, group, and whole-class work, all while gathering crucial information about the characteristics of individual learners. The one-hour process creates a pause to name and describe individual learning for new content. This can be particularly useful prior to rigorous content or to provide a "reboot" during long stretches of learning.

In short, drawing a JLP gives students a chance to reflect as a learner, naming and identifying themselves in terms of specific learner characteristics, and become empowered through sharing their skills, attributes, and feelings. For schools or classrooms adopting a social-emotional learning focus, a JLP might kick-start a formal social-emotional curriculum.

CREATING THE BASIC PROFILE: SIX SIMPLE STEPS

Step 1: Setting the Stage

Share the TEDx video "The Myth of Average."[3] This video will set the context for building a jagged learning profile. The video summarizes the barriers to access learning that occur when individuals are measured against an average and provides the background for Todd Rose's book *The End of Average*. Rose briefly addresses the jaggedness principle as it applies to public education and shares examples of a jagged learning profile. To improve accessibility for all learners, show the video using closed captions.

Step 2: Generating Ideas

Ask students to make a list of all the ways they learn. Individuals complete this process on their own, quietly, without talking about their ideas for three to five minutes. Students create this individual list first in order to avoid them auditing their thoughts based on their peers' thinking. Once students have an individual list, invite them to share with a partner or group of three and compare lists. This is an important step, since because it allows students to notice similarities and differences in the ways their peers learn. I often hear comments such as, "Wait. What?! I could never learn just by listening. I have to write it all down!" I remind myself to be patient with the chatter and let students ruminate and talk, changing partners often. Learning floats on a sea of talk! I encourage students to "steal" ideas from their friends to add to their own list if a friends' ideas resonate with them. To generate a collaborative list of ideas, I then ask students to write several ideas from their list on a large whiteboard, or share individual ideas on sticky notes to place on a large table or whiteboard for everyone to see. This closing step creates a master bank of ideas for students to choose from since, ultimately, they will include ideas that are not their strengths (which makes them jagged!).

Step 3: Curating Characteristics

After completing step 2, direct students or participants to select eight to ten items from the whiteboard that best describe and define their learning, —their ACTUAL learning. Encourage students to select a variety of categories: those that describe when they feel good as a learner and those that often require extra cognitive energy, focus, or perseverance. The idea is to promote ALL types of learning and thinking, even when it's challenging. Some question prompts might be useful: Which characteristics best describe how you learn? Is there a word that helps define a barrier to your learning? Question prompts usually result in a variety of both strengths and weaknesses, based on student perceptions, experiences, or the ways students feel they are "smart." Remind students that our learning changes over time, so they are picking ideas that resonate with them *right now*. Encourage them to be brave in their selection, knowing that the process will be repeated after cycles of learning so that they can see how their perceptions of learning change.

Step 4: Basic Steps for Creating a Jagged Learning Profile

- Using large sheets of butcher paper, students trace each other's bodies. Alternatively, students can sketch the outline of their body, use an image on a digital application, or be given a "gingerbread person" handout or cutout. Figure 23.1 shows how students work together to sketch a silhouette for the JLP.
- Students use the Curated Characteristics list generated in Step 3 and write the list down the center (or side) of the body outline.
- Students write "low" on the left side of the page and "high" on the right side of the page. You may also use other scoring terms, such as "weak/strong," "struggle/solid." The grade level and personality of a classroom might determine how students and teachers want to create meaningful measuring labels.

- Next, students score themselves in each category by drawing a dot that corresponds to each Curated Characteristic. Figure 23.2 shows a student "scoring" himself in each of the categories he self-selected.
- Last, students connect the dots, noticing the "jagged" nature of their own learning. Figure 23.2 also demonstrates this process.

Students can then participate in a guided gallery walk, noticing similarities and differences in their peers' jaggedness, looking for patterns and outliers, and asking peers to share their thinking about the self-assessment that makes their learning "jagged."

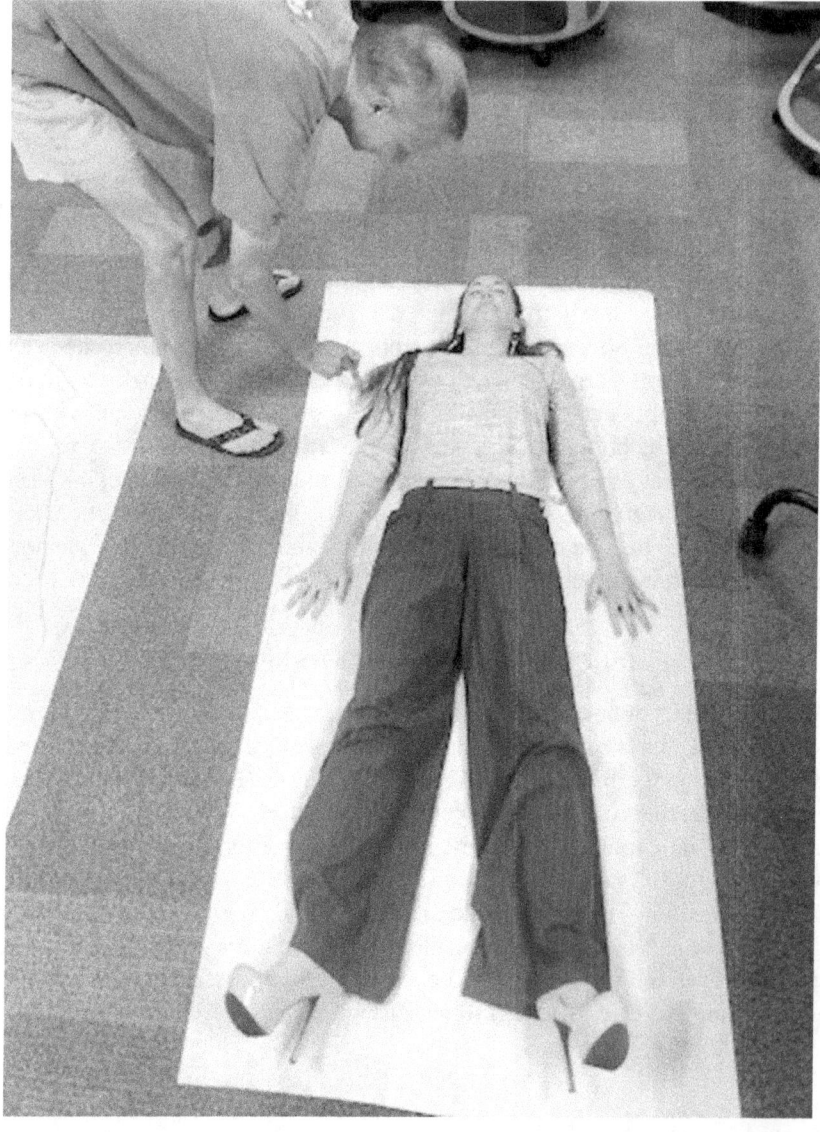

Figure 23.1. Master in Teaching students sketching a full-size jagged learning profile.

Figure 23.2. Mathematics teachers and instructional coaches name and describe the characteristics of their shared learners.

Students might also reflect in writing or in a video response such as FlipGrid about what they learned during the JLP process while their ideas are fresh.

ADAPTATIONS FOR CONTEXTS OUTSIDE THE K–12 CLASSROOM

Preservice Teachers

When I work with preservice teachers in teacher preparation programs, we use the language of diversity, differentiation, and content standard–specific terms, such as verbal, visual, spatial, social, comprehension, computational, symbolic, metaphor, analogy, large motor, small motor.

When I work with younger undergraduates, the "ways they learn" generally begin with vague terms that become more specific when the class makes a collaborative list. Characteristics undergraduates have listed include: hands-on, through repetition, by watching someone, by listening. I often guide students toward more specific descriptive terms to name their dimensions of learning; the naming process helps students describe themselves with additional specificity and nuance. For example, "by watching someone" might become "through modeling" or "think alouds."

In-service teachers

During a professional development session with secondary mathematics teachers, my goals for the teachers changed the JLP process by asking teachers to name the characteristics of their learners. I wanted teachers to notice and name diverse characteristics and their students' differentiated needs. When I asked teachers to name the dimensions of their learner, they became more aware of the characteristics that would drive instructional choices, and the profiles they visualized supported instructional development. Figure 23.3 shows a group of mathematics teachers and instructional coaches naming and describing the characteristics of their shared learners.

Figure 23.3. District administrators in Juneau School District identify characteristics based on cultural stakeholders.

School Administrators and Instructional Coaches

The jagged learning profile can be adapted for use with school administrators, counseling staff, curriculum directors, or instructional coaches. For example, the JLP has been successfully conducted with a team of district leaders implementing a new literacy program across multiple districts. In this example, twelve unique districts adopted the same curriculum, but needed a process to customize materials that aligned with the cultural and linguistic diversity of indigenous learners. In district teams, administrators and coaches created a "jagged culture profile" to determine the learning gaps that might exist between the adopted curriculum and the unique culture of their community of learners. Instead of using learner characteristics to build a profile, participants mapped stakeholder values to determine the jagged culture profile of their districts. This process helped educators make professional development decisions based on their jagged culture profile.

CONNECTIONS AND EXTENSIONS OF THE JAGGED LEARNING PROFILE

Connections with Students

Since the value of the JLP is its continual use, consider using the following connections with students over time.

Connection 1: In writing, in pairs and small groups, or in individual conferences, ask students: Why did you select the characteristics that make up your JLP? If you could add more, what would you add? On what would you like to focus during our class this week/month/semester/year?

Connection 2: Students write on the lines that connect the Curated Characteristics. Students might write a description of the characteristic, why they selected the term, or the relationship between words. For example, if a student has placed "distracted" and "focused" on their JLP, they might note the difference between the similar terms or under what circumstances "distracted" or "focused" might occur in their learning. Asking students to write ideas on the lines between dimensions can also prepare them to share verbally.

Connection 3: Invite students to add a new characteristic to their JLP or write a new dimension over the top of an old one, demonstrating how their learning changed or their perception of their learning changed.

Connection 4: When pairing or grouping students, suggest that students find collaborators with complementary profiles. Ask students to find others who perceive themselves as "weak" where they see themselves as "strong."

Connections with Disciplinary Skills

After students are comfortable with the process, a content-specific JLP can be used as a way to track perceived progress. Instead of Curated Categories based on ways students learn, substitute knowledge or skills from your content or an upcoming unit. Students can rate themselves as a form of preassessment. During and after a learning cycle, students can reassess their learning profile using a different color to see how learning has changed. Visually representing student thinking and perceptions of their learning is powerful motivation, decreases the feeling of making mistakes, and develops a safe culture for learning. When students are asked to self-assess, they are generally more critical. Reflect on the original JLPs frequently, over time, particularly as a debrief or reflection of learning—"How would you describe your jaggedness now?"

Be certain that this process is not conflated with any type of scoring or grading; it's intended to highlight a student's *perception* of their learning. The jagged learning profile should be maintained as a tool to track student perception of their learning, not as a grading tool.

Connections Over Time

One benefit of JLPs is making perceptions of learning visible over time. Since the process is not intended to score content understanding; for grading; or for purposes other than reflection regarding perceptions, experience, and growth, the JLP is perfect for a growing, culturally responsive classroom. There is space in the JLP for learners of all levels, languages, and cultures, and making this process visible both grounds learning in the unique prior learning experiences of individual students and upends the expectation that everyone's learning should look the same. It celebrates our differences and demonstrates (literally!) individual and collective growth mindfulness about learning. Students' perception of learning strongly influences their approach to learning and the quality of their learning outcomes.

CONCLUSION

Jagged learning profiles help teachers respond in real time to the cues and clues made visible by their learners' reflection on their talents and traits. When a student names their own abilities, they have a personal, identifying language to talk about their learning process. When we visualize and study our *own* JLPs as individuals and educators, we open the path to understanding our students' jagged profiles. Teachers who participate in the process also help build students' individual identity and model transparency in the classroom culture. The JLP process kick-starts powerful conversations about learning. It highlights learning through an individual's own perspective, and values cultural and linguistic diversities that are visualized, celebrated, and continually revised.

NOTES

1. Todd Rose, *The End of Average: How to Succeed in a World That Values Sameness* (New York: Harper Collins, 2016), 80.
2. TEDx Talks, "The Myth of Average: Todd Rose at TEDxSonomaCounty," YouTube, June 19, 2013, video, https://www.youtube.com/watch?v=4eBmyttcfU4.
3. Ibid.

BIBLIOGRAPHY

Rose, Todd. *The End of Average: How to Succeed in a World That Values Sameness.* New York: Harper Collins, 2016.

TEDx Talks. "The Myth of Average: Todd Rose at TEDxSonomaCounty." YouTube, June 19, 2013. https://www.youtube.com/watch?v=4eBmyttcfU4.

Chapter 24

Creating a Classroom Community That Values Disabled School Citizens

Steve Singer

A primary objective of schooling is to shape young people into citizens who appropriately contribute to US society, the democratic process, and to their world in general.[1] The school system reflects dominant ideologies that shape what appropriate means. In turn, future adult citizens maintain the system as is, by applying the ideas they have incorporated into their identities as US citizens. In itself, this is not necessarily a "bad" cycle. It even permits change through gradual shifts in cultural thought and practices as each new generation rises to power. However, it is also troubling because, in each generation, certain voices and experiences are valued more than others, often in ways that are not obvious. The same system that maintains US culture also conditions populations of people to take up their positions as privileged or marginalized, creating a cycle that is difficult to dismantle.[2] And through this mechanism, a substantial portion of what we (the people) might know remains unknown and unvalued.

Change is difficult and slow, but this does not mean it is unattainable. When educators consider how to stop ableism, it often appears to be a monolithic task. But there are more manageable things educators can do right now that have a lot of meaning. Rather than think about "stopping," we should think about "confronting"; rather than considering the nation at large, we should think about the spaces we create, such as classrooms. More precisely, I propose that rather than trying to reduce ableism, we create classrooms that promote a different model of knowledge creation that becomes part of students' indoctrination into US citizenship. Consequently, students will take the new model forward and slowly create wide-scale change.

Fifteen percent of school-aged children receive services for disabilities.[3] Most of these students spend all or at least part of their days in general education classrooms, where *we* include *them*. In many cases, *we* modify the curriculum for *them*. These statements, generally associated with forward thinking and inclusion, highlight that disabled students are not us. Attempts to solve the supposed problem of disabled students in classrooms are addressed by focusing on the existing policies and ideas created through dominant thought that created the problems. Disabled students are us, the United States, if we maintain that US society is based on a vision of people with diverse backgrounds coming together in a single democratic republic. Furthermore, we will all be disabled should we live long enough. It is time to acknowledge that disabled lives are American lives, even if for absolutely no other reason than to protect the rights of others and our diverse characteristics, also to be recognized as American lives.

This chapter aims to outline a way of *starting small* with strategies and activities that educators can immediately and relatively easily use to begin a shift in their classroom cultures. These strategies support disabled students in developing an increased understanding of self and their value as classroom citizens. As educators implement these strategies and foster the increased presence of disabled voices in their classrooms through modeling, they begin to shift what knowledge and experience hold credence in that space. When educators continually signal all citizens of the classroom of this value, the culture of that classroom shifts and becomes incrementally more equitable. Furthermore, a cultural shift in this way has implications for disabled students' psychosocial development, academic success, and planning for their future lives. I detail a three-step action plan that educators may use to initiate a classroom culture shift: Self-assessment and remediation, fostering disabled students' identity development, and cultural shift in the classroom through valuing multiple voices. Next, I discuss the challenges of enacting change and how educators can achieve and celebrate small victories. Finally, I conclude the chapter by discussing implications for educators, students, and beyond as they navigate revised meanings of inclusive citizenship.

SCHOOL CITIZENSHIP OF DISABLED STUDENTS

The premise of school citizenship is that students are actively involved in the maintenance and revision of the system. When all students practice citizenship, the system is more likely to reflect the values of its members and, in turn, benefit the members. In this way, citizenship includes following rules, developing the skills and knowledge to contribute to the system, and learning to assume personal responsibility to enact citizenship. However, not all students are equitably prepared to take on these roles or be perceived as equal citizens, especially disabled students.[4] In fact, disabled students' voices are largely absent in all components of school citizenship, with others speaking for them, highlighting their subjugated position.[5] Despite often being "in" classrooms, disabled students frequently do not experience inclusion due to peers' and teachers' negative attitudes regarding disability and ineffective learning supports.[6]

Scholarship about the citizenship of disabled students focuses primarily on rhetoric about this subjugated position and the individual developmental benefits of promoting citizenship for this population. There is scarce mention of how the absence of disability in acts of citizenship compromises the ability of any democratic system to serve its citizens, results in incomplete/ineffective general knowledge, and impedes social change. Furthermore, recommendations for increasing disabled students' citizenship focus on what disabled students might do, underemphasizing that poor reception of those acts by teachers and peers is a significant barrier. To improve the authentic participation of disabled students in citizenship, we must encourage participation and transform how all students and educators understand and value participation.

TRANSFORMING CLASSROOMS

In the remainder of this chapter, I outline the first steps teachers can take to transform their classrooms in ways that foster acts of citizenship by disabled students for the benefit of all classroom citizens. Table 24.1 provides an overview of this work.

Step 1: Self-Assessment

A challenging first step in shifting the culture of classrooms is to assess how we intentionally or unintentionally create a classroom culture that positions disabled students in the margins. Understanding how this happens allows us to answer the question, "How does my modeling shape students' conceptions of disability?" Table 24.2 asks three questions about how you construct what citizenship for disabled students means in your classroom. As you consider each question, list specific and observable examples of your practices, being sure to be critical.

Question 1: How Do I Talk to or About Disabled Students? Disabled students understand how people communicate with them or about them. They infer information from the content and the form of communication, which may suggest their lowered position in the classroom. Examples that suggest this position include: (1) Engaging disabled students only for instructional purposes rather than social ones, (2) Using simplistic and slow-paced language in a nonconfrontational way, and (3) Minimal engagement with contributions made by disabled students. Additionally, teachers and other professionals in the classroom sometimes talk about disabled students while they are present (e.g., performance or best practices), which leaves disabled students feeling like specimens. To assess these sometimes subtle behaviors, make mental notes of all your communications during a class period. After class, make a T-chart of communication with nondisabled and disabled students. Then, compare and contrast the exchanges for intent, form, content, and length/depth.

Table 24.1. Overview of Action Plan

Step 1: Self-Assessment
- Reflect on three questions
- Scrutinize your responses
- Create alternative strategies
- Develop an easy-to-use checklist

Step 2: Fostering Disabled Student's Identity Development
- Modify an existing unit of study
- Invite a disabled guest to serve as an expert
- Provide an additional opportunity for disabled students to engage in the topic and be experts in a space that centralizes disabled existence

Step 3: Classroom Cultural Shift through Valuing Multiple Voices
- Students map out their varied identifications using a graphic organizer
- Ask students to reflect on how any of their listed identifications inform a topic of study
- Synthesis of teacher-intended lesson and student contributions

Table 24.2. Self-Assessment Questions

1. How do I talk to or about disabled students?
2. How do students engage in citizenship in my classroom?
3. How do I generate knowledge in my classroom?

Question 2: How Do Students Engage in Citizenship in My Classroom?

Citizenship in the classroom looks different across grade levels and content areas. Citizenship involves students conducting tasks and following established rules (e.g., homework or turn-taking). This type of citizenship is generally applied consistently, even when there are modifications for disabled students. However, students also enact citizenship through discussion and other activities that construct meaning in the classroom community. How do students do this or perhaps don't do this? Do you lead discussions and ask students to reflect and respond? Do students generate information to complete projects or participate in activities? Can student voices affect change in the classroom (e.g., celebrate a new holiday or student-generated inquiry)? Do students have options, or can they create new ones for engagement? Conversely, are there rules they must follow? For example, if you teach chemistry for older students, applying scientific methods and following safety procedures are important aspects of citizenship.

Question 3: How Do I Generate Knowledge in My Classroom?

Now that you have examined how all students engage in citizenship, how do you use those acts combined with your established knowledge and experience to generate the understanding and skills that students need? If discussion is a part of your instructional technique, what happens after students offer their ideas? How do you juxtapose personal experience with evidence? Are ideas written down somewhere for use? Do you synthesize all the contributions in discussion or ask students to apply the concepts in a new way? Or perhaps you leave it to students to create meaning individually, using the connections they have made? What do you do when students' ideas conflict or contain information and opinions that defy generally agreed-upon facts? Once you have completed a course of study and negotiated what is part of that knowledge, how do you present the conclusions?

Now, you have an idea of how you create opportunities for active citizenship and how students enact that citizenship. Further, you have acknowledged how you engage disabled students, which may demonstrate some of the assumptions you have about them. Review each item and place a checkmark next to the ones you feel are constructive. Consider how these might make your disabled students feel, and whether access to the acts of citizenship you detailed is equitable. Reconsider if it should remain checked. For the remaining items, write an alternative strategy you might implement to increase equity. Understand that the characteristics of disabled students widely vary; thus, your reflections will vary from year to year, so respond to yourself by thinking about your current students.

With a better understanding of how you currently create a learning environment that prioritizes certain voices and experiences over disabled ones, make a short checklist to use when developing lesson plans. Later, I build on the strategies developed here to create a broader sense of cultural shift in the classroom. Drawing from your lists of strategies under each question above, generate a simple, broad question such as "Does this activity do [insert objective]?" Your developed strategies under this broad question serve as both actions you can take now and as reminders of what you want to promote in your lessons. As you create new lessons, work to ensure you can answer "yes" to each question. At first, it may seem laborious, but after a few concerted efforts to do this, you should find that you intuitively create lessons that align with your objectives and rely less on the checklist.

However, more than changing classroom practices is required to change classroom culture. Both nondisabled and disabled students have entrenched ideas of what it means to be disabled in the United States, developed over their lifetimes and reflected in most contexts. They are accustomed, perhaps unknowingly, to the practices that maintain these ideas. Like us, students also may acknowledge or theorize that there is a problem but struggle to understand how it is a problem beyond a critique of discourse about disabled people. Part of classroom cultural revision is necessarily also about actively revising students' perceptions, which I will discuss next.

Step 2: Fostering Disabled Students' Identity Development

It is not an easy task to support any of our students to reframe their schemas of disability. One problem is that classroom citizens, disabled or not, often do not know that what disabled students contribute has value or has value deeper than it appears. Below is a reasonable, demonstrative example:

> A class, including Sara, a blind student, debriefs from a visit to a planetarium. The teacher asks if students could identify constellations before the moderator showed the lines between the stars. Students respond, such as: "I saw the dipper, but didn't know if it was the big or little one," and then the teacher scaffolds how students discern the two. Sara offers an idea she realizes doesn't align with the question: "I couldn't see them, but he said Polaris is a bright star at the tip of the little dipper. It points northward. I wonder if I could see that?" The teacher responds, "That's right, Sara. Did anyone else see any constellations?"

Unpacking this a bit, we can identify a few things. The teacher might not have adequately planned for Sara's meaningful engagement. When Sara provided an answer that did not (couldn't have) responded to the prompt, the teacher acknowledged its accuracy, but didn't build knowledge from it like they did on the previous comment. Possibly, the teacher was nervous about engaging the student about a comment related to seeing, didn't recognize the benefit the comment could have to other students, didn't have a response, or didn't have time to respond to all comments. Realistically, Sara might not have responded because she knows that her peers are uncomfortable about her blindness, is accustomed to either not being held accountable to contribute, is despondent because of poor access, or doesn't recognize that her thoughts are important. Sara's peers did not have the opportunity to understand the value of her contribution. That value includes Sara pointing out the limited accessibility of the activity, modeling how students can expand their learning beyond the assigned task, evidencing how her experience as a blind person led to knowledge generation (curiosity about seeing the bright star with respect to how everyone can use that star), and making connections that other students might not have based on their respective sighted experiences. These are significant contributions. Instead, the students received another subtle message that disabled students are not equal citizens, adding to a long history of these messages. In turn, this guides their future behavior.

If this were your class, the checklist you developed in the previous section might have helped you predict some of these events, leading to a lesson revision. However, planning and modeling the value of disability-based knowledge is insufficient. To revise schemas of disability and what this characteristic brings to the classroom, disabled students, too, need to recognize their value. Like other students, disabled students often internalize their diminished positions in the classroom. While I shrink at the suggestion of placing the onus of change on disabled students, they need to develop a knowledge of self and the tools required to be active citizens. Students can accomplish this through fostering healthy identity development.

Fostering healthy disability identity development is a complex task, especially if disabled students are not surrounded by others who promote these ideas. Some objectives you might consider include increasing the following:

1. Exposure to other disabled people, particularly those who have a constructive understanding of disability.
2. Opportunities to engage others, especially disabled people, in a dialogue about how disabled people are perceived/treated, and that positions the student as an expert.
3. Understanding of the relationship between self/individual identity and group identity.
4. Opportunities for disabled students to use their developing knowledge in constructive ways.

Teachers can increase exposure to the messages above with only moderate revision of learning activities and projects. Table 24.3 provide guidelines for an inaugural unit of study.

Table 24.3. Developing a Unit That Promotes Healthy Disability Identity Development

1. Select a unit that explicitly connects to disabilities, such as the study of war, biology, or book/story analysis. Consider how including a disabled guest would bring a valuable perspective to the learning.
2. The students may focus on the guest's disabilities. Your objective for the activity is to refocus on the relationship between disability and the topic in ways that build an understanding of disability in a social context. For example, how did a nation manage an increase in disability after a war, or why did Bobby respond to Sally (disabled) that way in the story?
3. Develop one additional layer of engagement that provides disabled students with focused attention. For example, the disabled students engage the guest in a roundtable discussion, where lived disabled experience becomes a powerful debriefing tool.

While it is reasonable to think that this planning will benefit all students, be sure to prioritize the objective of supporting disabled students' identity formation, which may necessitate leaving nondisabled students out of a portion of the activities. Integrating disability into your curriculum is a fantastic secondary objective. Still, the intent is to support disabled students' ability to recognize and confidently contribute as valued classroom citizens.

Step 3: Classroom Cultural Shift through Valuing Multiple Voices

The final step is for disabled students to practice citizenship but within the context of all students doing so. As in step 2, the following subsections provides guidelines for a foundational lesson that should catalyze future planning. I provide substantial structure to classroom meaning-making, but this can be less formal as the process becomes routine. Teachers may adjust the exact presentation of this practice for specific age groups and content areas.

Students Map Their Varied Identifications Using a Graphic Organizer

Free identification graphic organizers are available online with instructions for their use. Students will generate many identifications (e.g., boy, Asian, disabled), so I suggest helping students to essentialize their lists to the identifications that significantly impact how they interpret/interact with their worlds. For example, it's likely helpful to focus on identifications that are associated with minority status in the school (e.g., disabled or racial identification) rather than ones that are common or not related to marginalized communities (e.g., child or athlete).

Students Reflect on How Their Identifications Inform the Topic of Study

Select a planned activity. following a discussion or after the students have conducted foundational work (e.g., describing historical facts), ask students to reference their graphic organizers and consider: (1) The relationship between their identifications and the content, and (2) If they are willing to share either their thoughts about these relationships or any relevant personal experiences. Teachers must scaffold this by asking questions such as "How might the colonists have responded if George Washington were a woman?" or "I wonder if the use of sign language will increase as we explore the solar system?" Teachers must not force students to disclose their thoughts because teachers cannot presume to understand their relationships with their identities. In time, the positive environment will encourage students to feel comfortable to volunteer their respective knowledge.

Teachers can scaffold this investigation by offering examples of how their identifications inform the study and making explicit connections between other identifications and the content. This practice presents an excellent opportunity for modeling to disabled students how their experiences or identity group history is relevant. Teachers must carefully mediate these conversations to ensure they are productive, respectful, and relevant. The objective is not to discuss diversity but to use human experience to understand and critique. Teachers should also help students revise statements that may be untrue, overgeneralized, or need translation to be relevant. Teachers can genuinely offer what they have yet to consider. This act dismantles the idea that the teacher is the only knowledge maker and provides evidence to students about the power of their contributions.

Synthesis of Teacher-Intended Lesson and Student Contributions

Eventually, the teacher will need to answer "So what," which is typical at the end of a lesson. Closings summarize and contextualize the content so students understand what to *do* with the knowledge they have created. An objective might be to re-story the lesson's content in a way that acknowledges the ideas generated in class as part of factual information. In many cases, it will be important to ask, "Why?" Why don't textbooks, videos, or other media reflect what the class discussed? What are the implications of this?

The lesson structure I provide is one introductory method for training all students to understand the relevance of their experiences and thoughts. This empowers students and suggests how to continue claiming that power. Teachers should predict that this first lesson will consume a lot of time and may result in unsatisfactory progress. They might also expect that the students won't effectively participate in the process. Neither should deter further efforts. Teachers and students will learn how to conduct this kind of work efficiently, with practice. They will also learn when it is important to engage content in this way or how to appropriately "call out" when the class fails to consider relevant perspectives. Teachers will figure out how to incorporate citizenship in ways that do not derail their lessons. Most importantly, students develop procedures that boost their citizenship, identity crystallization, and recognition of other students doing the same.

CONSIDERING VARIABLES

Change is difficult. Teachers will encounter obstacles as they implement the steps I have provided. Anticipating some of these challenges and maintaining a "starting small" vision helps make this process more manageable. No matter how noble the intent of classroom citizenship revision is, lasting change isn't likely to occur if the work becomes a burden. The intervention described in this chapter is a moderately labor-intensive starting point. Teachers should reflect on how the practices they and their students implemented here were successful and then integrate them in smaller ways moving forward.

In addition to navigating how to implement sustainable changes, teachers must understand that they are likely to fail in their early attempts to modify citizenship. At first, success is acknowledging a need for change and attempting it without giving up. Tell others about your efforts and celebrate the attempts. Consistent and authentic positive messages to yourself and your students about your efforts will create a positive relationship with the act of change that will pave the way for future success.

Disabled students have a dramatic range of characteristics, which create different life experiences. It may be easy to envision the steps above while working with disabled students who communicate and behave in normative ways, but it can be more challenging for those who don't. Citizens may struggle to recognize which behaviors are intentional communication or engage in a contribution presented in a way they find dissonant. For example, a class discusses making nutritious food choices. A disabled student offers the word "mom" and then repeats it several times, talking over other students. The students might not know how to respond and choose to ignore it. While it's possible the student's comment was unrelated to the discussion, the "least dangerous assumption"[7] is that the student communicated a connection. The teacher provides follow-up questions and expands the connection, such as how parents make nutritious food choices for their families. If the contribution was unintentional, perhaps the teacher's commentary helps the disabled student engage in the content. Teachers must actively participate in making communication repairs and assisting all students to interpret information in productive ways until they begin to perceive or excavate the value from contributions automatically.

Teachers must consider that disabled students have different orientations to their disabilities. Some may be proud of how disability has shaped their lives, and others may resent their disabilities. Therefore, these can be sensitive topics. Students' rights to privacy (FERPA) can complicate classroom-wide conversations about disability, even when the intent is increased citizenship. Parents have determined the best courses for their children, which may be assimilation rather than a disability gain narrative. Still, moving toward equity in the classroom means disabled students will grapple with disability in new ways, which makes them vulnerable. The objectives of healthy identity formation and acts of citizenship among peers are not to shape students in an idealized version of what disability could mean, but to support students in exploring who they are and asserting what they know and think in their communities.

CONCLUSION

Teachers should acknowledge that the position from which they start increasing the citizenship of disabled students is not effectively zero, but much lower. They must contend with the existing structures that have created and maintain disabled students as second-class citizens. Not only does policy mediate the experiences and treatment of disabled students, but also how schools have interpreted the inclusion of disabled students in the mainstream. Able-bodied thinking shapes disabled students' understanding of themselves and their roles in the classroom and continues to guide schools regarding how students engage in and evidence learning. Mostly, this is not the result of maliciousness but routine assumptions, and too few people resist it. This suggests that steps toward increased citizenship for disabled students will most certainly be met with resistance, even if that resistance is simply inertia, the tendency for things to remain the same. Teachers, too, will feel the effects of inertia as they face obstacles, or students are slow to take up new ideas and might be inclined to give up. However, success lies in regular and consistent practice until the mechanisms of citizenship students have developed become a predictable standard in their classrooms. Should teachers and student citizens fail to implement changes such as these, I fear little will change for disabled students and the adults they will become. Confronting ableism can effect change, but without retraining and revising how we participate and receive participation in democratic processes, the roots of ableism will remain.

However, if we are successful in this endeavor, we tap into a consciousness of life in the United States from which we have capitalized so little. It is difficult to predict the outcomes of expanding our collective knowledge in such a vast way. Beyond the benefits to US society, these efforts also serve our disabled students in ways we cannot predict. Further, it's possible that what we think we know about inclusive education could dramatically shift. Our current understanding is founded on stymied membership of disabled students in our classrooms, and the opportunity to grow could be genuinely transformative.

NOTES

1. Jacques Benninga and Brandy Quinn, "Enhancing American Identity and Citizenship in Schools," *Applied Developmental Science* 15, no. 2 (2011): 104–10.
2. Dan Lowe, "Privilege: What Is It, Who Has It, and What Should We Do About It?" in Bob Fischer (ed.), *Ethics: Left and Right* (Cambridge: Oxford University Press, 2020), 457–64.
3. National Center for Education Statistics, "Students with Disabilities. Condition of Education," U.S. Department of Education, Institute of Education Sciences, 2023, https://nces.ed.gov/programs/coe/indicator/cgg.
4. Bronwyn Hayward, *Children, Citizenship and Environment: School Strike Edition* (New York: Routledge), 2020.
5. Gerison Lansdown, Shane R. Jimerson, and Reza Shahroozi, "Children's Rights and School Psychology: Children's Right to Participation," *Journal of School Psychology* 52, no. 1 (2014): 3–12.
6. Cheryl M. Jorgensen and Laurie Lambert, "Inclusion Means More than Just Being In," *International Journal of Whole Schooling* 8, no. 2 (2012): 21–36.
7. Cheryl Jorgensen, "The Least Dangerous Assumption," *Disability Solutions: A publication of Creating Solutions, A Resource for Families & Others Interested in Down Syndrome & Developmental Disabilities* 6, no. 3 (Fall 2005).

BIBLIOGRAPHY

Benninga, Jacques, and Brandy Quinn. "Enhancing American Identity and Citizenship in Schools." *Applied Developmental Science* 15, no. 2 (2011): 104–10. DOI: 10.1080/10888691.2011.560816.

Hayward, Bronwyn. *Children, Citizenship and Environment: School Strike Edition*. New York: Routledge, 2020.

Jorgensen, Cheryl. "The Least Dangerous Assumption." *Disability Solutions: A Publication of Creating Solutions, A Resource for Families & Others Interested in Down Syndrome & Developmental Disabilities* 6, no. 3 (Fall 2005).

Jorgensen, Cheryl M., and Laurie Lambert. "Inclusion Means More than Just Being In." *International Journal of Whole Schooling* 8, no. 2 (2012): 21–36.

Lansdown, Gerison, Shane R. Jimerson, and Reza Shahroozi. "Children's Rights and School Psychology: Children's Right to Participation." *Journal of School Psychology* 52, no. 1 (2014): 3–12.

Lowe, Dan. "Privilege: What Is It, Who Has It, and What Should We Do About It?" In *Ethics: Left and Right*, edited by Bob Fischer, 457–64. Cambridge: Oxford University Press, 2020.

National Center for Education Statistics. "Students with Disabilities: Condition of Education." U.S. Department of Education, Institute of Education Sciences, 2023. https://nces.ed.gov/programs/coe/indicator/cgg.

Index

academic librarians: collaborative research project, 248–49; higher education librarian led PD, 249
ACCESS for ELLs. *See* Assessing Comprehension and Communication in English State-to State for English Language Learners
Adams, Abigail, 166
Advanced Placement Language and Composition (AP Lang) courses, 129; autonomy in assessment in, 131–32; ILP in, 132; metacognition and multiple choice test in, 130–31, *131*; Plato "Allegory of a Cave" and Thoreau *Walden* in, 130
AI. *See* artificial intelligence
AICL. *See* American Indians in Children's Literature
All American Boys (Reynolds), 228
"Allegory of a Cave" (Plato), 130
American Indians in Children's Literature (AICL) resource, for social studies classroom, 165
American Library Association, annual book awards of, 246
analytic rubrics, 203
Angelou, Maya, 79, 87
annual book awards: of American Library Association, 246; for YA literature, 245
Another (Robinson), *214*
AP Lang. *See* Advanced Placement Language and Composition
around-the-room activities, conferencing in high school STEM class during, 145–46

Articles of Confederation, 165
artificial intelligence (AI), teachers shifts in student assignments and, 152
ASCD. *See* Association for Supervision and Curriculum Development
Assessing Comprehension and Communication in English State-to State for English Language Learners (ACCESS for ELLs) exam, 58
assessments: AP Lang course autonomy in, 131–32; BAS of Fountas and Pinnell Literacy, 188; decision-making and available and required resources, 205–6, *206*; literacy transformation and digital program for, 115, 116; potential impact, 206–7; resource questionnaire in, *206*; RTI process and Classroom Assessments for Elementary Teachers class, 185–86; standards and formative, 153–54; of student for content or skill level in critical literacy, 166
asset-based teaching, mindset shifts from deficit model to, *3*
assigned partners, in talking procedures, 59
assignments: AI and teachers shift in student, 152; example based on standard, 153–56, *154*; journaling in critical literacy student engagement, 168; rubrics for, 202–3, 224; social sciences reading methods, 222, 225, *226*, 228; social sciences writing methods, 222, 225–26, *228*, 228–29
Association for Supervision and Curriculum Development (ASCD): curriculum design and, 158; Whole Child Framework, 158

authors, attending events with, 244
author studies, writing use of, 84
autonomy in assessment, of AP Lang course, 131–32

Balanced Literacy (BL) models: Fountas and Pinnell Classroom problematic in, 93; small changes for, 93–94; Units of Study from Teachers College Reading & Writing Projects problematic in, 93
banana slug in Redwood Forest, wonder walks and, *25*
Bandura, Albert, 101
BAS. *See* Benchmark Assessment System
Beane, James, 42
behavior, wonder walks and improvements in, 31
Benchmark Assessment System (BAS), of Fountas and Pinnell Literacy, 188
Bishop, Rudine Sims, 245
BL. *See* Balanced Literacy
Black Lives Matter (BLM) protests, 226; social justice in education and, 161
body position, in talking procedures, 60
Booklist, 245
Buck Institute for Education's Gold Standard PBL, 67
Bunker, Lisa, 176
burnout concern, for faculty members, 200

call back procedure, in talking procedure, 59, *60*
Callender, Kacen, 176
CCCs. *See* Crosscutting Concepts
change, Minor blue-print for: imagine look of, 174; measure plan impact, 174; plan and implement, 174; share of findings, 174; student formal and informal feedback, 180; study students for, 174
character education program, wonder walks and, 26
Chile public school system: COVID-19 pandemic impact on, 38, 40; curriculum integration in, 38; experimental education in, 37; test-to-the-test curriculum in, 37–38; UTP leadership in, 39. *See also* El Salitre public school
choice, PBL and incorporation of, 4, *5*, 7
citizenship, critical literacy in social science classroom on, 166

Classroom Assessments for Elementary Teachers class, RTI process incorporated into, 185–86
classroom community: disabled school citizens and, 261–70, *263*, *266*; in discourse-driven classroom, 62; ELA co-construction of, 124–25; writing to create, 83–86
climate change education, Nezhukumatathil on vanilla beans and, vii–viii
co-construction of units, scaffolding process of, 125
collaboration: for LGBTQ+ content curriculum change, 175. *See also* librarian collaboration
collaborative research project: with academic librarians, 248–49; for librarian collaboration, 247–49; with school librarians, 247
Common Core Standards: EE course curriculum alignment with, 113–15; state option to use, 152
community: LGBTQ+ book club development and, 180–81; PBL project on organisms within ecosystem in local, 70–74, *71*, *72*, *73*, 76; *semillero* initiative strong sense of, 42
conferencing: in elementary school writing instruction, 137; goal established in, 137–38; goals establishment in, 137–38, 141–42; independent work time and, 138; scaffolding and, 138; as small-group instructional technique, 137; structure for, 138, *138*; student invitation for, 138–42
conferencing, in high school STEM class, 137, 149; during around-the-room activities, 145–46; documentation for, *146*, *147, 148*, 149; during group projects, 145; during independent work, 145; during labs, 144–45; mentor text use, 142; new strategy introduction in, 143; organization techniques and, 143–44; reference materials use, 142–43; sample conference topics, 142–44; when to apply, 144–46
connections over time, with JLP, 258
Constitution with the Haudenosaunee Confederacy, 165
constraints and impacts identification, for decision-making, 205

content ideas examples, in discourse-driven classroom, *63*
cosmopolitanism, in international writing course, 212
course information sessions implementation, in post-secondary courses, 201–2
COVID-19 pandemic: Chile public school system impacts from, 38, 40; TCs impacted by, 234
critical literacy, in social studies classroom, 161; on citizenship, 166; dimensions of, 163; knowledge building component, 163, *163*, 163–67; outcomes of, 169; primary source use, 166–67; reflection component, 163, *163*, 168–69; sample intervention timeline, *165*; student assessment for content or skill level, 166; student engagement component, 163, *163*, 167–68
Crocker, Elizabeth, 101, 102, *107*
Crosscutting Concepts (CCCs), of NGSS, 50
cultural shift in classroom, for disabled school citizens, 262, *263*; students reflect on identifications inform study topic, 267–68; students varied identification using graphic organizer, 267; teacher-intended lesson and student contributions synthesis, 268
curating characteristics step, of JLP, 253, 254
curriculum: ASCD design of, 158; books for redesign of, 158; Chile public school system and, 37–38; connections in wonder walks, 26, 31; diversity in, 161–63; EE course alignment with Common Core Standards, 113–15; El Salitre public school experimentality for integration of, 37–45; scaffolding skills with creation of, 154
curriculum change strategies, for LGBTQ+ content, 173; collaboration for, 175; human rights focus of, 179, 180, 181; impact in, 180–81; LGBTQ+ book club and, 174, *174*; plan for, 175–76; support building for, 176–78; unit launching, 178–80; *Universal Declaration of Human Rights* and, 178
curriculum integration: of Beane for Winter School, 42–43; experimentality in, 37–45; lessons for, 45; results, 44, *45*

Daily Reading Workshop (RW), 93–94
daily share time, in writing to create classroom community, 85–86
DCIs. *See* Disciplinary Core Ideas
Deci, Edward L., 101
decision-making, for post-secondary courses: available and required resources assessment, 205–6, *206*; constraints and impacts identification, 205; potential impact assessment, 206–7; student feedback improvement, 204–5; with students in peer observations, 205; systematic self-reflection, 204
Dee, Barbara, 176
deficit model, mindset shifts to asset-based teaching, *3*
DEI. *See* diversity, equity, and inclusion
Dewey, John, 168
digital platforms for collaboration, of TLs in international writing course, 212, 214, 216
digital program for assessment, in literacy transformation, 115, 116
dimensions, of critical literacy, 163
disabled school citizens, classroom community for, 261, 270; challenges for enacting, 262; cultural shift in classroom for, 262, *263*, 267–68; disabled student identity development for, 262, *263*, 265–67, *266*; implications for, 262; school citizenship of disabled students, 262; self-assessment and remediation for, 262, 263–65, *264*; students right to privacy and, 269; Title I school special education, 102; variables for, 268–69
Disciplinary Core Ideas (DCIs), of NGSS, 50
disciplinary skills, JLP connections with, 257–58
discourse, described, 58
discourse-driven classroom, 64; community to encourage talk, 62; content ideas examples, *63*; discourse definition, 58; discourse-driven questions in, 59, 60; FEP status and, 57, 58, 59; ML and, 57, 58, 59; ML support on FEP status, 57; probing statements of "Are You Sure?," 61–62; scaffolding in, 59, 60–61, *61*; talking procedures in, 59–60, *60*; third grade estimation lesson example, 58

discourse-driven questions, in discourse-driven classroom, 59, 60
diversity, equity, and inclusion (DEI) initiatives, 204; ELA and, 123
documentation, for conferencing in high school STEM class, *146, 147, 148,* 149
Douglass, Fredrick, 166
Drama (Telgemeier), 176
Dueck, Myron, 158

early childhood learners, interactive, sensory-rich activities for, 3
EdCamp, 181, 183n21
Edutopia website, Student Engagement and Project-Based Learning section of, 158
EE. *See* English Essentials
ELA. *See* English Language Arts
elementary classroom: conferencing in writing instruction, 137; flip, switch, reverse process in writing assignment for, 223; JLP benefits for, 252; Number Talks in mathematics, 11–21; student storytelling at, 79; student storytelling in fourth-grade, 80, 84; student storytelling in kindergarten, 80–82, *81, 82, 86*; TCs in international writing course enrollment in, 211; TCs LS inclusion for social studies, 233–41, *238*
El Salitre public school, in Chile: background on, 38; learning with cinema curriculum integration project, 44; low attendance and low participation at, 39–40; MINEDUC on low-economic status of, 38; pedagogical reflection and action at, 40–41; public lessons plan for parents and families, 39–40, 41, *43,* 43–44; Teachers Council at, 39–40; Winter School plan for, 42–43
embedded and implicit phonics instruction, NCTQ on, 95–96
The End of Average (Rose), 251, 252
engage, explore, explain, elaborate, evaluate phases, of 5E Instructional Model, 51–52
English Essentials (EE) course, for literacy transformation: curriculum alignment with Common Core State Standards, 113–15; ten-day cycle for, *114*
English Language Arts (ELA), 113; classroom community co-construction in, 124–25; DEI initiatives and, 123; equitable practices initiatives and, 123–33; essential questions and writing tasks for, 125–27, *126; Of Mice and Men* in, 127–29; *Othello* in, 125, 127
English/Language Arts curriculum, LGBTQ+ content lacking in, 173
Escuela-Centro Experimental Carén project, of University of Chile, 42
Escuela de Invierno (Winter School) plan, for El Salitre: Beane curriculum integration, 42–43; working sessions for, 43
Ewing, Melissa, 101–2
experimental education, in Chile public school system, 37
experimentality for curriculum integration, 39–45; at El Salitre Chilean public school, 37–38

faculty members: administrative appointments of, 199; burnout concern, 200; work demands of, 199, *200*
Felix YZ (Bunker), 176
FEP. *See* Fluent English Proficient
5E Instructional Model, for inquiry-based science teaching, 50; of engage, explore, explain, elaborate, evaluate phases, 51–52
Floyd, George, 226, 227
Fluent English Proficient (FEP) status, 57; in discourse-driven classroom, 59
focus lesson step, in writing to create classroom community, 83–84
formative assessments, standards and, 153–54
formulate goals for student learning step, in LS, 236
Fountas and Pinnell Classroom, of BL, 93
Framework for High-Quality PBL criteria, 67

Gay Straight Alliance (GSA), 181
generating ideas step, of JLP, 252–53
Georgia state requirement for dyslexia student support, 185–86
Gephardt, Donna, 176
Giving Students a Say (Dueck), 158
Global Read Aloud (GRA), in international writing course, 213–14

goals, establishment in conferencing, 139–40; metacognition, 142; rapport and, 142–43; student independence and, 143
GR. *See* Guided Reading
GRA. *See* Global Read Aloud
Gracefully Grayson (Polonsky), 176
grading and student feedback, for post-secondary courses: quiz corrections with explanations, 203; value of rubrics for assignments, 202–3, 224
grading rubrics, 203
Grading Smarter Not Harder (Dueck), 158
group projects, conferencing in high school STEM class during, 145
growth mindset, Number Talks development of, 13
GSA. *See* Gay Straight Alliance
Guided Reading (GR), 94–95

higher education: academic librarians and, 248–49; faculty members demands in, 199, *200*; faculty members in, 199, *199*, *200*; JLP benefits for, 252; librarian-led PD, 249
High Quality Project Based Learning (HQPBL), 69
high school: conferencing in STEM class of, 137–49, *146*, *147*, *148*; JLP benefits for, 252
holistic rubrics, 203
Horn Book Guide, 245
The Horn Book Magazine, 245
Howe, James, 176
HQPBL. *See* High Quality Project Based Learning
human rights focus, of LGBTQ+ curriculum content, 179, 180, 181
Hurricane Child (Callender), 176
Hurricane Season (Melleby), 176

identity development, for disabled students, 262, *263*, 265–67, *266*
iEARN global partnership, for international writing course, 212
illustrators, attend events with, 244
ILP. *See* Individualized Learning Plan
implementation guide, for Number Talks, 16–17
independent work time, of students: conferencing and, 138; conferencing in high school STEM class during, 144

independent writing, to create classroom community, 84–85
Indian Brown Bat endangered species interest, 70
Indigenous people resources, for social studies classroom, 165
Individualized Learning Plan (ILP), AP Lang course, 132
informative texts, standards and projects for writing, 157
inquiry-based science teaching: challenges for science instruction locations, 54; 5E Instructional Model for, 50; key leaders for small steps in, 52–53; NGSS and UbD framework for, 49–50; at Philadelphia K-8 school, 49–55; reason for small steps in, 55; small steps to include science in, 53–54; STEAM instruction, 49
inquiry design model, for LS inclusion, 235
instructional coaches, JLP and, 257
interactive modeling, for wonder walks, 27
international writing course, cosmopolitan and critical perspectives in: background on, 211–12; book list and reading schedule for, *214*, 217; cosmopolitanism defined, 212; crafting writing mini-lessons, 214–15, 217–18, *218*; global partnership through iEARN, 212; GRA and, 213–14; KOSKO global project in, 212–13; next steps for, 215–16; NWP model for, 212; reflections on, 215; Short's Cultural X-ray activity, 213, *213*; small shifts enactments, 212–13; TC from United States and Argentina in, *211*, 211–17
iReady Reading Diagnostic for student data analysis, 188

Jacobson, Jennifer, 80, 102
jagged learning profiles (JLP), for culturally responsive classrooms: adaptations for contexts outside K-12 classroom, 255–57; connections and extensions of, 257–58; connections over time, 258; connections with disciplinary skills, 257–58; connections with students, 257; in-service teachers, 256, *256*; learning needs visual in, 251; on multiple dimensions of learning, 251; PSTs and, 255–56; Rose on, 251; school administrators and instructional coaches, 257

jagged learning profiles (JLP) steps: basic steps for creation of, 253, *254*, *255*; curating characteristics, 253, 254; generating ideas, 252–53; setting the stage, 252

Jigsaw Lesson Study. PASS protocol and, *237*, 237–38

JLP. *See* jagged learning profiles

journaling: assignment in critical literacy student engagement, 168; literacy and, 5

K-2 classrooms, PBL implemented in, 1–7

K-12 students: JLP adaptations for contexts beyond, 255–57; public library cards for, 248. *See also* elementary classroom

Kaba, Mariame, 229

King, Rodney, 227

Kirkus Reviews, 245

Knowing Our Students, Knowing Ourselves (KOSKO) global project, in international writing course, 212–13

knowledge building component, in critical literacy, *163*, 163–67

KOSKO. *See* Knowing Our Students, Knowing Ourselves

Kozelski, Courtney, 101

labs, conferencing in high school STEM class during, 146

language, PBL embedding of, 5–6, *6*, 7

Last Stop on Market Street (de la Pena), *214*

lesson planning, 151

lesson study (LS) inclusion, for elementary social studies TCs, 233, 241; context for, 234–36; difficulties and suggestions, 240; example of structure of, *238*; formulate goals for student learning step in, 236; inquiry design model and, 235; Jigsaw Lesson Study, *237*, 237–39; plan a lesson with goals step, 236; reflect on lesson step in, 236; teach and observe lesson step in, 236

LGBTQ+ book club development, 174, *174*; community buy-in for, 180; community impact in, 180–81; unit instructional cycles for curriculum in, *179*

LGBTQ+ content, absence in English/Language Arts curriculum, *173*

LGBTQ+ Gallery Walk, 178

LGBTQ+ unit launching: LGBTQ+ Gallery Walk, 178; making it public, 179–80; mentor texts curriculum changes in, 176; self-assessment, 178–79; student feedback on, 180

librarian collaboration: academic librarians, 248–49; attending events with authors and illustrators, 244; Bishop windows, mirrors, and sliding glass doors concept, 245; collaborative research project, 247–49; following annual book awards, 245–46; following book creators on social media, 245; reading a book but don't show illustrations, 245; reading a wordless book and have students write text, 245; school librarian—classroom collaborator, 247; YA literature and, 243, 246

library organizations annual events: NJASL, 244; NJEA, 244; NJLA, 244

Lilly, Todd, 101

Lily and Dunkin (Gephardt), 176

literacy: EE course for transformation of, 113–15; journaling and, 5; PBL embedding of, 5–6, *6*, 7; PBL enhancement of growth in, 2, 5; scaffolding activities to build skills in, 6; sentence stems and, 5; storytelling for, 5; upper elementary literacy methods course, 222. *See also* critical literacy

literacy transformation, in middle school: AP Lang courses, 129–32; digital program for assessment, 115, 116; EE course, 113–15, *114*; ELA course and, 113; initial meetings for, 114–15; ongoing professional learning and coaching in foundational literacy, 116–17; response to, 115–19; results of, 119–20; small steps replication, 120–21; small steps to, *116*; standards with resources and materials, 117, *118*, 119

literature circles, for writing motivation, 104

LS. *See* lesson study

"Making Curriculum Matter to Students" (Nerlino), 154

making time, in writing motivation: to notice, 105–8; to share, 108–10; to write, 102–5

Manzano, Sonia, 225

McTighe, Jay, 158

Melleby, Nicole, 176
mental health, wonder walks and improvements in, 32
mentor texts, 224; conferencing in high school STEM class use of, 142; LGBTQ+ curriculum changes, 176; in writing to create classroom community, 84
metacognition: in AP Lang course test, 130–31, *131*; goal in conferencing establishment, 140
middle school: absence of LGBTQ+ curriculum in, 175; JLP benefits for, 252; literacy transformation in, 113–21, *114*, *116*
Milo Imagines the World (de la Pena), *214*
mindfulness, wonder as component of, 23, 26, 33–34
mind map, for standards, 152–53, *153*
mindset: adjustment for PBL, 2, *3*, 7; shift from deficit model to asset-based teaching, *3*
MINEDUC. *See* Ministry of Education
mini-lessons, international writing course crafting of, 214–15
Ministry of Education (MINEDUC), on El Salitre low-economic status, 38
Minor, Cornelius, 173–74, 180
The Misfits (Howe), 176
ML. *See* multilingual learners
The Moon Within (Salazar), 176
MTSS. *See* Multi-Tiered System of Support
multilingual learners (ML), 57, 58; in discourse-driven classroom, 59; student storytelling at Title I elementary school with, 79
multiple choice test, in AP Lang course, 130–31, *131*
Multi-Tiered System of Support (MTSS), for RTI simulation activity, 187–88, *189*
"The Myth of Average" TEDx video, 252

National Center on Response to Intervention, MTSS definition from, 187–88, *189*
National Council on Teacher Quality (NCTQ) Contrary Content list: BL, 93–94; classroom reading and, 90, *90*; embedded and implicit phonics instruction, 95–96; GR and Daily RW, 94–95; RR, *91*, 91–93; SBRR and, 89; STR and, 89; *Teacher Prep Reading Foundations Technical Report 2023* of, 90
National Education Association of 1892, standards and, 152
national standards, in 2010, 152
National Writing Project (NWP) model, for international writing course, 212
NCTQ. *See* National Council on Teacher Quality
Nerlino, Erin, 154
Newbery Award, 246
new course and content area, flip, switch, reverse process, 230; assignment of elementary-age student writing assignment, 223; assignment of reading text related to social studies topic, 223; assignment of social studies topic and multimodal project, 223; change results, 223–29; change to social studies methods first, 222–23; context for, 221–22; Kaba and, 229; police brutality social studies topic, 226–29, *227*; Science of Reading and, 222; teaching upper elementary literacy methods course, 221
New Jersey Association of School Librarians (NJASL), 244
New Jersey Education Association (NJEA), 244
New Jersey Library Association (NJLA), 244
new strategy introduction, in conferencing in high school STEM class, 143
Next Generation Science Standards (NGSS), 49; CCCs dimension focus, 50; DCIs dimension focus, 50; SEPs dimension focus, 50–51
Nezhukumatathil, Aimee, vii–viii
NGSS. *See* Next Generation Science Standards
NJASL. *See* New Jersey Association of School Librarians
NJEA. *See* New Jersey Education Association
NJLA. *See* New Jersey Library Association
No More "I'm Done!" (Jacobson), 80, 101
Number Talks: advice for school administrators, 20; advice for teachers, 17–19; background on, 11–12; benefits of, 13; classroom vignette for, *14*, 14–16, *15*; in elementary mathematics classroom, 11–21; goals of, 13; growth mindset

development by, 13; implementation guide, 16–17; small start, regular practice for, 18; string of expressions table, *12*; Temple University development of, 13; tools for student support and, 18–19; turn and talk and sentence frames for, 18–19; writing extensions in, 19

NWP. *See* National Writing Project

Of Mice and Men (Steinbeck), 127–29
open-ended guiding questions, for PBL, 3–4, 7
organization techniques, in conferencing in high school STEM class, 143
Othello (Shakespeare), 125, 127

PASS. *See* Powerful Authentic Social Studies
PBL. *See* project-based learning
PD. *See* professional development
pedagogical reflection and action, at El Salitre public school, 40–41
peer observations of students, for decision-making, 205
de la Pena, Matt, *214*
plan, for LGBTQ+ content curriculum change, 175; LGBTQ+ vocabulary addressed, 176; texts used in, 176
plan a less for goals step, in LS, 236
police brutality social sciences topic, in flip, switch, reverse process: *All American Boys* reading assignment for, 228; BLM protests, 226; Floyd murder, 226, 227; King and, 227; magazine creation, 227, *227*; racism and, 226; reading methods assignment for, 228; Thirteenth Amendment, 227; writing methods assignment for, *228*, 228–29
policies and procedures, of post-secondary courses: change in late work policy, 201; changes to, 201–2; course information sessions implementation, 201–2; create template emails, 202; review of, 201; Syllabus quiz implementation, 201–2
Polonsky, Ami, 176
post-secondary courses improvement, small but meaningful framework for, 199–200, 203–7; changes to policies and procedures, 201–2
Powerful Authentic Social Studies (PASS), in Jigsaw Lesson Study process, *237*, 237–38

presentations, PBL literacy integration through, 6
preservice teachers (PSTs): JLP and, 255–56; support through RTI process, 185–96
probing statements of "Are You Sure?" in discourse-driven classroom, 61–62
professional development (PD), higher education librarian led, 249
project-based learning (PBL): characteristics of, 1; choice incorporation in, 4, *5*, 7; implementation challenges for, 2; K-2 classrooms implementation of, 1–7; literacy and language embedded in, 5–6, *6*, 7; literacy growth from, 2, 5; mindset adjustment for, 2, *3*, 7; open-ended guiding question for, 3–4, 7; presentations and reflection activities, 6
project-based learning (PBL), on organisms within ecosystem: anecdotes of outcomes, 74–75; Buck Institute for Education's God Standard PBL and, 67; building bat houses project, 70–74, *72*, *73*, *75*; context for, 68; drawing on student interest in, 69–70, 75–76; Framework for High-Quality PBL criteria and, 67; HQPBL criteria use, 69; Indian Brown Bat endangered species interest, 70; key vocabulary for, 68; situating project in local community, 70–74, *71*, *72*, *73*, 76; step-by-step guide to starting small, 75–76; student voice and public product focus, 69
projects: collaborative research, 247–49; conferencing during group, 145; El Salitre cinema curriculum integration, 44; example of standards related to, *155*, 155–56; example related to standards, *155*, 155–56; for writing informative texts, 157
PSTs. *See* preservice teachers
public libraries: bring public librarians to school, 247–48; collaborate events with public librarians, 248; as leisure reading collaborator, 247–48; public library cards for K-12 students and educators, 248

quiz corrections with explanations, 203

racism, 226
rapport, in conferencing, 141

reading methods assignment: for police brutality social sciences topic, 228; in upper elementary literacy methods course, 222; for Young Lords social studies topic, 225, *226*

Reading Recovery (RR): running records, three-cueing system and miscue analysis for, 91; small changes for use of, 92–93; SMV system method in, 91; use in Title I low SES schools, 91

reference materials, conferencing in high school STEM class use of, 142

reflection activities, PBL literacy integration through, 6

reflection component, in critical literacy, 163, *163*, 168–69; Dewey on, 168

reflect on lesson step, in LS, 236

"Remember the Ladies" letter, of Adams, 166

research: collaborative research project for librarian collaboration, 247–49; SBRR, 89

resources: assessment questionnaire, *206*; decision-making assessment of available and required, 205–6, *206*; indigenous people and social studies classroom, 165; middle school literacy transformation standards with, 117, *118*, 119; for students in STEM class, 142

response-to-intervention (RTI) process: incorporation into Classroom Assessments for Elementary Teachers class, 185–86; PSTs support through, 185–96, *189*, *190*, *191*, *192*, *193*; simulation activity for, 185–96

The Revolution of Evelyn Serrano (Manzano), 225

Reynolds, Jason, 228

Roberts, Justin, *214*

Robinson, Christian, 214, *214*

Rose, Todd, 251, 252

RR. *See* Reading Recovery

RTI. *See* response-to-intervention

rubrics, for case assignments, 202–3, 224

running records, RR use of, 91, *91*

RW. *See* Daily Reading Workshop

Ryan, Richard M., 101

Salazar, Aida, 176

Sanchez, Alex, 176

SBRR. *See* scientifically based reading research

scaffolding, 120; co-construction of units process, 125; conferencing and, 138; curriculum creation and skills of, 154; in discourse-driven classroom, 59, 60–61, *61*; in standards application, 157

scaffolding activities: for literacy skills, 6; of text through annotations, 103–4, 106; wonder walk samples, *29*, 33–34

school administrators: advice for Number Talks and, 20; JLP and, 257

school citizenship, of disabled students, 262

school librarians: as classroom collaborator, 247; collaborative research project, 247; school lesson plans and, 244; state standards support by, 244, 250n4; YA literature and, 247

School Library Journal, 245

science: as afterthought in education of, 49; wonder walk and instruction in, 26. *See also* inquiry-based science teaching

science, technology, engineering, and math (STEM) classroom: conferencing across grade levels for, 149; conferencing in high school, 137–49, *146*, *147*, *148*; metacognition goal in conferencing and, 141; student resources in, 141–42

Science, Technology, Engineering, Arts, and Math (STEAM), 49

Science and Engineering Practices (SEPs), of NGSS, 50; simple small-step principle for, 51; you explore, I guide, we learn approach to, 51

Science of Reading, 222

Science of Teaching Reading (STR), 89

scientifically based reading research (SBRR), 89

Section 1, Tier 1 of simulation activity for PSTs support, *189*; data from Fountas and Pinnell Benchmark Assessment System, 188; iReady Reading Diagnostic for student data analysis, 188

Section 2, Tier 2 of simulation activity for PSTs support, 188; break point data and intervention, *190*; data team meeting, *193*; progress monitoring planning guide, *191*; screener data for students, 190; six week data team protocol and student data set,

191, 191–92; student data set, *193*; twelve week data team protocol, 192, *192*
Section 3, Tier 3 of simulation activity for PSTs support, 194; SST meeting, 193
seedbed. *See semillero*
SEL. *See* social-emotional learning
self-assessment: for LGBTQ+ unit launching, 178–79; writing, *110*
self-assessment and remediation, for disabled students, 262, 265; how do I generate knowledge in classroom, 264, *264*; how do I talk to or about disabled students question, 263, *264*; how do students engage in citizenship question, 264, *264*
self-determination theory, of Ryan and Deci, 101
semillero (seedbed) initiative: El Salitre public school and, 42; El Salitre Teachers Council on curriculum integration after, 42; strong sense of community for, 42
sentence frames tool, 18–19
sentence stems, 5
SEPs. *See* Science and Engineering Practices
SES. *See* socioeconomic status
setting the stage step of JLP, "The Myth of Average" TEDx video, 252
Shanahan, Timothy, 94
Short's Cultural X-rays activity, in international writing course, 213, *213*
simulation activity, for PSTs support through RTI process, 185; advice for, 195–96; considerations for various classrooms, 195; designing of, 187; evaluation of, 196; example described, 187–94; MTSS introduction, 187–88, *189*; reflection on, 194–95; Section 1, Tier 1, 188, *189*; Section 2, Tier 2, 188, *190*, 190–92, *191*, *192*, *193*; Section 3, Tier 3, 193–94; use of, 186–87
Sit Spot activity, wonder walks and, 34
small but meaningful framework, for improving post-secondary courses, 199–200; changes for effective and efficient grading and student feedback, 202–3; changes to course policies and procedures, 201–2; for decision-making, 203–5
The Smallest Girl in the Smallest Grade (Roberts), *214*

small-group instructional technique, conferencing as, 137
small wins, Weick on, 37
Smithsonian National Museum of the American Indian, 165
SMV. *See* structure/meaning/visual
social cognitive theory, of Bandura, 101
social-emotional learning (SEL) strategies, Crocker use for writing motivation, 101, 102, *107*
social justice in education, BLM movement and, 161
social media: follow book creators on, 245. *See also* digital platforms; digital program
social studies classroom: AICL web blog, 165; Articles of Confederation resource, 165; Constitution with the Haudenosaunee Confederacy resource, 165; critical literacy and, 161–69; diversity in curriculum, 161–63; multicultural and culturally responsive education in, 162; Smithsonian National Museum of the American Indian resource, 165; White male perspectives in, 162
socioeconomic status (SES), RR use in Title I schools with low, 91
So Hard to Say (Sanchez), 176
sources, multimodal, 166–67
SST. *See* Student Support Team
standards: ASCD Whole Child Framework and, 158; books for curriculum redesign, 158; creating multiple pathways through, 151–59; example of assignment based on, 151–54, *154*; example of projects related to, *155*, 155–56; formative assessments and, 153–54; identification of connections between, 153; mind map for, 152–53, *153*; National Education Association 1892 and, 152; national standards in 2010, 152; projects for writing informative texts, 157; as roadmap for teacher, 140–52; scaffolding in application of, 157; school librarians support of state, 244, 250n4; states option to create, 152; themes exploration and, 158; UbD framework use for, 154, *155*; unit ideas based on, *156*, 156–57. *See also* Common Core Standards
Star-Crossed (Dee), 176

states: option to create standards, 152; school librarians support of standards by, 244, 250n4
STEAM. *See* Science, Technology, Engineering, Arts, and Math
Steinbeck, John, 127–29
STEM. *See* science, technology, engineering, and math
storytelling: literacy and, 5; transforming literary spaces through student, 79–82, *81*
STR. *See* Science of Teaching Reading
structure/meaning/visual (SMV) system, of RR, 91
student conferencing invitation, 138; discuss and teach during, 139–40; to try strategy individually, 140–41
Student Engagement and Project-Based Learning, of Edutopia website, 158
student engagement component, in critical literacy, 163, *163*; curriculum personalization for, 167; journaling assignment and class discussion for, 168; student freedom of choice, 167; written reflection and, 167–68
students: AI and teachers shift in assignments for, 152; assessment for content or skill level in critical literacy, 166; disabled school citizens right to privacy, 269; feedback for decision-making improvement, 204–5; feedback on LGBTQ+ unit launching, 180; formal and informal feedback in Minor blue-print for change, 180; identity development for disabled, 262, *263*, 265–67, *266*; invitation for conferencing, 138–40; JLP connections with, 257; journaling assignment in critical literacy engagement, 168; Minor blue-print for study, 174; Number Talks tools to support, 18–19; in peer observations, for decision-making, 205; resources in STEM class, 141–42; self-assessment and remediation for disabled, 262, 263–65, *264*
student storytelling, 83–87; at Title I elementary school with ML, 79; transforming literary spaces through, 79–82, *81*
Student Support Team (SST) meeting, in Section 3, Tier 3, 193–94

support building, for LGBTQ+ content curriculum change, 176–78
Syllabus quiz implementation, in post-secondary courses, 201–2
systematic self-reflection, for decision-making, 204

talking procedures, in discourse-driven classroom: assigned partners for, 59; body position, 60; call back, 59, *60*
TCs. *See* teacher candidates
teach and observe lesson step, in LS, 236
teacher candidates (TCs), LS inclusion for elementary social studies, 233–41; difficulty building inquiry-based lesson, 235
teacher candidates (TCs) from United States and Argentina: digital forms of collaboration for, 212, 214, 216; in international writing course, 211–17; Word cloud from, 211, *211*
Teacher Prep Reading Foundations Technical Report 2023, of NCTQ, 90
teachers: AI and shift in student assignments, 152; -intended lesson, for disabled school citizens, 268; JLP in-service, 256, *256*; mind-map for standards by, 152–53, *153*; Number Talks advice for, 17–19; PSTs, 185–96, 255–56; RTI process in preparation programs for, 183; standards as roadmap for, 151–52; TCs, *211*, 211–17, 233–41
Teachers Council, at El Salitre public school, 39–40; on curriculum integration learning plan, 42; pedagogical reflection by, 41
technical-pedagogical unit (UTP), leadership in Chile public school system, 39
Telgemeier, Raina, 174
template emails, for post-secondary courses, 202
Temple University, Number Talks development by, 13
texts through annotations, scaffolding activity of, 103–4, 106
theme exploration, standards and, 156
Thirteenth Amendment, 22
Thoreau, Henry David, 130
Title I schools: Ewing as literary coach at, 101–2; RR use in low SES, 91; special

education for students with disabilities at, 102; storytelling at elementary, 79
transforming literary spaces, through student storytelling, 79; in fourth-grade classroom, 80, 84; getting started advice, 86–87; in kindergarten classroom, 80–82, *81*, *82*, *86*; prioritize time to write, 82–83; writing to create classroom community, 83–86
turn and talk tool, 18–19

UbD. *See* Understanding by Design
Understanding by Design (McTighe and Wiggins), 158
Understanding by Design (UbD): inquiry-based science teaching use of template of, 50; use for standards and planning, 154, *155*
unit ideas, based on standards, *156*, 156–57
Units of Study from Teachers College Reading & Writing Projects, of BL, 93
Universal Declaration of Human Rights, 178
upper elementary literacy methods course, in flip, switch, reverse process: one-third reading methods in, 222; one-third social studies methods in, 222; one-third writing methods in, 222; police brutality social sciences topic, 226–29, *227*; Young Lords social studies topic, 224, 224–25, *226*
UTP. *See* technical-pedagogical unit

Van Gogh, Vincent, 199

Walden (Thoreau), 130
website, for Young Lords social studies topic, 224, *224*
We Got This (Minor), 173–74, 180
Weick, K. E., 37
"What to the Slave Is the Fourth of July?" (Douglass), 166
White male perspective, in social studies classroom, 162
Wiggins, Grant, 158
windows, mirrors, and sliding glass doors concept, of Bishop, 245
Winter School. *See Escuela de Invierno*
wonder, as mindfulness component, 23, 26, 33–34

wonder walks, 23–34; banana slug in Redwood Forest, *25*; behavior improvements from, 31; building routines for, 33; character education program and, 26; curricular connections in, 32; interactive modeling for, 27; mental health improvement, 32; personal wonder in, 33; sample scaffolds for, *29*, 33–34; scaffolding activities and, 33–34; science instruction aligned with, 26; Sit Spot activity, 34; student noticing in, *28*, *30*, *31*; suggestions and considerations for, 32–34; sunset in Black Canyon, *25*
word cloud use, by TCs from United States and Argentina, 211, *211*
work demands, for higher education faculty members, 199, *200*
workshops, writing motivation incorporation of, 102
writing, to create classroom community: daily share time, 85–86; focus lesson step, 83–84; independent writing, 84–85; use of mentor texts and author studies, 84
writing extensions, in Number Talks, 19
writing instruction, conferencing in elementary school on, 137
writing methods assignment: for police brutality social sciences topic, *228*, 228–29; for upper elementary literacy methods course, 222; for Young Lords social studies topic, 225–26
writing motivation, through self-efficacy development: Bandura social cognitive theory and, 101; Lilly and, 101; literature circles for, 104; making time to notice, 105–8; making time to share, 108–10; making time to write, 102–5; Ryan and Deci self-determination theory and, 101; scaffolding text through annotations, 103–4; workshops incorporated in, 102; writing self-assessment, *110*
written reflection, student engagement component in, 167–68

YA. *See* young adult
you explore, I guide, we learn approach, to SEPs, 51
You Matter (Robinson), *214*

young adult (YA) literature: annual book awards for, 245; LGBTQ+, 173; librarian collaboration and, 243, 246; school librarians and, 247

Young Lords social studies topic, in flip, switch, reverse process: description of Young Lords group, 224–25, *225*; reading methods assignment for, 225, *226*; *The Revolution of Evelyn Serrano* reading assignment for, 225; website for, 224, *224*; writing methods assignment for, 225–26

About the Editor

Lauren Madden is a professor of elementary science education at The College of New Jersey. She holds a BA in earth sciences–oceanography, an MS in marine science, and a PhD in science education. Dr. Madden's work advocates for scientific literacy and the health of our planet through teaching and learning. Her research has been supported by grants from the New Jersey Sea Grant Consortium, the National Science Foundation, and the U.S. Environmental Protection Agency. She has written a textbook on elementary science teaching methods along with more than forty peer-reviewed journal articles and book chapters. She was named the 2021 Outstanding Science Teacher Educator of the Year by the Association for Science Teacher Education and received the inaugural I CAN STEM Role Model Award from the New Jersey STEM Pathways Network. In recent years, her work has focused directly on K–5 climate change education, and she was the lead author of *Report on K-12 Climate Change Education Needs in New Jersey* from the New Jersey School Boards Association and Sustainable Jersey Schools. Her expertise in climate change education in New Jersey has been featured prominently in many media outlets, including *The New York Times, The Washington Post, The Guardian, NPR,* and *The Star-Ledger.*

About the Contributors

Carolyn Davidson Abel is a professor of reading and teaches courses on literacy development at Stephen F. Austin State University. With over fifty years in education and having been recognized for teaching excellence, she received the Margaret Hoover Perkins Professorship, which supported her as first author and principal of the research *Leaping the Language Gap: Strategies for Preschool and Head Start Teachers*.

Natalia Albornoz is a psychologist with a master's in educational psychology from the Universidad de Chile and a PhD in Psychology from the Pontificia Universidad Católica de Chile. She also teaches learning and development at the School of Education of the Universidad de O'Higgins and is currently a researcher for Escuela-Centro Experimental Carén of the Universidad de Chile. Her research areas are learning and development of historical thinking from a Vygotskian approach, experimental pedagogy, and theoretical psychology. She has worked on various research projects using qualitative methods, such as ethnography, photo-elicitation, and microgenetic devices.

Clancy Bishop, a devoted first-grade teacher at Hendrix Elementary School in Boiling Spring, South Carolina, serves with over twelve years of classroom experience. Initially certified at Winthrop University with a BA in early childhood education, Bishop holds an MEd, accompanied by an additional thirty graduate hours. She constantly seeks ways to enhance her teaching skills and enrich her students' learning experiences. An advocate for efficiency for both teachers and students, Bishop truly believes that every student reaches their potential when exposed to highly effective teaching practices. Furthermore, she models her instructional and professional practices to promote student and teacher success and strives to empower others to reach their full potential. Beyond her own classroom, she is passionate about collaboration and enjoys working with fellow teachers in order to enhance the educational experience for all students.

Lauren Bsales is a high school technology teacher at the Hanover Park Regional High School District. Through her college and graduate training at The College of

New Jersey, she has gained experience in the STEM field and is certified to teach elementary, K–12 technology education, and K–12 Deaf/HOH Education. Bsales, who is currently a graduate student in The College of New Jersey's iSTEM Master of Education program, works to integrate research-based elementary strategies into her technology education classroom by scaling effective elementary practices to meet the needs of high school students. Lauren is.

Alexander S. Butler, PhD, is an assistant professor of elementary social studies education at Bowling Green State University in the School of Inclusive Teacher Education. He earned his PhD in curriculum and instruction from Indiana University. His research focuses on several topics, including: teacher candidates, the purposes of social studies in the field of education, and K–12 students' perceptions of the Caribbean. He was recently awarded a Midwest Teaching with Primary Sources grant through the Library of Congress and selected as 2024 Caribbean Digital Scholarship Summer Institute Recipient.

Amy L. Clay is the director of the French Basic Language Program and an assistant teaching professor of French at the University of Illinois Urbana-Champaign. She teaches French language and culture and teaches graduate student courses on language teaching methods and literacies pedagogy. Her academic work focuses on literacies pedagogy, decolonization and inclusivity in French language teaching, and teacher education.

Tiffany Coleman is a dedicated fourth-grade teacher in South Carolina with sixteen years of experience in elementary education. She holds an MEd in literacy and a BA in early childhood education. Coleman is passionate about fostering her students' identities as readers and writers. She prioritizes getting to know her students and their interests, ensuring they remain engaged and enthusiastic about learning.

Nikki Collins is a kindergarten teacher at Hendrix Elementary School in South Carolina. She holds an MEd +30 in education and a BA in early childhood education. In her twenty-six years of experience, Collins has taught first and second grade, but her passion lies with kindergarten students. She loves to begin fostering the love of reading and writing with her students from the very beginning of their education.

Elizabeth Crocker began teaching in church-based preschool programs and retired from public education after more than twenty-four years of service. Currently, she teaches courses in classroom management and literacy methods at the University of South Carolina. Her experience includes elementary and middle-level teaching, instructional coaching, gifted education, and administration. She holds an EdD in curriculum and instruction from the University of South Carolina. Her passion is promoting student self-efficacy and motivation through the integration of collaborative classroom practices and social-emotional learning.

Steph N. Dean is an assistant professor in the Department of Teaching and Learning at Clemson University. She works with pre- and in-service teachers, supporting the implementation of authentic and meaningful science education. Dean is interested in school-based outdoor learning, and she uses qualitative methods to more fully understand what it is like to teach, learn, and play within a natural environment. Dean's other areas of inquiry include pedagogies of place, integral nature-based thinking, and wonder. She received her PhD in science education research from George Mason University.

Maggie Demarse is a PhD student in the Curriculum, Instruction, and Teacher Education program at Michigan State University. Her research focuses on interdisciplinary project-based learning (PBL), specifically in elementary science and social studies education. Currently, she teaches undergraduate courses in social studies methods, science methods, and social justice foundations. Prior to working with preservice teachers, she was an elementary and middle school science and literacy teacher in Dayton, Ohio.

Ewa Dziedzic-Elliott serves as the subject librarian for all departments in the School of Education at The College of New Jersey. She has ten years of experience as a K–12 librarian, including work in both elementary and high school settings. She holds an MLIS from Rutgers University and an MA in Polish Language and Literature with a minor in speech therapy from Jan Kochanowski University, Poland, EU. She has published in the *Journal of Academic Librarianship*, *Political Librarian*, and *Library Connections*. She currently serves on the board for New Jersey Association of School Librarians (NJASL) and is a member of an editorial team for the *Political Librarian Journal*.

Abby C. Emerson is an assistant professor in Elementary Special Education at Providence College. Her research and teaching centers on anti-racist and abolitionist teacher education, a critique of whiteness in education spaces, parenting as a site of social change, and arts-based research methodologies. Previously, she was an elementary school teacher for ten years in New York City public schools. During that time she was named the 2018 National Association for Multicultural Education's Critical Teacher of the Year. Her writing about teaching and learning can be found in *Radical Teacher*, *Whiteness and Education*, *Review of Research in Education*, and the Bank Street College of Education Occasional Paper Series.

Melissa Ewing is a literacy coach at Hendrix Elementary in Boiling Springs, South Carolina. She holds an EdD in curriculum and instruction, an MEd in curriculum and instruction with an emphasis in triple literacy and ESOL, a BA in special education, and an NBCT in literacy. With over twenty years in education, she is passionate about partnering with teachers. She works to foster a culture of efficacy and joy in teaching writing, while also developing students' identities as readers, writers, and thinkers. Her research focuses on cultivating these cultures of efficacy in writing for both teachers and students.

Magnolia Guerrero is currently the principal of Escuela El Salitre in Chile. She has been an elementary teacher for more than forty years in several schools, professional development programs, and teacher education programs. She holds a master's in curriculum and assessment from Universidad Mayor (Chile). Her extensive experience includes elementary classroom teaching, student counseling, pedagogical school leadership, elementary teaching for adult learners, teacher education curriculum courses, teacher professional development, and school principalship. Since 2022, she has been an active collaborator in the project Escuela-Centro Experimental Carén from Universidad de Chile.

Anne-Lise Halvorsen is a professor of teacher education at Michigan State University. Her scholarship focuses on developing and field-testing innovative and justice-oriented social studies curricula. She is the coauthor of *Reasoning with Democratic Values: Ethical Issues in American History*, coauthor of *Powerful Social Studies for Elementary Students*, and the author of *A History of Elementary Social Studies: Romance and Reality*. Her work has been published in *American Educational Research Journal, Journal of Curriculum Studies, Teachers College Record, Theory & Research in Social Education, Social Education*, and *Social Studies and the Young Learner* and has been funded by the George Lucas Educational Foundation, the Michigan Department of Education, and the Spencer Foundation. She is a former kindergarten teacher and a former curriculum writer for the State of Michigan.

Kristin Hord is a nationally board certified veteran elementary classroom teacher, with over a decade of classroom experience. She most recently has served nine years as a third-grade teacher and currently works as an academically and intellectually gifted teacher in Raleigh, North Carolina. She provides direct and indirect instruction to students in grades K–5 and challenges students to think critically and outside the box. Hord graduated from Niagara University with a bachelor's degree in early childhood and childhood education and from State University of New York at Oswego with a master's in literacy education birth–sixth grade.

Tanner Huffman is an associate professor in the Department of Integrative STEM Education and director of the Center for Excellence in STEM Education in the School of Engineering at The College of New Jersey. He holds a PhD from Purdue University and started his career as a middle and high school technology and engineering teacher in central Pennsylvania. Before joining the faculty at The College of New Jersey, Huffman was the director of research, assessment and special projects at the International Technology and Engineering Educators Association. He is a strong advocate for K–12 engineering education with a focus on social relevance and empowerment. From 2017 to 2020, he led the development of the Framework for P–12 Engineering Learning (www.p12engineering.org/framework) published by the American Society of Engineering Education.

Heather West Jerez is a senior mathematics learning scientist at Amplify, where she works closely with the research team to support the development of mathematics curriculum and assessment. She earned her PhD in teacher education and learning sciences with a concentration in elementary mathematics education from North Carolina State University. She earned her master's degrees from Teachers College, Columbia

University, and George Mason University and her bachelor's degree from Penn State University. Her research interests include elementary mathematics curriculum and instruction, children's mathematical thinking, and teacher education. Jerez is a former elementary school teacher with experience in public schools in grades PreK–5.

Grace Kang has taught at the K–6 grade levels for ten years. She is an associate professor of elementary literacy at Illinois State University. Grace teaches various literacy methods courses at the undergraduate and graduate levels and her research explores culturally sustaining pedagogies, broadening definitions of literacy, and social justice-oriented teacher education, specifically in writing. Some of her research has been published in *The Reading Teacher*, *Language Arts*, *JOLLE*, and *Written Communication*.

Courtney Kozelski is a middle and high school special education teacher and coordinator in Charleston, South Carolina. Holding a doctorate in curriculum and instruction from the University of South Carolina, a master of education in literacy from The Citadel Graduate College, and dual bachelor's degrees in special education and sociology, she has devoted her career to fostering inclusive and personalized learning environments. Her experience includes roles as a special education coordinator, personalized learning coach, and special education teacher, specializing in data-driven instruction and literacy. Kozelski has worked in diverse educational settings, including public, private, public charter, and Montessori schools, with students from pre-K through grade 12. She is dedicated to continuous improvement and collaborative resource development, ensuring high-quality education for all students. K–

Emily S. Meixner is a professor of English and the coordinator of the secondary English education program at The College of New Jersey. She earned her PhD in curriculum theory and multicultural teacher education from the University of Wisconsin–Madison and regularly teaches courses on secondary reading and writing pedagogy as well as children's and young adult literature. Her research interests include secondary literacy best practices, LGBTQ+ children's and young adult literature, and novice teacher professional development.

Serena Morales, PhD, is an associate clinical professor in the College of Education at Boise State University. She works in both teacher preparation and graduate studies in education, with a focus on building relevant assessment architectures that provide visible evidence of learning in secondary classrooms. A former middle school English language arts teacher, she works to balance on the swinging bridge between theory and practice and to humanize learning experiences in higher education.

Briana Pelton is a middle school principal with Wake County Public Schools in Raleigh, North Carolina, and has served as a principal in elementary and middle school settings for fourteen years. She was a 2008 Kenan Fellow and worked to research and develop curriculum to support educators with facilitating inquiry science learning experiences. Pelton has undergraduate and graduate degrees from the University of North Carolina at Chapel Hill in English and elementary education, along with a master's in school administration. Pelton is a former elementary school teacher with experience in kindergarten through fourth grades with many years teaching in a Spanish/English dual immersion program.

Jillian Plum is an EL specialist and adjunct professor at Oral Roberts University in Tulsa, Oklahoma. She earned her EdD in educational practice and innovation from the University of South Carolina, her MS in teaching, learning, and leadership at Oklahoma State University, and her BS in elementary and early childhood education at Oral Roberts University. She has worked in public education as a teacher, multilingual learner (ML) instructional coach, and ML curriculum specialist. Her research focuses on supporting teachers to utilize and encourage instructional discourse with their ML students to support their language development.

Ashley Pollitt, PhD, is an assistant professor in the Department of Special Education, Language, and Literacy at The College of New Jersey. She earned her PhD in teacher education and teacher development from Montclair State University. She draws on her experiences as a former high school English special education teacher to engage current and future teachers in critical conversations about disability and ableism. Her research is grounded in disability studies in education.

Erin Riley-Lepo, PhD, is a visiting assistant professor in the Educational Administration and Secondary Education Department at The College of New Jersey. She earned her PhD in teacher education and teacher development from Montclair State University. Before making the move to higher education, she was a secondary English language arts teacher for over twenty years. Her research interests include equitable, effective classroom assessment and researcher-practitioner partnerships.

Tiffany Robles is the director of curriculum and instruction for the nonprofit Gaining Ground Literacy. She holds an EdD in educational practice and innovation from the University of South Carolina, an MEd in curriculum studies from Oklahoma State University, and a BS in elementary education and a BBA from Oklahoma Christian University. She has worked in public education as a classroom teacher, reading specialist, and instructional coach. Her research focuses on providing engaging curriculum and instruction for all students in an effort to narrow the educational opportunity gap.

Ivan Salinas is associate professor in the Department of Pedagogical Studies at Universidad de Chile in Santiago, Chile. He holds a PhD in teaching and teacher Education from the University of Arizona with a minor in language, reading and culture. He teaches in elementary and high school teacher education programs in the areas of science learning, science teaching, and research in education. His research includes teacher learning, teacher education policies, science teaching learning, curriculum integration, and climate change education.

Rachel Scupp-Jorge is an eighth-grade English teacher at Thomas R. Grover Middle School in New Jersey. In her fifteen years of teaching, she has revised her pedagogical practice to focus on social justice and advocacy. Students in her class analyze texts through social justice lenses and apply their knowledge to advocate for important issues through their writing. In the 2022–2023 school year, she was awarded the New Jersey PTA Outstanding Educator Award for her focus on social justice and inclusivity in the West Windsor-Plainsboro School District.

Samantha Shane is a career and technical education teacher at Morris County School of Technology in Denville, New Jersey. Shane is shaping relevant and engaging career and technical education experiences that empower students to take charge of their learning. Her focus is empowering student choice in learning, ensuring each lesson equips students with meaningful, real-world skills that prepare them for their chosen career paths. Shane aims to bridge the gap between theory and practice. In 2023, she was named an ASCD Emerging Leader.

Steve Singer is an associate professor of deaf education at The College of New Jersey and former family and consumer sciences middle school teacher. He earned an MS from Rochester Institute of Technology in secondary education of deaf students and a PhD from Syracuse University in cultural foundations of education/disability studies. His scholarship focuses on identity and the experiences of disabled or deaf people, often where these intersect, which has been published in domestic and international scholarly journals and book chapters. Being deaf disabled informs his practice and scholarship.

Jennifer Tymkin is a veteran K–5 educator with decades of teaching experience in Raleigh, North Carolina, with Wake County Public Schools. Students in her classroom are routinely challenged to think flexibly about math concepts, regularly engaged in discourse around problem-solving strategies, and consistently empowered to become confident, independent learners. She earned her BA in psychology and elementary education certification from Thiel College.

Temple A. Walkowiak is an associate professor of mathematics education at North Carolina State University. Prior to her appointment at NC State, she worked as a teacher and mathematics specialist for nine years in Virginia public schools. She earned her PhD in mathematics education from the University of Virginia and her bachelor's and master's degrees from James Madison University. Her research focuses on the measurement of mathematics teaching practices in elementary classrooms as well as elementary teacher development of knowledge, beliefs, and teaching practices in mathematics. She especially enjoys partnering with local elementary schools on initiatives to support and empower teachers in their mathematics teaching.

Zora M. Wolfe is the associate dean of the College of Health and Human Services and associate professor in educational leadership at Widener University, Chester, Pennsylvania. She earned her MA in secondary science education from Teachers College, Columbia University and an EdD in educational leadership from the University of Pennsylvania. Her career has spanned teaching kindergarten in an American school in Taiwan to teaching high school math and science in New York City and Denver,

Colorado. She was part of the founding staff and principal of a charter high school and also has experience as an assistant principal and curriculum director at the K–12 levels.

Ashley Wright is a high school social studies teacher in Fort Lauderdale, Florida, where she teaches United States government, psychology, and international relations. She earned an EdD in curriculum and instruction from the University of South Carolina, an MA in political science from Florida Atlantic University, and a bachelor's degree with a double major in political science and history also from Florida Atlantic University. Using her background in the social sciences and her role in education, she hopes to promote the importance of social studies in the classroom. Her research focuses on the impact social studies instruction can have in educating students on issues of social justice and civic engagement.

Tingting Xu, PhD, is a professor of early childhood education in the Department of Education Studies at Stephen F. Austin State University. She holds a master's in early childhood education and a PhD in curriculum and instruction, specializing in early childhood education, from Florida State University. Her research interests encompass areas in the early childhood field and teacher preparation.

Mona Zignego, PhD, is a researcher, author, professional development facilitator, and specialist in literacy and data analysis. As a national and international presenter, she has a demonstrated history of working in the K–12 setting and as a teacher educator in adult education. Her research focuses on connecting research to practice to improve the teacher educator's work with in-service and preservice teachers.

www.ingramcontent.com/pod-product-compliance
Lightning Source LLC
Chambersburg PA
CBHW081825230426

43668CB00017B/2375